W9-BNP-585

Jesus Christ

God's Revelation to the World

AVE MARIA PRESS AVE Notre Dame, Indiana

The Subcommittee on the Catechism, United States Conference of Catholic Bishops, has found that this high school text, copyright 2016, is in conformity with the *Catechism of the Catholic Church* and that it fulfills the requirements of *Core Course I: The Revelation of Jesus Christ in Scripture* of the *Doctrinal Elements of a Curriculum Framework for the Development of Catechetical Materials for Young People of High School Age.*

Nihil Obstat: Reverend Monsignor Michael Heintz, PhD
                          Censor Librorum

Imprimatur: Most Reverend Kevin C. Rhoades
                          Bishop of Fort Wayne–South Bend

Given at: Fort Wayne, Indiana, on 5 February 2015.

The *Nihil Obstat* and *Imprimatur* are official declarations that a book or pamphlet is free of doctrinal or moral error. No implication is contained therein that those who have granted the *Nihil Obstat* or *Imprimatur* agree with its contents, opinions, or statements expressed.

Scripture texts in this work are taken from the *New American Bible with Revised New Testament and Revised Psalms* © 1991, 1986, 1970, Confraternity of Christian Doctrine, Washington, DC, and are used by permission of the copyright owner. All rights reserved. No part of the *New American Bible* may be reproduced without permission in writing from the copyright owner.

English translation of the *Catechism of the Catholic Church* for the United States of America copyright © 1994, United States Catholic Conference, Inc.—Libreria Editrice Vaticana. English translation of the *Catechism of the Catholic Church: Modifications from the Editio Typica* ©1997, United States Catholic Conference, Inc.—Libreria Editrice Vaticana. Used with permission.

Catechetical Writing Team
Michael Pennock
Christine Schmertz Navarro
Michael Amodei

Theological Consultant
Rev. Msgr. Michael Heintz, Ph.D.
Director, Masters of Divinity Program, Department of Theology
University of Notre Dame

Pedagogical Consultant
Michael Boyle, PhD
Director for Catholic School Effectiveness
Assistant Professor, Research and Psychology in the Schools
Loyola University Chicago

Theology of the Body Consultant
Sr. Helena Burns, fsp

© 2010, 2016 by Ave Maria Press, Inc.

All rights reserved. No part of this book may be used or reproduced in any manner whatsoever, except in the case of reprints in the context of reviews, without written permission from Ave Maria Press®, Inc., P.O. Box 428, Notre Dame, IN 46556.

Founded in 1865, Ave Maria Press is a ministry of the United States Province of Holy Cross.

Engaging Minds, Hearts, and Hands for Faith® is a trademark of Ave Maria Press, Inc.

www.avemariapress.com

Paperback: ISBN-13 978-1-59471-621-8

E-book: ISBN-13 978-1-59471-622-5

Cover image © SuperStock.

Cover and text design by Andy Wagoner.

Printed and bound in the United States of America.

ENGAGING MINDS, HEARTS, AND HANDS FOR FAITH

An education that is complete is the one in which hands and heart are engaged as much as the mind. We want to let our students try their learning in the world and so make prayers of their education.

Bl. Basil Moreau
Founder of the Congregation of Holy Cross

In this text you will find:

 knowledge about how Jesus Christ is the unique Word of Sacred Scripture and how God's mission of Salvation is revealed in both the Old Testament and the New Testament

 ways to quench the human desire to know and love God, especially through praying with Sacred Scripture

 Scripture-inspired lessons and exercises to help you participate in sharing Christ's social mission in the world

SEARCHING FOR GOD

TRUE HAPPINESS

Gallup, a leading international polling firm, found that Americans who say that **religion** is an important part of their daily lives and attend a place of worship at least every week or almost every week score significantly higher on the Gallup-Healthways Well-Being Index than the moderately religious and the nonreligious.

The *very religious* rate their lives more positively, are less likely to suffer from depression, and have fewer negative emotions in their daily lives. They also tend to make better health choices than those who are less religious or not religious at all. Specifically, having relationships with church friends increases life satisfaction.

Religiosity seems to improve five specific elements of well-being: career, social, financial, physical, and community.

In an earlier survey, twenty-eight percent of those who attended religious services weekly said that they were extremely satisfied with their lives compared with twenty percent of those who did not go to a place of worship.[1]

religion The relationship between God and humans that results in a body of beliefs and a set of practices: creed, cult, and code. Religion expresses itself in worship and service to God and by extension to all people and all creation.

1

FOCUS QUESTION

How can you FIND HAPPINESS?

INTRODUCTION
The Pursuit of Happiness

MAIN IDEA
You are naturally religious because, like all human beings, you search for happiness.

As a human being, you use both your heart and your mind to search for happiness. This chapter will explore some different ways that people approach the lifelong search for happiness.

Restless Human Hearts

Modern psychology claims that you will not be happy until a certain number of your basic needs—such as food, health, safety, love, and self-esteem—are met. However, even if you are lucky enough to have all of your needs met, do you think that you could ever be *perfectly* fulfilled? Although the church-going religious people in the survey you read about at the start of the chapter were happier than their less religious peers, they were not completely happy.

You share with all human beings the deep yearning to be happy, satisfied, and complete. Yet the truth is that nothing in this life—no matter how good—can make you fully content or perfectly happy.

Questioning Minds

In addition to having a restless heart, you also have an active, questioning mind. Have you ever looked up at the sky on a star-filled night and wondered what is way out and beyond what you see? If you've experienced the death of a close friend or relative, did you question why they had to die and where they are now? Do you ever think about where your life is going? Do you wonder what will happen to you after you die? These are often known as "ultimate questions," and many of them are religious.

NOTE TAKING

Self-Reflection. This section poses a few "ultimate" questions about the meaning of life. As you read the section, create a list like the one here and list the questions in your notebook. Add three of your own ultimate questions about the meaning of life.

Ultimate Questions about the Meaning of Life
How can God have no beginning or end?

You are religious by nature. Your questions lead you to searches. You are able through your own natural reason to discover true and certain knowledge about the one, true God. Because of disordered human appetites which are the result of Original Sin (see Chapter 4), you absolutely do need God's Revelation to understand the truths of religion. It is by coming to know God through natural reason that you are able to form a foundation to receive the gift of faith so as to better understand what God reveals.

Throughout history, other humans have also discovered that they are not whole or complete persons until they are connected, bound to, or related to the **divine**. All humans have shared your search for God and have given expression to their quests through their beliefs and behavior. Countless religions through the ages have produced prayers, sacrifices, rituals, meditations, and so on to express belief in a divine being who created them and the universe. However, it is only in the salvific religion, revealed first to the Chosen

divine Relating to or proceeding directly from God.

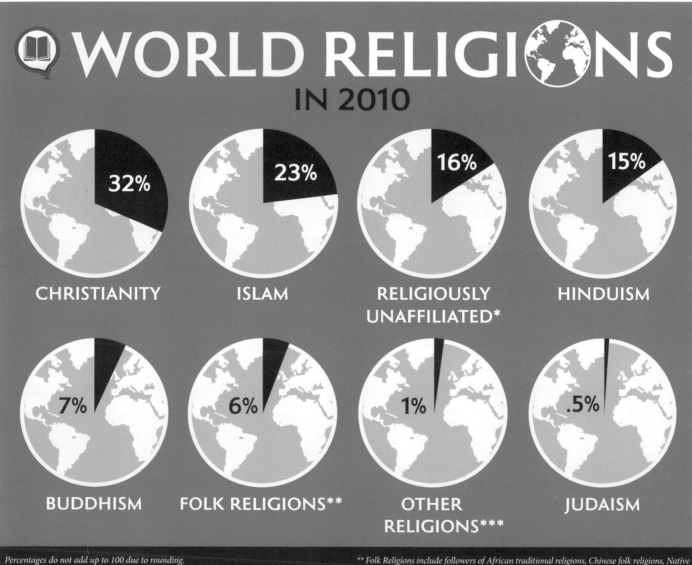

WORLD RELIGIONS IN 2010

CHRISTIANITY	ISLAM	RELIGIOUSLY UNAFFILIATED*	HINDUISM
32%	23%	16%	15%

BUDDHISM	FOLK RELIGIONS**	OTHER RELIGIONS***	JUDAISM
7%	6%	1%	.5%

Percentages do not add up to 100 due to rounding.

* The religiously unaffiliated number 1.1 billion or one-in-six people worldwide. They include atheists, agnostics, and people who do not identify with a particular religion in surveys. Many of the religiously unaffiliated have some religious belief.

** Folk Religions include followers of African traditional religions, Chinese folk religions, Native American religions, and Australian aboriginal religions.

*** Other Religions include Bahai, Jain, Sikh, Shintoist, Taoist, followers of Tenrikyo, Wiccan, Zoroastrian, and many other faiths.

Optional: Update this chart with more current statistics.

People of the **Old Testament**, that came to fruition in the coming of a Savior, Jesus Christ, that humans can know God more accurately and intimately.

Even though you encounter **secularism** frequently in society, the vast majority of people still belong to an organized religion. The religions with the greatest number of followers are Christianity, with approximately 2.2 billion members, and Islam, with 1.6 billion followers.[2]

> **Old Testament** The forty-six books of the Bible that record the history of Salvation from Creation through the old alliance or covenant with Israel, in preparation for the appearance of Christ as Savior of the world.
>
> **secularism** An indifference to religion and a belief that religion should be excluded from civil affairs and public education.

SECTION ASSESSMENT

NOTE TAKING

Use the list you created to help you complete the following item.

1. Which of the "ultimate questions" you considered do you think is the most ultimate? Why?

VOCABULARY

2. Define *religion*.

COMPREHENSION

3. What does it mean to say that you are religious by nature?

SECTION 1
Why People Desire God

MAIN IDEA
Only God can satisfy your yearning for happiness.

You want to be joyful, content, and satisfied. How are most people around you searching for happiness? People search for happiness in different ways. Some chase wealth. Others try to be successful in a career, while others try to attract the perfect husband or wife by looking beautiful or handsome.

Money, a successful career, looking good, and marriage are certainly not bad goals in and of themselves. When you view these things as *the* road to happiness, however, you will be disappointed, because these "achievements" cannot make you perfectly or completely happy. A person searching for perfect happiness cannot find it in this limited, imperfect material world. He or she must look to the Divine.

> The desire for God is written in the human heart, because man is created by God and for God. (*CCC*, 27)

Only God can fill your yearning for happiness. God created you with a desire for him that nothing else can satisfy so that you would search for him and find him. St. Augustine expressed his own need for God by

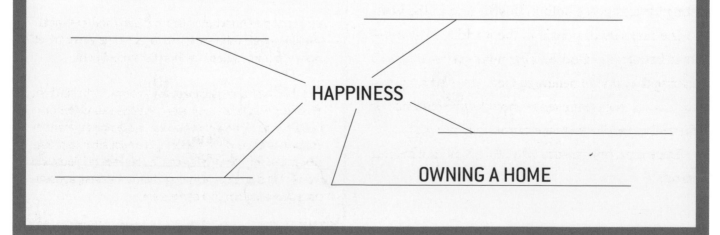

NOTE TAKING

Brainstorming. Create a design in your notebook like the one below. At the end of each of the spokes, write down some of the things, people, and events that many people in society think will bring them happiness. Add an asterisk to any of your examples that you think really do bring happiness.

HAPPINESS

OWNING A HOME

St. Teresa of Ávila said: "It is presumptuous in me to wish to choose my path, because I cannot tell which path is best for me. I must leave it to the Lord who knows me to lead me by the path that is best for me, so that in all things his will be done."

saying, "Our heart is restless until it rests in you." God created you to share in his own life of love—he wants you to be happy. Jesus said, "I am the way and the truth and the life. No one comes to the Father except through me" (Jn 14:6). God is the true road to happiness because he created you and he created happiness. Any other path disappoints. Only in God can you find lasting joy and peace both in this life and in the next.

The majority of people in the world are **theists**—that is, believers in God. Smaller numbers are **atheists**, meaning they do not believe in God. Yet others, known as **agnostics**, are on the fence about God's existence or believe that God's existence cannot be known.

These are a few reasons why atheists do not believe in God:

- Some have trouble believing in God because they see so much suffering in the world.

- Others look at the sins of believers and see them as hypocrites.

> **theist** A person who believes in a personal and provident God. However, a theist may believe in one god or many gods.
>
> **atheist** A person who denies in theory and/or practice that God exists. Atheism is a sin against the virtue of religion, a requirement of the First Commandment.
>
> **agnostic** A person who practices a form of atheism that often expresses an indifference to the search for God. In some cases, an agnostic may make no judgment of God's existence while declaring it impossible to prove, affirm, or deny. When it rejects God and the religious and moral truths attainable through human reason, agnosticism, like atheism, is a serious sin.

- Some are too busy, lazy, or indifferent.
- Still others are afraid that if they did believe in God they would have to change their behavior.

There are several forms of atheism. The most common form of atheism—known as "practical materialism"—restricts all a person's hopes and dreams to the particular time and place of his or her earthly life. Another version is *atheistic humanism*, which holds that a person alone determines his or her own fate. A third form of atheism preaches the liberation of humanity by social and economic means independent of religion and God.

Agnosticism also has several forms. An agnostic may profess no judgment about God's existence, while at the same time declaring it impossible to prove, affirm, or even deny. Agnosticism is most often equivalent to practical materialism.

Atheism and agnosticism in all their forms are a sin against the virtue of religion (*CCC*, 2125). This sin is not only a rejection of God, but of all the religious and moral truths available to a person through natural reason.

SECTION ASSESSMENT

NOTE TAKING

Use the results of your brainstorming activity and the information in your chart to complete the following task.

1. Create a pie graph to visually indicate your own estimate of the percentage of all people who seek happiness primarily in each of the particular ways you named, including through God.

VOCABULARY

2. Define *theist*.

COMPREHENSION

3. Explain the similarities and differences between an atheist and an agnostic.
4. Name two reasons why people might have trouble believing in God.

REFLECTION

5. Why is it not possible for a person to find perfection in this material world?
6. Why do you think God created people with a yearning that cannot be satisfied during their life on earth?

SECTION 2
Knowing God through Natural Revelation

MAIN IDEA
It is possible to determine that God exists using your reason and your senses.

Christians have always believed that it is possible to use human reason to discover that there is a God. Consider how Johannes Kepler used logic to convince his friend of God's existence.

Johannes Kepler (1571–1630) was a famous German astronomer who discovered that the earth and planets travel around the sun in elliptical orbits. One of his closest friends insisted that God did not exist and that the universe began and operates by its own means.

Kepler made a model of the sun with the planets circling around it. When the friend saw the ingenious model, he commented, "How beautiful! Who made it?"

Tongue-in-cheek, Kepler answered, "No one made it; it made itself."

His friend rejected this answer and insisted that Kepler tell him who made the model.

The famous astronomer then answered: "Friend, you say that this toy could not make itself. But listen to yourself. This model is but a very weak imitation of this vast universe, which I think you said made itself."

NOTE TAKING

Assessing Arguments. Create a chart like the one below. As you read this section, list the proofs that God exists. Then rate the strength of each argument.

Proof	Weak		Strong
1. God is the Unmoved Mover	←	✗	→
2.	←		→
3.	←		→
4.	←		→
5.	←		→

Kepler made his point. *Something* does not come out of *nothing*. There must be a creator behind everything that exists.

You can figure out that God exists through **Natural Revelation**—that is, through your senses and reason. (The word *revelation* means unveiling something hidden.) Using your senses and reason, you can uncover that God exists and identify some of God's attributes. The bishops of the First Vatican Council (1869–1870) captured this truth:

> The same Holy Mother Church holds and teaches that God, the source and end of all things, can be known with certainty from the consideration of created things, by the natural power of human reason. (*Dei Filius,* chapter 2, quoted in *CCC*, 36)

Contemplating the magnificence of the universe and the complexity of human beings are two ways to learn about God through Natural Revelation.

Contemplate Creation

The writer of the Old Testament Book of Wisdom suggests that those who cannot determine that there is a God from his creation are fools.

> Foolish by nature were all who were in ignorance of God,
> And who from the good things seen did not succeed in knowing the one who is. (Ws 13:1)

From Genesis 1:1, the first verse of the **Bible**, you learn that God is the Creator of the universe. By looking at the natural universe, you can discover the Creator's work. St. Paul's Letter to the Romans emphasizes that humans can discover the existence of God by studying his creation:

> Ever since the creation of the world, his invisible attributes of eternal power and divinity have been able to be understood and perceived in what he has made. (Rom 1:20)

God gave you intelligence. Think about the beautiful world in which you live. Curiosity will lead you to ask, "Where do all of these beautiful things come from?" St. Augustine suggested this path of inquiry:

> Question the beauty of the earth, question the beauty of the sea, question the beauty of the air distending and diffusing itself, question the beauty of the sky . . . question all these realities. All respond: "See, we are beautiful." Their beauty is a profession. These beauties are subject to change. Who made them if not the Beautiful One who is not subject to change? (St. Augustine, *Sermo* 241, 2:PL 38, 1134; quoted in *CCC*, 32)

St. Thomas Aquinas (1223–1274) (see photo on page 9), a **Doctor of the Church** and one of the greatest scholars in the Church's history, offered five proofs for God's existence. Note that these are not proofs in the sense that science would define them today. Rather they are "converging and convincing arguments" for the existence of God.

Natural Revelation The knowledge of the existence of God and his basic attributes that can be derived by human reason while reflecting on the created order.

Bible Sacred Scripture; the books that contain the truth of God's Revelation and were composed by human writers inspired by the Holy Spirit.

Doctor of the Church A title officially conferred on a saint by the pope or by a general council declaring that person to be holy, wise, learned, and therefore a source of sound theological teaching for the Church. See page 370 for a complete list of the Doctors of the Church.

God is the Unmoved Mover.

The world is in motion in time and space. For the world to move forward there must have been a "First Mover" who started everything. That "unmoved mover" is God.

God is the First Cause.

Nothing causes itself. As in Kepler's example above, even a model requires a creator. Everything that exists results from something or someone that came before it. Logically, there has to be a first cause or "uncaused cause" that is eternal and started the universe off.

Everything comes from something, and God is the Something.

"Nothing" cannot create "something." For anything to exist, there must be a necessary, eternal being (God) who always existed and brought other beings into existence.

God is the Supreme Model.

You can recognize different degrees of goodness, truth, justice, beauty, and so on in the world. Think of the words "good, better, best" or "most beautiful." You can only speak of such different qualities by comparing them to a supreme model or reference point: God.

God is the Grand Designer.

The world contains beauty, symmetry, order, and power that only a Grand Designer could create. Prominent scientists marvel at the statistical impossibility of human life forming in the universe out of chance alone. Someone must have put the laws into nature that make human life in a well-ordered universe possible. That Someone is God.

Some scientists remain skeptical that God created the universe. Not one of them, however, has been able to prove that the universe just created itself or evolved from matter. There is more evidence that God is the Creator than there is that he is not.

CARING FOR GOD'S Creation

Knowing God as Creator naturally leads you to take care of his creation. One way to do that is by recycling. Consider these facts:

- When you recycle a used aluminum can, it can be back on a shelf again in as little as sixty days. There is no limit to the number of times aluminum can be recycled.
- When you recycle one aluminum can, you can save enough energy to run a television for three hours.[3]
- By recycling just one glass bottle, you save enough electricity to power a hundred-watt bulb for four hours.
- On average, a US citizen recycles 338 pounds of paper per year.[4]

On your own or with classmates, devise a recycling project to protect the environment. For example, collect empty ink cartridges and turn them in at an office supply store or some other recycling center. Calculate how much of the resources of God's good earth you have preserved.

Contemplate the Human Person

Of course, when you think about God's creation, you must also think about the human person. Is it an accident that human beings possess a longing that the material world cannot satisfy? You probably sense that life has meaning because *your* life has meaning. Your study, hard work, self-discipline, and desire to develop your talents all mean something because they help you become the person God created you to be. Contemporary arguments based on your openness to several of the following elements of your humanity are other ways to lead you to God:

- *Beauty and truth.* God gives you a taste of Heaven here on earth. Think of a beautiful piece of music or some song lyrics that seem to take you out of yourself. Your experiences of joy in the presence of beauty and your insights into truth are but hints of what God's beauty and truth are like. God is the source of beauty and truth. In Christ, "the whole of God's truth" is brought to light (*CCC*, 2466).

- *Moral goodness, voice of conscience, and freedom.* Inside of you, you feel the call to do good and to avoid evil. As you look within, do you sense a God of goodness and justice who teaches you how to act as a being created in his image and likeness? This voice of conscience serves as an inner moral compass that explains, for example, why you feel disgusted and angry when you hear of thieves who defraud poor people or terrorists who kill innocent civilians. You sense deep inside that some behaviors are simply wrong because they go against how God made people. Accompanying the right to act in conscience is the gift of freedom to be able to make personal, moral, and just decisions.

- *Love and intelligence.* Along with free will, these are spiritual realities that cannot be explained by the existence of the material universe alone, but must come from a Supreme Being.

You know that you are not God. You may, however, get the sense that you are part of something bigger than you are. This "aha" is another way to realize that there is a God.

Though honest thinking can help you discover God's existence, the human reason and senses that can help you learn about God can also confuse you. Your mind is hampered from discovering naturally knowable truths by passion, imagination, and sin. Sin can lead you to persuade yourself that one of God's revealed truths is actually false. In order to avoid these dangers and enter into an intimate relationship with God, you need the help of God's grace. Building on what you discover through human reason, with God's grace, you can freely accept God's Revelation of himself by faith.

♥ Finding God in Nature

Nature is essential to human life. Without air, sunlight, water, and the food that the earth provides, you could not live. God created the natural world to sustain humanity and for humanity's enjoyment. Nature also helps you to discover God because he is its Creator.

Take a walk by yourself in a favorite place outdoors. On your walk, become aware of God's presence. Take note of all that you see, smell, hear, taste, and touch. Enjoy God's goodness in nature: his beauty, power, creativity, majesty, love.

Take some photos of objects or scenes that strike you—such as a flower, an interesting rock formation, grass blowing in the wind, or a majestic tree. Develop a collage with your photos. Use the collage to help you write a prayer. For example, you might praise God for his goodness in the natural world or thank him for giving you the gift of sight to see his splendor in creation. Share your collage and prayer with your classmates.

SECTION ASSESSMENT

NOTE TAKING

Use the chart you made to help you answer the following questions.

1. Which proof of God's existence do you think is the strongest? Explain why.
2. Which proof of God's existence do you think is the weakest? Explain why.

VOCABULARY

3. Define *Natural Revelation*.

REFLECTION

4. How do you know God wants you to be happy?
5. How can your own sense of moral goodness, voice of conscience, and freedom lead you to believe that God exists?
6. When you think about the meaning of your life, does the meaning extend beyond you or is it limited to you? Explain your response.

COMPREHENSION

7. Explain what St. Thomas Aquinas meant in describing God as the Supreme Model.

Knowing God through Divine Revelation

> **MAIN IDEA**
> God must reveal himself to you for you to go beyond simple knowledge of his existence.

It is clear that you can know on your own that God exists. You can also identify some of God's qualities through Natural Revelation. However, left to yourself, you cannot get a true and complete picture of who God really is. When you try to talk about God, you recognize that human language is inadequate to describe him. God transcends, or goes beyond, all creation and creatures. God is a mystery beyond human understanding. Human intellect and language can provide insight about God, but always fall short of describing who God really is.

Luckily, God does not leave you to your own limited knowledge from Natural Revelation. The *Catechism of the Catholic Church* teaches that "God willed both to reveal himself to man and to give him the grace of being able to welcome this revelation of faith" (*CCC*, 35). God speaks to you through Divine Revelation. The next section offers further definition of and insight into Divine Revelation.

What Is Divine Revelation?

Amazingly, the all-powerful and infinite God wants to make himself known to you and to invite you into relationship with him. God not only created you; he wants to communicate his own divine life to you. By doing this, God makes it possible for you to know him, respond to him, and love him beyond what you could ever do on your own. He never stops calling you to him, even if you forget about him.

God broke into human history to reveal himself; this unveiling is called **Divine Revelation**. A synonym for Divine Revelation might be "Supernatural Revelation," not in a paranormal sense, but rather indicating that God shares with you his mysterious Self at a level that you could never discover through nature or natural means.

> **Divine Revelation** The way God communicates knowledge of himself to humankind, a self-communication realized by his actions and words over time, most fully by his sending us his divine Son, Jesus Christ.

NOTE TAKING

Summarizing Main Ideas. Develop an organizer like the one below in your notebook. As you read this section, list at least one quality each for God the Father, God the Son, and God the Holy Spirit.

God the Father ⟶ Creator
God the Son ⟶
God the Holy Spirit ⟶

Salvation History and the Holy Trinity

God revealed himself gradually to humanity, preparing people to welcome Jesus Christ, the perfection of his Revelation. Of course, God did not reveal himself to humanity for his own sake! If that were the case, he would resemble some of the ancient Greek or Roman gods, who only wanted humans to worship and serve them. Instead, God revealed himself to enter into relationship with you.

The real God could not be more different from the ancient gods of myths who fought among themselves and imposed retribution on the lives of humans who displeased them. Instead, God is not only a God of love, God is the **Holy Trinity**: Father, Son, and Holy Spirit. There are Three Divine Persons in one God. The Holy Trinity is also often referred to as the "Blessed Trinity."

The Trinity is a mystery of the highest kind, but try thinking of it this way: since God is love, does it make sense that he would be just one, alone? Love is active. Two people, such as a married couple, have an exclusive love. Other people are not part of this relationship. When the couple has or adopts a child, for example, the two need to open their exclusive love for each other to include the child. Becoming a family encourages each person to become more outward and selfless in his or her love. The mystery of the Holy Trinity is one way to understand that God loves in an outward and selfless way.

The Father, the Son, and the Holy Spirit are equal and have existed for all eternity, meaning that the Holy Trinity has no beginning or end. Humans have attempted to describe the roles of the Three Persons:

- God the Father created the world and directs all of **Salvation History**.
- God the Son saved the world from sin and death.
- God the Holy Spirit sustains the Church now that Jesus is not physically on earth.

More information on the Three Persons of the Holy Trinity follows.

God the Father

This course will invite you to learn more about and come into closer relationship with each person in the Trinity. People did not come to know about the Trinity overnight. Although all Three Persons always acted together, the Bible talks about God the Father's work during the story of Creation and throughout the Old Testament. The Israelites, God's Chosen People, were unique because—unlike their neighbors who were **polytheistic**, meaning they worshipped multiple gods—the Israelites were **monotheistic**, or believed in one God.

You have probably heard or read the story of Adam and Eve in the Book of Genesis and learned about the consequences of giving in to the temptations of the devil, the enemy of God and humankind, and disobeying God. As that Scripture account shows, God the Father created the first humans to live in a state of holiness and justice (see *CCC*, 375), but they sinned. Right away, the Father promised that he would redeem their descendants so that he could give them eternal life after death.

Holy Trinity The central mystery of the Christian faith; there are Three Divine Persons in one God: Father, Son, and Holy Spirit.

Salvation History The story of God's saving action in human history.

polytheism The belief, in opposition to Christian doctrine, that there are many gods.

monotheism From the Greek words *monos* (one) and *theos* (God); the belief in one all-powerful God. Christianity, Judaism, and Islam are the three great monotheistic religions.

From the beginning, it was clear that sin damages relationships. As the human family grew, God saw that sin was shattering relationships—primarily through **idolatry**. With relationships damaged by sin, people kept hiding from God out of fear, as did Adam and Eve, and fleeing his call. Noah, however, was a righteous man. After saving Noah, his family, and pairs of creatures from destruction by flood, God made a **covenant** with Noah in which he promised never again to destroy the world by flood. This covenant was an early sign that God wanted to save *all* peoples (nations) from the punishment of sin.

Later, God called Abram from his homeland, promising that Abram would be the father of a great nation, and renamed him "Abraham." Abraham would have descendants who would be stewards of God's promises to him. God later reaffirmed the promise he made to Abraham with Abraham's son, Isaac, and grandson Jacob, who was renamed "Israel." The People of Israel are the priestly People of God, the first people whom God called and the first to hear his Word.

---

idolatry Worshiping something or someone other than the true God.

covenant A binding and solemn agreement between human beings or between God and people, holding each other to a particular course of action.

Incarnation The assumption of a human nature by Jesus Christ, God's eternal Son, who became man in order to save humankind from sin. The term literally means "being made flesh."

Christ A Greek translation of the Hebrew *Messiah*, which means "anointed one." It became the name proper to Jesus because he accomplished perfectly the divine mission of the priest, prophet, and king, signified by his anointing as Messiah, "Christ."

Resurrection The rising of Jesus from the dead on the third day after his Death on the Cross. Jesus was able to conquer death because he is God.

When Abraham's descendants, the Israelites, became slaves in Egypt, God freed them, created a covenant with them on Mount Sinai (called the *Sinai Covenant*), and gave them his Law so that they could serve him faithfully and prepare for the arrival of his Son. He gave them a land of their own and protected them from their enemies, except when they were unfaithful to him. When the Israelites fell into sin, God sent prophets to further form his people so that he could save them and prepare them for a New Covenant written on their hearts. The prophets called God's People to purification and redemption and announced that God wanted to save all people. The prophets spoke of Jesus' coming centuries ahead of his birth.

The last and greatest prophet was Jesus' cousin, John the Baptist. Through his preaching and baptizing of many, and later through his martyrdom, John paved the way for Jesus' own ministry. The Holy Spirit worked through him and in him so that the people would be ready for the Lord. John was able to announce that the prophecies he spoke of would occur in his lifetime. He initiated the restoration of humanity into God's "divine likeness," a process that sin had interrupted early on.

God the Son

The **Incarnation** is a second mystery of faith that you cannot fully grasp with a limited human mind: "The Church calls 'Incarnation' the fact that the Son of God assumed a human nature in order to accomplish our salvation in it" (*CCC*, 461). Jesus, the only Son of God the Father, was born into the world of the Virgin Mary through the power of the Holy Spirit. His followers called Jesus "the **Christ**" because they realized that he was the Messiah, the "anointed one" for whom the Jewish people had been waiting. Jesus had enemies, primarily among the Jewish leadership, and they convinced the Romans that Jesus could cause a riot, so the Romans crucified him. Nevertheless, he rose from the dead, and this **Resurrection** is the key to

JESUS IS THE WORD

In American English slang, "Word" has had several meanings. Some years ago, people used "Word" to indicate agreement, as in "That test was hard!" with the response, "Word." The Bible and Christian **theology** use "Word" to mean Jesus Christ in a way that also bears some explanation. John's Gospel opens with this verse (bracketed text added).

In the beginning was the Word [Jesus]
and the Word [Jesus] was with God,
And the Word [Jesus] was God. (Jn 1:1)

Jesus is the Word, the *Logos* in the original Greek text. In Greek philosophy, the *Logos* was reason, the controlling principle of the universe. To some of Jesus' Jewish contemporaries, the *Logos* meant divine wisdom, which shows itself in all of creation. God inspired the author of John's Gospel to write that Jesus is the divine wisdom in creation and that he had always existed with God the Father.

> **theology** The study of the nature of God and religious truth. Theologians are people who conduct this study.

Notice in the following quotation how the author of the Letter to the Hebrews connects *Logos* and speech:

In times past, God spoke in partial and various ways to our ancestors through the prophets; in these last days, he spoke to us through a son, whom he made heir of all things and through whom he created the universe,

who is the refulgence of his glory,
the very imprint of his being,
and who sustains all things by his mighty word. (Heb 1:1–3)

Jesus is the perfect Revelation of God. Everything that God revealed in the Old Testament prepared the way for the *Logos*, the Word, God's greatest Revelation.

your Salvation. After the Resurrection, Jesus' followers understood that Jesus is God.

There will be no further Revelation now that Jesus has suffered, died, risen from the dead, and ascended into Heaven. This does not mean that God stepped out of human history after Jesus' Ascension, but rather that Jesus has fulfilled the goal of Salvation History by redeeming all human beings. Now, the Church is the means for humans to connect with God.

"Then there appeared to them tongues as of fire, which parted and came to rest on each one of them" (Acts 2:3).

Pentecost A Greek word that means "fiftieth day." On this day, the Church celebrates the descent of the Holy Spirit upon Mary and the Apostles. It is often called the "birthday of the Church."

Apostle A term meaning "one who is sent." Jesus called twelve of his disciples to become his Apostles, chosen witnesses of his Resurrection, and the foundation on which he built the Church. As Jesus was sent by the Father, so he sent his chosen disciples to preach the Gospel to the whole world.

God the Holy Spirit

Immediately after the Romans crucified Jesus, his followers hid because they were afraid. While they were hiding, the Holy Spirit came to them on **Pentecost** (see Acts 2). The Holy Spirit filled the **Apostles** with courage, the ability to speak publicly, the authority to baptize, and the enthusiasm to share the Good News or Gospel about Jesus Christ. After a time, the early Christians came to understand that the Holy Spirit was divine as well.

Jesus had told his followers that he and the Father are one (see Jn 10:30). In some mysterious way, the early Christians realized that the Father, the Son, and the Holy Spirit are one, yet distinct from each other. Early Christian leaders articulated the theology of the Trinity at the First Council of Constantinople in 381, though the relationship between the Son and the Holy Spirit was still a question at that point.

The Trinity and You

The results of Salvation History are the reason you are sitting at your desk or lounging on the couch, reading this book. The Father created you. The Son saved you from sin. The Holy Spirit works in your life, inspiring you to love. This is another way of saying that all Three Divine Persons are involved in the work of Creation, Redemption, and Sanctification. These special roles attributed to the Father (Creator), Son (Savior), and Holy Spirit (Sanctifier) are known as the divine missions of the Blessed Trinity. You need to learn about each person of the Trinity, but especially about Jesus Christ: because he is fully human and fully divine, Jesus *perfectly* reveals to you who God is. His goal is for you and every other person to come into communion with the Trinity. God wants to share his powerful divine love with you. You can experience it now. You can experience it for eternity.

SECTION ASSESSMENT

NOTE TAKING

Use the characteristics of the Father, the Son, and the Holy Spirit that you identified to complete the following item.

1. Describe the Trinity.

COMPREHENSION

2. What made the Chosen People different from their neighbors?
3. Who is the last and greatest prophet?
4. What is the key to your Salvation?
5. How did the coming of the Holy Spirit affect the Apostles?

CRITICAL THINKING

6. Why is Jesus God's perfect Revelation to human beings?

REFLECTION

7. Describe a time when you have experienced the presence of the Holy Spirit.

Handing Down Divine Revelation

MAIN IDEA
As successors of the Apostles, the bishops preserve Sacred Scripture and Sacred Tradition for all the faithful.

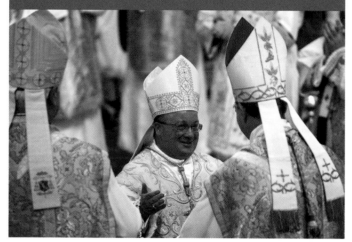

Are you interested in your own family's story? When did you, your parents, grandparents, or great-grandparents or beyond come to live in this country? Where did they come from? Why did they leave their native countries? What were their jobs and accomplishments once they arrived? You can learn the answers to these and other questions about your family's story by talking to relatives, viewing photos and letters, researching your family tree, and reading family diaries.

NOTE TAKING

Supporting Main Ideas. As you read this section, jot down at least three examples that illustrate the importance of trust between members of the Church.

How do you learn about the story of Salvation History, a narrative that grounds the Catholic faith yet occurred thousands of years ago? After the Father revealed himself fully through his Son, Jesus Christ, Jesus then entrusted Revelation or the **Deposit of Faith** to his Apostles. Inspired by the Holy Spirit, the Apostles handed the Revelation on to the early Church leaders and their successors (see image at left).

The Church's Deposit of Faith consists of both **Sacred Scripture** and **Sacred Tradition**. Both flow from the same source (God) and have the same goal (human Salvation through Christ). (See, also, pages 362–365 in the Appendix: Catholic Handbook for Faith.)

Sacred Scripture

The early Christians passed on the Good News of Jesus Christ orally as well as in writing. Sacred Scripture is the written form of the Good News that the Apostles and the early Christians preached. (Chapter 2 presents a full overview of Sacred Scripture. Chapter 3 explains how and why important aspects of the oral preaching were put into writing.)

You can be confident that when you read Sacred Scripture you are reading God's Word. As an introduction, you can think of Sacred Scripture, or the Bible, as

Deposit of Faith "The heritage of faith contained in Sacred Scripture and Sacred Tradition, handed down in the Church from the time of the Apostles, from which the Magisterium draws all that it proposes for belief as being divinely revealed" (*Catechism of the Catholic Church*, Glossary).

Sacred Scripture The *written* transmission of the Church's Gospel message found in the Church's teaching, life, and worship. It is faithfully preserved, handed down, and interpreted by the Church's Magisterium.

Sacred Tradition The *living* transmission of the Church's Gospel message found in the Church's teaching, life, and worship. It is faithfully preserved, handed down, and interpreted by the Church's Magisterium.

The modern body of Catholic Social Teaching began with Pope Leo XIII's (left) encyclical Rerum Novarum *("of revolutionary change") in 1891 and continues through Pope Francis's 2015 encyclical on the climate,* Laudato si' *("Praise Be to You").*

the speech of God as it is put down in writing under the breath of the Holy Spirit. . . . The books of Scripture firmly, faithfully, and without error teach that truth which God, for the sake of our salvation, wished to see confided to Sacred Scriptures. (*Dei Verbum*, 11, quoted in *CCC*, 107)

Sacred Scripture recalls the events of Salvation History and the covenants God made with humanity. Sacred Scripture includes the Old Testament and the **New Testament**.

The forty-six books of the Old Testament recall the history of God's Chosen People, the Israelites. They tell of God's promise to send a Savior, which you know is Jesus Christ. The twenty-seven books of the New Testament tell the story of God the Father's saving action through his Son and the Holy Spirit's work through the early Church.

> **New Testament** The twenty-seven books of the Bible written by the sacred authors in apostolic times, which have Jesus Christ, the incarnate Son of God—his life, his teachings, his Passion and glorification, and the beginnings of his Church—as their central theme.

Sacred Tradition

Although the Bible speaks to people's hearts today, it remains a collection of writings by and about people who lived two thousand or more years ago. Christians have not added to the Bible over the centuries. Circumstances have changed greatly over time, however, meaning that the Church has needed to interpret the Good News in ways that were not relevant in biblical times.

For example, teachings came from Church councils in the first centuries of Christianity defining the theology of the Trinity and the Incarnation. Saints lived holy lives and the Church recognized their stories as important for other Christians to know about and follow. The Church determined the best way to celebrate the Mass and the proper ritual for the Sacrament of Penance and Reconciliation. Although much of Sacred Tradition is based in Sacred Scripture, Sacred Tradition is a body of written literature that grows over time as times change. Its major teachings do not change, but the application of these truths evolves and expands.

The word *tradition* in Sacred Tradition means "handing down" rather than custom or common practice. The Church's responsibility through the ages is to "faithfully preserve, expound, and spread . . . by their preaching" (*Dei Verbum*, 9, quoted in *CCC*, 81) the gift of faith given to the entire Church.

Apostolic Succession

Before Jesus ascended into Heaven, he commissioned his Apostles to proclaim the Good News to all nations, not just in the first century AD but for all times. Jesus meant the Gospel to be the source of saving truth and moral discipline. The early Christians spread the Good News first orally and later in writing.

In their later years, the Apostles passed their teaching authority to their successors—the **bishops**—to ensure that the Gospel would be spread until the end of time. Under the guidance of the Holy Spirit, the bishops preserve the Sacred Tradition (including doctrine,

practice, and worship) they receive. The Holy Trinity supports the bishops in this stewardship and sustains the People of God in belief century after century.

The Magisterium of the Church

Although God specifically charges the bishops to be stewards of Sacred Scripture and Sacred Tradition, the heritage of the Catholic faith belongs to the whole People of God. God asks the bishops together with the bishop of Rome, the pope, to interpret God's Word authentically in the name of Jesus Christ. When they do so, they act as the **Magisterium**—that is, the teaching authority of the Church.

bishop One who has received the fullness of the Sacrament of Holy Orders, which makes him a member of the episcopal college and a successor of the Apostles. He is a shepherd of a particular church entrusted to him.

Magisterium The official teaching authority of the Church. Christ bestowed the right and power to teach in his name on Peter and the Apostles and their successors. The Magisterium is the bishops in communion with the successor of Peter, the bishop of Rome (the pope).

The Church's magisterial teaching can be found in encyclicals, pastoral letters, sermons, and the like. Because Christ gave the hierarchy the right to teach, Catholics give religious assent to magisterial teaching through prayerful listening and obedience.

LOOK NO FURTHER
THAN THE CATECHISM OF THE CATHOLIC CHURCH FOR

Sacred Tradition!

I. THE PROFESSION OF FAITH
- Nicene Creed
- Teachings about the Holy Trinity and the Church

II. THE CELEBRATION OF THE CHRISTIAN MYSTERY
- The Seven Sacraments

III. LIFE IN CHRIST
- Moral Teachings
- Ten Commandments
- Beatitudes

IV. CHRISTIAN PRAYER
- Prayers from Scripture and Tradition
- Our Father
- Devotions to Mary and the Saints

It is important to emphasize that the bishops do not simply interpret Scripture and Tradition on their own: they have God's help. As stewards, they carefully consider God's Revelation and receive the guidance of the Holy Spirit. Christ told his Apostles that people should listen to them as if they were listening to him. The People of God have the same responsibility to listen to the bishops because they are the Apostles' successors.

The People of God are called to listen to all that the bishops teach, most especially when they teach dogmas. Dogmas are truths contained in or connected to Divine Revelation. You must believe dogmas. Dogmas are close to the heart of the Faith; other truths are related to and based on these central teachings. Dogmas strengthen your faith, and your faith strengthens your ability to receive, understand, and live dogmatic truths.

SECTION ASSESSMENT

NOTE TAKING

Use the examples you collected of the importance of trust between members of the Church to complete the following item.

1. Identify a reason why trust is important for handing on the Faith. Explain.

VOCABULARY

2. Use *Magisterium* in an original sentence.
3. Define *Sacred Tradition*.

COMPREHENSION

4. What are the two elements of the single Deposit of Faith?
5. What is the relationship between the Apostles and the bishops?

CRITICAL THINKING

6. Why is the *Catechism of the Catholic Church* a good example of Sacred Tradition?

SECTION 5
Faith: Your Response to Divine Revelation

MAIN IDEA
Faith is the free acceptance of Divine Revelation and God's love.

When a friend does something kind for you, you naturally say "thank you." It is natural and right to show gratitude for good things that happen to you. So it is with the Good News of your Salvation in Jesus Christ. It is a privilege to hear the Good News, especially when you live it within a community of believers, the Church. Gratitude naturally leads to a positive response to God's invitation that is called **faith**.

To have faith means that you take a leap of sorts. Your belief now extends beyond what you can discern with your senses to include the supernatural—that is, God, who transcends the material world. In Scripture, faith is defined as "the assurance of things hoped for, the conviction of things not seen" (Heb 11:1).

> **faith** One of the theological virtues. Faith is an acknowledgement of an allegiance to God.

Personal Faith

Faith is both a human act and a gift from God. Prior to your yes to faith, the Holy Spirit has already been at work in you, opening "the eyes of your mind" so that you can accept and believe the truth. However, your human will and mind need to cooperate with God's grace and the Holy Spirit's work.

NOTE TAKING

Understanding Concepts. As you read through this section, create a chart like the one here and list what faith enables you to do. Choose three examples, identify the one that most interests you, and explain why it does.

Faith enables me to . . .	Example
believe in God and all that he has revealed	The birth of my nephew was inspiring.

What does faith enable you to do? Simply, it enables you to respond yes to Divine Revelation. In addition, faith

- enables you to believe in God and all that he has revealed;

- makes it possible for you to accept Jesus Christ as your Lord;

- helps you imitate Jesus and put his teachings into practice;

- enables you to partake of the life of the Holy Spirit, who enlightens you as to who Jesus is;

- opens up the gates of Heaven to you—faith is necessary for your Salvation;

- helps you accept Church teaching; and

- enables you to commit yourself totally to God with both your intellect and your will.

When you use the gift of faith and live a Christ-like life, you are on the path to eternal life—a life of union with God. It is important to emphasize that God does not force you to have faith. Divine Revelation is God's gift, as is our free will. This means that you are free to accept or reject God's love. By responding affirmatively to Divine Revelation through faith in Jesus Christ, you position yourself for happiness both in this life and forever in eternity. You will not need to constantly search for happiness.

The Faith of the Church

With the help of the Holy Spirit, all members of the Church support the bishops in understanding and passing on revealed truth. The *sensus fidei* is the truth that the Church faithful as a whole—laypeople to bishops—cannot be wrong about matters of belief. The People of God, guided by the Magisterium, follow the faith of the Church and apply it to everyday life.

Because of the presence of the Holy Spirit, the Faith of the entire Church grows. The presence of the Holy Spirit helps each person in the following ways:

- You pray about and study the faith of the Church that scholarly research and thought explain.

- You bring your spiritual experiences to your reading of the Bible and understand those experiences better from having read Scripture.

- You hear the preaching of bishops who preach the truth (see image on page 26).

Sacred Scripture, Sacred Tradition, and the Church's Magisterium support one another. With the help of the Holy Spirit, they provide what you need to gain eternal life.

SECTION ASSESSMENT

NOTE TAKING

Refer to your chart listing all that faith enables you to do to answer the following question.

1. Which achievement do you find most compelling? Why?

ANALYSIS

2. What meaning do you find in the expression "the eyes of your mind"?

3. Explain the meaning of the following Scripture verse: "Faith is the assurance of things hoped for, the conviction of things not seen" (Heb 11:1).

REFLECTION

4. Describe a faithful person whom you know personally. How does that person manifest the gift of faith?

Section Summaries

Focus Question

How can you find happiness?

Complete one of the following:

 Name some ways you can discover happiness through a relationship with God.

Why do you think some religious people choose to live in fear rather than happiness?

Make assumptions based on the happiness level of religious people versus nonreligious people. What types of things make each kind of person happy? What is your opinion of each type of happiness?

How can prayer and faith in God help you at times when you feel down because of a problem at home or at school?

INTRODUCTION (PAGES 3–5)

The Pursuit of Happiness

You are naturally religious because you, like all human beings, search for happiness. The search for happiness, however, can lead you to realize that you are neither whole nor complete until you are in relationship with God. Knowing that the majority of people worldwide are religious also supports this reality.

 Although nothing in this life can make you completely happy, some people, places, or things in your life can help lead you to God. Name at least two and explain how they help you grow closer to God.

SECTION 1 (PAGES 6–8)

Why People Desire God

Only God can fill your yearning for happiness. People often seek happiness through material things that do not really satisfy. Who knows better how to make you happy than the One who created you? God is relational and wants to extend himself to you, his own creation.

 People will often consult an owner's manual for a vacuum or car, yet rely on themselves to figure out how to best live their lives. Why do so many people not seek the help of God to figure out the best course for their lives?

SECTION 2 (PAGES 9–13)

Knowing God through Natural Revelation

It is possible for you to determine that God exists using your reason and your senses. Creation and the human person are hard to explain without a God. There are several persuasive rational arguments for God's existence. While it is possible to know that God exists and deduce some of his attributes, our understanding of God remains limited.

 Name the two rational arguments for God's existence that most clearly resonate with you.

SECTION 3 (PAGES 14–19)

Knowing God through Divine Revelation

While you may be able to figure out that there is a God on your own, God must reveal himself to you for you to go beyond knowledge of his existence. Divine Revelation means that God breaks into the human world to reveal himself. The subject of Divine Revelation is the Holy Trinity: Father, Son, and Holy Spirit.

 Why did God break through into the human world to reveal himself?

SECTION 4 (PAGES 20–24)

Handing Down Divine Revelation

As successors of the Apostles, the bishops preserve Sacred Scripture and Sacred Tradition, the Deposit of Faith. Therefore, you can be confident that Catholic teachings stay faithful to Divine Revelation. The bishops, as successors to the Apostles, preserve, interpret, and teach Divine Revelation.

 How do you think the bishops' communion with one another resembles and differs from the collaboration of business colleagues?

SECTION 5 (PAGES 25–27)

Faith: Your Response to Divine Revelation

Faith is your free acceptance of Divine Revelation and God's love. After learning about God's Revelation, a person can say yes to this Revelation or reject it. Faith is both a divine gift and a human act. The Holy Spirit works in the human heart, preparing it to be open to Revelation, but a person's will must also assent.

 Share at least three practical ways a person says yes to the gift of faith.

Chapter Assignments

Choose and complete at least one of these assignments to assess your understanding of the material in this chapter.

1. Assess the Happiness Survey

 Take some time to further assess the happiness survey referred to on page 1. Follow the directions below:

1. Search and examine the results of the latest Gallup poll on happiness mentioned on page 1.

2. Compare elements of other surveys on happiness you are able to discover. Include information like the following as the basis of your comparison:

   - Date(s) administered

   - Number of people interviewed

   - Pool of people interviewed (a survey of American women will differ from one for men and women, for example)

   - Criteria used to determine happiness

   - Questions asked

3. Research and cite challenges to the Gallup poll results.

4. Summarize: What do you think is missing from the Gallup poll on happiness? What are some other questions you could use to gauge happiness? Answer these questions and develop a summary of your research, concluding with your own reflections.

2. Capture "the Search"

Chapter 1 describes the search for happiness as a shared human quest. It also mentions an emptiness that causes people to search.

Create a multimedia collage about "the search." Include a mix of music, Internet or print headlines that you can scan, photos (either your own or others), and other visuals you can find or create. Make sure that your collage has a clear theme, such as the human search in general, teens and the search, or your own search for happiness. Include at least ten visual elements in your presentation.

3. A Visual "Proof" of God's Existence

In order to help his friend understand that God exists, Kepler made a model of the sun with the planets circling around it. Think of a three-dimensional way that you could help someone who does not believe in God begin to believe. If you have a friend who does not believe, try to understand the reasons why he or she does not believe. If you do not know an unbeliever, choose the obstacle(s) to belief yourself. It is important that your model or process challenge the stated doubts directly.

 Create your 3-D object, sketch it, or explain it in detail if it does not lend itself to imagery. Write a one-page summary of how this object could help promote belief in God.

Faithful Disciple

Blessed John Henry Newman

John Henry Newman was born on February 21, 1801, in London, the eldest of six children. At an early age, Newman read classic novels and works by philosophers such as Voltaire, David Hume, and Thomas Paine. At age fifteen, Newman read works from the English Calvinist tradition and became an evangelical Calvinist who believed that the pope was an evil force in the world.

John Henry Newman later joined the Church of England (the Anglican Church), became a deacon, and then was ordained an Anglican priest. He became a curate or assistant priest at St. Clement's Church in Oxford.

Newman was a leader in the Oxford Movement, a group of influential Anglicans who wished to return the Church of England to many of its former Catholic beliefs and practices. Newman suggested that Anglicans' concerns about Catholicism were a response not to the true creed of Roman Catholics but rather to misinformation about Roman Catholic belief.

On September 19, 2010, Pope Benedict XVI declared that "venerable Servant of God John Henry, Cardinal, Newman priest of the Congregation of the Oratory, shall henceforth be invoked as Blessed."

His proposal that Anglicans reconnect with the Roman Catholic Church understandably put Newman at odds with the Anglican Church. Newman subsequently withdrew to live in an Anglican monastery. There he wrote *Essay on the Development of Christian Doctrine,* in which he withdrew his former negative critique of Roman Catholicism. In 1845, Newman left the Church of England to become a Roman Catholic. Unfortunately, this conversion cost him relationships with his family members and friends. A year later, in Rome, he was ordained a Roman Catholic priest.

At this time, anti-Catholicism in England was on the rise. People attacked Catholic priests as well as Catholic churches. In response, Newman gave nine lectures demonstrating the false origins of anti-Catholic ideology and advising Catholics how to respond to anti-Catholicism.

John Henry Newman became rector of the newly established Catholic University of Ireland, now University College, Dublin, and published *The Idea of a University*, a philosophy of education. He was an important figure in the late nineteenth century Catholic Church in England and was named a cardinal.

Today, many non-Catholic colleges and universities have "Newman Centers" modeled on a Catholic center originally founded at Oxford University in England. These centers offer Masses, other sacraments, and social opportunities for Catholic students. Check these centers out when you visit colleges.

Cardinal John Henry Newman died in 1890 after a bout with pneumonia. He was beatified by Pope Benedict XVI on September 19, 2010, during his visit to the United Kingdom.

Reading Comprehension

1. When Bl. John Henry Newman was an evangelical Calvinist, how did he view the pope?

2. In which two churches was Bl. John Henry Newman a priest?

3. What is an area of theology that Bl. John Henry Newman wrote about after he became a Catholic priest?

Writing Task

- During Bl. John Henry Newman's life, strong anti-Catholicism in England arose from misinformation. Do similar attitudes exist today? Why?

Explaining the Faith
Isn't the Bible just another piece of literature?

While the Bible contains many literary forms and types of literature—poetry, history, stories, letters, Gospels—it is not just another piece of literature. The Bible is the inspired Word of God. God is the author of Sacred Scripture; he inspired its human writers to compose the biblical books. His inspiration ensures that the Bible is the truth.

Christians value the Bible as Divine Revelation and as the living Word of God, rather than as being relevant only at the time the biblical authors wrote. By reading Sacred Scripture, people encounter God and grow in relationship with him.

Reading the Bible accurately today, however, requires being attentive to the Holy Spirit, who inspired the original writers and guides your understanding today. Understanding what God wanted to reveal through the biblical authors is essential to your faith.

There are several means by which the People of God grow in faith through Scripture. Biblical scholars use *exegesis* (a detailed study or explanation of a biblical book or passage) to better understand and explain the meaning of Sacred Scripture in terms of the Bible's formation and editing, historical and cultural context, and literary genres. They do so in service of the whole Church. In addition to scholars, individual believers experience spiritual realities that help faith grow in the Church. Preaching by bishops also helps people understand the Scriptures in greater depth.

Ultimately, the task of interpreting the Word of God is the responsibility of the Magisterium—the pope and the bishops in communion with him. The Magisterium, Sacred Scripture, and Sacred Tradition work together to lead people to Salvation under the guidance of the Holy Spirit.

Reflection

- How does being an active, practicing Catholic help you to read the Bible?

Prayer
Prayer of Praise

Come, let us sing joyfully to the Lord;

cry out to the rock of our salvation.

Let us come before him with a song of praise,

joyfully sing out our psalms.

For the Lord is the great God,

the great king over all gods,

Whose hand holds the depths of the earth;

who owns the tops of the mountains.

The sea and dry land belong to God,

who made them, formed them by hand.

Enter, let us bow down in worship;

let us kneel before the Lord who made us.

For he is our God,

we are the people he shepherds,

the sheep in his hands.

—Psalm 95:1–7

INTRODUCTION TO SACRED SCRIPTURE

A CLOSER READING of the Bible

For a period of time, there was an active website called *No Question Left Behind*, a site where Catholic teens responded to other teens' questions about issues related to Catholicism. A teen submitted this question: "Where does the Bible deal with or talk about the evil of porn?"

Since pornography requires modern technology such as photographs and video, how could the Bible have anything to say about pornography?

Having read the Bible closely, a boy named Austin responded:

In the times of the Bible there really wasn't pornography like we have now. Back then they obviously didn't have photographs, the Internet, or television. There was adultery in those times, and according to the Bible (see Mt 5:27–29) pornography falls under adultery. In these three verses Jesus says: "You have heard that it was said, 'You shall not commit adultery.' But I say to you everyone who looks at a woman with lust has already committed adultery with her in his heart." When Jesus says "lust" he means thoughts of immoral behavior or behaving immorally.

So if you like someone, or feel attracted to somebody, that's not adultery. It becomes the sin of adultery when you lust over someone or an image. In the Bible, St. Paul says to the Corinthians in 6:18–20, "Flee from sexual immorality. All other sins a man commits are outside his body, but he who sins sexually sins against his own body. Do you not know that your body is the temple of the Holy Spirit, who is in you, whom you have received from God? You are not your own; you were bought at a price. Therefore honor God with your body." . . . .

There might be more about adultery and subjects related to it in the Bible, but those verses seem the most clear about teachings on pornography. So, those quotes from Jesus and Paul basically address your question. In a few sentences, Jesus and Paul tell us pornography is adultery. Adultery goes against the law of God.[1]

FOCUS QUESTION

How does the Bible
teach you HOW TO LIVE TODAY?

INTRODUCTION
The Bible Is the Inspired Word of God

MAIN IDEA
Inspired by God, many human authors wrote the Bible, a collection of writings that reveal who God is.

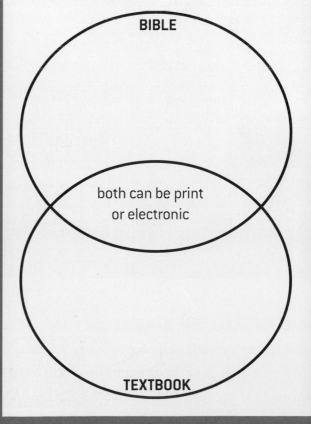

How does the Bible teach you how to live today? Sometimes you may wonder how the Bible relates to your life, since it was written about two thousand years ago. How can you gain insights from the Bible about how to deal with school or relationships?

Learning more about the Bible, reading it more closely, and asking for the help of the Holy Spirit can help you address issues in your life today. In the example on page 37, Austin does a good job of interpreting the Bible. He realizes that while the Bible does not address pornography directly, the Bible does address lust, which is at the heart of pornography. Jesus said that looking at another person with lust is adultery, so clearly pornography falls into this category.

Austin takes the topic a step further. Realizing that some readers might confuse physical attraction with lust, he looks at St. Paul's writings. To distinguish between healthy physical attraction and lust, he offers a biblical quote that suggests you can reflect, pray, and

NOTE TAKING

Compare and Contrast. Draw a Venn diagram like the one below to illustrate what you understand to be the similarities and differences between the Bible and a textbook. The overlapping area will contain similarities, and the remaining space in each circle will illustrate differences.

BIBLE

both can be print or electronic

TEXTBOOK

St. Matthew

St. Mark

St. Luke

St. John

consider whether your thoughts and actions honor God, another person's body, and your own body.

As you will read in this chapter, the biblical authors do not address all modern issues, but they do address common human emotions and dynamics that transcend time. In addition, the Bible is relevant because you are not simply reading words that God "once said." Instead, God speaks to you directly now through the Bible.

What Is Inspiration?

You are familiar with the words "inspired" and "inspirational" in everyday speech. Saying that God *inspired* the writers of the Bible, however, employs the term more technically. Used in this sense, "inspiration" means that while God is the true author of the Bible, he worked through many different human authors to reveal himself. God inspired human authors to write those truths that are necessary for your Salvation, and to do so without error.

The Catholic Church does not teach that God *dictated* the Bible to the authors, but rather that he *worked through them* as they wrote, collected, and edited the biblical books. Under the influence of the Holy Spirit, the human authors drew on their own background, education, skills, and talents, using everyday vocabulary and examples to communicate what God wanted his people to know. God respected the freedom of the human writers, but in every case, the Holy Spirit guided the author in the truth. The product is the inerrant ("without error") Word of God. These are true statements about Sacred Scripture:

- God is the author of the Bible.
- The Holy Spirit inspired the writers of the Sacred Scripture.
- The Sacred Scriptures teach the truth.

Because God inspired authors to write the Bible, you can truly come to know him through it.

SECTION ASSESSMENT

NOTE TAKING

Use your completed Venn diagram to answer the following question.

1. What do you consider the most important difference between the Bible and a textbook?

COMPREHENSION

2. Why can people encounter God in the Bible in a way they cannot in other types of writing?

CRITICAL THINKING

3. Why is it important that God worked through human authors to create the Bible rather than dictating it to them?

4. If human authors drew on their own background, education, skills, and talents to write the Bible, what do you think the reader must do to understand their contributions to the Bible?

SECTION 1
Not All Bibles Are the Same

MAIN IDEA
Many Bibles have been published; the primary differences between them stem from the process of translating ancient biblical texts into modern languages.

If you have ever looked to purchase a Bible for yourself or for someone else, you know that there are hundreds of Bibles. You may ask the following questions about all these choices:

1. What distinguishes one translation from another?
2. Why do Protestants and Catholics have different Bibles?
3. Once I choose a Bible, how do I know how to explore it?
4. Once I know how to explore the Bible, how do I figure out what it means?

Biblical Translations

You might ask, "Why do we need so many translations? Isn't the Bible the Bible, plain and simple?" Once you realize that about seven thousand different languages are spoken around the world, you will understand one reason why many biblical translations are necessary. The question, made clear on any visit to a bookstore, then becomes "Why there are so many *English* Bible translations, such as the *King James Version* and the *New American Bible Revised Edition*?"

NOTE TAKING

Getting to Know Your Bible. As you go through this section of the text, look at your own Bible, create your own chart, and fill out the right-hand column of the chart with answers to the questions in the left-hand column. This table provides a full example.

What is the name of your Bible?	*Anselm Academic Study Bible*
What is its translation?	*New American Bible Revised Edition*
Does your Bible have a table of contents or an index?	yes
Can you find this passage? John 11:35	yes

PERCENTAGE of Languages WHICH APPEAR IN EACH TESTAMENT OF THE BIBLE

Vulgate St. Jerome's fourth-century translation of the Bible from Greek into the common language of the people of his day, Latin.

Dead Sea Scrolls Old Testament manuscripts discovered in 1947 in a cave near the Dead Sea along with other writings. The manuscripts have proved very valuable to scholars studying the Old Testament and have revealed some Jewish practices in Jesus' day.

	OLD TESTAMENT	NEW TESTAMENT
Aramaic	20%	40%
Hebrew	40%	15%
Greek	40%	45%

The nature of the original languages is the primary reason for the variety. The authors of the Old Testament wrote in three languages: Hebrew, Aramaic, and Greek. Though most authors wrote in Hebrew, seven Old Testament books are exclusively in Greek. The New Testament authors wrote in *Koine* or "common" Greek, the spoken language of the first-century Roman Empire. Later, the common spoken language of the Roman Empire changed from Greek to Latin. St. Jerome's fourth-century translation of the Bible from Greek to Latin, known as the **Vulgate**, was the Church's official translation for many centuries.

Translators also work with Scripture copies found hundreds of years after the original texts were written. For some Old Testament books, translators use versions from AD 1000, and for the New Testament, copies dating from AD 300. Fortunately, the **Dead Sea Scrolls** (discovered in Israel in the late 1940s) reproduced some Old Testament books that predate the birth of Christ.

For most of Christianity's history, bibles have been COPIED BY HAND.

Does viewing a handwritten page from the Bible (see image on page 39) help you to understand or appreciate it better than a type-set one?

Translation is complicated, as you may know from studying a foreign language. To translate well, in addition to knowing the language's vocabulary and grammar, you also must be familiar with its nuances and figures of speech. If translating your Spanish homework word for word is not always possible, you can imagine the challenge of translating the ancient languages of the Bible.

Scripture scholars do their best to perform the most authentic biblical translations. Despite their careful research, they do not always agree among themselves about the meaning of a word or phrase. They have to make decisions about whether to translate a phrase word for word or to find a comparable phrase in English.

Audience

Bibles also differ because translators gear the English vocabulary to their readers. Children require a simpler translation. Some teens and adults want basic translations, while others prefer a more academic style. If you include translations of individual books of the Bible, there have been almost five hundred new translations or revisions of older English versions of the Bible.

Protestant and Catholic Bibles

Protestant Bibles and Catholic Bibles differ in that they do not have the same number of Old Testament Books in their **canon**. The word *canon* comes from the Hebrew for "measure"; in this case, it refers to the standard list of books recognized by a religious community to be genuine and inspired. The Church discerned the inspired books for the biblical canon through her Sacred Tradition.

If you think that it was easy for Christian leaders to identify the inspired writings, you are probably not considering the presence of other documents of the time that resembled the four Gospels yet often reflected heretical beliefs. For example, Gnostics—who believed in two gods and in Salvation based on secret knowledge rather than on faith in Jesus—wrote several texts that contained some material that was in the Gospels but also included content that reflected their belief system.

Although the current canon took a while to be officially approved, much of the Church accepted it early in Church history. Two North African Church councils (at Hippo in 393 and at Carthage in 397) approved the Old Testament and New Testament canons that you have in your Catholic Bible.

Meanwhile, Jewish leaders at the end of the first century AD noted that some material—even whole books—had been added on to some versions of the Hebrew Scriptures. They decided that they would keep only the original thirty-nine books in their canon that had been written in Hebrew and let go of the seven books written in Greek. Approximately two centuries later, because Greek was more widely spoken than Hebrew, Jewish leaders translated the entire Old Testament from Hebrew to Greek; the name of their translation is the **Septuagint**.

In the sixteenth century, leaders of the Protestant Reformation adopted the Jewish canon of thirty-nine books, while Catholic leaders at the Council of Trent affirmed the forty-six books of the original Septuagint. Sometimes you will find a Protestant Bible that also

canon The official list of inspired books of the Bible. Catholics list forty-six Old Testament books and twenty-seven New Testament books in their canon.

Septuagint A second-century BC Greek translation of the Hebrew Bible made at Alexandria, Egypt. The term is from a Latin word meaning "seventy" for the legendary seventy scholars who worked on the translation.

contains the seven Greek books; they are usually put in the back of the Bible in a section called the **apocrypha**. Catholics call the seven Greek books *deuterocanonical*, which means "second canon," to acknowledge that they are not part of the Jewish canon.

Now you are aware of the origins of different versions of the Bible. Note in the following feature several important English translations of the Bible.

PROTESTANT
TRANSLATIONS OF THE BIBLE

For centuries, Protestants have been using the popular *King James Version* (1611) of the Bible. Other Protestant translations include the following:

NEW REVISED STANDARD VERSION (1989)

Using a good sense of English and sound modern scholarship, this is the most important modern revision of the *King James Version*.

REVISED ENGLISH BIBLE (1992)

This is the British equivalent of the *New Revised Standard Version*.

NEW INTERNATIONAL VERSION (1973–1978)

This is a conservative translation by scholars from thirty-four different Protestant denominations.

CATHOLIC
TRANSLATIONS OF THE BIBLE

Until the twentieth century, Catholics relied heavily on the *Douay-Rheims* version (1582–1609) of the Bible, a translation of St. Jerome's Latin Vulgate. In 1943, however, Pope Pius XII wrote a document called *Divino Afflante Spiritu* (Inspired by the Holy Spirit) that encouraged a new translation of the Bible from the original languages. The following are two prominent English translations by Catholic scholars:

NEW AMERICAN BIBLE, REVISED EDITION (2010)

The Church uses this translation for the readings at Mass and other liturgies in the United States. It is solid, faithful to the original text, readable, and scholarly. The revision date of 2010 refers to the Old Testament; the translation of the New Testament contained in this edition was made in 1986. The NABRE is the translation used in this textbook.

NEW JERUSALEM BIBLE (1985)

This translation borrows heavily from the French *La Sainte Bible*, which in turn is an important and scholarly translation from the original languages. It contains many helpful introductions and notes to guide the reader.

At the **Second Vatican Council** in 1965, the document *Dei Verbum* (Word of God) further explained the Church's understanding of biblical interpretation, and in 1994, the Pontifical Biblical Commission issued *The Interpretation of the Bible in the Church*. The understanding of Scripture continues to be vital to the life of the Church, and using a good translation is vital to understanding Scripture.

> **apocrypha** A word that means "hidden." The term describes the extra section of Protestant Bibles where the additional Old Testament books of the Greek Septuagint from Catholic Bibles are placed.
>
> **Second Vatican Council** A conference of bishops from around the world called by St. John XXIII to consider the Church in the modern world. It took place from 1962 to 1965.

HOW TO LOCATE AND READ BIBLE REFERENCES

To read the Bible, you must first know how to find biblical references. A typical Bible reference looks like this: Jn 1:1–18. Follow these steps to locate and read the passage:

1. "Jn" is an abbreviated title of the book, in this case the Gospel of John. (Common abbreviations for the books of the Bible can be found in your own Bible or on page 363. If you are not familiar with the order of the books, look in the front of the Bible for a table of contents.)

2. The first number listed is the chapter number; the verses follow the colon (:). For this example, look at chapter 1 of the Gospel of John, verses 1 through 18.

3. A dash (–) indicates that you should read several chapters or verses in sequence. Study these two examples:
   - Gn 1–2 (Genesis, chapters 1 through 2)
   - Ex 32:1–5 (Exodus, chapter 32, verses 1 through 5)

4. A semicolon (;) separates two distinct references; a comma (,) separates two verses in the same chapter. Study these two examples:
   - Lk 6:12–16; 7:18–23 (Luke, chapter 6, verses 12 through 16 and Luke, chapter 7, verses 18 through 23)
   - Is 9:1, 3, 8 (Isaiah, chapter 9, verses 1, 3, and 8)

5. Sometimes you will see something like this: Prv 6:6f. "f." means the following verse; "ff." means an indeterminate number of subsequent verses. So, Prv 6:6f. means Proverbs, chapter 6, verses 6 and 7. Prv 6:6ff. means Proverbs, chapter 6, verse 6 and several verses that follow.

PRACTICE

Write in your notebook the full citations for the following biblical passages. Follow the format of the examples given above.
- Ps 8:1–5; 9
- Ps 8; 50; 145
- Jl 1:1ff; 2:28–3:17
- Is 40:12–41:4; 65:17f.
- 1 Cor 10:1–13; 12:1–13:13

STORIES OF A FAMILY BIBLE

Research the history of a family Bible. Visit with your parents or grandparents (or with a neighbor or parents of a friend if your family doesn't have a Bible). Ask questions like these:

- How long has the Bible been in your family?

- How did this Bible come to your family?

- How do you remember using the Bible with your family?

- What is another interesting story from your family's experience that connects with this Bible?

  Also, note and write down the following:

- the year the Bible was published

- its particular translation

- whether or not it is a Catholic Bible

- other unique elements of its design

  After you have completed your visit, write a one page summary titled "Our Family Bible." Make three copies of your report. Turn in one copy to your teacher. Give a second copy to the family member or friend who owns the Bible. Seal a third copy of your report in an envelope, and slip it into the pages of the family Bible itself.

SECTION ASSESSMENT

NOTE TAKING

Use the chart you made to help you answer the following questions.

1. What did you learn about your Bible after reading this section?

2. What translation of the Bible are you using?

3. What does John 11:35 say?

COMPREHENSION

4. What discovery in the late 1940s contained copies that predate the birth of Christ of Old Testament books?

5. What is the biblical canon?

CRITICAL THINKING

6. Why do you think it would be difficult for two scholars or members of the Magisterium, working separately, to come up with the exact same English translation of the Bible?

APPLICATION

7. Do you think the differences between the Catholic and Protestant Bibles would make it challenging for Catholic and Protestant teens to do a Bible study together? Why or why not?

SECTION 2
What Does the Bible Mean Literally?

MAIN IDEA

Christians disagree about the best way to interpret Scripture. The Catholic Church values the work of scholars and members of the Magisterium who search for the biblical texts' literal meaning.

You may know that not all Christians read the Bible the same way. Some Christians, for example, view biblical passages as God's dictation to the biblical authors and apply them word for word to their lives.

In contrast, the Catholic Church asks you to read Sacred Scripture carefully, prayerfully, and with an awareness that the scriptural authors wrote biblical passages in different cultural and historical settings. *Critical interpretation*, or **exegesis**, means studying the passages in depth in order to learn what God is revealing. Exegesis requires that you ask questions such as these:

- What is the type, or **literary genre**, of writing? What does this tell me about how to understand the text's content?

- What occurred historically at the time this was written that might shed light on what this passage means?

> **exegesis** The process used by scholars to discover the literal meaning of the biblical text.
>
> **literary genre** A type of writing that has a particular form, style, or content.

NOTE TAKING

Asking Questions. Create your own version of this chart (without the examples). As you learn about each type of biblical criticism in this section, imagine using a similar technique for subjects other than biblical studies, and write the example in the middle column. Then develop a corresponding question that you might ask the original authors of the Bible.

Type of Biblical Criticism	Modern Application	Question for Biblical Author
Form Criticism		
Historical Criticism	The more I know about Europe in the 1980s, the better I understand the fall of the Berlin Wall.	What was Jerusalem like at the time of Jesus?
Source Criticism		
Redaction Criticism		

- Who first wrote this material?
- How did these texts come to be in the Scriptures?
- How was this material gathered and edited?
- If any changes were made, why were they made?

Exegesis involves detective work. In a sense, the exegete "interrogates" the biblical passage, gathers additional information, assesses its relevance to the passage, and uncovers material that helps you understand what God wanted to reveal. You may not personally have the knowledge and skills of a bishop or a scholar, but you too can learn more about God's Revelation through biblical exegesis.

Your everyday life prepares you to examine the biblical text because you regularly interpret oral and written communications. Anytime someone communicates with you, you ask yourself questions about what was said. You assess whether the person is reliable and whether he is communicating his own idea or what someone else wants him to say. You might question whether this person is being serious or joking around with you. Questions about the source of a communication, its form, its origin, and whether it has been modified are questions that you usually answer without even having to think about them.

The Magisterium and Catholic Scripture scholars search for the literal meaning or **literal sense** of the biblical text. "The *literal sense* is the meaning conveyed by the words of Scripture and discovered by exegesis, following the rules of sound interpretation" (*CCC*, 116). The Church uses the techniques explained in the sub-sections that follow to find the literal meaning of a Scripture passage.

> **literal sense** (of the biblical text) "The meaning conveyed by the words of Scripture and discovered by exegesis, following the rules of sound interpretation" (*CCC*, 116).
>
> **oral tradition** The process of sharing stories and other important pieces of information by word of mouth.

Form Criticism

Scripture experts use *form criticism* to determine how each biblical book took shape in the period of **oral tradition** before authors put it into writing. Form criticism also identifies the literary genres.

A text's form provides you with clues about its content. A literary genre is a type of writing that has a particular style. As you identify a literary genre, you adjust your expectations about the content you will find. Think about how you can immediately tell if a series of numbers is a phone number or a social security number. Based on the number of digits and the placement of hyphens, you know whether you can use this information to call a person on the phone or to verify that person's identity.

Within biblical books, you can find short examples of different literary genres. Several examples follow:

ALLEGORY: an extended comparison in which many elements of a story stand for deeper realities like abstract ideas, moral qualities, or spiritual realities (see Prv 9:1–6)

CREED: a formal statement of religious belief (see Dt 26:5–10)

ETIOLOGY: a story that gives the cause of something (see Gn 32:22–32)

FABLE: a brief story with a moral, often involving animals that act and speak like human beings (see Jg 9:7–15)

HISTORY: a chronological narrative or record of events, as in the life or development of a people, country, or institution (see 1 Kgs 1–2)

LAW: a rule of conduct or standard of behavior established by proper authority, society, or custom (see Ex 20:1–17)

PROPHECY: an inspired utterance made by a prophet that expresses God's will (see Am 1–2)

GENEALOGY: a record of one's ancestry (see Mt 1:1–17)

RIDDLE: a question or statement that teases the mind, requiring thought and application (see Mt 11:11)

PARABLE: a vivid story told to convey religious truth, often with a surprise ending (see Mt 13:33)

Consider the **parable** of the Good Samaritan (see Lk 10:25–37). Because Jesus used the literary form of a parable, you can assume that he was not speaking of actual, *historical* persons when he told the story. Rather, he used the story to make the point that people should be compassionate and loving to all, even enemies. Because Jesus' lesson was so important, the early Christians repeated this parable among themselves. The author Luke then emphasized the story's significance by including the parable in his Gospel.

Fundamentalism *and the* BIBLE

You may have heard the term *fundamentalist* in connection with Bible reading and study. What exactly does the term mean, and how does it differ from how a Catholic understands and reads the Bible?

Christians known as fundamentalists believe that there is no higher authority than Scripture. They also allow for private interpretation and *literalist* reading of biblical texts. However, Christian faith is not a "religion of the book"; rather, it is a religion of the living Word of God. Catholics seek the Revelation of Jesus Christ in both Scripture and Tradition. Further, the Church relies on the Magisterium to arrive at an authentic interpretation of Scripture that all believers can share.

Fundamentalists read the Bible in a *literalist sense*. There are important differences between a *literal* and a *literalist* reading. The literal interpretation considers what the author intended to convey. For example, an author writing "It's raining cats and dogs" has used a figure of speech to tell the reader "It's raining hard." But a literalist interpretation takes into account only the exact meaning of the words without considering any other factors. By this measure, "It's raining cats and dogs" means that cats and dogs are falling from the sky.

The primary purpose of the Bible is to present the religious truths that God wishes to reveal through the events of Salvation History. Under the guidance of the Magisterium, biblical scholars and individuals work to find the literal sense of the biblical passages—what the author intended to convey. Literalism falls short of this goal because it does not penetrate the text's true meaning.

Historical Criticism

Using *historical criticism*, Scripture experts try to determine the historical and cultural context of the biblical text. Historical criticism uses archaeological and historical research to discover more about the time period in which a text was written.

For example, you may be familiar with the **Ark of the Covenant** from the Old Testament. Why do you think that people do not know where the Ark is today? Historical research reveals that the Ark of the Covenant was a wooden chest, built by the Chosen People after Moses received the Ten Commandments. (Exodus 25:10–22 describes its design. Exodus 37:1–9 describes its construction.) It would have measured approximately four feet by two-and-a-half feet. The original tablets of the Ten Commandments—and nothing else—were in the Ark. The Ark traveled with the Israelites in the desert until King David brought it to Jerusalem around 1000 BC.

The last time the Old Testament mentions the Ark is when the Babylonians demolished the Jerusalem Temple in 587 BC. There was no mention of the Ark when the Jews rebuilt the Temple about seventy years later. The scholarly consensus is that the Babylonians destroyed the Ark and melted it down for its gold.

Source Criticism

If God did not dictate the Bible to its authors, then where did the authors get their material? When scholars and the Magisterium use *source criticism*, they attempt to find out where biblical material came from. For example, some believe that the history in the Book of Kings came from court records written by royal **scribes**. In the New Testament, source criticism reveals that the author of Luke's Gospel used three main sources in his writing:

- the Gospel of Mark

- a collection of writings also found in Matthew's Gospel

- material unique to Luke

Redaction Criticism

An expert using *redaction criticism* focuses on the editor or editors who collected and arranged sources in a biblical chapter or book. Redaction criticism also tries to determine how a given biblical author's theology or understanding of God influenced the way that he organized the material.

For example, consider the genealogy of Jesus. When the **Evangelist** Luke recorded Jesus' family tree, he traced his lineage back to Adam, the common ancestor of *all* people, to show that his Gospel was written for **Gentile** Christians. The author of Matthew's Gospel, on the other hand, traced Jesus' ancestry to Abraham, the father of Judaism, and so displayed a different but not conflicting theology. Because he was writing for a predominantly Jewish-Christian community, Matthew included material showing that Jesus Christ fulfilled the prophecies made to the Chosen People.

---

parable From the Greek *parabole*, meaning "placing two things side by side in order to compare them"; a short story that illustrates a moral or spiritual lesson.

Ark of the Covenant The most important symbol of the Jewish faith. It served as the only physical manifestation of God on earth. The Ark was built while the Israelites wandered in the desert and was used until the building of the First Temple.

scribes People trained to write using the earliest forms of writing before literacy was widespread.

Evangelist One who proclaims in word and deed the Good News of Jesus Christ. "The Four Evangelists" refers to the authors of the four Gospels: Matthew, Mark, Luke, and John.

Gentile A term for non-Jews.

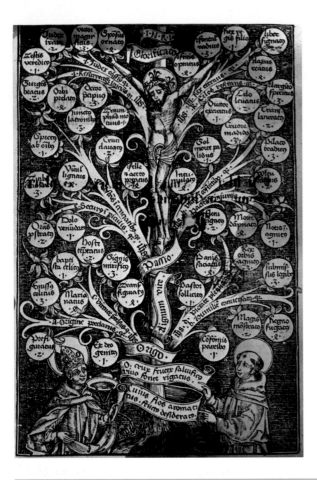

Among other reasons, the Bible is complex because it was written for different audiences, its events occurred in different times and cultures, and it was written in different languages. While you should not think that the Bible is too difficult for you to read yourself, you should also realize the value of Scripture scholarship. The Church's Magisterium, itself made up of Scripture scholars, relies on Scripture scholarship for the most authentic reading of the Bible.

This tree, written in Latin and reminiscent of Bonaventure's Tree of Life, *includes events from Jesus' life such as* Maria natus, *"Mary born," as well as descriptions of Jesus' life such as* dignum vite, *"a worthy life."*

SECTION ASSESSMENT

NOTE TAKING

Use your chart to help you complete the following item.
1. Identify the two questions that you think are the most important when studying the Bible critically.

VOCABULARY

2. What is the literal sense of the biblical text?

3. What is a literary genre? Define the term and list three examples.

COMPREHENSION

4. List three types of biblical criticism. Explain how each approaches the Bible.

5. Summarize the difference between a literal and a literalist interpretation of the Bible.

REFLECTION

6. What is one book, story, person, or event in the Bible about which you would like to learn more? Which form of biblical criticism would help you most in your search?

SECTION 3
What Does the Bible Mean Spiritually?

MAIN IDEA
After discovering the closest literal interpretation of the biblical text, Catholics must read individual passages as religious truths, in the context of the Church, and according to the spiritual senses of Scripture.

As you learned in the previous section, a full understanding of Scripture includes knowing the historical context and literal sense. Still, the main reason for seeking this literal knowledge is to get to the heart of religious truth. Your primary reason for opening the Bible is to learn about God and the story of Salvation as God and the biblical authors intended. And, primarily, the Bible is a book of prayer (see "The Bible and Prayer" on page 56). This section expands on these ways for reading and studying the Bible.

Understanding Religious Truth in the Bible

Think about how you look for specific types of information in the print or electronic books you use. You may take out a cookbook for recipes or use a dictionary to find word meanings. Each type of book provides the information you want and sticks to that area of knowledge. You have no expectation that a cookbook contains definitions or that a dictionary should offer recipes. Predictably, when readers look for answers to historical and scientific questions in the Bible, they can run into difficulty.

NOTE TAKING

Summarizing Content. The section provides guidelines for reading the Bible as God's Revelation rather than simply as a piece of literature. Copy the chart. For each guideline, write a summary sentence of the text material.

Guideline	Summary
Look for religious truth in the Bible.	The Bible is Divine Revelation; it answers religious questions, not necessarily historical or scientific ones.
Read the Bible according to the Spirit.	
Seek the Bible's deeper spiritual meaning.	

It is very important to remember that the Bible is neither a science book nor a history book. The Bible is a written record of Divine Revelation. God inspired its authors to reveal religious truths through their writing. These religious truths reveal who you are in relation to God and the world he created. They tell you that you are a material and spiritual being made in God's image and likeness. In addition, they reveal your destiny—eternal life in union with a loving, Triune God. Because some people look for scientific or historical truth in the Bible, they find themselves at odds with the scientific and historical academic communities. In truth, there is no need for this opposition.

One of the Magisterium's responsibilities is to identify the truths of the Faith revealed in Sacred Scripture and explain how they relate to academic scientific and historical research. The Catholic Church welcomes and encourages the research of historians and scientists because "truth does not contradict truth"—scientific evidence does not conflict with religious beliefs. For example, consider the work of historians who have looked for evidence or records that support the events depicted in the New Testament. Nothing is more important for a Christian than being certain that Jesus existed. Was there really such a person? Or was he just the invention of the early Christians, as some claim? Historians, including non-Christians, have looked into these questions. Drawing on records from Roman and Jewish historians, they have affirmed the following historical information:

- Jesus of Nazareth did indeed exist.
- The Romans under the prefect Pontius Pilate crucified Jesus.
- Jesus established a Church that persists to this very day.

Cardinal Caesar Baronius (1538–1607) put it well when he said, "The Bible teaches us how to go to Heaven, not how the heavens go." Simply put, scientific research and Christian faith do not contradict one other. They neither prove nor disprove one another. In the words of the *Catechism of the Catholic Church*:

> Though faith is above reason, there can never be any real discrepancy between faith and reason. Since the same God who reveals mysteries and infuses faith has bestowed the light of reason on the human mind, God cannot deny himself, nor can truth ever contradict truth. Consequently, methodical research in all branches of knowledge, provided it is carried out in a truly scientific manner and does not override moral laws, can never conflict with the faith, because the things of the world and the things of faith derive from the same God. The humble and persevering investigator of the secrets of nature is being led, as it were, by the hand of God in spite of himself, for it is God, the conserver of all things, who made them what they are. (*CCC*, 159)

Read the Bible according to the Spirit

Because Sacred Scripture is inspired, it "must be read and interpreted in the light of the same Spirit by whom it was written" (*Dei Verbum*, 12 § 3, quoted in *CCC*, 111). In other words, if you want to understand the Bible, you must ask for the guidance of the Holy Spirit while reading it. The documents from the Second Vatican Council teach Catholics three ways of interpreting Scripture in accordance with the Holy Spirit.

FIRST, read specific passages with the whole content and unity of Scripture in mind. Jesus Christ is the center and heart of Sacred Scripture as the Word of God. The Old Testament prefigures Christ and illuminates the New Testament. It would not make sense to read the New Testament without a good knowledge of the Old Testament, because the Old Testament is important Divine Revelation. As St. Augustine put it, "the New Testament lies hidden in the Old, and the Old Testament is unveiled in the New" (quoted in *CCC*, 129).

SECOND, "read the Scripture within 'the living Tradition of the whole Church'" (*CCC*, 113). Recall that Sacred Scripture is one of two parts of a *single* Deposit of Faith that also includes Sacred Tradition. You might find it surprising that God did not give the authority to interpret Sacred Scripture to individuals but rather to the whole Church, through the Magisterium. Therefore, to interpret the Bible properly, you should read it within the Tradition of the Church. If you were to interpret a Scripture passage in a way that contradicts Sacred Tradition, your personal interpretation is more likely to be wrong.

> **Exodus** A foundational event in the history of the Chosen People that occurred when Moses led the Hebrews out of Egypt and slavery.

THIRD, pay attention to the *analogy of faith*: the unity "of the truths of the faith among themselves and within the whole plan of Revelation" (*CCC*, 114). Simply put, Sacred Scripture cannot reveal religious truths that contradict one another. God's revealed truths make sense, one with the other. Therefore, when interpreting the Bible, do so in a way that is in harmony with all of God's Revelation, including the teaching of the Magisterium.

Seek the Bible's Deeper Spiritual Meaning

You can look to the deeper meaning of various scriptural passages as part of God's overall plan of Salvation using the *spiritual senses*. However, the Bible's spiritual senses depend on the literal sense achieved by good exegetical work. There are four senses of Scripture: the literal sense and the three spiritual senses. Read below to understand these four senses more fully.

1. *The literal sense.* As you read in the previous section, the literal sense is not necessarily an exact word-for-word reading, but is the meaning the author intended to convey. You understand the literal sense of Scripture when you know what the biblical author meant to communicate.

2. *The allegorical sense.* An allegory is a metaphor, or sustained comparison. In an allegorical work of literature, you can see that the story line conveys more than one level of meaning. In an allegorical reading of Scripture, you look at the entire Bible, especially the Old Testament, in light of its fulfillment in Christ. Knowing of Christ's victory over sin, for example, it is possible to recognize that the **Exodus** crossing of the

THE BIBLE AND PRAYER

The Bible is central to the Church's life. The Bible enables you to hear God speak to your heart and strengthens and nourishes the Church as a whole. Consequently, the Bible has a central role to play in your prayer life.

- Scripture readings are integral to every Mass and to all the other **sacraments**. Because the first Christians were Jews, they continued to pray in accordance with Jewish custom. Like the Jewish rites, the Liturgy of the Word in the Mass contains readings to which the assembly listens, psalms to which the assembly gives a response, and prayers of praise and intercession for people living and dead.

  At Mass, first you hear a reading from the Old Testament (or Acts of the Apostles during the Easter season), and then you respond to a psalm. Next, you hear a reading from the New Testament. Then the priest or deacon reads the Gospel. After the Gospel reading comes the homily, in which the priest or deacon further connects the common theme of the readings and applies them to contemporary life. The Liturgy of the Word concludes with the prayers of the faithful or the prayers of intercession.

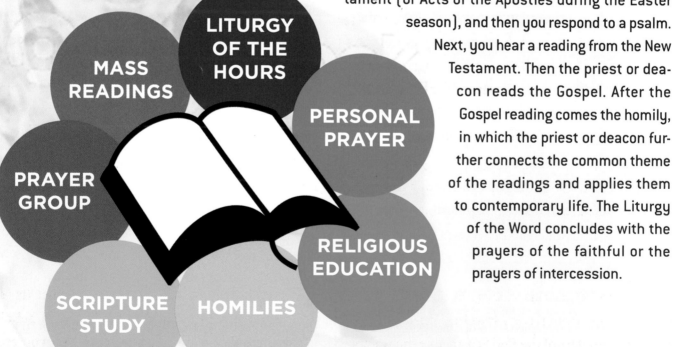

LITURGY OF THE HOURS

MASS READINGS

PERSONAL PRAYER

PRAYER GROUP

RELIGIOUS EDUCATION

SCRIPTURE STUDY

HOMILIES

- Scripture is also at the heart of the **Liturgy of the Hours,** or Divine Office, which is the public prayer of the Church that praises God and sanctifies the day. It consists of Morning and Evening Prayer, Daytime Prayer, and Night Prayer and features the psalms.

  Because you speak the prayers aloud, you unite your heart and voice. This prayer practice leads to a greater understanding of **liturgy** in general and in particular a greater appreciation for the psalms. The Liturgy of the Hours helps you stay "in tune" with the liturgical seasons, the flow of the day, and any feast being celebrated that day, which in turn readies you for silent prayer and meditation on God's Word.

  Although you may be unfamiliar with the Divine Office, the Church intends for all the People of God to pray it.

- The Church encourages Catholics to use the Bible in personal prayer. **Lectio divina** is one meditative approach to Scripture. (See pages 64–65.)

- Many parishes foster Scripture study and prayer groups as a way to grow in holiness (see image on page 53). St. Jerome pointed out the importance of the Bible when he said that "ignorance of the Scriptures is ignorance of Christ." The Church echoes this saying: it "forcefully and specifically exhorts all the Christian faithful . . . to learn 'the surpassing knowledge of Jesus Christ,' by frequent reading of the divine Scriptures" (*Dei Verbum*, 25, quoted in *CCC*, 133).

- Parishes usually teach about Scripture in a variety of ways. Religious education for children includes stories from Scripture. People going through the Rite of Christian Initiation for Adults (RCIA) to become Catholic in adulthood learn about the Bible as they learn about the Catholic Church. Finally, the priest's homily during Sunday and weekday Masses helps the congregation understand the readings better and applies the message of the readings to everyday life.

> **sacrament** A sign and source of grace instituted by Jesus Christ and entrusted to the Church by which divine life is bestowed on us through the Holy Spirit.
>
> **Liturgy of the Hours** The prayer of the Church at specific times of the day; also known as the Divine Office. The Liturgy of the Hours uses readings from Scripture, particularly the psalms, and hymns.
>
> **liturgy** The official public worship of the Church. The liturgy is first Christ's work of Redemption, and of his continuing work of Redemption as he pours out his blessings through the sacraments. The Holy Spirit enlightens our faith and encourages us to respond. In this way, the liturgy is the participation of the People of God in the work of the Trinity. The sacraments and the Divine Office constitute the Church's liturgy. Mass is the most important liturgical celebration.
>
> **lectio divina** A Benedictine prayer tradition of "sacred reading"; its intent is for the person praying to meet God through the Scriptures.

Prayer should always accompany your growing knowledge of Scripture so that, through Scripture, you can talk with God and God can talk with you. Reading Scripture can lead you to meditate, and meditation can lead you to contemplation, a very high form of prayer.

Red Sea prefigures this victory. Because the Exodus was an escape from slavery into freedom, it is easy to see that the waters of the Red Sea are like the waters of Baptism that free us from our slavery to sin.

3. *The moral sense.* God's Word teaches its readers to live good lives and to act justly on behalf of God and other people. Therefore, when you read a prophet urging the Israelites to live according to the

Commandments, for example, you can pray and determine how this prophet is also challenging you to honor your relationship with God.

4. *The anagogical sense.* This sense helps you see earthly events and other realities in the context of your journey to Heaven. Your ultimate goal in life is to get to Heaven, and the Bible shows you the way. (The word *anagogical* comes from the Greek word for "leading.") For example, when the person finds a treasure in a field and sells all that he owns to buy the field, the treasure is a symbol of eternal life, and the story shows you that to achieve eternal life you must put God first (see Mt 13:44). You can also see the Church as a symbol of the heavenly Jerusalem. The Church, which is the Body of Christ, leads all to eternal life.

In summary, there are four senses of Scripture, three of which are spiritual:

1. The *literal sense* helps you understand what the biblical authors intended to communicate to their audiences.

2. The *allegorical sense* teaches what individual passages mean in the larger context of Salvation History.

3. The *moral sense* teaches you how to live your life.

4. The *anagogical sense* reminds you where you are going, building up the virtue of hope while leading you to Heaven.

SECTION ASSESSMENT

NOTE TAKING

Use the chart you created to help you answer the following question.

1. How do you read the Bible according to the Holy Spirit?

COMPREHENSION

2. What is one of the main responsibilities of the Magisterium?

3. What are three pieces of historical information about Jesus affirmed by Roman and Jewish historians?

ANALYSIS

4. What does it mean to read the Bible in the moral sense?

Section Summaries

Focus Question

How does the Bible teach you how to live today?

Complete one of the following:

 Look up today's Scripture readings for Mass (see www.usccb.org/bible/readings). Write two or three sentences that either explain one of the readings or apply a lesson from a reading to your own life today.

 Identify a contemporary moral issue and find relevant biblical passages that apply to this issue by searching an online concordance for key words. What did you learn from the Scriptures about this topic?

Your browser does not support the video tag. If you wanted to know what Sacred Tradition teaches about a given subject, how could you find that out? Explore the documents at the Vatican website (www.vatican.va) for answers.

INTRODUCTION (PAGES 39–41)
The Bible Is the Inspired Word of God

The Bible is a collection of writings that reveal who God is. God is the author of the Bible, but he worked through human authors who contributed to the inerrant Word of God.

 How can any writing by human authors be inerrant?

SECTION 1 (PAGES 42–47)
Not All Bibles Are the Same

There are many different Bibles. Sometimes Bibles differ because the translators chose different wording. Others differ because the vocabulary chosen is geared toward a particular audience. Protestant Bibles differ from Catholic Bibles because Protestant Bibles do not include seven books originally written in Greek, while Catholic Bibles do.

 Given what you have learned in this chapter, name three criteria you would look for if you were out to purchase a new Bible for yourself.

SECTION 2 (PAGES 48–52)

What Does the Bible Mean Literally?

Christians do not agree on the way to read and interpret the Bible. In contrast to fundamentalists, the Catholic Church's Magisterium supports biblical scholarship that uses exegesis to critically interpret the Scriptures and obtain the literal sense of the Bible. There are several types of biblical criticism within exegesis: form, historical, source, and redaction criticism.

 How might a fundamentalist reading of the story of Creation differ from the Catholic understanding?

SECTION 3 (PAGES 53–58)

What Does the Bible Mean Spiritually?

The Bible shares religious truth rather than scientific or historical truth. Scripture is interpreted only through the Holy Spirit and in the collective wisdom of the Church, to whom the Scriptures have been entrusted. Finally, you need to discern what the Bible says about the truths of our faith, about moral issues, and about our final destination: Heaven.

Identify several beliefs that a Catholic must profess in order to allow the Holy Spirit to guide his or her reading.

Chapter Assignments

Choose and complete at least one of these assignments to assess your understanding of the material in this chapter.

1. Research and Report

 Research one of these topics in greater depth, and develop a creative way to share the information with your teacher and the class.

- Report about some of the complexities of translating the Bible.

- Research the Dead Sea Scrolls. Learn more about their history and significance.

- Look into the "Dead Sea Scrolls Digital Project," a partnership between the Israel Museum and Google that allows users to search and read high-resolution images of the scrolls as well as view short videos that explain and provide background about the manuscripts.

- Explore biblical archaeology, and learn more about how this discipline helps scholars and Bible readers understand more about the Bible.

2. Create a Bible Game

Create a game that helps people get to know the Bible, inviting them to practice their skills of locating and reading Bible references and using the table of contents and possibly the index. Note the translation of the Bible you are using. Try out your game on other students.

3. Make an Illuminated Manuscript

Locate one or more of your favorite Scripture passages. Create a parchment-like, elegant illustrated manuscript of your biblical passage using heavy-bond paper. Transcribe the verse in ink in your best handwriting, or use an appropriate computer font. Create an illustration that visually captures the spirit of your passage.

Faithful Disciple

St. Jerome

St. Jerome

St. Jerome, an important **Church Father**, translated the Bible from its original languages into Latin.

Jerome was born in northeast Italy. He went to Rome as a young man to study Latin and Greek literature and had an early devotion to some non-Christian scholars. This education in the classics inspired him to lifelong study. At the age of eighteen, Jerome was baptized. After further travels and study, he entered a strict monastic community near his home at Aquileia. There he mastered Hebrew, a difficult language. Later, in Antioch, Jerome had a vision that criticized him for his devotion to secular learning, for being "a follower of Cicero and not of Christ." Prior to going to Rome, he became a priest in Antioch.

As the pope's secretary in Rome, Jerome displayed both his strengths and his weaknesses to the pope. Jerome had an explosive temper, often using his sharp pen to write fierce letters to his opponents. However, the pope saw beneath Jerome's sometimes prickly personality. He discovered in Jerome a man of deep holiness, learning, and integrity. As a result, the pope commissioned him to translate the Bible into Latin, a task that eventually took Jerome to Bethlehem.

Laboring relentlessly in a cave, Jerome, with the help of his disciples, completed his translation of the Bible into Latin with a commentary—a task that took twenty-three years. The Church used this translation, known as the Latin Vulgate (382–405), as its official translation from that time on.

In his later years, Jerome also wrote against various heresies and corresponded regularly with St. Augustine. He died peacefully as an old man, worn down with a number of infirmities. The Church recognizes him as one of her greatest minds and defenders of the Faith. Augustine said of him, "What Jerome is ignorant of, no man has ever known."

💡 Reading Comprehension

> **Church Father** A theologian of the first eight centuries of Christianity whose teachings made a lasting mark on the Church.

1. What was the message St. Jerome received in his vision?

2. How long did it take St. Jerome to complete his translation and commentary on the Bible?

✒️ Writing Task

- Write a short essay explaining what St. Jerome meant when he said that "ignorance of the Scriptures is ignorance of Christ."

Explaining the Faith

Isn't the Bible just a story about the past? Why do people today think it applies to them?

The Bible is the *living* Word of God. What does this mean? Although Christians greatly value the Bible, they value it insofar as it leads them to Jesus Christ, the Word. The Bible lives because God still reveals himself to you through it and because you still encounter him in it. Because you can encounter Christ in the Scriptures, they should be an important part of your personal prayer, and you should listen attentively when a lector or priest proclaims the readings from Scripture at Mass and during other liturgical celebrations.

You can relate the Bible's message to aspects of your life even if its authors lived long ago and far away. The Bible's message is timeless, just as Jesus Christ and the Salvation he won are timeless. Although the content of the Bible is rooted in specific historical events, the message of Sacred Scripture will never grow old or become irrelevant.

Reflection

- Can you think of any other piece of writing that could accurately be called "living"? Why or why not?

Prayer

Lectio Divina

A time-honored way to pray the Sacred Scriptures—and to meet the living God—is the devotional reading of the Bible. For centuries, Catholics have practiced a method of prayer derived from the Benedictine tradition known as *lectio divina*; that is, "sacred reading." The purpose of the sacred reading of God's Word is not necessarily to cover a lot of territory or to use study aids or take notes. Its purpose is simply to *meet* God through his written word and allow the Holy Spirit to lead you into a deeper union with him. Therefore, it is best to take a short passage, read it slowly and attentively, and let your imagination, emotions, memory, desires, and thoughts engage the written text.

Pray with the Bible using lectio divina. Select your Scripture readings from the Mass readings for the day (see www.usccb.org/bible/readings). Then follow these steps:

Read (lectio). Select a short Bible passage. Read it slowly. Pay attention to each word. If a word or phrase catches your attention, read it to yourself several times.

Think (meditatio). Savor the passage. Read it again, reflecting on it. This time, feel any emotions that may surface. Study the pictures that arise in your imagination. Pay attention to any thoughts or memories the passage might call forth from you.

Pray (oratio). Reflect on what the Lord might be saying to you in this passage. Talk to him as you would to a friend. Ask him to show you how to respond to his Word. How can you connect this passage to your daily life? How does it relate to the people you encounter every day? Might there be a special message in this Scripture selection just *for you* today? Pay attention to any insights the Holy Spirit might send you.

 Contemplate (contemplatio). Sit in the presence of the Lord. Imagine him looking on you with great love in his heart. Rest quietly in his presence. There is no need to think here; just enjoy your time with him, as two friends would who quietly sit on a park bench gazing together at a sunset.

Take an insight that you gained from your sacred reading, and apply it to your life. Perhaps it is simply a matter of saying a prayer of thanks. Perhaps you need to be more patient with someone in your life. Let the Word the Holy Spirit spoke to you come alive in your life.

SURVEYING THE BOOKS OF THE BIBLE

LISTENING TO THE
MOST WIDELY READ BOOK

Recently, Litchfield Associates has enabled people to listen to the *King James Version* of the Bible through the Scourby Audio Bible App. Alexander Scourby, named by the *Chicago Tribune* as "the best audio-book narrator," has offered his recorded narration of this Bible. This means that the Bible, often known as the "greatest story ever told," has now encountered the greatest voice ever recorded.

The Bible app also has a visual component. As Scourby reads, the text that he is reading is highlighted in yellow, so it is possible to follow along on the screen of your smartphone, tablet, or other mobile device.

With this app, Litchfield hopes to provide people with additional opportunities to "read" the Bible through listening. Users can create daily bookmarks to listen to while driving and during work breaks, opening up time for scriptural prayer that was previously unavailable. Future versions of the app will include a sleep timer for night listening, repeat and search functions, and playlist capability.

FOCUS QUESTION

How does the Bible **CHANGE WITH THE TIMES** yet **ALSO REMAIN UNCHANGED?**

Chapter Overview

Introduction	**Best Seller**
Section 1	**Formation of the Old Testament**
Section 2	**Survey of the Old Testament Books**
Section 3	**Formation of the New Testament**
Section 4	**Survey of the New Testament Books**

INTRODUCTION
Best Seller

MAIN IDEA
Though the media, language, or features of the Bible change, God's Revelation does not change.

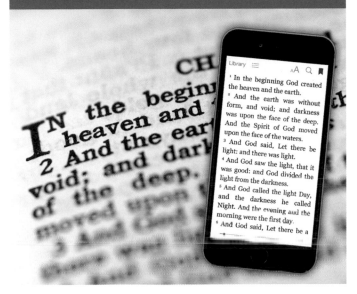

NOTE TAKING

Brainstorming. Record the question below in your notebook. As you read the section, list at least three more possible answers not included in the section.

Name at least three different media used to transmit the Bible today.

1. Printed text

2.

3.

4.

The Bible is the most-read book in history (see image at left). People have translated the Bible into more than two thousand languages, and it is always at the top of any best-seller list. In 2009, the Bible sold twenty-five million copies in America alone—twice as many as the final Harry Potter book!

The Bible has had a great impact on our language and culture. Do you recognize these common phrases that come from the Bible? Could you add any of your own to the list?

- "Do not . . . throw your pearls before swine." (Mt 7:6)
- "One does not live by bread alone." (Dt 8:3; Mt 4:4)
- "It is more blessed to give than to receive." (Acts 20:35)
- "Am I my brother's keeper?" (Gn 4:9)
- "For the love of money is the root of all evils." (1 Tm 6:10)
- "Labor of love" (1 Thes 1:3)
- "The truth will set you free." (Jn 8:32)
- "Many are invited, but few are chosen." (Mt 22:14)

The Bible contains knowledge, wisdom, and truth. The more you read Sacred Scripture, the more you discover God's plan for your happiness.

An amazing truth is that God is revealing himself to you through the Bible just as he did to biblical readers hundreds and thousands of years ago, and yet he is revealing something new at the same time. God does not change. The Bible does not change, but humanity does. A monk in a medieval monastery would have approached the Bible with questions and concerns that differ from your own.

The Bible's languages, features, media, covers, and prices may change, but God's Revelation does not change. This chapter provides an overview of the books of the Bible.

THE BIBLE IN DOLLAR$ AND ¢ENTS

A German, Johannes Gutenberg, printed the first Bibles in 1456. These Bibles, known today as Gutenberg Bibles, are the rarest and therefore most expensive printed books that book collectors can buy. A first-edition Bible would cost $25 to $35 million, says a rare book expert from the PBS program *Antiques Roadshow*. Single pages from these volumes cost $25,000 each.

You can consider your own Bibles to be a real bargain, given this market![1]

Johannes Gutenberg

SECTION ASSESSMENT

NOTE TAKING

Use the list you created to help you answer the following question.

1. Of the different media forms (e.g., printed, digital, audio) that the Bible takes, which one works best for you? Explain why.

ANALYSIS

2. What might be some positive benefits of listening to the Bible while you sleep? Would you try it?

REFLECTION

3. Which common biblical phrases do you hear most often, and under what circumstances?

SECTION 1
Formation of the Old Testament

MAIN IDEA
Because the Old Testament represents the Chosen People's faith experience over nine hundred years, the editors' role was especially important in the three-stage process of its formation.

The Old Testament is the first part of the Bible and centers on the covenant God made with his Chosen People. Recall that there are forty-six books in the Old Testament and that God inspired multiple authors to record Salvation History in the Old Testament prior to the coming of Jesus Christ. The "Old" Testament has its name for two reasons. First, the Old Testament reveals God's Revelation prior to Jesus' coming. Second, the

Pentateuch A Greek term for the first five books of the Bible.

term distinguishes the covenant that God made with the Jewish people from the new one made by Jesus Christ.

The Old Testament consists of several sections with multiple books in each one: first the **Pentateuch** (or Torah, meaning "Law")—the first five books; and then the *historical*, *wisdom*, and *prophetic* books. Their recounting of Salvation History does not progress in sequence like a modern news report. Some events were not recorded in writing until long after they occurred. Oral tradition preserved the history and wisdom of the Chosen People until God inspired authors to record the material in writing.

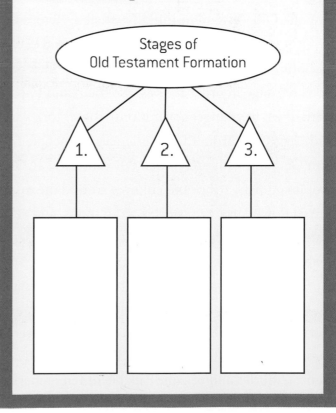

NOTE TAKING

Understanding Main Ideas. In a chart like the one below, list the three main stages in the Old Testament's formation, and write what you think is most important to know about each stage.

Stages of Old Testament Formation

1.   2.   3.

Oral Tradition

Do you have a good memory? You are lucky if you do. But because you have access to so much information, it almost does not matter if you forget even significant pieces of information, such as assignment due dates or homework. Your teacher probably has the information posted online, or a friend probably caught the assignment at the end of class and can text it right to you.

In the ancient world, most people had no access to writing implements, and few could read or write. They preserved information in their minds. This is how the Old Testament initially existed. Before the physical writing took place, there was a period of oral tradition. The Chosen People told stories of their religious heritage in order to preserve them and to pass them down to younger generations. These stories and traditions came from the experiences the people had with God and with each other. For centuries, ancient peoples of many tribes and cultures around the world passed down laws, told stories, sang songs, and celebrated sacred events through oral tradition to preserve the history of their peoples.

Is oral tradition an effective method of preserving history? Today we rely on technology to capture every detail, so that we sometimes forget the power of human memory. Illiterate people depended greatly on their memories and became capable of remembering quite a bit of information. Many of the biblical traditions were in story form because it was easier to remember stories.

Written Form

Historians believe that the Chosen People began to write down their stories during the reign of King Solomon, perhaps around 950 BC. Solomon's court would have been wealthy enough to employ scribes who did the actual writing. Scholars believe that the scribes first wrote down the oral traditions about Israel's history from the creation of the world up to the conquest of Canaan. This material is in the first section of your Bible, the Pentateuch.

The scribes then recorded the stories of the kings. They wrote first about the early kings such as King Saul and King David. These are the historical books. Next came the writings of the prophets. Some of the prophets wrote their own books. Their disciples and secretaries, however, were often the ones to collect and record their prophecies, sayings, and teachings.

Editing

In the sixth century BC, editors collected, combined, and improved the texts. Many of the Old Testament books are compilations, the work of several writers and editors. The last of the Old Testament books dates to around 100 BC.

When you consider that authors formed and edited the Old Testament over the course of about nine hundred years, it is easy to understand why many of the Old Testament books are compilations. This long formation process also clarifies why some books repeat themselves and explains why other books like the Psalms and Proverbs are really collections of wisdom from many people over the years.

SECTION ASSESSMENT

NOTE TAKING

Use the chart you created to help you complete the following task.

1. Summarize the Old Testament's formation in one sentence.

COMPREHENSION

2. When were the first Old Testament books committed to writing?

3. What are the four major divisions of the Old Testament?

APPLICATION

4. Here are the abbreviations for several Old Testament books. Identify the full name of each book: Lv, 2 Chr, Jos, Jb, Sir, Is, Mi, Mal.

REFLECTION

5. How does knowledge of the Old Testament formation process change your understanding of the Old Testament?

SECTION 2
Survey of the Old Testament Books

MAIN IDEA
The Old Testament consists of four sections with different types of literature to help you come to know God.

The Old Testament prepares people for the coming of the Savior, Jesus Christ. Every book of the Bible underscores God's love, which comes to its fullness in Christ. The following sections provide a survey of the forty-six books of the Old Testament. Notice that the abbreviations for the books are next to the names.

> **Law** The Law helped the Israelites live in conformity to God's will. There are 613 laws listed in the last four books of the Pentateuch.

NOTE TAKING

Remembering Key Details. Transcribe this list of Old Testament books by category. After you have read the section, fill in as many of the books as you can without looking. Then go back and check the text to fill in the rest of the list.

THE PENTATEUCH
Genesis
_____
_____
_____
_____

THE HISTORICAL BOOKS
Joshua
_____
_____
First Book of _____
Second Book of _____
First Book of _____
Second Book of _____
_____
_____
_____
_____
_____
_____
First Book of _____
Second Book of _____

THE WISDOM BOOKS
_____
_____
Ecclesiastes
_____
_____

THE PROPHETIC BOOKS
I _____
J _____
L _____
B _____
E _____
D _____
Twelve Minor Prophets

Penta in Greek means "five" (e.g., a pentagon is a five-sided shape). *Pentateuch* means "five books."

GENESIS (GN)

The word *genesis* means "beginning." The first eleven chapters of Genesis contain stories of prehistory: God's Creation of the world, the sin of Adam and Eve, Cain and Abel, Noah and the Flood, and the Tower of Babel. The last chapters of Genesis relate the story of the patriarchs: Abraham, Isaac, and Jacob.

EXODUS (EX)

This central book of the Old Testament tells how the Egyptian pharaoh enslaved Israel's descendants and how God freed the Israelites from slavery in the great event known as the Exodus. The Book of Exodus tells that God met with Moses on Mount Sinai, where he entered into a covenant with his Chosen People, giving the Israelites the **Law**. The Law helped the Israelites understand how to serve God.

LEVITICUS (LV)

The third book of the Pentateuch examines the particulars of the Law and focuses on holiness in all aspects of life.

NUMBERS (NM)

This book's name comes from two censuses detailed in chapters 1 and 26. The Book of Numbers continues the story of the Israelites in the desert until they come to the border of the Promised Land.

DEUTERONOMY (DT)

Deuteronomy means "second law." The Book of Deuteronomy repeats much of the material of the three previous books through sermons attributed to Moses.

Sampling Scripture

ABRAHAM, FATHER OF FAITH

Abraham and Sarah are pivotal Old Testament figures. They were living in Haran (present-day Iraq) when God called them to leave their home. Abraham is a symbol of faith, of one who trusted God totally. Abraham was willing to sacrifice his only son, Isaac, to God, though God prevented the human sacrifice (see Gn 22). Abraham is "the father of a multitude of nations" (Gn 17:5). Both Christians and Jews consider Abraham the father of their faith. Jewish people are ancestors to Christians, since they have been the trustees of God's promise from the beginning. St. Paul described the special role of the Jewish people:

> They are the Israelites; theirs the adoption, the glory, the covenants, the giving of the law, the worship, and the promises; theirs the patriarchs, and from them, according to the flesh, is the Messiah. (Rom 9:4–5)

Muslims also profess that Abraham is the father of their faith. Muslims understand Ibrahim (Abraham) to be the father of the Arab people, and they consider him a prophet, placing him on the same level as Moses, Jesus, and Muhammad. The Qur'an tells that Ibrahim almost sacrificed Ishmael, his son by Hagar.

Reflect on each of the following questions. Write responses.

- How important is trustworthiness in a friend?
- Imagine that you are Abraham or Isaac. Describe what thoughts and feelings you might have on the journey to the sacrifice.

The Historical Books narrate the events of Salvation History, namely how God remained faithful to the covenant and how the Israelites struggled over time to live according to the Law. The Historical Books cover almost nine hundred years of history from about 1020 BC to 142 BC. Recall that although these books are called the Historical Books, you want to look for religious rather than historical truth in them.

JOSHUA (JO)
Joshua, a military leader, led the Israelites into the Promised Land, conquered it, and divided the land among the various tribes.

JUDGES (JGS)
The Israelites fall into the cycle of apostasy in the Book of Judges. God sends a judge to deliver Israel and to lead the troops.

RUTH (RU)
The Book of Ruth is a short story about Ruth, a Gentile, who showed great fidelity to her Jewish mother-in-law, Naomi.

FIRST AND SECOND SAMUEL (1 AND 2 SM)
The First and Second Books of Samuel tell of Israel's transition from the judges' leadership to the monarchy. God allowed Samuel to anoint Saul as king while warning the people that they would regret having a king. Saul disobeyed God, so Samuel then anointed David.

FIRST AND SECOND KINGS (1 AND 2 KGS)
After David's death, his son Solomon took the throne. He built the Temple in Jerusalem, but managed his resources poorly. After Solomon died, the kingdom split into two: the northern kingdom of Israel and the southern kingdom of Judah. The remaining chapters tell the stories of both the northern and the southern kingdoms until they fell to outside nations.

FIRST AND SECOND CHRONICLES (1 AND 2 CHR)
These books retell many of the stories of the First and Second Books of Samuel and Kings, but focus primarily on the southern kingdom from the time of King David until the Babylonian conquest of Judah.

EZRA AND NEHEMIAH (EZR AND NEH)

Scholars believe that "the Chronicler" wrote Ezra and Nehemiah as well as First and Second Chronicles. Ezra and Nehemiah tell the story of the Jews after they returned from exile in Babylon.

TOBIT, JUDITH, AND ESTHER (TB, JDT, AND EST)

These three books are inspiring works of fiction. Tobit is on a romantic quest. Judith conquers a powerful army. Esther saves her people from genocide. Their authors wrote these books to encourage the Jewish people.

FIRST AND SECOND MACCABEES (1 AND 2 MC)

The First and Second Books of Maccabees give an account of events in the second century BC when various groups tried to suppress Judaism in Palestine, causing a revolt among the Jews. A period of Jewish independence followed.

Sampling Scripture

LESSONS FROM RUTH

You can find the Book of Ruth between Judges and First and Second Samuel because it is set during the era of the **judges**. The book tells the story of Ruth, a Moabite woman who became the great-grandmother of King David. This story shows that God's love extends not only to the Chosen People, but to everyone.

Naomi had gone to Moab with her immediate and extended family to escape a famine. The men of the family died, leaving Naomi with two daughters-in-law, Ruth and Orpah, who had no husbands or children. When the famine ended, Naomi wanted the women to remain with their own people because they were Gentiles. Orpah did just that, but Ruth insisted on returning with her mother-in-law to her native Bethlehem. Ruth's faithfulness was rewarded when she married Boaz, a rich landowner. Their son, Obed, was King David's grandfather.

judges Military leaders who led Old Testament Israelite tribes in battles against their oppressors.

- Read the entire Book of Ruth. List three qualities that describe Ruth's character, recording the verses that support your descriptions.

Wisdom literature addresses the ways that God works in individuals' everyday lives.

JOB (JB)

This famous story tells the trials of an innocent man and raises the question of why bad things happen to good people. The Book of Job teaches that God's ways are not human ways.

PSALMS (PS(S))

The Psalms are a collection of five books of poetry or song lyrics that were composed over a period of five hundred years. Those worshiping at the Temple sang many of the 150 psalms. The psalms praise and thank God, petition him for help, and express sorrow and repentance. A psalm is read at every Mass during the Liturgy of the Word.

PROVERBS (PRV)

The Book of Proverbs contains short sayings for moral living. The proverbs educate you about how to live a good life.

ECCLESIASTES (ECCL)

In this book, a fictional character named Qoheleth teaches important lessons about living through questions, sayings, and proverbs.

SONG OF SONGS (SG)

The Song of Songs is a poem that celebrates the ideal of romantic love and is an allegory of God's love for his People.

WISDOM (WS)

The Book of Wisdom, written about a hundred years before the coming of Jesus Christ, encouraged Jews living in Egypt to remain faithful to their heritage.

SIRACH (SIR)

Sirach was likely a sage. He recounted many wise lessons and sayings.

Sampling Scripture
EXPLORING PROVERBS

One of the most familiar sayings from the Book of Proverbs is this: "Fear of the LORD is the beginning of knowledge" (Prv 1:7). To know God, then, means that you are humble and know your place before him. This attitude leads to true wisdom.

King Solomon was famous for being wise. Biblical scholars believe that Solomon was the author of the second and fifth parts of the Book of Proverbs. Other authors also contributed to this work, which editors likely put together in the early part of the fifth century BC.

Proverbs is a poetic book. The authors used parallelism, in which the second line of a couplet restates, contrasts, or advances the thought of the first line. An example of *contrasting parallelism* is this proverb: "A wise son gives his father joy, but a foolish son is a grief to his mother" (Prv 10:1). Parallelism makes it easier for you to remember the wise saying; its purpose is to encourage you to live a virtuous life and to avoid sin that leads you astray.

Read Proverbs 25:1–29:27, the second collection of proverbs ascribed to Solomon. From your reading, identify five of your favorite proverbs and write or type them out. Then rewrite these proverbs in a form that would appeal to a person your own age today, and illustrate one of them.

God sent prophets to encourage the people of Israel to stay faithful to their covenant with him.

A prophet spoke to the People on behalf of God and sometimes spoke to God on behalf of the People. Prophets generally tried to keep kings or the Chosen People in line when they strayed from the covenant with God.

ISAIAH (IS)

The Book of Isaiah spans three centuries, with the Prophet Isaiah and his disciples addressing different audiences. The book is divided according to prophecies for Jerusalem, the Exile, and the return.

JEREMIAH (JER)

Jeremiah came from a priestly family. He delivered words of warning and hope to Jews living in Jerusalem prior to the Babylonian Exile (a period the Jews were held in captivity), then to the Jews living in Egypt during the Exile. He shared the news that God was going to make a New Covenant with his people.

LAMENTATIONS (LAM)

Lamentations, a book that may be the work of Jeremiah, consists of five poems lamenting the fall of Jerusalem. (A lamentation is an expression of deep sorrow.)

BARUCH (BAR)

Although Baruch was probably Jeremiah's scribe, it is more likely that other authors wrote this book in his name. It serves as a reminder that the Exile occurred because of the people's infidelity to God.

EZEKIEL (EZ)

God called Ezekiel to be a prophet in Babylon, where the Jewish people were in exile. Once the Babylonians had destroyed Jerusalem, Ezekiel promised Salvation and a New Covenant if the Jews returned to God. Ezekiel often acted his prophecies out dramatically.

DANIEL (DN)

The Book of Daniel is an **apocalyptic** text, placed among the prophetic books because Christians initially interpreted it as prophetic literature.

apocalyptic *Apocalypse* is a Greek word for "revelation." It also refers to a type of highly symbolic literature that contains apparitions about the future and the Final Judgment. This form of literature was used to give hope to a persecuted people that God's goodness will triumph over evil.

TWELVE MINOR PROPHETS

The prophets discussed above are considered the "major prophets" because their works are longer than the minor prophets' books, not necessarily because they are more important. The books of the minor prophets are Hosea (Hos), Joel (Jl), Amos (Am), Obadiah (Ob), Jonah (Jon), Micah (Mi), Nahum (Na), Habakkuk (Hb), Zephaniah (Zep), Haggai (Hg), Zechariah (Zec), and Malachi (Mal).

Sampling Scripture
MICAH'S MESSAGE OF JUDGMENT

The prophet Micah came from a small country village and prophesied during the reigns of Kings Jotham, Ahaz, and Hezekiah. His poetic images come from rural life and show his outrage over the injustices landowners committed against the poor.

The first three chapters of Micah condemn the leaders of both the northern kingdom of Israel and the southern kingdom of Judah. Micah railed against their sins, their hatred of good and love of evil (3:2). Micah also offered hope, saying that a ruler would come from Bethlehem to lead Israel to peace and justice. This ruler would gather God's "**remnant**," a righteous group that would survive God's chastisement of the nation.

The Book of Micah ends on a positive note. Micah reminds the people of God's unending mercy.

- Read Micah. Answer these questions: What are some of the social evils that the prophet criticizes (see Mi 2)? What roles will the future ruler and remnant have (see Mi 5)?

remnant A name for the exiles and former exiles who remained faithful to God during the time of the Babylonian Captivity and who were expected to restore Jerusalem.

SECTION ASSESSMENT

NOTE TAKING

Use the chart you created to help you answer the following questions.

1. Tell which category of Scripture the following books belong to: 1 and 2 Samuel, Jeremiah, Proverbs, Baruch, Ezekiel.

2. Which books were written by an author known as "the Chronicler"?

3. Why is the Book of Daniel categorized with the prophetic books?

COMPREHENSION

4. What does every book of the Bible underscore?

5. Which section of the Old Testament has the greatest number of books? The fewest?

ANALYSIS

6. What do you think of Ruth's decision to stay with Naomi?

7. Could Micah's description of the sins of his time apply to any aspects of our society today?

SECTION 3
Formation of the New Testament

MAIN IDEA
Although Jesus' followers primarily shared the Good News orally, it became evident some years after Jesus' Death that writing down the Gospel was very important.

The New Testament's name describes its content. These books describe the Good News of Jesus Christ and his New Covenant with humanity. The **Gospels** share

Gospel A word meaning "Good News." *Gospel* refers to three distinct but interrelated concepts: Jesus Christ himself is the Gospel; his message is the Gospel; and the four written accounts of his Life, Death, Resurrection, and Ascension in the New Testament are Gospels.

this Good News. The Acts of the Apostles, Epistles (Letters), and Revelation talk about the spread of the Gospel in the early Church.

The Gospels are the heart of the New Testament—and of the whole Bible—because through them you can know Jesus Christ, the Son of God, and learn how to live as his disciple. Think about how you stand in Mass when the priest reads the Gospel but sit for the other readings. This is just one way in which you honor the Gospels as the most important biblical texts.

The Evangelists did not produce the Gospels like news reports after Jesus' Ascension. There were three stages in the formation of the Gospels: (1) the time of Jesus' own life; (2) the years when the Apostles and

NOTE TAKING

Compare and Contrast. As you read about the formation of the New Testament, compare it to the Old Testament's formation. Design a Venn diagram like the following and use it to capture what is unique to each one's development and what is common to both.

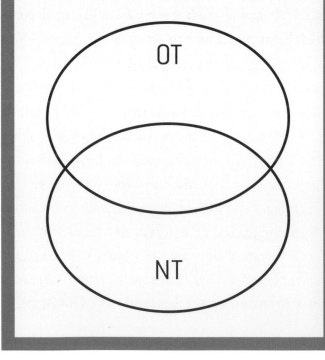

early disciples of Jesus orally preached the Good News; and (3) the actual writing of the Gospels.

While Nazareth has changed from the time when Jesus was a child there, images of the city such as this one remind us of Jesus' historical life as well as his childhood and early life that we know so little about.

Stage 1: The Historical Jesus, 6 BC to AD 30/33

Scholars estimate that Jesus was born in 6 BC. Remember that the years BC, or "before Christ," are numbered in reverse. According to the research of historians, Herod the Great was appointed as king of the region of Judea by the Romans and reigned from 37 to 4 BC. The Gospels record that Herod was alive at the time of Jesus' birth and died when Jesus was still a small child, which helps the Church to arrive at the date of 6 BC.

Jesus lived the typical life of a Jewish boy growing up in Nazareth, a town in **Galilee**. As a child, he learned the carpenter trade from his foster father, Joseph. He came onto the public scene probably about AD 28. During his public ministry, he traveled the countryside around Galilee and Judea and visited the small towns where he taught, healed, and proclaimed the coming of God's Kingdom. At the instigation of some religious leaders who saw Jesus as a threat, the Roman prefect Pontius Pilate crucified him. Three days later, Jesus rose from the dead and visited his Apostles,

revealing himself completely as the Son of God. In summary, Jesus is the Good News.

Stage 2: Oral Tradition, AD 30 to 50

The Apostles believed that Jesus was the awaited Messiah and the Son of God. They followed Jesus' command to "go into to the whole world and proclaim the gospel to every creature" (Mk 16:15). While remaining pious Jews themselves, the early Christians believed that Jesus was the fulfillment of God's Old Testament promises. The Apostles first announced the marvelous things God had accomplished in Jesus to their fellow Jews. Later, they found that Gentiles were also receiving the Holy Spirit. Early Christians then began to preach to both Jews and Gentiles throughout the Roman Empire.

Their preaching took three key forms:

1. The **kerygma**, or preaching to unbelievers

The Acts of the Apostles records several sermons that Sts. Peter and Paul preached about Jesus. In their preaching, they presented a basic outline of Jesus' Life, Death, Resurrection, and Ascension. They used passages from the Hebrew Scriptures to show that Jesus fulfilled prophecies made about the Messiah. During this period, some disciples began to assemble collections of material about Christ, such as miracle stories, his parables, and the Passion narratives. Later, the four Evangelists would draw on these sources to help compose their Gospels.

> **Galilee** A large region in the north of the modern nation of Israel, north of Samaria at the time of Jesus.
>
> **kerygma** The core or essential message of the Gospel that Jesus Christ is Lord. One example is Acts 2:14–36.

2. The *didache*, or further teaching to those who had accepted Jesus

The *didache* was further catechetical instruction for those who had already accepted Jesus. *Catechesis* literally means to "sound down"; that is, to repeat the message and explain it in greater depth. Early converts needed additional instruction about how to live a more Christ-filled life. Originally, this instruction was shared orally. Eventually it was written down.

In 1873 Philotheos Bryennios—a Greek Orthodox theologian and bishop—discovered an early copy of The Didache *or* The Teaching of the Twelve Apostles. *The oldest surviving written catechism, it was lost for centuries before his discovery.*

3. The liturgy, or Christian worship

Belief and prayer are closely related. Early Christians recalled Jesus' central moments, teachings, and prayers in their Eucharistic celebrations. Some examples include Jesus' words at the Last Supper, the Lord's Prayer, and his Passion.

The early Church preached the Gospel that Jesus lived and proclaimed. The Church's primary interest

> **didache** A Greek word that means "teaching." In a Christian context this term refers to the earliest known writing in Christianity aside from the New Testament.

was to interpret the *meaning* of Jesus' main deeds and sayings and to share the Good News with as many people as possible. In some cases, local communities slightly varied the wording of liturgical prayers. However, they faithfully recounted the spirit of what Jesus did and said.

Stage 3: The New Testament Writings (AD 50 to ca. 120)

Luke told his reasons for writing his Gospel in its very first verses:

> Since many have undertaken to compile a narrative of the events that have been fulfilled among us, just as those who were eyewitnesses from the beginning and ministers of the word have handed them down to us, I too have decided, after investigating everything accurately anew, to write it down in an orderly sequence for you, most excellent Theophilus, so that you may realize the certainty of the teachings you have received. (Lk 1:1–4)

The final stage of the formation of the New Testament was the writing down of the Gospel. Remember that the four Gospels, the Acts of the Apostles, and the Book of Revelation were written in the latter half of the first century to the early second century. Although the four canonical Gospels were composed between AD 65 and 100, oral preaching about Jesus carried on well into the second century. Some of the first New Testament books written were the letters of St. Paul.

Luke's quote describes how the Evangelists formed the Gospels: they examined the sources, including those from eyewitnesses, and then organized the material into a written account.

All four Gospels share the Good News: the Salvation and Redemption from sin that God accomplished for us through his Son, Jesus Christ. The Gospel writers (represented by the symbols on page 84) told the

Corinth is mentioned many times in the New Testament. It was located in what is now southern Greece. St. Paul lived in Corinth for eighteen months (see Acts 18:1–18).

story differently to different Christian communities. Mark highlighted Jesus' *suffering*, portraying a man who freely gave his life for humanity. Matthew emphasized Jesus as a *teacher* who perfectly fulfilled the Jewish prophecies made about him. Luke presented Jesus as a *Savior* for all people, one who reaches out especially to the poor and neglected. John's Gospel, written approximately ten to thirty years later than the others, focused on Jesus' *divinity*.

Why Wait before Writing?

Why did the early Church wait years after the events of Jesus' Life, Death, and Resurrection before writing anything down? Recall that in those days many Jews could not read, so oral transmission was the main means of conveying knowledge. Students needed to remember what their teachers taught them. Knowing

that his audience would want to remember his teachings, Jesus used vivid stories, short sayings, striking images, and poetic language to present his truth in a memorable way.

Eventually, the early Christians realized that the Good News about Jesus also had to be committed to writing for three main reasons.

1. The end of the world was not coming as quickly as anticipated.

Many of the earliest Christians expected that Jesus would come back "to judge the living and the dead" in their lifetimes. They had more urgent tasks—such as preaching the Gospel and preparing for the Lord's return—to attend to than writing. But the first Christians were mistaken about the timing of Christ's Second Coming. And people who had heard Jesus speak firsthand began to die, some becoming martyrs. The early Christians began to see the need to preserve an accurate apostolic testimony about Jesus for the future.

2. Some people were distorting the true Gospel.

The New Testament letters reveal that after the Apostles preached in certain communities, others would sometimes distort the original, authentic message. In his Second Letter to the Corinthians, St. Paul wrote that he was "afraid that, as the serpent deceived Eve by his cunning, your thoughts may be corrupted from a sincere commitment to Christ" (2 Cor 11:3). To combat heretical teachings and to clarify Jesus' true message, early Christians needed an authoritative written record of the Good News.

3. Christians needed more instruction.

A written record of the Apostles' teaching would help to instruct Christians about the Faith in a consistent way. Such writings could also serve as guides for liturgy. The Church included the **epistles** and Gospels in the Eucharistic liturgy. Finally, the Church could send writings—such as St. Paul's letters—to new and growing local churches.

> **epistle** A letter. In the New Testament, epistles are letters intended for public reading.

SECTION ASSESSMENT

NOTE TAKING

Refer to your Venn diagram to answer the following question.

1. What are the similarities and differences between the formation of the Old and New Testaments?

COMPREHENSION

2. Why are the Gospels the heart of the Bible?

ANALYSIS

3. Each Gospel writer focused on a different aspect of Jesus' story (pages 86–87). What do you suppose was going on in each of their communities for the Evangelists to choose these themes?

REFLECTION

4. How do you respond when you hear predictions that the end of the world is coming?
5. Why is the story of Jesus Christ Good News to you?

SECTION 4
Survey of the New Testament Books

MAIN IDEA
The New Testament shares the Good News about Jesus Christ in the Gospels and then illustrates more concretely how the Good News should be lived in the Acts of the Apostles, the Pauline Letters, and Revelation.

The New Testament canon developed over time. Under the inspiration of the Holy Spirit, the Apostles and their successors determined which writings belonged in it. By AD 200, Church leaders had discerned that God had inspired the four Gospels, the Pauline Epistles, Acts, and some of the other epistles. By 367, the canon consisted of the twenty-seven books in the New Testament. The Council of Trent (1543–1565, shown on the left), a gathering of the bishops of the world called to address the Protestant Reformation, reemphasized that this canon was the inspired Word of God. The canon is affirmed as a matter of Catholic doctrine, which all Catholics are called to embrace.

All twenty-seven books of the New Testament were first written in *Koine* (common) Greek, the spoken language of the ordinary people in the Roman Empire. Biblical scholars are uncertain as to the exact dates of the various New Testament books. The chart below lists the New Testament books and their approximate dates of composition, with short summaries for some books.

NOTE TAKING

Asking Questions. As you read this section, list in your notebook three questions you have about the New Testament.

1. _____

2. _____

3. _____

THE BOOKS OF THE New Testament

Gospels (4)

"The Gospels are the heart of all the Scriptures 'because they are our principal source for the life and teaching of the Incarnate Word, our Savior'" (*CCC*, 125).

MATTHEW (MT)
80–90 (+/– 10 years)

MARK (MK)
60–75 (most likely 68–73)

LUKE (LK)
85 (+/– 5 years)

JOHN (JN)
80–110 (probably in the 90s)

Acts of the Apostles (1)

The Acts of the Apostles is really the second part of the Gospel of Luke.

ACTS OF THE APOSTLES (ACTS)
Acts (85, +/– 5 years) tells the history of the early Church and reports the spread of the Gospel from Pentecost to the imprisonment of St. Paul in the late 50s.

One of the central debates in the early Church was whether Gentiles could join the Church without becoming Jewish. The Council of Jerusalem (Acts 15) determined that Gentiles did not need to be Jewish in order to be Christian. The three missionary journeys of St. Paul feature prominently in Acts.

The Pauline Letters (The New Testament Letters) (13)

St. Paul or his disciples wrote these epistles—formal, finely written letters meant to teach a person or group, in this case individual Christian leaders or local churches. The epistles appear in the Bible in order of length, from longest to shortest.

Each of Paul's writings addressed the needs of the community to which he was writing.

Some call Paul's letters to Philemon, to the Colossians, and to the community in Ephesus the "prison letters" because Paul wrote them while in prison. Those letters thought to be written by Paul himself are marked in this chart with the letter *P*. Those that were likely written by his disciples are marked *D*.

ROMANS (ROM)
The Letter to the Romans (P—57/58) is Paul's longest letter and contains his most advanced theological reflection on Jesus. The letter stresses the necessity of faith in Jesus Christ, who justifies and saves all believers. It also offers instructions on Christian living.

1 AND 2 CORINTHIANS (1 COR AND 2 COR)

In the First (P—56/57) and Second (P—57) Letters to the Corinthians, Paul addressed problems his converts were having in Corinth. In the First Letter, he gave important instructions on the Eucharist and Jesus' Resurrection (see 1 Cor 11:23–24). He also wrote a beautiful passage on the meaning of love (see 1 Cor 13:1–13). In the Second Letter, Paul encouraged the Corinthians to forgive each other and to be generous in a collection for the church in Jerusalem. He also defended his work as an Apostle.

GALATIANS (GAL)

In the Letter to the Galatians (P—54–55), Paul defended his role as a true Apostle of Jesus Christ. He also said that Christians should preach the Gospel to Gentiles because Christ's love extends to all.

EPHESIANS (EPH)

The Letter to the Ephesians (D—61–63 or 90s) develops the theme of the Church as the Body of Christ and the Bride of Christ. It also emphasizes the unity of Gentiles and Jews in Christ, teaching how Christians should live in God's Spirit as his children.

PHILIPPIANS (PHIL)

Paul wrote the Letter to the Philippians (P—56) from prison to Christians in northern Greece (Macedonia). In this deeply personal and joyful letter, Paul told his readers to rejoice in Christ the Savior, the one who teaches us the meaning of true humility.

COLOSSIANS (COL)

The Letter to the Colossians (D—61–63 or 80s) instructs the Colossians to reject false teachings and to accept only Jesus Christ as the true Lord of creation and the source of new life.

1 AND 2 THESSALONIANS (1 THES AND 2 THES)

The First Letter to the Thessalonians (P—50) is the oldest piece of writing in the New Testament. It reminds Paul's converts how to live until Christ comes again. The Second Letter to the Thessalonians (D—50 or 90) reminds converts that they need to keep working for the Kingdom of God and tries to quell a rumor that the end times had begun.

1 AND 2 TIMOTHY, TITUS (1 TM , 2 TM, TI)

The Letter to Titus (D—65 or 95–100), the First Letter to Timothy (D—65 or 95–100), and the Second Letter to Timothy (D—64–67 or 95–100) are called "pastoral letters" because they are correspondences between those who "shepherded" or "pastored" Christians. These letters are also unique because they were written to individuals, not entire communities.

These letters give advice on issues of Church leadership (e.g., the qualifications of bishops), Church organization, Christian worship, and moral living. They also warn against certain false teachings and the need to be faithful to the true doctrine passed on by the Apostles.

Hebrews (1)

Though identified as Paul's Letter to the Hebrews, it is more likely a sermon or homily by someone else.

HEBREWS (HEB)

The Letter to the Hebrews (60s if by Paul; or before the turn of the century, most likely the 80s, if by someone else) emphasizes Christ's superiority over all creation. Christ is the High Priest whose perfect sacrifice in dying on the Cross took away sin, fulfilling all the promises made in the Old Testament.

The Catholic Epistles (7)

The Catholic Epistles are letters intended "for all."

These letters are **catholic**, or universal, because they contain general advice that is helpful to all the churches.

Also, these letters can help you to understand better how the Church was founded and formed in the first century. The names of the letters reflect their authorship.

> **catholic** With a lowercase *c*, *catholic* means universal.

JAMES (JAS)

The Letter of James (62 or 80s or 90s) advises its readers to treat people justly, to take care of the poor, and to control their speech. Faith in Jesus should lead to good works.

1 AND 2 PETER (1 AND 2 PT)

The First Letter of Peter (60–63 or 70–90) emphasizes that Christians should imitate Jesus when they suffer by not returning evil for evil. Good example will lead others to Christ. The Second Letter (ca. 130) uses much of Jude's material and encourages its readers to remain strong and faithful to true teaching.

1, 2, AND 3 JOHN (1, 2, AND 3 JN)

The Letters of John (ca. 100) were identified with the early Church with the Apostle John. The first two letters focus on love as proof of our faith in Jesus as well as the need to love others. The third letter was written to a Church leader who needed to support missionary efforts.

JUDE (JUDE)

The Letter of Jude (90s) warns Christians to remain firm in their faith against false teachers. It speaks of the punishment that will come to false teachers.

REVELATION (RV)

In this highly symbolic work, written in 95 or 96, John relates visions he has of God, the Risen Christ, and the future. The purpose of the book was to encourage Christians who were undergoing persecution for their faith in Jesus Christ. Using apocalyptic language, the author reassures his readers that Christ will reward the faithful with a heavenly home at the end of time.

SECTION ASSESSMENT

NOTE TAKING

Refer to the questions you recorded to complete the following item.

1. Have you learned the answers to your three questions? If so, list the answers here. If not, where could you go (on your own) to find answers to these questions?

COMPREHENSION

2. Who wrote the Acts of the Apostles?

3. How are Paul's letters arranged in the New Testament?

4. Why are some of the New Testament letters called "catholic"?

CRITICAL THINKING

5. Why do you think that biblical scholars approximate the years when various New Testament books were written? What might allow these scholars to make closer approximations?

Section Summaries

Focus Question

How does the Bible change with the times yet also remain unchanged?
Complete one of the following:

Although translations, supplemental materials, and media do not ever change the Bible's Revelation, what might be some ways that they could distort Revelation?

People often use biblical texts in music, art, and film. Name a time when a biblical verse surprised you by turning up in popular media. Share the occasion and whether the verse was used appropriately in your opinion.

"God's Word is eternal." Explain how this statement is true for the Bible as a whole.

INTRODUCTION (PAGES 69–70)

Best Seller

The Bible has influenced the culture, and in turn, the culture has influenced the way the Bible is made, distributed, and even read. The Bible is an all-time best seller and is published in many different editions and translations.

Can you envision other ways that technology in the future may share the biblical texts?

SECTION 1 (PAGES 71–73)

Formation of the Old Testament

The formation of the Old Testament involved three steps. For many years, the Israelites preserved their history through oral tradition. Then scribes wrote down the oral tradition. Finally, editors took the different writings and compiled them into the books you read today.

Name a contemporary three-step process of communicating a message today that is comparable to the "teach-write-edit" process employed in the formation of the Old Testament.

SECTION 2 (PAGES 74–83)

Survey of the Old Testament Books

The Old Testament is divided into four main sections. In the Pentateuch, you learn how God called Abraham and later saved his People from slavery. The historical books recount Israel's relationship with God as they moved both toward and away from him. Over the years, the Israelites gathered stories and sayings into the wisdom books that they used to teach important lessons. The prophetic books reminded the people and their leaders how they should be living.

 What comparison can you make between the way the books of the Old Testament are arranged and a library?

SECTION 3 (PAGES 84–88)

Formation of the New Testament

The Apostles preached about Jesus himself as the Good News, and after his Ascension, they took his message out to the Mediterranean world. They preached according to the needs of the early Christians and worshipped according to Jesus' instructions. They eventually wrote down the Gospel because the end of the world had not come as they had anticipated, and people were distorting the message.

If you thought that the end of the world was coming in the next few years, how would your behavior and your relationship with God change?

SECTION 4 (PAGES 89–93)

Survey of the New Testament Books

The Gospels are at the heart of Scripture because they allow you to know Jesus. The Acts of the Apostles and the epistles help you get a sense of the early Christian Church. The Book of Revelation reminds you that being Christian could be dangerous; in the Church's early years, apocalyptic language became necessary for this reason.

 When are times when less formal writing is appropriate for use in books? Why do you think using *koine* Greek as the language for much of the New Testament would have been helpful to the first-century readers?

Chapter Assignments

Choose and complete at least one of these assignments to assess your understanding of the material in this chapter.

1. Explore Biblical Places

Create a slide show or multimedia presentation of key biblical locations mentioned in the Old Testament or New Testament. Cite a biblical passage that mentions each place, and choose at least ten photos of the different places. In writing, discuss how these photos affect your thinking about biblical times.

Websites to help you complete this project include the Ave Maria Press website at www.avemariapress.com/resources/revelation and the following:

- Pictures of Palestine: www.trekearth.com/gallery/Middle East/Palestine/

- Bible Places: www.bibleplaces.com

2. Map Biblical Stories

Choose either the travels of the patriarchs or the journeys of Jesus in one of the Gospels, and map them:

- For the patriarchs, begin with Abram's call to leave Haran (Gn 12), and finish with Joseph and his brothers in Egypt (Gn 50).

- Follow the path of Jesus through an entire Gospel. Whichever Gospel you choose, note that Jesus' life course leads to Jerusalem, specifically Calvary, the site of his Death that led to Salvation for humankind.

A *biblical atlas* provides maps to help you navigate around the ancient biblical world. Your Bible might contain some good maps. You can also find maps online. Print, photocopy, or create your own map of the ancient world either during the time of Abraham or during Jesus' time.

See the Ave Maria Press website www.avemariapress.com/resources/revelation for some helpful resources for completing this assignment. Here are two other useful websites:

- http://ancienthistory.about.com/od/biblicalmaps/qt/BiblicalMaps.htm

- www.bible.ca/maps

3. Use a Biblical Commentary

A *biblical commentary* analyzes, evaluates, and explains biblical texts. Some can be quite scholarly, such as the *Anchor Bible* series. Others are designed for beginning Scripture students. Two time-tested Catholic biblical commentaries are the *Collegeville Bible Commentary* and the *New*

Jerome Biblical Commentary. The *Catholic Study Bible*, second edition, also has extensive commentaries.

Read about Noah's Flood in Genesis 7–8. Locate one of these biblical commentaries, read what it has to say about the Flood, and write a two-page summary.

Faithful Disciple

St. Edith Stein

St. Edith Stein

Born in 1891, St. Edith Stein grew up in a large Jewish family in Poland. From early childhood, Edith was very bright. As a young woman, Edith earned a doctorate, *summa cum laude*, in philosophy from the University of Freiburg in Germany. She worked closely with a prominent philosopher, Edmund Husserl, whose work would later influence the thought of Karol Wojtyla (St. John Paul II). Edith's adult years coincided with World Wars I and II.

Despite her admiration for her mother's Jewish faith, Edith had become an atheist by the time she was in high school, though she continued her search for truth. After reading the autobiography of St. Teresa of Avila, she decided that she wanted to become Catholic and was baptized in 1922 at the age of thirty-one.

After her conversion, Edith spent her time lecturing and writing. She earned a name for herself as a brilliant philosopher and author. For some time, however, she had been yearning for the solitude of the Carmelite monastery. Because of her Jewish ancestry, the Nazis restricted her public activities, so the time was right for her to enter the cloister of the Discalced Carmelite monastery at Cologne-Lindenthal at the age of forty-two. Her religious name was Teresa Benedicta of the Cross.

When she realized that her presence in the monastery posed a threat to her sisters, Edith asked to move to a cloister in Holland. Although the Nazis had occupied Holland, it was a neutral nation. In response to a Dutch bishop's pastoral letter protesting the deportation of Jews, however, the Nazis arrested all Catholics of Jewish extraction in Holland, including Edith. The Nazis sent her to Auschwitz, where she died in the gas chambers on August 9, 1942.

St. John Paul II canonized Edith Stein in 1998. She is one of six patron saints of Europe. There was some controversy as to whether the Church should consider Edith a martyr because some suggested that she died because of her Jewish background rather than her Christian faith. The Nuremberg Laws of 1935 had created racial, not religious, definitions of what it meant to be Jewish. The position of the Roman Catholic Church is that she died because the bishops in Holland publicly condemned Nazi racism: she died for the sake of a Catholic moral position.[2]

Reading Comprehension

1. Which saint inspired St. Edith Stein's conversion?

2. What was her religious name?

3. Why did St. Edith Stein move to a cloister in Holland?

4. How did the Nuremberg Laws define Jewish identity?

Writing Task

- As a young person, how did St. Edith Stein give up her faith yet still remain on a faith journey?

Explaining the Faith
Why do Catholics believe in things and do things that are not in the Bible?

The belief that Mary is the Mother of God is an example of Sacred Tradition. Some venerations of Mary and the saints are small-t traditions.

The Bible is not the only means God uses to hand down the truths of Revelation. The bishops transmit Revelation through the ages in two ways: Sacred Scripture and Sacred Tradition. Both of these elements of the Deposit of Faith come from God and have human Salvation as their goal, so Catholics must give them equal authority. Just as the Holy Spirit inspired the biblical authors to write down what God wanted, so the Holy Spirit inspires Sacred Tradition. While some Catholic beliefs are not written in the Bible, they also do not contradict the content of Sacred Scripture.

However, do not confuse Sacred Tradition with theological, disciplinary, liturgical, or devotional traditions that have become popular over time in local churches. These small-*t* "traditions" include things like Advent wreaths, Nativity scenes, and Holy Week processions.

Over time, the Church shifts its disciplines and practices to emphasize different aspects of truth without losing focus on the big picture of Divine Revelation.

 ## Reflection

- Why do Americans believe in human rights that are not covered in the Bill of Rights? How does this compare to Catholics' beliefs in practices and truths that are not completely spelled out in Scripture?

Prayer
Priestly Blessing

The Book of Numbers contains Moses's instructions to Aaron and the priests about how to bless the Chosen People. A blessing conveys prosperity and well-being. Receiving God's blessing is a great honor. It reveals the great dignity you have as God's child. Meditate on the words of this familiar blessing:

> The LORD bless you and keep you!
> The LORD let his face shine upon you,
> and be gracious to you!
> The LORD look upon you kindly and give
> you peace!
> —Numbers 6:24–26

THE PENTATEUCH:
CREATION, COVENANT, AND THE EXODUS

A COLLEGE SIGNS A
COMMUNITY COVENANT

On November 3, 2012, during halftime of the Utah State University–Texas State football game, administrators from Utah State joined members of the US military as well as representatives from the university's Reserve Officers Training Corps (ROTC) program to sign a community covenant.

> Community Covenant is an Army program designed to foster and sustain effective state and community partnerships with the Army to improve quality of life for soldiers and their families. It is a formal commitment of support by state and local communities to soldiers and families of the Army, in active guard and reserve. It is part of a national initiative to link the community and military in supporting families and veterans.[1]

Although Community Covenant is an Army program, it extends to the other military services as well. The Utah State University Extension program will be especially helpful since it offers "educational resources and programs in financial literacy, relationships and family life, and family resource management, to name a few."

In addition to Utah State, 125 Utah cities and twelve counties have signed the community covenant.[2]

103

FOCUS QUESTION

What does GOD WANT FOR YOU?

Chapter Overview

| Introduction | Agreements, Deals, Contracts, and Covenants |

| Section 1 | Formation of the Pentateuch |

| Section 2 | Creation, the Fall, and the Promise of Redemption |

| Section 3 | God's Call, Promise, and Covenants |

| Section 4 | The Exodus and the Giving of the Law |

Agreements, Deals, Contracts, and Covenants

What Is a Covenant?

A covenant resembles an agreement, a deal, or a contract, but these words are not synonyms for covenant.

- An agreement between two parties means that both parties know exactly what they are consenting to, verbally or in a formal document. To agree is to come to terms.

- A deal is a transaction, bargain, or contract between two or more parties, often a business or legal arrangement.

- A contract is a binding agreement between two or more persons or parties, especially one that is legally enforceable. For example, a prenuptial agreement is a contract because it is binding by law. The word *contract* is impersonal.

As you will see, a biblical covenant involves commitment by two individuals or groups as well as a strong desire for the well-being of others.

MAIN IDEA
Though a covenant resembles an agreement, a deal, or a contract, it is unique in that it is a loving commitment to the well-being of other persons.

You know that military personnel and their families have special needs during a deployment and when soldiers return to the United States as veterans. What do other US citizens owe their fellow Americans who are risking their lives for the well-being of the country?

You may wonder why the Army used the word *covenant* for the Community Covenant program. Why not use *agreement*, *deal*, or *contract*? Isn't covenant a religious term? *Covenant* has actually been used in both secular and religious settings. This chapter explains the nature of biblical covenants, especially the covenant God made with the first humans and more formally later with his Chosen People.

NOTE TAKING

Word Association and Comparison. Use the material in this section to help you to write words you associate with agreements, deals, contracts, and covenants. Circle those words that apply to two terms; put a rectangle around words that apply to three; and underline any word that relates to all four terms.

Example:

Agreement: relationship

Deal: transaction, relationship

Contract: binding, relationship

Covenant: binding, relationship

SECTION ASSESSMENT

NOTE TAKING

Use the word association and comparison notes you created to answer the following questions.

1. Did you find that any of the four terms—agreement, deal, contract, covenant—have word associations in common? If so, what are they?

2. Did one of the four terms seem to be significantly different from the other three? If so, which one?

COMPREHENSION

3. What is the Community Covenant designed to do?

4. What are other uses for the term *covenant* besides religious uses?

CRITICAL THINKING

5. This introductory section distinguishes between closely related words. Why is a word's specific meaning important in communication?

6. What alternate name might you give the Army program in the news story, instead of Community Covenant? Explain your answer.

SECTION 1
Formation of the Pentateuch

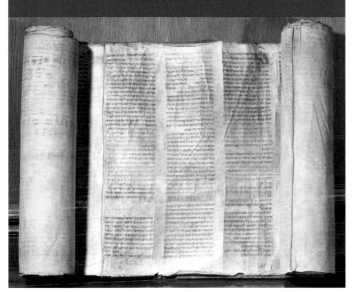

MAIN IDEA
Different inspired authors and editors created the Pentateuch.

As you know, the first five books of the Bible have the name *Pentateuch*, meaning "five books." Although its books consistently focus on the Chosen People and their relationship with God, the Pentateuch contains different types of literature: myth, laws, stories, speeches, and songs. It does not tell a continuous story like a trilogy. Instead, the Pentateuch is a gathering of different kinds of writings from different authors or sources.

Redaction and Source Criticism: Sources of the Pentateuch

Recall that a biblical scholar using source criticism is interested in the origins of biblical material: where did these writings come from? Redaction criticism focuses on the editors who put together sources and arranged them in a biblical chapter or book. Both of these approaches are important for learning about the Pentateuch.

Biblical scholarship holds that editors wove four main sources into the Pentateuch. Four sources can be identified because each contributes very differently. At times, the editors did not attempt to coordinate the inconsistencies between different accounts of the same story. Consequently, there are places in the Bible where

---

NOTE TAKING

Summarizing Main Ideas. As you study each of the four sources for the Pentateuch, write a sentence that will best help you distinguish each one from the others.

Source	Sentence
Yahwist	The Yahwist uses human characteristics for God.
Elohist	
Deuteronomist	
Priestly	

there are two versions of the same event. (See the two Creation accounts of Genesis 1:1–2:3 and 2:4–2:25.)

The four main sources are called the Yahwist (J), Elohist (E), Deuteronomist (D), and Priestly (P) sources.

THE FOUR SOURCES FOR THE Pentateuch

YAHWIST (J)

- You can recognize this source when the Pentateuch uses the name **YHWH** for God. (In German, YHWH is *Jahweh* which is why the abbreviation is J.)

- This source uses a vivid, earthy style of writing, often attributing human emotions and physical traits to God. This approach is called *anthropomorphism*.

- The Yahwist provides the basic outline for the Pentateuch, with accounts of the first humans, the patriarchs, the Exodus from Egypt, the Israelites' journey in the desert, the covenant at Mount Sinai, and the entry into the Promised Land.

ELOHIST (E)

- This source uses the term **Elohim** for God.

- Abraham is a central figure.

- The Elohist retells stories from the northern kingdom's point of view with emphasis on the kings.

- It is believed that, around 750 BC, an editor combined the J and E sources. This editor kept some repetitions and contradictions.

DEUTERONOMIST (D)

- The term *Deuteronomist* comes from Greek words meaning "second law."

- Most likely, priests of the northern kingdom composed this material, placing great emphasis on morality.

- This source portrays Israel's history as a cycle of reward for faithfulness to the covenant and punishment by YHWH for sin.

- The D source especially highlights Moses's speeches.

PRIESTLY SOURCE (P)

- This source contains census lists, genealogies, numbers, dates, descriptions of proper ways to worship, and the proper use of clean and unclean animals. Like the Elohist, the Priestly source refers to God as Elohim.

- This is probably the latest of the four sources and likely contributed a coherent framework to the Pentateuch.

While the editors wove together the four sources into the Pentateuch, there are still some rough edges, such as repetitions or narrative gaps.

YHWH God's sacred name, revealed to Moses; it means "I am who I am" or "I AM" and is never pronounced by Jews.

Elohim A common Semitic word for God used in the Bible. Elohim appears in Hebrew names like Mich-a-el, Dan-i-el, and Ari-el.

SECTION ASSESSMENT

NOTE TAKING

Use your notes to answer these questions.

1. Name one difference between the Yahwist and the Elohist sources, besides their use of different names for God.

2. What is one difference between the Deuteronomist and the Priestly sources?

VOCABULARY

3. Define *YHWH*.

CRITICAL THINKING

4. Why do you think that the editors of the Pentateuch decided, in some cases, to include more than one version of the same story?

Creation, the Fall, and the Promise of Redemption

MAIN IDEA
The first three chapters of Genesis explain what God wanted for humanity, how sin affected humans, and how God offered people a promise of Salvation.

The two creation stories in Genesis tell you what God wanted for you and for all human beings. Subsequent chapters tell of the first humans' loss of paradise through sin. Immediately after this loss, however, God promised to save humanity from sin.

Creation

When you open your Bible to the first pages of Genesis, you find the stories about God's creation of the world and human beings. Most ancient cultures had creation stories. While the Genesis creation stories resemble creation stories of other civilizations, the radical differences between Genesis and the others are most important:

- The Genesis stories reveal one God rather than the many gods of other religions.
- Genesis tells you that God created humans out of his own goodness, not as a by-product of conflict between warring gods.
- The relationship between God and the people in the Bible is positive rather than adversarial.

The two creation stories in Genesis are complementary rather than contradictory, each revealing something important about God. They reflect religious truth rather than historical or scientific truth.

NOTE TAKING
Summarizing Main Ideas. As you read through this section, write a sentence that summarizes each event.

Sequence of Events	Summary Statement
Creation	God created the world and human beings to live with him in paradise.
Sin and the Fall	
Punishment	
The Promise	

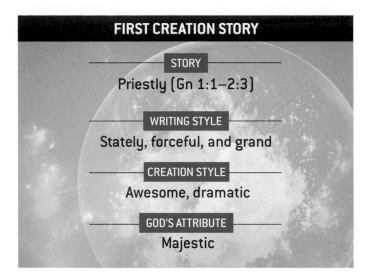

FIRST CREATION STORY

STORY
Priestly (Gn 1:1–2:3)

WRITING STYLE
Stately, forceful, and grand

CREATION STYLE
Awesome, dramatic

GOD'S ATTRIBUTE
Majestic

Differences between the

FIRST and SECOND

CREATION STORIES

SECOND CREATION STORY

STORY
Yahwist (Gn 2:4–2:25)

WRITING STYLE
Lighter in tone

CREATION STYLE
Down-to-earth

GOD'S ATTRIBUTE
Anthropomorphic

God wanted paradise for Adam and Eve. God wanted them to experience a close relationship with him and others, to be at peace within themselves, and to be in harmony with nature. Adam and Eve experienced this state, called **Original Holiness and Original Justice**.

Sin and the Fall

God blessed Adam and Eve in many ways. He also forbade them to eat from one tree. Genesis 3:1–13 describes Adam and Eve's rebellion against God. After hearing a snake's explanation of what would happen if they ate the fruit from the one tree, Adam and Eve believed the snake's promise over God's command. The snake is representative of Satan or the **devil** in the story.

God had given Adam and Eve **free will**. Only with free will could they truly respond to God's love. But they wanted to do things their own way. This story illustrates the lure of sin and its results. Simply defined, people sin when they make choices that are not in line with what God wants for them, other people, and the natural world. The term **Original Sin** uses the term *original* in the sense of "first." Adam and Eve committed the initial sin, but their choice affects all of their descendants.

In addition to naming the first sin, Original Sin also describes the brokenness in human experience—inner conflict, discord with other people, apathy toward creation, and separation from God.

Original Holiness and Original Justice The state of Adam and Eve before sin. The grace of Original Holiness was for people to share in God's life. The main gifts of Original Justice were that people would not have to suffer or die. Original Justice also guaranteed an inner harmony of the human person, the harmony between man and woman, and the harmony between Adam and Eve and all of creation.

devil The name for the fallen angel who refused to accept God or his Kingdom. Another word for the devil is Satan, or the "Evil One."

free will The capacity to choose among alternatives. Free will is "the power, rooted in reason and will . . . to perform deliberate actions on one's own responsibility" (*CCC*, 1731). True freedom is at the service of what is good and true.

Original Sin The sin of disobedience committed by Adam and Eve that resulted in their loss of Original Holiness and Original Justice and their becoming subject to sin and death. Original Sin also describes the fallen state of human nature into which all generations of people are born. Christ Jesus saved humanity from Original Sin. The Sacrament of Baptism restores Original Holiness, but not Original Justice (see *CCC*, 400).

"The 'tree of knowledge of good and evil' symbolically evokes the insurmountable limits that man, being a creature, must freely recognize and respect with trust" (CCC, 396).

The Promise

Protoevangelium is a Latin term meaning "first gospel." It is the initial sign of the very Good News that God did not abandon humanity's first parents or their descendants after they committed sin. Even with the dire consequences of Original Sin—including the deprivation of Original Holiness and Justice for all people—God did not abandon the human race. Although God punished people for their sin with suffering, exile, and death, he embedded a promise within that punishment. Addressing the devil, God said:

> I will put enmity between you and the woman,
> and between your offspring and hers;
> They will strike at your head,
> while you strike at their heel. (Gn 3:15)

Here, God promised that the woman's offspring would destroy the snake, who represents sin and death. (If the snake can only nip at the humans' heels, but the humans can strike his head, the humans have the clear advantage.) Jesus Christ is the "New Adam" who will defeat Satan and gain eternal Redemption and life for humanity. The sinless Virgin Mary is the "New Eve" because she helped reverse the original Eve's sin by bearing and raising Jesus.

The **Fall** is a short form of "the Fall of Adam and Eve" and describes their move from paradise in the Garden of Eden to exile. They "fell" from the state of Original Holiness and Justice into the state of Original Sin, giving up a life of peaceful harmony.

Punishment

Sin usually brings its own punishment, as you may have experienced. (For example, lying to a friend might seem to have immediate positive consequences, but ultimately injures that relationship.) After Adam and Eve had sinned, they could no longer stay in paradise. They could no longer walk and talk with God, be at peace internally, connect well with each other, and simply live off of nature.

God expelled the humans from the garden. Yet God also cursed the devil and indicated that one of Eve's descendants would conquer him. God indicated that sin would have these consequences: suffering in childbirth, oppression, hard labor, and death.

> **Fall** A short form of "the Fall of Adam and Eve" which describes their explusion from paradise in the Garden of Eden into exile as a consequence of their disobedience. They symbolically "fell" from the state of Original Holiness and Original Justice into the state of Original Sin.
>
> **Protoevangelium** A Latin term meaning "first gospel" and is the initial sign of the very good news that God did not abandon humanity's first parents or their descendants after they committed sin. Eve's offspring (Jesus) would someday destroy the snake (sin and death).

After Adam and Eve

The Book of Genesis describes clearly how sin spread in the world following the Fall. Genesis also points out how God never abandons human beings.

- *Cain and Abel (Gn 4).* This story about the sons of Adam and Eve reveals that sin can lead to the serious crime of murder and, even worse, *fratricide*—the killing of one's own sibling. God exiled Cain to a nomadic or wandering life, but the "mark of Cain" (see Gn 4:15) spared him from death. You can see that God does not abandon sinners, even if they deserve punishment. The Lord God, though a just Judge, is faithful and loving.

- *Noah and the Flood (Gn 6:5–9:29).* Sin shattered humanity. People lived in different nations. In the story of the Great Flood, God destroyed all humanity except Noah and his children, who would repopulate the earth. God entered into the first biblical covenant with Noah and all his descendants, promising that never again would he destroy the world by flood. The sign of this covenant is the rainbow. This covenant remained active for the Gentiles until the time of Jesus Christ.

SECTION ASSESSMENT

NOTE TAKING

Use your summaries to help you complete the following item.

1. Which two events in the sequence of events described in this section do you think are most important? Craft a statement that communicates your answer.

VOCABULARY

2. Define *Original Sin*.

COMPREHENSION

3. Why is the story of Adam and Eve's expulsion from the Garden called the Fall?

4. Who is the offspring who "will strike at your head, while you strike at their heel"?

REFLECTION

5. Why do you think that Adam and Eve listened to Satan's assessment of the tree of knowledge and good and evil over God's description of the tree and his explanation of the punishment of eating from it?

God's Call, Promise, and Covenants

MAIN IDEA
God called Abraham and his descendants, the Chosen People, to be in a covenant relationship with him.

The divine-human covenants in the Bible resemble political suzerainty covenants in the Ancient Near East. A *suzerainty covenant* occurred when one people or geographical area was under the rule of a more powerful nation. The more powerful group was the *suzerain*. The weaker group was the *vassal*. Although the suzerain might dictate the vassal's political dealings, the vassal retained some autonomy. Suzerainty covenants had these characteristics:

- The suzerain initiated the covenant.
- The suzerain expected loyalty from the vassal.
- The vassal had obligations specified in the covenant treaty.
- The suzerain had a right to punish the vassal if the vassal disobeyed. In the Ancient Near East, the usual punishment for violating a covenant was death.

The biblical covenants retained key elements of these treaties. It is no surprise that in the Bible, God was the suzerain and Israel was the vassal.

- God initiated the covenants with Noah, Abraham, and Moses.
- God expected the Chosen People to be faithful to him.
- The Law God gave Moses on Mount Sinai explained Israel's obligations.
- The biblical authors at times suggested that God punished the Chosen People for their violation of the Law and covenant. Much of the time, however, the Chosen People brought disaster upon themselves by straying from God. God never broke the covenant, however, and waited for his People to return.

Though the divine-human covenant and the suzerainty covenant share similarities, you can imagine that God's loving covenant with humanity far exceeds any human type of contract, agreement, or covenant.

The Covenant with Abraham

Chapters 1–11 contain the prehistory portion of Genesis—the part that took place before recorded history. The remaining chapters in Genesis tell the story of the **patriarchs** and their families. Abraham, Isaac, and Jacob are the "fathers" of the Chosen People because of the significant roles they played in the history of the Israelites.

NOTE TAKING

Supporting a Statement. As you read through this section, jot down arguments for and against this statement: "Abraham is a model of faith."

Example: The fact that Abraham believed that God would still give him a son even in his old age *supports* the statement.

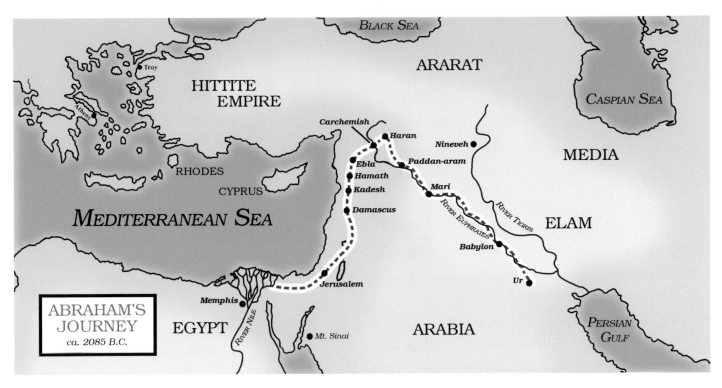

ABRAHAM'S JOURNEY ca. 2085 B.C.

God called a man named Abram to leave his home and travel to a new land that God would show him (see image on page 114):

> I will make of you a great nation, and I will bless you; I will make your name great, so that you will be a blessing.
>
> I will bless those who bless you and curse those who curse you. All the families of the earth will find blessing in you. (Gn 12:2–3)

Abram believed and obeyed God's summons. Genesis 15 describes God's covenant with Abram. To seal the covenant, Abram cut animals in half in the ancient covenant ritual, which suggested that if either party violated the covenant, they would be split apart like the animals. Then Abram fell into a deep sleep. In his dream, God told him what would happen to his

> **patriarchs** A name to describe "fathers of the faith," male rulers, elders, or leaders. The patriarchs of the faith are Abraham, Isaac, and Jacob.
>
> **circumcision** The surgical removal of the male foreskin; it was the physical sign of the covenant between God and Abraham.

descendants and promised him a specific piece of land (Gn 15:18–21). In the dream, Abram saw a smoking fire pot and a flaming torch—symbols of God's presence—pass between the animals. God's sealing of the covenant with Abram through a dream formalized God's promises to him.

In Genesis 17, God changed Abram's name to *Abraham* to signify that he would be the "father of a multitude of nations" (Gn 17:4). He also changed Abraham's wife's name from Sarai to Sarah to show that the pair was beginning a completely new life together. God added that kings would be among Abraham and Sarah's descendants. He repeated the terms of his covenant with Abram and added to them.

> I will maintain my covenant between me and you and your descendants after you throughout the ages as an everlasting covenant, to be your God and the God of your descendants after you. (Gn 17:7)

God required that Abraham and his male descendants undergo **circumcision**, an act that was often used as a rite of passage at puberty in the ancient world. By requiring it in infancy, the covenant emphasized the lifelong and eternal nature of relationship to God:

> Every male among you, when he is eight days old, shall be circumcised, including houseborn slaves and those acquired with money from any foreigner who is not of your descendants. . . . Thus my covenant will be in your flesh as an everlasting covenant." (Gn 17:12–13)

God fulfilled his promise that Abraham and Sarah would have a son. Against all odds, Abraham's wife, Sarah, who had been unable to have children, conceived their son Isaac in her old age.

God tested Abraham's faith in Genesis 22 when he asked Abraham to offer his son Isaac to him as a human sacrifice. Abraham trusted and obeyed God without protest, bargaining, or hesitation, but agreed with a heavy heart. At the last minute, the Lord's angel gave Abraham a ram to use for the sacrifice instead of his son. God did not actually want Abraham to kill Isaac. Abraham is a model of faith, one who put aside his own desires to follow his God.

In several ways, Isaac prefigures Jesus—that is, he foreshadows or represents Jesus before the Incarnation takes place. These are some parallels between Isaac and Jesus:

Abraham loved his son Isaac, just as God the Father loved Jesus.

Isaac carried wood for his own sacrifice, just as Jesus carried the wood of the Cross for his execution.

Isaac asked where the lamb for sacrifice was. Prophetically, Abraham said that God would provide the lamb. Later, God did provide Jesus as the Lamb of God, his beloved Son, the perfect sacrificial offering for the Salvation of all people. (Lambs were a common animal sacrifice in the ancient world.)

Isaac, his son Jacob, and his grandson Joseph were the patriarchs who were responsible for being stewards of the promises that God gave to Abraham. The Catholic Church considers these men saints even though they were born before Jesus came into the world.

It probably will not surprise you that the author of the Letter to the Hebrews in the New Testament emphasizes Abraham's faith. Hebrews mentions Abraham's response to God's call, his belief in God's promise, his courage to live in a foreign land, and his faith in following God's request to sacrifice his son. For the writer of Hebrews, Abraham fit the definition of faith perfectly: "Faith is the assurance of things hoped for, the conviction of things not seen" (Heb 11:1, quoted in in *CCC*, 146). Jesus Christ would be even greater than Abraham.

The Patriarch Israel

Later in Genesis, Isaac's wife Rebecca gave birth to twins, Esau and Jacob. Although Esau was the first-born son, due to receive a position of honor in his family and a double portion of his father's estate, Jacob was able to trick his brother out of his inheritance and special blessing. This deception angered Esau, so Jacob fled to work his uncle's land, where he married his cousins Leah and Rachel. (In the ancient world, *polygamy*—marriage to more than one wife—and matrimony between cousins were not unusual.)

Three Names for the Chosen People

Throughout the Old Testament, the biblical authors refer to God's People by three primary names: Hebrews, Israelites, and Jews.

Hebrews

The authors first called God's Chosen People the **Hebrews**, most likely after Eber, the ancestor of several Semitic peoples who lived in Canaan (a territory that included modern-day Israel and Jordan, the Sinai desert, Lebanon, and the coastal areas of Syria).

Israelites

After God changed Jacob's name to Israel, his descendants were known as the *Israelites* (see, for example, Exodus 1:1, 7). Later in Israel's history, after the united kingdom of Israel split in two, the northern kingdom—made up of ten of the twelve tribes of Israel—took on the name Israel, while the southern kingdom of two tribes became Judah. A citizen of the modern state of Israel is known as an *Israeli*.

Jews

After the Chosen People entered the Promised Land, those who lived or were born in ancient Judea were known as **Jews**.

Genesis recounts that Jacob had two important encounters with God. On the road to Bethel, Jacob had a remarkable dream (Gn 28:10–22) in which God reaffirmed with him the terms of his covenant with Abraham. Years later, Jacob wrestled with a mysterious person all night (Gn 32:23–33). He refused to stop fighting until he received a blessing from his opponent. Instead of blessing him, the stranger gave him a new name—*Israel*—meaning "one who contends with God." This meeting blessed Jacob and transformed him from a crafty deceiver into an honorable man.

Israel made his home in Canaan and fathered a large family, including twelve sons.

Joseph, the Favored Son

While having more than one wife was complicated for Israel, you can imagine that the dynamics between the wives' sons could be complex as well. Jacob's favorite wife, Rachel, gave birth to Joseph, who then became his favorite son. As he grew older, Joseph showed off his status and abilities. His brothers were jealous and tried to rid themselves of Joseph by selling him to a slave trader heading for Egypt.

> **Hebrews** The first name given by biblical authors to the Chosen People, most likely after Eber, the ancestor of several Semitic peoples who lived in Canaan.
>
> **Jews** The term for people who lived or were born in ancient Judea.

Although Joseph had trials in Egypt, his ability to interpret dreams enabled him eventually to become Egypt's chief governor. The pharaoh's dream had predicted a famine that affected Canaan as well. When his brothers came to Egypt in search of food, Joseph tested them to determine whether they had remorse for what they did to him. Satisfied, Joseph requested that his brothers bring his father and his younger brother, Benjamin, to Egypt.

This story explains how Israel and his family came to Egypt, setting the stage for the Book of Exodus.

In several ways, Joseph also prefigures Jesus:

- Both are beloved sons.
- Both go to Egypt because of persecution.
- Both are betrayed for pieces of silver.
- Both are falsely accused.
- Both forgive those who hurt them.

SECTION ASSESSMENT

NOTE TAKING

Use your notes to help you answer the following questions.

1. What are two examples of Abraham's faith?
2. Why do you think that Abraham should be considered a "model of faith"?

VOCABULARY

3. Expand on the glossary definition (page 381) of *covenant* from what you learned in this section. Write a new, more in-depth definition.
4. What is the title for Abraham, Isaac, Jacob (or Israel), and Joseph that describes the significant roles they played in the history of the Hebrew people?

COMPREHENSION

5. What did God require of Abraham and his descendants for their side of the covenant?
6. List and explain the three names used to describe the Chosen People.

CRITICAL THINKING

7. How did biblical covenants resemble and differ from the suzerainty covenants of the Ancient Near East?
8. Explain how Joseph and Jesus resembled each other. From what you know about both, how did they differ?

REFLECTION

9. What is your reaction to God's request that Abraham sacrifice his son?

SECTION 4
The Exodus and the Giving of the Law

MAIN IDEA
God freed his people from slavery and gave them the Law so that they could deepen their covenant relationship with him.

There is a four-century gap in the Bible's story of the Israelites after Israel and his sons came to Egypt. The Book of Exodus picks up the Israelites' story again when a new Egyptian pharaoh, who did not know about Joseph, began to enslave foreign inhabitants, including the Israelites.

God heard the cries and suffering of his people and called Moses to lead the Israelites out of Egypt and end their slavery through the Exodus—God's saving act to free the Israelites from slavery in Egypt.

Moses

After God, Moses is the main figure in the Exodus story. Though an Israelite, Moses grew up in the home of an Egyptian princess who raised him as her own. Although raised by royalty, Moses knew his real identity. In fact, the event that forced Moses to flee Egypt was his murder of an Egyptian who mistreated an Israelite slave. He fled to Midian (a region bordering Egypt on the east), where he met and married Zipporah and fathered a son, Gershom (Ex 2:11–22).

While Moses was shepherding his father-in-law's flocks, God called him to lead God's Chosen People out of Egypt, appearing to Moses in a burning bush (see image at left). God introduced himself as "the God

NOTE TAKING **Identifying Biblical Books.** This section mentions the four biblical books that come after Genesis. For each book, note down a unique characteristic to help you remember and distinguish them from each other.

Book	Unique Characteristic
Exodus	
Leviticus	This book is about the Law.
Numbers	
Deuteronomy	

of your father . . . the God of Abraham, the God of Isaac, and the God of Jacob" (Ex 3:6).

God said, "I have witnessed the affliction of my people in Egypt and have heard their cry against their taskmasters, so I know well what they are suffering" (Ex 3:7). God then asked Moses to go to Pharaoh to lead his people out of Egypt. In response, Moses shared several practical concerns about the mission as well as a lack of self-assurance. After Moses protested repeatedly about his inability to speak well, God appointed his brother Aaron to be his spokesperson.

Moses and Aaron shared God's plan with the Israelite elders and the Egyptian pharaoh. The pharaoh, however, had other plans: after speaking with Moses he redoubled the Israelite slaves' workload. Only after God sent ten plagues (see Ex 7–12) was the pharaoh finally persuaded to free the Israelites.

OLD TESTAMENT NAMES FOR...

HELLO my name is

GOD

Before God revealed his name to Moses, the Chosen People used a common Semitic name for a deity, *El*, to refer to God. Originally, the Canaanites had a god named El, the father of all other gods and of all creatures. *Elohim* is a plural form of El and can refer to "the god" or multiple gods. The Chosen People typically spoke of God as "the God of Abraham, of Isaac, and of Jacob."

Although the J source author of Genesis used the name YHWH to refer to God from the beginning of time, the P and E traditions point out that God did not reveal this name until he did so to Moses. The pronunciation of YHWH is uncertain because, out of respect for Almighty God, the Jews never said the name aloud. Instead of reading or saying the divine name aloud, the Israelites substituted the word *Adonai* (translated "Lord" or "master").

The patriarchs believed in the existence of one God. Only YHWH created, revealed, judged, entered, saved, and set up the kingdom of which YHWH alone is Master.

Adonai A name for God meaning "Lord" or "master," which the Israelites used out of respect for the sacredness of the name YHWH.

The Passover

The final plague sent by God, the death of the first-born, struck fear into the Egyptian people and their pharaoh (see Ex 12). The Israelites themselves escaped this plague by following God's instructions: they killed unblemished lambs and smeared their blood on the doorposts and lintels of their houses. They ate their evening meal quickly with bitter herbs and unleavened bread because bread made with yeast would take too long to rise. The Lord said,

> This is how you are to eat it: with your loins girt, sandals on your feet and your staff in hand, you will eat it in a hurry. It is the LORD's Passover. For on this same night I will go through Egypt, striking down every firstborn. . . . But for you the blood will mark the houses where you are. Seeing the blood, I will pass over you; thereby, when I strike the land of Egypt, no destructive blow will come upon you. This day will be a day of remembrance for you, which your future generations will celebrate with pilgrimage to the LORD; you will celebrate it as a statute forever. (Ex 12:11–14)

The **Passover** meal was the last that the people would eat before leaving Egypt. The Lord led the people out of Egypt through the Red Sea into the wilderness. The Israelites belonged to the **Twelve Tribes of Israel**, meaning that they were descendants of Israel's

---

Passover A sacred feast that first occurred prior to God's saving the Israelites from the Egyptians. The angel of death "passed over" the houses with lambs' blood smeared on their doorposts and lintels. The Passover then became a religious celebration reminding the Chosen People of God's deliverance, Salvation, fidelity, and love.

Twelve Tribes of Israel The descendants of the twelve sons of Jacob (Israel). See Exodus 1:2–5, Numbers 1:20–43, or 1 Chronicles 1:1–2.

♥ The Significance of PASSOVER

The Passover event is central to both Jewish and Christian faiths. The Passover celebration reminds Jews of God's deliverance, fidelity, and love. Christians celebrate the Passion, Death, and Resurrection of Jesus Christ as the fulfillment of the Passover: Jesus Christ liberates all people from the slavery of sin. "Every time Passover is celebrated, the Exodus events are made present to the memory of believers so they may conform their lives to them" (*CCC*, 1363). When the Church celebrates the Eucharist, she commemorates and makes present Christ's Last Supper, which was a Passover meal. Jesus is the unblemished Lamb who delivers the world from the slavery and death of sin. You commemorate Jesus' sacrifice and saving actions every time you celebrate the Eucharist.

twelve sons. (After several hundred years, you can imagine that this family had grown into quite a large group of people!)

There were hardships in the desert, and the people complained to Moses, who turned to God. The Lord answered Moses by providing the Israelites water, food in the form of quail and *manna*, and protection from local peoples who tried to destroy them.

The Sinai Covenant

In the third month after they fled Egypt, God communicated with the Israelites through Moses on Mount Sinai. There, God made a covenant with the people. The prophets summarized this covenant in variations of one simple line: "You shall be my people, and I will be your God" (Jer 7:23, Ez 11:20, and Hos 2:25). This important covenant, known as the **Sinai Covenant**, involved these elements:

- It bound God and the Chosen People in a personal, loving union.
- It revealed God's special love and mercy for them.
- It stipulated that God's People were to respond to his love through obedience to the Law, summarized in the **Ten Commandments**, and to be faithful to God in conduct and worship.

The Israelites agreed to the terms of the Sinai Covenant. Moses sealed it by building an altar with twelve pillars to represent the Twelve Tribes and by sacrificing some young bulls and splashing their blood on the people and the altar. (Blood here symbolizes life, and the altar is a symbol of God.)

The Ten Commandments (Ex 20:1–17) summarized the Law, serving as a basic guide for the Israelites to follow in order to keep their commitment to the covenant. Chapters 20–23 of Exodus report the duties the Chosen People needed to observe. Over the years, the Lord inspired other laws to help the people adapt to new situations.

There are 613 laws listed in the last four books of the Pentateuch. Some of those laws may appear unnecessary or strange to you today, but the Israelite laws reflected a major advance over their neighbors. Some of the Old Testament laws resemble the famous Babylonian *Code of Hammurabi*, written in 1780 BC. Through divine inspiration, the Israelites reshaped their neighbors' laws to reflect their belief in the one true God who rescued and sustained them. While the Code of Hammurabi regulated society, the Ten Commandments went a step further and prescribed the type of culture Israel should have as God's People.

The rest of the Israelites' sojourn in the desert was rocky. The people grew impatient with Moses, and his brother Aaron even helped the people create a golden calf to worship. This worship was idolatrous, a major breach of the First Commandment. Although Moses was angry, he also appealed to God on his people's behalf, and God renewed the covenant (see Ex 34:10–11).

The biblical authors devote Exodus 25–31 and 35–40 to instructions for building the Ark of the Covenant (to contain the Ten Commandments) and the **tabernacle**, the structure where God would meet Moses.

Sinai Covenant The covenant God made with his Chosen People through Moses on Mount Sinai; it bound God and his Chosen People in a loving union and gave the Israelites the Law so they would know how they were to stay faithful to the covenant.

Ten Commandments The Ten Commandments summarize the Law, serving as its basic guide.

tabernacle The portable sanctuary in which the Jews carried the Ark of the Covenant throughout their travels in the desert.

LIVING THE TEN COMMANDMENTS

The Ten Commandments tell you how to respond in love to God and neighbor. Reflect on the applications for each of the commandments. Then, write your own personal resolutions for the commandments, explaining how you are applying them to your life.

1 I AM THE LORD YOUR GOD: YOU SHALL NOT HAVE STRANGE GODS BEFORE ME.

- I put God before all else.
- I am loyal to the Lord more than I am to my successes, prestige, popularity, possessions, etc.

2 YOU SHALL NOT TAKE THE NAME OF THE LORD YOUR GOD IN VAIN.

- I respect God's name and everything else that is holy.

3 REMEMBER TO KEEP HOLY THE LORD'S DAY.

- I make sure I go to Mass on Sunday.
- I renew my spirit through rest, healthy activities, and prayer on the Lord's Day.

4 HONOR YOUR FATHER AND YOUR MOTHER.

- I honor and obey the wishes of my parents.
- I respect other family members.
- I listen to others who have proper authority over me.

5 YOU SHALL NOT KILL.

- I respect all life as a gift from God.
- I don't do anything that would harm others or myself.
- I show care for those who most need love.

6 YOU SHALL NOT COMMIT ADULTERY.

- I respect my own sexuality.
- I do not tell inappropriate jokes, watch sexually explicit movies, or visit Internet sites that degrade sexuality.

7 YOU SHALL NOT STEAL.

- I am honest in all my dealings.
- I do not cheat on my schoolwork.

8 YOU SHALL NOT BEAR FALSE WITNESS AGAINST YOUR NEIGHBOR.

- I tell the truth.
- I refrain from gossip, taking care to protect the reputation of others.

9 YOU SHALL NOT COVET YOUR NEIGHBOR'S WIFE.

- I guard against lustful thoughts.

10 YOU SHALL NOT COVET YOUR NEIGHBOR'S GOODS.

- I am not envious of another's good fortune.
- I am not a jealous person.

The Book of Numbers

The Book of Numbers continues the story of the Israelites' forty years of wandering in the desert. Throughout that period God cared for the Israelites by meeting their needs.

This book also recounts the constant "murmuring" of the Israelites—their complaints, discontent, and rebellion against Moses, God's chosen leader. They complained about their food, said they wanted to return to Egypt, and doubted God's ability to defeat their enemies.

You may be somewhat shocked at the Israelites' lack of gratitude. Although the Israelites were not setting a fine example of covenant fidelity, their story can reassure you that though you may sin, abuse your freedom, and doubt God, God remains faithful to you. He does not abandon you. The Father has sent his Son to offer reconciliation to the world. The Holy Spirit remains with you, guiding you.

The Books of Leviticus and Deuteronomy

You may recognize the name Levi, one of the sons of Israel, in the title of the Book of Leviticus. The tribe of Levi was the priestly tribe in charge of Israel's public worship, animal sacrifices, and ritual offerings. The Priestly source composed Leviticus, a book that stresses the theme of God's holiness and the human obligation to worship him with respect and love. There is also an emphasis on the holiness of God's Chosen People that involves seeing God as part of daily life. The laws in the Book of Leviticus govern various aspects of daily life, including sex, birth, disease, and death.

The biblical authors attributed many of these later laws to Moses because the laws grew out of the Sinai Covenant. The Book of Deuteronomy is a restatement and further development of Mosaic Law; it is the result

There were many kinds of sacrifices made by ancient Hebrews, including whole offerings, that is, "wholly burned" sacrifices, where the entire animal except its hide was consumed in fire on the altar.

of a reform movement in the northern kingdom shortly before its defeat by the Assyrians. Deuteronomy centers on God's love of Israel and his unhappiness with the people for worshiping false gods and not responding to him with their whole hearts. The book challenges the nation to choose between *obedience* to God and the Law, which brings life, and *disobedience*, which brings death.

In summary, the Pentateuch reveals God's incredibly patient and constant love for you and all humanity. The Creation stories reveal that God created a beautiful world and wanted Original Holiness and Original Justice for Adam and Eve. Even after their sin, God promised to be with Adam, Eve, and their descendants and pledged that evil would be overcome. God invited Abraham, Isaac, and Jacob to make a covenant with him, promising that their family would be great. When God heard their descendants' cries of suffering in slavery, he sent Moses to lead the people out of Egypt and into the wilderness, where he cared for them and led them, giving them the Law so that they knew how to live as his people.

SECTION ASSESSMENT

NOTE TAKING

Use your chart to help you answer these questions.

1. What is unique about the Book of Exodus?
2. How does the Book of Leviticus differ from the Book of Deuteronomy?

VOCABULARY

3. Define the *Exodus*.
4. What is the *tabernacle*?

COMPREHENSION

5. How did God know not to kill the firstborn of the Israelites before their departure from Egypt?
6. What are three elements of the Sinai Covenant?
7. What is the relationship between the Passover and the Eucharist?

REFLECTION

8. List at least three names that Catholics use for God today. Do you think that having multiple names for God as they did in the Old Testament confuses or helps people understand God?
9. Which of the Ten Commandments do you think people your age have the hardest time following? Why?

Section Summaries

Focus Question

What does God want for you?

Complete one of the following:

 From your life experience, what else do you think God wants for you?

 Research *discernment*, a prayerful process that helps you get a sense of what God wants for you specifically. Write three things you learned about discernment.

 Spend personal time reflecting on God's saving act in the Exodus. What is something to which you feel enslaved? Write a prayer for liberation from whatever enslaves you.

INTRODUCTION (PAGES 105–106)

Agreements, Deals, Contracts, and Covenants

Though a covenant resembles an agreement, a deal, and a contract, it is unique in that it is a *loving* commitment to the well-being of the other person or party. While "covenant" can be used in a completely secular way, this section looks at covenant in a religious sense.

 Write about a personal promise to God that you have made or would like to make.

SECTION 1 (PAGES 107–109)

Formation of the Pentateuch

Inspired by God, authors and editors created the Pentateuch from different sources. Redaction criticism helps biblical scholars identify at least four main sources for the Pentateuch: the Yahwist, Elohist, Deuteronomist, and Priestly sources.

 How did the four sources of the Pentateuch become one narrative?

SECTION 2 (PAGES 110–113)

Creation, the Fall, and the Promise of Redemption

The two Creation stories in the Book of Genesis reveal that paradise consisted of loving relationships with God and others as well as inner peace and harmony with nature. The disobedience of Adam and Eve to God damaged the right relationships they originally had. Even though the first humans' disobedience brought Original Sin to their descendants, God did not abandon Adam and Eve nor humanity. God promised that evil would be defeated.

 Describe how the two Creation accounts point in a veiled way to the coming of Christ.

SECTION 3 (PAGES 114–118)

God's Call, Promise, and Covenants

God called Abraham, Isaac, and Jacob (Israel) and their descendants, his Chosen People, to be in a covenant relationship with him. The similarities between the biblical covenants and the suzerainty covenants of the Ancient Near East highlight how unique God's deep love is for his people.

 What was a key difference between the biblical covenant and the suzerainty covenants of the Ancient Near East?

SECTION 4 (PAGES 119–125)

The Exodus and the Giving of the Law

God called Moses to lead his people to freedom from slavery in an event called the Exodus. In the Sinai Covenant, God gave the Israelites the Law so that they could live in a covenant relationship with him. The Ten Commandments summarize that Law.

 How can having and following a law bring freedom?

Chapter Assignments

Choose and complete at least one of these assignments to assess your understanding of the material in this chapter.

1. Stage the Debate between God and Moses

With a classmate, write and perform a skit between God and Moses in which Moses tries to convince God not to destroy the disobedient Israelites. (See, for example, Exodus 32:30-35.) Use humor if you wish, but make sure Moses wins the argument!

Memorize and rehearse your parts. Arrange for some simple costumes. Plan a time to share your skit before the rest of your class.

2. Explain *Covenant* in Context

Covenant House is an international nonprofit organization that helps and houses homeless children and teens. The organization has houses in twenty-two cities in the United States, Canada, and Latin America.

Research and read about Covenant House. Find out the number of homeless youth the organization serves, its mission and services, and its hopes for the youth. Next, write about each of the following elements of this chapter in the context of Covenant House, making connections between the chapter and this organization. See the example under the heading "Creation" for ideas on how to do this.

- Creation

  Example: *When God created the world, he said that all that he had made was good. Many of the young people at Covenant House have been treated badly at home or on the street, an experience that can make them feel ashamed and worthless rather than good and valuable. Covenant House staff affirm the goodness of the young people so that they will regain their self-esteem.*

- The Fall/sin

- God's call and covenant

- Slavery in Egypt

- God's deliverance of the Israelites

- The Sinai Covenant

Write a reflection about how the word *covenant* reflects the purpose of the organization. Your reflection can be presented in different creative ways.

3. Understand Yom Kippur

Read Leviticus 16. It tells of Yom Kippur, the Day of Atonement, which purified the Israelites and their land of sins and transgressions committed in the previous year. The ritual of the scapegoat (Lv 16:20–28) transferred the people's sins to the animal. The goat was led to the desert, believed to be the home of Satan, to die. With the animal's death, the people's sins returned to the evil spirit, and their guilt was taken away. Write a report on the modern-day Jewish feast of Yom Kippur, comparing it to its origins in Leviticus.

After St. Caedmon woke from his vision, his ability to write poems in praise of God was unparalleled by any other poet at the time. The verses he sang in his vision are today known as Caedmon's Hymn.

Faithful Disciple

St. Caedmon

St. Caedmon lived in seventh-century England. He was working as a herdsman at a monastery when he received his gift of religious poetry. Caedmon could not read, nor did he think he could sing, so he would usually leave when other servants played the harp and sang. One night, he had a vision that a man was calling him by name and asking him to sing. Caedmon protested, but the man asked Caedmon to sing about creation, at which point Caedmon began to sing in praise to God in verses that he had never heard before.

Caedmon shared his dream with St. Hilda, the abbess, and the educated men of the monastery, and they concluded that he had received a divine gift. He became a monk, and as he learned sacred history, he turned the stories into verse. His poems treated Genesis, Exodus, other stories of the Old Testament, and important moments in the New Testament.

Caedmon died between 670 and 680. The Caedmonian poems were published in 1655 by Francis Junius, a friend of Milton. Although St. Caedmon may not have written all of the poetry himself, other poets followed who wrote in his style: "St. Bede tells us that many English writers of sacred verse had imitated Caedmon but that none had equaled him."[3]

Reading Comprehension

1. What was St. Caedmon's occupation before he became a monk?

2. What was his divine gift?

3. What did St. Caedmon use as the subject of his poetry?

4. How long after St. Caedmon lived were his poems published?

Writing Task

- Write a poem about a story in Genesis or Exodus.

Explaining the Faith

What is the natural law? How is the natural law related to the Ten Commandments?

The natural law is the expression of what a person knows in his or her own soul to be right or wrong. Because of sin, however, not every person automatically understands these moral guidelines. God created the natural law. Grace and Divine Revelation enable people to accept it with confidence. The basic principles of the natural law extend to the entire human race. Natural law corresponds to three basic human drives and needs: (1) preserving life; (2) developing as individuals and communities; and (3) sharing life with others. The Ten Commandments provide the principal ways to apply the natural law.

 Reflection

- How is your ability to decipher natural law enhanced by the development of a moral conscience?

Prayer

Prayer to St. Caedmon

This prayer is especially appropriate given Moses's lack of confidence in his own gifts.

St. Caedmon,

We pray for your intercession on behalf of all who feel unworthy. Satan tries to steal so many souls by making them feel they have nothing to offer, or convincing them that God could never really love them. Please help these souls to realize that God loves us all and that he has given each of us gifts that can only be discovered by turning to him. We pray that all his children may turn to him today and receive the gifts he longs to give.

Amen.[4]

KINGS AND PROPHETS AWAIT THE MESSIAH

LIFELONG FRIENDS

Jerzy, a Jew, and his friend Lolec, a Catholic, lived in Poland in the 1920s. Lolec and Jerzy met before they turned five years old, skied and hiked together, played on the same soccer team, visited each other's homes almost daily, and participated in religious festivities together.

Jerzy Kluger

This close friendship then took an unexpected turn. The two became separated during World War II when the Russian army captured Jerzy and his father, who then fought with the Allies against Nazi Germany. Meanwhile, Lolec entered an underground (secret) seminary to become a priest.

The two were out of touch for many years. Jerzy Kluger studied engineering and married. Lolec became an archbishop. In the 1960s, during the Second Vatican Council, Jerzy heard that Lolec was in Rome, where he then lived, and got in touch. Jerzy, by then also a successful business-man, and Lolec stayed in contact from then on. In September 1978, Lolec, also known as Karol Wojtyla, was elected pope. He chose the name John Paul II. (Pope John Paul II was canonized a saint in 2013.)

St. John Paul II granted Jerzy and his family the first audience (or visit) of his pontificate. Because of their lifetime friendship, Jerzy became a sounding board, confidant, and go-between as St. John Paul II pushed the Roman Catholic Church to heal strained relations with Jews. In 1994, they stood together as the pope welcomed the first Israeli ambassador to the Holy See. Later, St. John Paul II was the first pope to go to a synagogue. He referred to Jews as "our elder brothers." Jerzy was with him for each of these monumental events.

St. John Paul II was the celebrant at Jerzy's daughter's wedding, baptized his granddaughter, and let Jerzy's grandchildren play with his skullcap. The two friends did shout at one another in their later years, but certainly not as enemies. It was only because neither of them could hear well.[1]

FOCUS QUESTION

What is GOD WILLING TO DO FOR YOU?

Chapter Overview

Introduction	Qualities of Friendship
Section 1	Conquest of the Promised Land
Section 2	The Monarchy in Israel
Section 3	God Sends Prophets
Section 4	Prophets of Hope: The Babylonian Exile
Section 5	The Southern Kingdom after the Exile

INTRODUCTION
Qualities of Friendship

MAIN IDEA
Friendship is an apt description for the relationship between God and the Israelites.

True friendship has many faces. Lolec and Jerzy were great friends as children. Even though they were out of touch as young adults, they resumed their friendship later. St. John Paul II was able to improve Catholic-Jewish relationships in part because of this friendship.

One key quality of friendship is loyalty. Native Americans describe a friend as "one-who-carries-my-sorrow-on-his-back." Friends, it has been suggested, know everything about you, but still like you anyway.

The theme of friendship appears regularly in the Old Testament, especially describing the relationship God had with his Chosen People. You may feel that the friendship God had with the Israelites was one-sided. The Israelites were not always faithful friends to the God who

- rescued them from slavery
- guided them with his Law
- gave them a land
- sent judges and kings to defend them from their enemies
- gave them prophets to correct them when they went astray

The Lord God always remained faithful to Israel, kept his promises to them, and sent them a Savior.

NOTE TAKING

Compare and Contrast. Draw a Venn diagram in your notebook like the one below. As you read the section, write in the circles characteristics of the friendship of St. John Paul II and Jerzy Kluger and those pertaining to the friendship between God and the Israelites. Put common characteristics in the overlapping portion.

Human Friendship

Divine-Human Friendship

In this chapter, you will survey the story of God's friendship with his Chosen People. The history covered in this chapter stretches from the thirteenth century BC to the time approaching Jesus' birth. You will see that God continually offers friendship to his people no matter what they have done.

The Bible on Friendship

Read these quotes from the Old Testament about friendship. For each quality, share a personal anecdote about you or someone you know who has put that quality into practice.

- *Putting the other first*: "Jonathan then said to David, 'I will do whatever you say'" (1 Sm 20:4, see image on page 137).

- *Confidentiality*: "One who slanders reveals secrets, but a trustworthy person keeps a confidence" (Prv 11:13).

- *Dependability*: "A friend is a friend at all times" (Prv 17:17).

- *Humility*: "Do nothing out of selfishness or out of vainglory; rather, humbly regard others as more important than yourselves, each looking out not for his own interests, but everyone for those of others" (Phil 2:3–4).

- *Positive influence*: "There are friends who bring ruin, but there are true friends more loyal than a brother" (Prv 18:24).

SECTION ASSESSMENT

NOTE TAKING

Answer this question based on the information you gathered in your Venn diagram.

1. Compare and contrast the friendship between Lolec and Jerzy with the one between God and the people of Israel.

ANALYSIS

2. How does the description of friendship as "one-who-carries-my-sorrow-on-his-back" compare with the common phrase that a friend "has my back"?

REFLECTION

3. What do you think is the most important quality of friendship? Write a paragraph describing how you have exhibited this quality in one of your friendships. Write another paragraph explaining how God has shown this quality to you.

4. Read John 15:13. Jesus said that a willingness to lay down one's life for a friend is the greatest love. How can you do this? For whom would you do this?

SECTION 1
Conquest of the Promised Land

MAIN IDEA
In their early years in the Promised Land, the Israelites learned the hard way that obeying God brought them success while disobeying God brought them ruin.

In Chapter 4, you studied the story of the Israelites from creation through their forty years wandering in the desert after the Exodus. In this chapter, you will familiarize yourself with what happened to the Israelites once they arrived in the land God promised to Abraham. This part of the story roughly covers the years 1250–1030 BC.

The Old Testament Books of Joshua and Judges present the Israelites' history from the time of Moses's death to the beginning of the monarchy. These books tell the story of the Israelites' settlement in the Promised Land and their interactions with their Canaanite neighbors.

The Books of Joshua and Judges present two different time frames of Israel's conquest of Canaan. In Joshua, results come quickly, and the Israelites take over the city. This highlights a major theological theme and religious truth: the Lord fought for Israel—without his help, the Israelites would never have settled in the "land flowing with milk and honey" (Jos 5:6). The Book of Judges presents a more accurate historical record: the conquest spanned approximately two hundred years and involved several major battles before the Israelites gained a foothold in the land.

After Moses's death, Joshua led the Israelites across the Jordan River, and they conquered the city of Jericho (see image at left). The Book of Joshua emphasizes that the Israelites had God's support against their enemies, but only when they were faithful. Obedience to God was the key to success. When the Israelites obeyed,

---

NOTE TAKING   **Analyzing Content.** As you read through this section and biblical verses, record some behaviors of the Israelites that please and displease God.

Behaviors That Please God	Behaviors That Displease God
Obeying God's commands like Joshua	Worshiping false gods

they were victorious. When they ignored God and followed their own will, they failed.

Joshua led the Israelites into the Promised Land, staying close to the Lord, celebrating a Passover meal before the invasion, and always obeying the Lord's commands. Joshua was victorious.

Joshua and other leaders distributed land to the Twelve Tribes (see Jos 13–21). The Book of Joshua concludes at Shechem with a renewal of the covenant and a farewell speech from Joshua:

> Today, as you see, I am going the way of all men. So now acknowledge with your whole heart and soul that not one of all the promises the Lord, your God, made to you has remained unfulfilled. Every promise has been fulfilled for you, with not one single exception. (Jos 23:14)

After Joshua's death, the various tribes had to contend with the ongoing resistance of hostile neighbors. In the absence of a strong central authority, God raised up various local military leaders called *judges*. The history of the Israelites during the period of the judges centers around a *cycle of **apostasy***, which typically followed these stages:

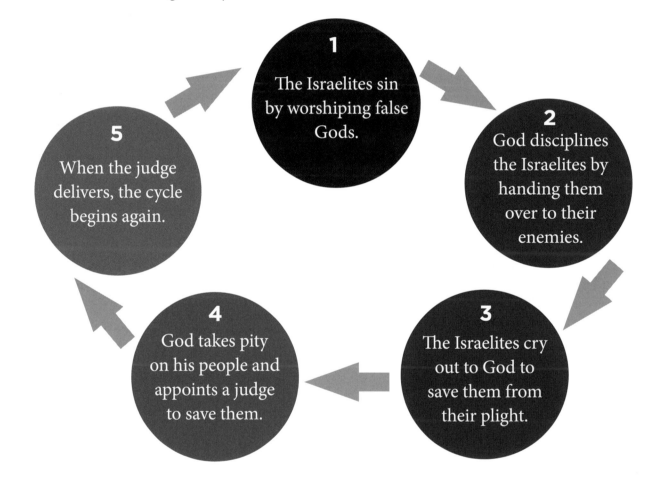

1 The Israelites sin by worshiping false Gods.

2 God disciplines the Israelites by handing them over to their enemies.

3 The Israelites cry out to God to save them from their plight.

4 God takes pity on his people and appoints a judge to save them.

5 When the judge delivers, the cycle begins again.

apostasy The denial of God and the repudiation of faith.

This pattern shows that even though the Israelites were God's Chosen People, their inclination to sin led them to prefer their own way over God's way. (This preference may remind you of Adam and Eve or of many people today.) God's faithful love remained constant. Time and time again, God rescued Israelites,

Sampling Scripture
JOSHUA AND JUDGES

Read the following Scripture passages. Write your answers to each question.

READ JOSHUA 2-4, 6, 24.

1. What role did Rahab play in helping the Israelites conquer the Promised Land?

2. Describe the fall of Jericho.

3. What symbolized Joshua's renewal of the covenant?

READ JUDGES 2, 6-8, 13-16.

1. Summarize the Israelites' behavior after Joshua's death and God's response to it.

2. How did Gideon respond to God's call (Jgs 6:11–24)? What led to his ruin (Jgs 8)?

3. What do you find most appealing about Samson's character? What do you find to be his greatest character flaw?

even raising up leaders for them. These three judges had well known accomplishments:

- *Deborah* was a prophetess who instructed the general Barak to lead the army in a successful holy war (see Jgs 5).

- *Gideon*, a young man, objected that he was too weak and unworthy to be a leader, but God led Israel to victory through him (see Jgs 6–8).

- *Samson* fought bravely against the neighboring Philistines, a group that settled in southern Canaan in about the twelfth century BC and conducted raids throughout the Mediterranean area. Though a hero, Samson had many personal failings that led to infidelity and suffering. His own life followed the apostasy cycle (see Jgs 13–16).

Despite the judges' help, Israel fell apart because of its overall unfaithfulness and lawlessness. "In those days there was no king in Israel; everyone did what was right in their own sight" (Jgs 21:25). The Israelites wondered what life would be like if they had a king and a more central form of government like other groups of people they were neighbors to.

SESSION ASSESSMENT

NOTE TAKING

Use your chart to help you answer this question.

1. How do the behaviors you discovered match the cycle of apostasy discussed in this section?

COMPREHENSION

2. Who led the Israelites after Moses's death?

3. Name two important judges, and list at least one of each of their accomplishments.

COMPARE AND CONTRAST

4. How does the cycle of apostasy resemble the experience of a penitent Catholic? How does it differ?

REFLECTION

5. Gideon claimed that he was too weak and unworthy to lead Israel. Describe a time when you thought you were unable to do something asked of you, but you came through it successfully.

The Monarchy in Israel

MAIN IDEA
Although the kings made positive contributions to the people of Israel, the negative effects of the kings' reigns—especially King Solomon's—split the once-united Israel.

The First and Second Books of Samuel cover the story of the Israelites from the period of the judges until the last years of King David's reign, approximately 1075–970 BC. The First and Second Books of Kings relate the history of the Israelites beginning with the death of King David (ca. 970 BC) and continuing with the split into two kingdoms in 922 BC, Assyria's destruction of the northern kingdom in 721 BC, and the Babylonian Captivity (Exile) of the southern kingdom in 587–586 BC. The religious theme during the period of the monarchy is familiar: fidelity to God leads to success; disobedience leads to disaster.

Samuel, Israel's Final Judge

Samuel, a priest and prophet, was Israel's last and most significant judge. The circumstances of Samuel's birth indicated that he was a special gift from God (see 1 Samuel 1–2; compare Hannah's prayer in 1 Samuel 2:1–10 to Mary's hymn of praise in Luke 1:46–55). Samuel ruled wisely as a judge, helping the people turn away from idolatry. Toward the end of his life, though, the people requested a king who would rule them like the kings of other nations.

Why do you think that the Israelites wanted a king when they already had a king in God? You have likely encountered this type of reasoning: "If other people have it or do it, it must be good for me too." But Israel was special—they were God's own people. Samuel

NOTE TAKING

Compare and Contrast. Design a model in your notebook that differentiates between the faults and triumphs of the kings as described in this section. For example, in the model here, the bricks scattered on the ground represent the faults of the kings; the bricks forming the foundation of a building represent the kings' triumphs.

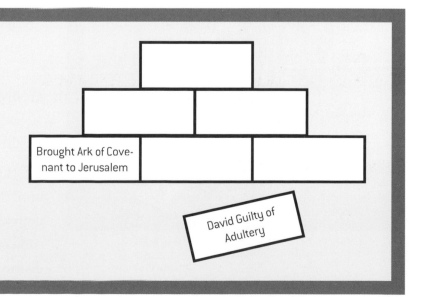

Brought Ark of Covenant to Jerusalem

David Guilty of Adultery

warned the people that a human king would draft Israelite children into his army, tax them, and treat them like slaves. He also told them that they were offending God by requesting a human king. Despite these warnings, the people still persisted. Samuel received a message from God to anoint a human king.

Anointing a King—Saul

When you think of the elaborate electoral system in the United States, the selection method for Israel's first king might seem odd. Samuel assembled the tribes to choose a king, most likely by a decision process known as casting lots (see 1 Sm 10:17–27). Saul was selected with God's approval. At first, Saul was successful in his military exploits and in his efforts to unite the tribes. Unfortunately, Saul's pride reversed these trends. Saul began to take privileges that were only reserved for priests. He also disobeyed certain commands from God.

Samuel anoints Saul as first king of Israel (see 1 Sm 16:13).

Samuel anointed David to replace Saul while Saul was still king. From that anointing, "the spirit of the Lord rushed upon David" (1 Sm 16:13). In the end, Saul paid a steep price for his sins: he lost the crown to David, the greatest of all Israel's kings, and God's spirit departed from Saul, who began to suffer psychological torments.

David, Israel's Greatest King

At the time of Saul's death, Israel was in turmoil. David became king of Judah in the southern portion of the kingdom and reigned for seven years. One of Saul's sons ruled in the north. After a period of political intrigue, David became the sole king of Israel, uniting all the tribes into a single nation for thirty-three years. During this time, David selected Jerusalem to be Israel's capital. David brought the Ark of the Covenant to Jerusalem (see image on page 143) to witness God's permanent presence to the new nation.

God made a covenant with David ensuring that a leader from his family would always rule Israel. This is often called the *Davidic covenant* to distinguish it from the Sinai Covenant given to Moses. God spoke to the prophet Nathan, who passed this message on to David:

> Moreover, the Lord also declares to you that the Lord will make a house for you: when your days have been completed and you rest with your ancestors, I will raise up your offspring after you, sprung from your loins, and I will establish his kingdom. . . . Your house and your kingdom are firm forever before me; your throne shall be firmly established forever. (2 Sm 7: 11–12, 16)

The Davidic dynasty lasted four hundred years until the Babylonians conquered the southern kingdom in 586 BC. Later generations looked to David as someone God used in a special way to work out his divine plan and to his reign as a golden age for Israel.

The PSALMS

The Book of Psalms is part of the wisdom literature of the Bible. Most likely, you are familiar with the psalms from hearing them read or sung during Sunday Mass, between the first and second readings. (Daily Mass also includes a psalm, but no second reading.) The cantor sings the body of the psalm, while the congregation sings the refrain. Psalms are effective individual prayers as well, often capturing your sense of anxiety, joy, frustration, or gratitude.

People connect differently to the psalms than to other books in the Old Testament. The psalms include hymns of praise and thanksgiving. Other psalms petition God directly, either individually or communally. Still others are prophetic oracles or take up problems of human living. Though individual psalms might be tied to specific events, they continue to be relevant for people today. A special category of psalms speak of a coming Messiah; for example, Psalms 2, 72, and 110 are the ones the New Testament quotes the most frequently.

There are 150 psalms in the Bible. Because he was a gifted poet and musician who also was king, David is associated with the authorship of the Book of Psalms. From your study of the Old Testament to this point, do you think that King David composed all of these psalms? Like many other parts of the Old Testament, the psalms are compilations. King David introduced music into the sanctuary and likely did compose many of the psalms: seventy-three psalms are attributed to him.

The Book of Psalms or *Psalter* ("Praises") is actually composed of five books. These books formed the hymnbook of ancient Israel, since most of the psalms were poems meant to be sung, typically as part of the Temple's worship service. Because they came from the people and were expressed in communal worship, the psalms not only expressed the prayers of the ancient Israelites but also nourished their spiritual lives. Jesus himself prayed the psalms, and they remain central to the Church's prayer.

Sampling Scripture

1 AND 2 SAMUEL

Read the following Scripture passages. Write your answers to each question.

READ 1 SAMUEL 16:1–20:42.

1. How does God's judgment differ from human judgment?
2. Name three qualities of David shown in these chapters. Explain each one with an example.
3. Discuss the friendship between David and Jonathan.

READ 2 SAMUEL 11:1–12:15.

1. What were David's sins?
2. How did he own up to them?
3. What was his punishment?

The Davidic covenant led the Israelites to believe that the **Messiah** would come from the house of David and would save the Chosen People from their enemies.

Despite his greatness, King David also had his faults. Second Samuel 11–12 describes King David's attraction to Bathsheba, the wife of one of his soldiers. David called for Bathsheba and conceived a son with her. After trying to trick her husband Uriah into having intercourse with his wife to hide the adultery, David put Uriah in the front lines of battle, where he was killed. After a period of mourning for her husband, Bathsheba married King David.

The prophet Nathan confronted the king about his sins of adultery and murder. Nathan said that the Lord would punish King David: his child with Bathsheba would die. David repented, begging for God's forgiveness, but his son still died. David and Bathsheba then had a second son, Solomon, who succeeded David as king.

King Solomon and a Divided Kingdom

Chapters 1–11 of 1 Kings describe King Solomon's reign. Solomon was a powerful and wealthy king with few rivals in the ancient Mediterranean world. He had a generally peaceful and prosperous reign. He was known as a great builder; his greatest achievement was building the Temple in Jerusalem, the center of Israel's religious life.

Pleased with Solomon, God told him, "Whatever you ask I shall give you" (1 Kgs 3:5). Solomon asked God for the gift of wisdom. He prayed to the Lord for an understanding heart to judge the people and a spirit to discern right from wrong. "Moreover, God gave Solomon wisdom, exceptional understanding, and knowledge, as vast as the sand on the seashore" (1 Kgs 5:9).

Despite his wisdom, however, power and the splendor of his office corrupted Solomon over time. He overextended himself economically by keeping many wives whom he had to support in luxury. Furthermore, some of his foreign wives introduced their gods and priests into the land and subsequently led many Israelites to false worship. Because Israel had a large army with many soldiers and Solomon initiated many building projects, Solomon taxed the Israelites heavily and conscripted many to forced labor.

Solomon's excesses led to hard times for him and for all of Israel. Rebellions plagued the kingdom. After his death in 922 BC, the united kingdom split in two. Rehoboam, Solomon's son, ruled the *southern kingdom*, the **kingdom of Judah**, commanding the loyalty of the tribe of Judah and some descendants of Simeon. Solomon's servant Jeroboam ruled the northern ten tribes, which formed the *northern kingdom*, the **kingdom of Israel**.

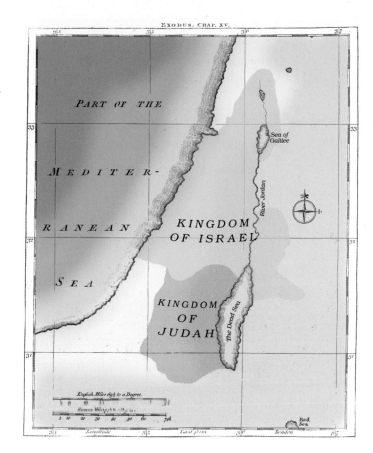

Idolatry eventually caused the northern kingdom's downfall. King Jeroboam centered worship at two ancient shrines—Dan and Bethel—rather than in the holy city of Jerusalem. A subsequent king, Ahab, allowed his wife, Jezebel, to erect altars to Baal, the pagan god of Israel's neighbors, who was thought to bring rain. These practices spread idolatry throughout the kingdom. In later years, Jews would explain Assyria's destruction of the northern kingdom by pointing to the northern kingdom's sin of idolatry.

Messiah The "anointed one" promised by the Old Testament prophets. He would be a descendant of David who would set up an ideal kingdom ruled by an adopted son. He would preach the Law in truth and would sacrifice his life for the people. Jesus Christ fulfills the prophecies about the Messiah.

kingdom of Judah The name of the southern kingdom after the splitting of the monarchy. It included the territory originally belonging to just two of the twelve tribes, Judah and Benjamin.

kingdom of Israel The name of the northern kingdom that split with Judah after the death of Solomon.

SECTION ASSESSMENT

NOTE TAKING

Use the information you gathered on the positive and negative elements of the reigns of the kings of Israel to help you complete the following item.

1. Tell how any of the positive elements foreshadow God's everlasting Kingdom.

VOCABULARY

2. Describe the kingdom of Judah and the kingdom of Israel after Solomon's reign.

COMPREHENSION

3. What was one of David's main accomplishments as king?
4. How did God's covenant with David influence the Jewish belief in the Messiah?
5. What was King Solomon's greatest achievement?
6. What was one of the problems caused by Solomon's many wives?

REFLECTION

7. When God called out to Samuel in a dream, Samuel replied, "Speak, for your servant is listening" (1 Sm 3:10). Write a short reflection about ways that the Lord speaks to you personally.
8. If God asked you to choose one gift, what would that gift be?

SECTION 3
God Sends Prophets

MAIN IDEA
The prophets God sent to his people warned them to stay faithful to him alone, challenged injustices, asked his people to repent, and consoled them when they were suffering.

Israel and Judah's decline and the Babylonian Exile gave rise to Israel's greatest prophets. Everyone needed to hear the basic message of the prophets: repent and be saved. Failure to heed the prophets' words brought doom.

Who were the prophets? The ancient Hebrew word for prophet is *nabi*, which means "one who speaks for another" or "mouthpiece." Although the more than twenty prophets in the Old Testament can be grouped in different ways, this chapter will categorize them by three basic time periods:

1. This section introduces prophets who lived and preached before the conquests of the northern and southern kingdoms, such as Isaiah, pictured to the left (*preexilic prophets*).

2. Section 4 looks at prophets who spoke during the exile of the southern kingdom (*prophets of the exile*).

3. Section 5 considers prophets who exhorted Israel after the exile of the southern kingdom (*postexilic prophets*).

It is also important to distinguish between prophets of the northern kingdom and the southern kingdom. Because the northern kingdom fell more quickly than

NOTE TAKING

Summarizing Main Ideas. In your notebook, make a chart like the one here that organizes the names and messages of the prophets by the era they were active. Fill in the names and messages of the prophets from this section. *Note*: You will need to complete this chart for the Exile and Postexilic prophets when covering the material in Section 4 (pages 157–163) and Section 5 (pages 164–168).

Prophets			
Era	**Names**	**Message**	**Method**
Preexilic	Elijah	Fidelity to God	Called on God to send fire to consume sacrifice
Exile			
Postexilic			

the southern kingdom, there are more prophets for the southern kingdom. In addition, the Bible no longer speaks of the people in the northern kingdom after the Assyrians conquer them: their defeat solidified the Jews' belief that the northern tribes abandoned the covenant with God. Jews who later compiled the Bible were from the southern kingdom and no longer considered the northern kingdom's faith to be authentic to YHWH because they did not worship in Jerusalem.

The Prophets' Basic Message

You may wonder what motivated the prophets to accept God's call. It was often a thankless vocation. The prophets' responsibility was to challenge the ruling authorities and tell them what they were doing wrong, a task that made the prophets quite unpopular. At times, prophets told the whole people to shape up. God asked them to share unusual and unwelcome messages, sometimes in odd ways. For all these reasons, the prophets stood out. Additionally, and most importantly, the prophets called the people to repentance.

The prophets of the Old Testament all received an irresistible call from God through dreams, visions, or internal inspirations. They preached their messages through stories, poetry, proverbs, satire, and other literary devices. The Old Testament prophets preached the following themes:

PROPHETS WANTED!
Can You Preach These Themes?

- Worship the one true God.
- Be just, especially to the poor.
- Know that God will ultimately triumph.
- Accept God's love and mercy.

YES! **NO**

The next sections provide brief background on the major prophets of the northern kingdom of Israel and the southern kingdom of Judah.

Preexilic Prophets of the Northern Kingdom

You know that after King Solomon died, the northern ten tribes crowned Jeroboam, one of Solomon's servants, king. Recall that the holy city of Jerusalem was located in Judah in the southern kingdom. *All* of God's Chosen People, however, were supposed to worship at the Temple. Because Jeroboam feared that allowing his people to worship in Jerusalem might inspire them to return their loyalty to the southern king, he decided to set up his own places of worship in the north.

Unfortunately, what this meant was that Israel's own king led his people away from God. King Jeroboam made two golden calves and placed one each in the northern kingdom's cities of Dan and Bethel, telling his people that the cows were the God who brought the people out of the land of Egypt. Naturally, the calves inspired idolatry among the members of the northern tribes.

Because of his insecurity, Jeroboam put the northern kingdom in a tenuous relationship with God from the start by violating the First Commandment. Many of Jeroboam's successors also "did what is evil in the Lord's sight" (1 Kgs 15:34).

Elijah

Elijah was an important prophet of the ninth century BC in Israel during the reign of the wicked King Ahab and his wife Jezebel: "Ahab, son of Omri, did what was evil in his sight more than any of his predecessors" (1 Kgs 16:30). King Ahab allowed pagan religion to take hold in Israel. Elijah called down a famine on the land in the hope that this would shock Israel back to fidelity. In a well-known scene (see 1 Kgs 18), Elijah challenged the prophets of Baal to ask their gods to send down fire to consume a sacrifice. Predictably, their

The prophet Elijah denouncing Ahab in 1 Kings 21:20–24.

gods were powerless to do anything. God, on the other hand, vindicated Elijah by sending fire to consume the sacrifice as well as the altar on which it lay. The people were awestruck, falling prostrate and proclaiming, "The LORD is God! The LORD is God!" (1 Kgs 18:39).

While Elijah's success inspired the people, it enraged Queen Jezebel, who threatened to kill him. Elijah fled to the southern kingdom.

Next to Moses, Elijah was the greatest of the Old Testament prophets. Because he was taken to Heaven in a whirlwind (see 2 Kgs 2:9–18), the Jews believed that Elijah would, at the end of time, bring peace to the world. The Jews understood Elijah as the precursor and partner of the Messiah. The New Testament records the impact of this great prophet: many people thought that Jesus himself was Elijah.

Elisha

The prophet Elisha succeeded Elijah. He performed many miracles as he carried on Elijah's work. Like Elijah, Elisha sided with the poor (see 2 Kgs 4:1–2).

Elisha cured Naaman, a foreign army commander, of leprosy. Hearing of Elisha's greatness from an Israelite servant girl, Naaman made the journey to Israel to seek healing, finally finding his way to Elisha's house. Elisha told Naaman that he needed only to wash seven times in the Jordan to become well. At first, Naaman thought that this suggestion was not spectacular enough to work, but he tried it anyway and was cured. He brought back some of Israel's soil to his homeland so that he could worship the God of the Israelites on it.

The stories of Elijah and Elisha set the stage for two prophetic books that are likewise important to the Old Testament: Amos and Hosea. When King Jeroboam II and his successors came to power, they were religiously and morally bankrupt. They permitted the worship of the Baals and allowed the rich to exploit the poor. Amos and Hosea—two prophets of social justice— challenged them.

Elijah and Elisha, like Samuel and Nathan, fall into the *nonwriting* group of prophets because they did not leave behind their own writings. Amos and Hosea, however, wrote their own books and are therefore called *writing prophets*.

Amos

Though he was from the southern kingdom, Amos received God's call to preach in the north around 750 BC. His basic message was that the worship of God must show itself in concrete deeds of mercy and justice to the weak and the poor. Amos fearlessly warned that the many sins of the northern kingdom—sins like genocide, dishonesty, greed, sexual excess, robbery, violence, injustice, and pride—would lead to the people's destruction. He called the nation to repent, saying:

> Hate evil and love good,
> and let justice prevail at the gate;
> Then it may be that the Lord, the God of hosts,
> will have pity on the remnant of Joseph. (Am 5:15)

Amos did not believe the people would repent in time to avert God's punishment, yet he still maintained hope. He foresaw that a small remnant would survive the impending destruction (see Am 3:12). God would sift out the bad and raise up the kingdom of David (see Am 9:11).

Israel's leaders did not appreciate Amos's message, so they banished him from the land (see Am 7:12). His message challenged Israel to repent before the day of doom descended on the nation. Amos's message stands today to challenge all nations, especially wealthy ones, to serve the poor.

Hosea

The prophet Hosea was a native of Israel. His preaching began during the last years of Amos's ministry (around 745 BC) and continued until the fall of Israel. Hosea's wife abandoned him—it is not known whether to worship false gods, to pursue infidelity, or to become a prostitute; in Hosea's writing, marital unfaithfulness symbolizes false worship. Hosea drew on his painful marital situation to describe God's relationship with Israel: Israel had become an unfaithful lover who ignored God's covenant love. Like Amos, Hosea saw Israel's worst crimes as idolatry and ruthless oppression of the poor.

Hosea accused Israel of sin, infidelity to God, and crimes like perjury, lying, murder, theft, and adultery. Sin resulted from not truly knowing God and all the good he has done for the people. Not knowing God led people to go through the motions in worship and exploit the poor. The antidote is clear:

> For it is loyalty that I desire, not sacrifice,
> and knowledge of God rather than burnt offerings. (Hos 6:6)

> **Lost Tribes of Israel** The ten tribes of the northern kingdom who disappeared from history after being enslaved and exiled by the Assyrians.

The life and ministry of the prophet Hosea overlapped the life and ministry of Amos. Both prophets seemed to anticipate the fall of Israel to the Assyrian Empire in 722 BC.

Israel's crimes deserved punishment, so Hosea prophesied that the nation would perish. Despite their actions, God still loved the Chosen People with a steadfast love, like that of a husband for his wife or a father for his son. God would never abandon his people irrevocably.

Fall of the Northern Kingdom

Assyria captured Babylon and marched to Egypt. Israel's kings foolishly tried to ally themselves with Egypt, leading to the northern kingdom's destruction in 722 BC. The king of Assyria deported more than twenty-seven thousand Israelites into exile. These exiles are the famous **Lost Tribes of Israel** who eventually intermarried with the peoples of their new lands and lost their identity as God's Chosen People. The northern kingdom had met its end.

Sampling Scripture

1 KINGS, AMOS, AND HOSEA

Write your answers to each question

READ 1 KINGS 3, 6, 8.

1. What is Solomon's request in 1 Kgs 3:9?

2. How does Solomon prove his wisdom in 1 Kgs 3:16–28?

3. How was the Temple decorated? What were some of the objects placed in the Temple?

4. List three petitions Solomon prayed for in his prayer of dedication.

READ 1 KINGS 17-19.

1. What does Elijah do for the widow?

2. How did Elijah taunt the false prophets of Baal?

3. Where did Elijah find the Lord God?

READ AMOS 7-8; HOSEA 1-3.

1. What is the meaning of Amos's visions?

2. List some of the sins of Gomer (Israel). See commentary in the *New American Bible Revised Edition* for more information.

3. What does Hosea 3 say about the outcome of the love between God and Israel?

Preexilic Prophets of the Southern Kingdom

The southern kingdom's demise came in 586 BC at the hands of the Babylonians, who would eventually take much of the population into exile. God sent prophets to warn the nation prior to the Babylonian Exile. Prophets of this era were Isaiah, Micah, Jeremiah, and Ezekiel. Jeremiah and Ezekiel preached both words of warning before the exile and words of consolation and hope after the nation was taken into captivity. Their stories will be covered on pages 158–160. Some of the successors to King Solomon tried to keep God's covenant, but eventually the kings intermarried with the northern kingdom's Ahab-Jezebel family, which led to the same offenses as before: idolatry, injustice, and religious worship marked by formality without a godly spirit.

Isaiah

Isaiah was an influential Hebrew prophet. The book that bears his name is the longest of all the prophetic books, with sixty-six chapters. Isaiah is unique in a number of ways.

The Book of Isaiah is actually a collection of prophecies spanning 250 years. Of course, the prophet Isaiah did not live that long. Much of the collection of the Book of Isaiah was written by later anonymous prophets. Hence, the Book of Isaiah is divided to reflect the different eras:

- Chapters 1–39 are credited to the prophet himself, who preached in the preexilic era from 742 to 700 BC.

- Chapters 40–55 reflect a message of compassion and were written toward the end of the Babylonian Exile. A second prophet writing in this section foretold the return of God's People to Jerusalem and said that all the nations would come to recognize YHWH as the one true God.

"The vineyard of the Lord of hosts is the house of Israel, and the men of Judah are his cherished plant" (Is 5:7a).

- Chapters 56–66, likely the work of another anonymous prophet, were written after the Babylonian Exile.

The first chapters reveal information about the prophet Isaiah himself. Early in his life he had a vision of God in all his glory in the Jerusalem Temple. This vision convinced him that the Chosen People must imitate God's holiness by righteous living, true worship, and turning from the abuses that oppressed the poor. He asked the people to repent during King Jotham's reign (742–735 BC):

> Wash yourselves clean!
> Put away your misdeeds from before my eyes;
> cease doing evil;
> learn to do good.
> Make justice your aim: redress the wronged,
> hear the orphan's plea, defend the widow.
> (Is 1:16–17)

Unfortunately, Isaiah knew that his people would not repent. In a beautiful story (see Is 5:1–7), the prophet compares the nation to a vineyard that God cultivates. Because the vines refuse to bear fruit, the vinedresser (God) has to prune it so that a future generation might bear fruit. This pruning will involve defeat by outside nations of both the northern kingdom and the southern kingdom.

When the people became afraid that God's covenant with David was coming to an end, Isaiah promised a sign: "the young woman, pregnant and about to bear a son, shall name him Emmanuel" (Is 7:14). And later,

They name him Wonder-Counselor, God-Hero, Father-Forever, Prince of Peace. (Is 9:5)

Isaiah's reference to *Emmanuel* (meaning "God is with us") is a prophecy about Jesus Christ, the Son of God, the promised Messiah.

Micah

Micah, Isaiah's contemporary, also preached a message of hope. Although he warned of the coming judgment, Micah also told of a time when God would bring a universal reign of peace:

They shall beat their swords into plowshares, and their spears into pruning hooks;
One nation shall not raise the sword against another,
    nor shall they train for war again. (Mi 4:3)

Micah added to and affirmed the hope that Isaiah had given the people.

- Micah foretold a coming Messiah who would lead Israel to peace and justice.
- This Messiah would come from Bethlehem and would rule by the strength of the Lord.
- He would gather God's remnant, a righteous group who would survive the Babylonian Captivity.

Micah's message of hope led to his belief that this remnant would lead the nations to true worship of God.

Sampling Scripture

ISAIAH

Read the following Scripture passage. Write your answers to each question.

READ ISAIAH 1–7.

1. What will happen in days to come (see Is 2:4)?
2. To what does Isaiah compare the nation (see Is 3:16f.)?
3. Interpret the allegory in Isaiah 5:1–7.

SECTION ASSESSMENT

NOTE TAKING

Use the chart you created to help you answer the following question. After finishing your chart using material from Sections 4 and 5, complete the following item.

1. Compare the message of the prophets who spoke to the people prior to their conquest with the message of those who preached during the exile of the southern kingdom. What similarities and differences do you observe?

VOCABULARY

2. What is the connection between the splitting of the kingdoms after Solomon's reign and the Lost Tribes of Israel?

COMPREHENSION

3. Why did the northern kingdom have fewer prophets than the southern kingdom?

4. How did Hosea's unfortunate marriage help him deliver his message?

APPLICATION

5. Which four themes preached by the prophets are still relevant today? Explain.

6. King Jeroboam's insecurity about losing his people to the king of Judah led him to set up alternate sites of worship for his people as well as golden calves for worship. Describe a time (in your experience or in the news) when one person's insecurity ruined something essential for a group.

7. Queen Jezebel wanted to kill Elijah because of his success as a prophet. Name another historical example of a prophet killed because his or her words were too threatening.

8. What do you think it means to "hate evil and love good" (Am 5:15) in your life today?

REFLECTION

9. If you could meet one of the prophets from this section, whom would you choose, and what question would you ask him?

10. In the larger picture of Salvation History, why were the prophets necessary to pave the way for Jesus?

SECTION 4
Prophets of Hope: The Babylonian Exile

MAIN IDEA

Once the Jews were suffering for their infidelity to the covenant, the prophets and some of the Jews themselves looked with hope to the future.

Jerusalem and the Temple were destroyed in 586 BC, and the Baylonian King Nebuchadnezzar deported most of its residents to Babylon. Those left behind in Jerusalem were poor, weak, and leaderless; some of them fled to Egypt for safety. One tradition reports that Jeremiah was stoned to death.

For pious Jews, living in a foreign land was difficult. While some of the Chosen People intermarried, others feared a loss of identity and encouraged only marriage between Jews. The northern kingdom had lost its identity first through idolatry and then through assimilation into the Assyrian society.

To distinguish themselves from their captors, many of the Jewish exiles studied the Law, observed the **Sabbath**, and continued the practice of circumcision. Without a Temple, there was no place for sacrifice, so they met in **synagogues** where they studied and prayed together. Scribes gathered Israel's oral traditions and committed them to writing as a permanent record of God's love toward his people. Many of these texts became part of the Jewish Scriptures.

> **Sabbath** A day of rest and prayer for the Jewish people on the seventh day of the week.
>
> **synagogue** A meeting place for Jews for study and prayer to foster study of the Law and adherence to the covenant code.

NOTE TAKING

Specifying a Theme. As you read through this section, identify the message of hope of the prophets of this period. Copy a graphic organizer like the one below in your notebook. Write the words of hope in the appropriate place.

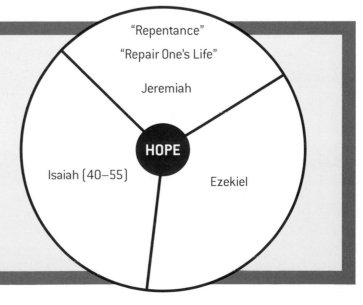

"Repentance"
"Repair One's Life"
Jeremiah

HOPE

Isaiah (40–55)

Ezekiel

Southern Preexilic Prophets Who Also Spoke during the Exile

Both Jeremiah and Ezekiel's lives spanned the fall of Judah to the Babylonians and the Exile. Note that their prophecies changed from calls to repentance and warnings of doom before the Exile to words of consolation and hope once doom had struck.

Jeremiah

Jeremiah consistently preached a message of repentance, warning that the People's sins would lead to sorrow and death. His message shouted out the love of a God who desperately wanted the Chosen People to repent before catastrophe struck. Even when the people ignored his message and Jerusalem fell to Babylon, Jeremiah preached hope.

Jeremiah taught by enacting living parables. In one example, Jeremiah compared God to a potter (see Jer 19). Unless the people repented, God would break the nation as a punishment. In a dramatic gesture, Jeremiah shattered a clay flask in front of the elders and priests. This served to warn the nation that God would destroy those who had abandoned him.

Jeremiah's life resembled that of the New Testament prophet, John the Baptist:

- Both are forerunners of the Messiah.
- Both accomplish what many might have thought impossible if not for the grace of God (see Jer 32:27; Lk 1:37).

There are also parallels between Jeremiah's life and Jesus' life.

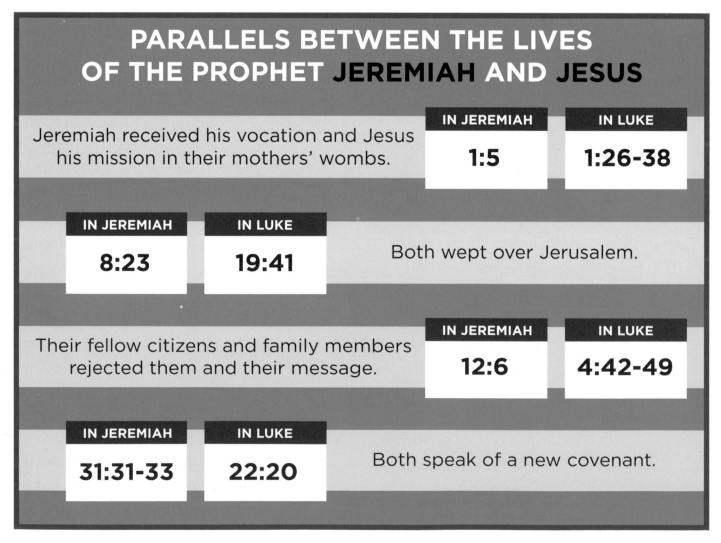

PARALLELS BETWEEN THE LIVES OF THE PROPHET JEREMIAH AND JESUS

Jeremiah received his vocation and Jesus his mission in their mothers' wombs.

IN JEREMIAH	IN LUKE
1:5	1:26-38

IN JEREMIAH	IN LUKE
8:23	19:41

Both wept over Jerusalem.

Their fellow citizens and family members rejected them and their message.

IN JEREMIAH	IN LUKE
12:6	4:42-49

IN JEREMIAH	IN LUKE
31:31-33	22:20

Both speak of a new covenant.

Sampling Scripture

JEREMIAH

Read the following Scripture passages in the Book of Jeremiah. Write your answers to each question.

1. What evils does Jeremiah describe? Why does the nation deserve punishment (see Jer 5)?

2. Why is God unhappy with the way worship is taking place (see Jer 7)?

3. Does Jeremiah prophesy good news or bad news? Explain (see Jer 31).

4. Interpret the following "living symbols" in these verses:

- loincloth (Jer 13:1–11)
- potter's vessel (Jer 18:1–12)
- broken flask (Jer 19:1–15)

Jeremiah said,

> See, days are coming—oracle of the LORD—when I will make a new covenant with the house of Israel and the house of Judah. It will not be like the covenant I made with their ancestors. . . . I will place my law within them, and write it upon their hearts; I will be their God, and they shall be my people. . . . Everyone, from least to greatest, shall know me—oracle of the LORD—for I will forgive their iniquity and no longer remember their sin. (Jer 31:31–34)

This famous passage gave great hope to the suffering Chosen People. It told them that God would show the initiative, giving people a new heart so that they could be open to him. Knowledge of God would no longer come from tablets of stone (as in Exodus) or law books (as in Deuteronomy). Jesus' Life, Death, and Resurrection inaugurated the New Covenant.

Ezekiel

Ezekiel's life overlapped with Jeremiah's, but he spoke from a different perspective. Born into a priestly family, he placed great value on the Temple and its worship, with a special focus on the need to keep the Sabbath and follow the law of holiness. In addition, while Jeremiah remained in Jerusalem during the Babylonian Exile, Ezekiel accompanied the exiled Jews to Babylon.

Ezekiel's behavior was eccentric. He reported outrageous visions and used symbolic actions to communicate his message. Chapter 1 of the Book of Ezekiel reports that the prophet had a fantastic vision of God involving a chariot and four winged creatures, each having four faces, representing the attributes of God: courage (lion), strength (ox), swiftness (eagle), intelligence (man). This vision struck Ezekiel dumb: a vision of God's glory was too much for him to take in.

Before the fall of Jerusalem, Ezekiel censured the Chosen People and the nations for their sinful conduct. He engaged in symbolic actions to shock the people into turning from their sins. One involved cutting his hair and dividing it up as a sign of the fate of the people (see Ez 6:1–4).

After Jerusalem fell, Ezekiel told the exiled Jews of a new king (see Ez 33–39), of a shepherd who would make a covenant of peace with the people, and of a time when God would restore the nation. In a famous vision, Ezekiel reported standing in a field of dry bones. His interpretation of the dream gave great hope to the nation:

> These bones are the whole house of Israel! . . . Thus says the Lord GOD: Look! I am going up to open your graves; I will make you come up out of your graves, my people, and bring you back to the land of Israel. You shall know that I am the LORD, when I open your graves and make you come up out of them, my people! I will put my spirit in you that you may come to life, and I will settle you upon your land. Then you shall know that I am the LORD. I have spoken; I will do it. (Ez 37:11–14)

Ezekiel also prophesied the building of a new Temple, a New Jerusalem, and the nation's return. Ezekiel is often considered to be the father of the Jewish religion. His emphasis on God's holiness and obeying the rules of holiness greatly influenced Judaism after the Exile.

Prophet of the Exile (Is 40–55)

Isaiah 40–55 was written during the period of the Jews' Exile in Babylon. One or more anonymous authors, writing in the spirit of the prophet Isaiah around 550 BC, encouraged the Jews in exile with a hope-filled message. The author understood that the Babylonian Empire was on the verge of collapse and that the leader of the Persian Empire, Cyrus, would soon conquer the Babylonians. In 538 BC, this scenario in fact played out, and God's remnant journeyed back to Jerusalem.

Sampling Scripture
EZEKIEL

Read the following Scripture passages in the Book of Ezekiel. Write your answers to each question.

1. Describe Ezekiel's vision of the Lord's chariot. What else happens to the prophet? What is his function supposed to be (see Ez 1–3)?

2. Interpret the symbolic actions Ezekiel performs (see Ez 4–5).

3. How does Ezekiel speak of personal responsibility (see Ez 18)?

🖐 Promoting Justice

Consider the prophetic method of acting out the message one is sending to the audience. Choose an issue of injustice that you see. Decide how you might act out the message to fight the injustice, and then act it out solo or with others.

THE SUFFERING SERVANT SONGS

There are four distinct poems in Isaiah 40–55 that deal with a specific individual called "the servant." These poems describe how God will use the servant to usher in a glorious future.

Christians see prophetic images of Jesus in these servant passages, because he is the Servant whose sufferings redeemed all people. Jesus' understanding that the Messiah would suffer and serve differed from the traditional view that the Messiah would be surrounded by glory and would dominate others. Here is a brief description of the Servant Songs:

- The first song (Is 42:1–4) speaks of God's chosen one who will bring justice to the world and treat the bruised reed, Israel, tenderly.
- The second song (Is 49:1–6) tells that God chose the servant before his birth. The servant's strength is his prophetic word.
- The third song (Is 50:4–9) describes how God's special messenger meets with resentment. People beat and spit on him and pluck his beard. Yet the servant suffers quietly.
- The final song (Is 52:13–53:12) has remarkable parallels to Jesus Christ's suffering, Death, and Resurrection. Without complaint, the servant accepts a painful, humiliating death so that through him the world can be saved.

These magnificent servant songs stress God's love for all people and deliver one of the Old Testament's most important messages: God is a saving God, a Lord who forgives and forgets the sins of his people.

God indicated through the prophet that Israel had paid the price for its sins and that the Lord was coming to save his people:

Comfort, give comfort to my people,
   says your God.
Speak to the heart of Jerusalem, and proclaim to her
      that her service has ended,
      her guilt is expiated. . . .
      A voice proclaims:
In the wilderness prepare the way of the LORD!
   Make straight in the wasteland a highway for our God!

Every valley shall be lifted up,
   every mountain and hill made low. . . .
Then the glory of the Lord shall be revealed.
(Is 40:1–5)

King Cyrus of Persia was the Lord's instrument because he allowed the Jews to return to Judah and Jerusalem. The prophet of Isaiah 40–55 made it clear that it was the all-powerful Creator God, the source of everything, who truly delivered his Chosen People. Through them he wanted to draw all people to himself: "I will make you a light to the nations, that my salvation may reach to the ends of the earth" (Is 49:6).

Sampling Scripture
ISAIAH 40-55

Read the following Scripture passages. Answer each question.

READ ISAIAH 40-44; 52:13-53:12.

1. Type or write out at least five verses that speak of God's mercy and tenderness to the Chosen People.

2. Note three ways the Servant Songs apply to Jesus.

3. Read the entire chapter of Isaiah 43:1–28. Pick out verses that express God's power and majesty. Then do one of the following:

   • Write a poem or song that describes God's glory.

   • Design a collage or multimedia presentation that illustrates the passage from Isaiah 43.

   • Report on a contemporary group of people or an individual who has rebounded from pride and sinfulness to reclaim the righteousness given by God.

SECTION ASSESSMENT

NOTE TAKING

Use your notes to help you complete the following task.

1. Describe ways that the prophets' messages supported the Jews who were trying to retain their religious and cultural identity.

COMPREHENSION

2. How does Jeremiah's life resemble the life of John the Baptist?

3. Give an example of a living symbol used by Jeremiah or Ezekiel.

4. Why is Ezekiel often considered the father of the Jewish religion?

VOCABULARY

5. What is the difference between the Temple and a synagogue?

APPLICATION

6. How can persecution strengthen religious identity today as it did for the Jews in Babylon?

REFLECTION

7. How is Ezekiel's vision of the dry bones relevant today?

SECTION 5
The Southern Kingdom after the Exile

MAIN IDEA
The Jews who returned to Jerusalem were serious about rebuilding the Temple and Judaism.

The Babylonian Exile taught the Chosen People an important lesson: God does not tolerate idolatry and pagan worship. After returning to Judah, the Jews were more faithful to their vocation of witnessing to the nations by keeping the Law. Led by Zerubbabel, a descendant of King David, and the priest Joshua, the returning Jews rebuilt the Temple and Jerusalem, reestablished the worship of YHWH, and renewed the covenant. In rebuilding the Temple (see image at left), they refused the help of the **Samaritans**, a mixed population of Israelite and Assyrian descent who continued to worship God at Dan and Bethel. Mutual distrust between the Jews and Samaritans festered for centuries and was evident in Jesus' time.

Many Jewish exiles chose to remain in Babylon, Egypt, and elsewhere. Though they looked to Jerusalem for leadership, paid taxes to the Temple, and made pilgrimages to the Holy City, they were more open to Gentile ideas. In fact, because more Jews lived outside of Palestine (a term for the Holy Land that first came into use around the fifth century BC), than within, the synagogue became an even more important

> **Samaritans** Descendants of a mixed population of Israelites who survived the Assyrian deportations and various pagan settlers imported after the northern kingdom fell. They worshipped YHWH on Mount Gerizim but considered only the Pentateuch to be divinely inspired.

NOTE TAKING **Ordering Events.** As you read this section, create your own timeline of events. Use a model like the one below. Add more dates, people, and events.

Jews return to Jerusalem	Old Testament takes shape	Alexander the Great	Maccabees	Herod the Great

institution. **Rabbis** and scribes became increasingly important religious figures, both within and outside the Holy Land.

Postexilic Judaism

The decades after the return to Jerusalem were a time of consolidation, reflection, and recommitment. Prophets wrote about issues such as the rebuilding of the Temple, the role of priests, and proper worship. Strong personalities like Ezra, the reformer-scribe, and Nehemiah, the Persian-appointed governor of Judah, helped shape postexilic Judaism. Their basic tasks were to rebuild the Temple and to renew the covenant in the hearts of the people.

The Old Testament began to resemble its present form as scribes compiled and edited earlier texts and oral traditions. The Pentateuch was completed, and the historical books reached their final form. The works of the prophets were organized. This period also produced some of its own writings, like the historical books of Chronicles, Ezra, and Nehemiah, as well as various other prophetic books.

Ezra

Ezra was a priest and religious reformer who likely came to Jerusalem around 398 BC. He helped solidify Jewish identity by forbidding marriages between Jews and non-Jews and unnecessary mingling with foreign nations. He also publicized the content of the Torah, making it the constitution for Judaism. Fidelity to the Torah set the spiritual tone of the postexilic Jewish community and helped Judaism survive to our own day.

> **rabbi** A Hebrew word for a Jewish master or teacher of the Torah.

Ezra, a Jewish high priest, reading the book of the Law to the people.

Other Postexilic Prophets

Other postexilic prophets in Judah included Zechariah, Haggai, the anonymous prophet(s) who authored Isaiah 56–66, Joel, Obadiah, and Malachi. Zechariah predicted a Messianic age to come. The prophet-disciple of Isaiah looked to a future day when God's light would shine on the Jewish nation and attract all people to God. A restored Jerusalem would bring glad tidings to the lowly, heal the brokenhearted, and proclaim liberty to captives, release to prisoners, and comfort to those who mourn (see Is 61:1–3). All of the prophets of the postexilic period in one way or another referenced and prefigured Jesus Christ, who did all of this and more, bringing Salvation to the world.

MINOR PROPHETS

Read the following Scripture passages. Write your answers to each question.

READ ZECHARIAH 8:1-23.

1. Note five things that will take place in the Messianic age.

READ EITHER THE BOOK OF JOEL OR THE BOOK OF MALACHI.

1. Read the introduction to the book in your Bible.

2. Briefly summarize what the book is about.

3. Copy at least five verses that speak a powerful message to you.

Jewish History Prior to the Birth of Christ

When they were ruled by the Persians, the Jews were not required to practice the official Persian religion, *Zoroastrianism*, a dualist system based on the visions of a tenth-century BC figure called Zarathustra.

Alexander the Great toppled the Persian Empire in 334 BC. In his conquered territories, he established a cultural union of East and West known as **Hellenism**. He wished all his conquered people to be one nation, with classical Greek culture serving as the unifying force. Thus, he introduced common (*Koine*) Greek as the official language of these conquered lands.

After Alexander's death, two competing families fought over his empire: the Ptolemies of Egypt and the Seleucids of Syria. The Ptolemies ruled Palestine from 323 to 198 BC. Their rule was generally benevolent, with no concerted effort to impose Hellenistic culture. In Palestine, some Jews adopted Greek customs, while

> **Hellenism** The diffusion of Greek culture throughout the Mediterranean world after the conquest of Alexander the Great.

others viewed this adoption as a desertion of the faith of their ancestors.

The Seleucids ruled Palestine from 198 to 63 BC. In general the Seleucid rulers, especially Antiochus IV (175–164 BC), tried to impose unity on their subjects. Antiochus IV wanted to build a mighty army and force Greek culture on all the people, including the Jews. He twice robbed the Temple and forbade Jews to engage in religious practices central to their faith: circumcision, Sabbath observances, Temple sacrifices, and abstinence from pork. Worst of all, he engaged in what the Jews termed "the abomination of desolation" by installing a statue of Zeus on the altar of holocausts in the Temple (167 BC).

The Maccabean Revolt

Antiochus IV's cruel rule led to a revolt by the Maccabee family, headed by Mattathias and his five sons. Judas Maccabeus was a remarkable leader who recaptured Jerusalem and rededicated the Temple in 164 BC. The December feast of **Hanukkah**, the Festival of Lights, commemorates this event in Jewish history.

Under the Maccabees, the **Hasmonean Dynasty** formed. The independent if short-lived Jewish dynasty governed the Jews until 63 BC, the time of the Roman conquest under General Pompey. The dynasty brought glory and political freedom to the Jews. Unfortunately, the regime became corrupt. When Palestine fell to Rome, the Roman army deposed the Hasmoneans and appointed a puppet king.

Herod the Great served as the king of Judea from 37 to 4 BC. He was in some ways a brilliant ruler; he was famous for his great building projects, including the rebuilding of the magnificent Jerusalem Temple. He was also a bloodthirsty ruler, who called for the execution of male Jewish children. Sometime toward the end of his reign, perhaps between 6 and 4 BC, one of the young boys who escaped Herod's

This Hanukkah menorah is located in front of the Western or Wailing Wall in Jerusalem.

wrath, Jesus Christ, was born in Bethlehem. The birth of the Messiah fulfilled all the Old Testament prophecies.

Hanukkah The Jewish Feast of Dedication, which celebrates the recovery and purification of the Temple from the Syrians in 164 BC. It is an eight-day feast that takes place during December. Jews usually give gifts at this time. Hanukkah is also called the Festival of Lights.

Hasmonean Dynasty Descendants of the Maccabees who ruled in Judea after the ousting of the last of the Syrians in 141 BC until the establishment of Roman authority in 63 BC.

A Deeper Look at the
MACCABEAN REVOLT

The Maccabean Revolt lasted for a total of three years. After that time, the Temple was cleansed, and the Jews gathered to celebrate its rededication (Hanukkah). Also, Judas Maccabeus was successful in negotiating a peace treaty with the Syrians. Because of the revolt, the Jews remained an independent nation until 63 BC.

Read the cited Scripture passages from the First Book of Maccabees. Use the citations to help you answer each of the questions.

1. What was the pact the Jewish Hellenizers initiated with the Gentiles? (Read 1 Maccabees 1:11–15.)

2. What were some of the crimes Antiochus committed against the Jews? (Read 1 Maccabees 1:20–62.)

3. Describe the incident that led to Mattathias's revolt. (Read 1 Maccabees 2:15–30.)

4. What led to Mattathias's decision to fight against the Gentiles? (Read 1 Maccabees 2:31–41.)

SECTION ASSESSMENT

NOTE TAKING

Use the timeline you created to help you answer the following question.

1. How did each of these men impact the history of the Jewish people in the centuries before the birth of Christ: Alexander the Great, Antiochus IV, Judas Maccabeus, and King Herod?

COMPREHENSION

2. Identify Ezra. Describe two of Ezra's accomplishments.

3. What is meant by the "abomination of desolation"?

ANALYSIS

4. What challenges do all religions face in preserving their identities in the midst of secular culture?

REFLECTION

5. How did the Jewish effort to compile the Bible after the Exile resemble the Jewish effort to rebuild the Temple?

6. What is a value from secular culture that you have personally incorporated into your life?

7. What is a personal value that opposes secular culture today?

Section Summaries

Focus Question

What is God willing to do for you?

Complete one of the following:

 Who in your life inspires you to be the best you can be?

 Make a list of the blessings God has given you in your life.

 Which of your current friends do you think you are most likely to maintain a lifelong friendship with? Why so?

INTRODUCTION (PAGES 137–138)

Qualities of Friendship

Friendship is a good word to describe the relationship between God and the Israelites. In the Old Testament, God revealed his desire to be in a loving friendship with his Chosen People. Although at times the People returned this friendship, they struggled to be loyal, an important element of friendship. Despite their infidelities, God always called the people of Israel back to him.

 What does it mean to be God's friend?

SECTION 1 (PAGES 139–142)

Conquest of the Promised Land

During the time of their conquest of the Promised Land, the Israelites learned lessons of obedience to God. After the successes that the Israelites had under the faithful Joshua, the Chosen People fell into a cycle of apostasy. When they strayed from God, they fell on hard times and called out to him. God sent a judge to save them, but when the judge died, so did the people's fidelity.

 Identify a situation involving a cycle of sin that resembles the cycle of apostasy. Why is this cycle so common in human life?

SECTION 2 (PAGES 143–148)

The Monarchy in Israel

While Samuel told the Israelites that having a king would harm the nation, the people still wanted a human king like the neighboring nations. King Saul's pride ended up being his downfall. King David united the tribes of Israel and brought the Ark of the Covenant to Jerusalem. King Solomon built the Temple but caused his people to rebel because of the hardships he imposed on them. Although Kings David and Solomon made positive contributions to the people of Israel, the negative effects of Solomon's rule destroyed the unity of Israel.

 How might "peer pressure" be an apt way to describe Israel's insistence on having a human king?

SECTION 3 (PAGES 149–156)

God Sends Prophets

All of the Old Testament prophets warned God's People to stay faithful to him alone, to challenge injustices, and to repent. The prophets who came before the fall of the northern and southern kingdoms specifically called the people to return to the covenant, repenting of common sins such as idolatry, indifference to poverty, and approaching worship as a formality without heart.

The prophets delivered a message of "repent or be doomed." Why are harsh words sometimes necessary to break a person away from sinful or self-destructive behavior?

SECTION 4 (PAGES 157–163)

Prophets of Hope: The Babylonian Exile

After the Jews were taken into exile in Babylon, the message of the prophets became one of compassion and hope. Jeremiah spoke of a New Covenant. Ezekiel used the imagery of new life returning to dry bones. The anonymous prophet of Isaiah 40–55 defined the expected Messiah as a "Suffering Servant." Many exiled Jews studied the Law, observed the Sabbath, and circumcised their sons.

The Jews anticipated the hopeful future prophesied by the prophets and worked to preserve their culture. What are signs in the Church and world today that Jewish culture and religion have been preserved?

SECTION 5 (PAGE 164–168)

The Southern Kingdom after the Exile

Though only a remnant of the people and their descendants who went into exile returned to Jerusalem under Cyrus of Persia, those who did return put their efforts toward rebuilding the Temple and their lives of faith. Jews came to know the Torah better and tried to separate themselves from Gentiles. Later, those in political power once again inhibited the Jews in their ability to practice their faith. Antiochus IV desecrated the Temple, prompting a revolt led by the Maccabees. Sixty years before Jesus' birth, the Romans came to power.

 What would you do if the government repressed your ability to practice your religion?

Chapter Assignments

Choose and complete at least one of these assignments to assess your understanding of the material in this chapter.

1. Write a Biography of a Modern-Day Prophet

Identify a person you know personally or have heard about recently who you think possesses prophetic qualities. This person must be living now or have died within the last ten years. Include the following material in your essay:

- a definition of what makes a prophet (use Chapter 5 material for reference)
- a short narration of the person's life
- a connection of your person's prophetic actions to at least two of the four themes of prophetic preaching on page 150
- a short reflection about why this person inspires you personally

2. Understand Rahab as an Ancestor of Faith

Write a two-page essay that details the biblical character of Rahab and her role as an ancestor of Jesus and the Christian faith. Include the following information in your report:

- biographical background on Rahab (check a Bible encyclopedia)
- the connection of Rahab and Jesus (see Mt 1:1–16)
- Rahab's place in Christian history (see Jos 2; Jas 2:24–25)

3. Draw a Comparison

Throughout this chapter about the kings and the prophets, it has become clear that when people stray from love of God and neighbor (as laid out in the Ten Commandments), they begin to abuse their own power. Compare and contrast King Solomon's abuse of power with an abuse of power that occurs today. You may present this as a writing assignment or an artistic presentation.

Faithful Disciple

St. María Micaela of the Blessed Sacrament

St. María Micaela was born on January 1, 1809, in Madrid, Spain. María's parents were members of the Spanish nobility. María Micaela spent many years attending parties and social events and riding horses at various royal palaces with her brother, Diego.

María Micaela did not want to marry, though she received pressure to do so. When she was thirty-five years old, María Micaela made a life-altering discovery: she met a banker's daughter who had been deceived into prostitution and now lived in poverty on the edge of society. This situation horrified María Micaela, and within a year she opened a shelter for young girls and women who had lived on the street and needed help. She established the Sisters of Adoration, Slaves of the Blessed Sacrament and of Charity, for the mission of caring for these young women. This ministry was controversial at the time because of the type of people it served. María Micaela died in 1865 from cholera while helping her sisters attend to people who were sick with the disease.

St. María Micaela

In the present day, the religious order founded by St. María Micaela has more than 1,100 sisters in twenty-two countries. The order's name describes the two principles of its mission: continuous worship of Jesus in the Eucharist and release of women exploited by prostitution or any kind of slavery. The sisters work primarily in Europe and on the west coast of South America. They also minister in India, Japan, Thailand, and the Philippines.

In 2005, the United States Department of State mentioned the Sisters of Adoration, Slaves of the Blessed Sacrament and of Charity, in its "International Best Practices" document for monitoring and combating human trafficking. In addition to the resources that the sisters provide for women in the sex trade, the State Department commended the sisters' courage: "Members of the order regularly search dangerous city streets at night seeking girls and women who are trapped in prostitution and offer them opportunities for a better life."[2]

Reading Comprehension

1. Describe St. María Micaela's life in Spain prior to founding her first shelter.

2. What is a mission of the Sisters of Adoration, Slaves of the Blessed Sacrament?

3. Why was this mission controversial at the time of St. Maria Micaela?

Writing Task

- Why do you think the story of the banker's daughter touched St. María Micaela so deeply?

Explaining the Faith
Why should Catholics bother reading the Old Testament?

"In Jesus, the same Word of God that had resounded on Mount Sinai to give the written Law to Moses, made itself heard anew on the Mount of the Beatitudes" (CCC, 58).

For some people, the word *old* communicates that something is out of date or irrelevant. Did you ever think that this is the attitude Catholics should have toward the Old Testament? Since Jesus Christ fulfilled the Old Testament in his Life, Passion, Death, and Resurrection, you might consider the Old Testament out of date or irrelevant. The Church, however, affirms the Old Testament's value. The Old Testament is important to Catholics for several reasons:

- God inspired the Old Testament.

- The books of the Old Testament prefigure and prepare for Jesus' coming and are part of the Salvation History that led to the New Covenant.

- There is unity between the Old and New Testaments. Familiarity with the New Testament helps a person uncover new things in the Old

Testament. In addition, the New Testament has to be read in light of the Old Testament. St. Augustine explained that the New Testament lies hidden in the Old and the Old Testament is unveiled in the New.

Catholics value the Old Testament and find it relevant to life today.

Reflection

- What attitude can you bring to help you read the Old Testament as the living Word of God?

Prayer
Prayer for Justice

Prayerfully reflect on these verses of Psalm 54, which appeal to God for justice. Their message is timeless.

> O God, by your name save me.
>> By your strength defend my cause.
> O God, hear my prayer.
>> Listen to the words of my mouth.
> Strangers have risen against me;
>> the ruthless seek my life;
>> they do not keep God before them.
> God is present as my helper;
>> the Lord sustains my life.
> —Psalm 54:3–6

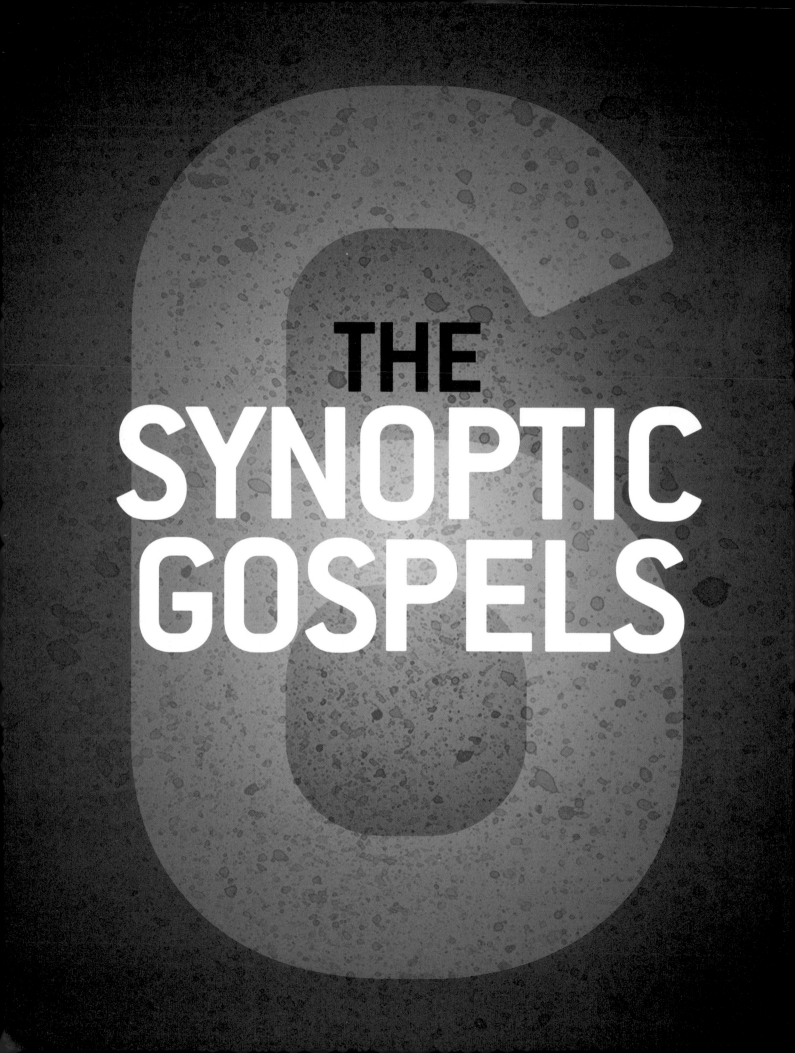

THE SYNOPTIC GOSPELS

PUTTING OTHERS FIRST

Spanish athlete Iván Fernández Anaya's goal was to become a member of the international Spanish cross-country team. He positioned himself in a cross-country race in Burlada Navarre, Spain, to win the race and make the team. He barely trailed Abel Mutai, a runner from Kenya. All of a sudden, close to the finish line, Mutai just stopped, thinking that he had already crossed it. The crowds lining the race tried to tell him to keep running, but a language barrier prevented him from understanding what they were saying. When Fernández Anaya reached Mutai, he used gestures to urge the Kenyan to keep going so that Mutai would finish first.

Fernández Anaya could easily have won the race and been in a better place to compete against the elite Spanish cross-country runners, but he said, "I didn't deserve to win it. I did what I had to do. He was the rightful winner. He created a gap that I couldn't have closed if he hadn't made a mistake. As soon as I saw he was stopping, I knew that I wasn't going to pass him."

His coach thought that this was a very honest gesture but would have coached Fernández Anaya to win. "But even if they had told me that winning would have earned me a place in the Spanish team for the European championships, I wouldn't have done it [passed Mutai to win] either," Fernández Anaya said.[1]

FOCUS QUESTION

What do the synoptic Gospels REVEAL ABOUT JESUS?

INTRODUCTION
Good News

MAIN IDEA
Good news about human beings is inspiring, but the greatest news is the Gospel of Jesus Christ.

Are you familiar with the Chicken Soup for the Soul series that has been popular for the last two decades? You may have read one or more books yourself or heard stories from the series. These books are popular, in part, because the books share "good news" stories about courage, perseverance, sacrifice, heroism, and love. Bad news sells, so the media often spend extra time on it, but plenty of good news is happening, too.

The story of Fernández Anaya and Mutai is an example of a "good news" story. In a world that thrives on competition, Fernández Anaya did the right thing and did not take advantage of his rival's confusion. While Fernández Anaya could clearly have snatched the win from Mutai, he put the other person first. Instinctively, you can recognize the goodness of his action.

The life of Jesus Christ is the perfect illustration of putting others first. He is *the* Good News, the best news that the world has ever heard. The word *gospel* means "good news," and in fact there is only one gospel running through the entire Bible—the Gospel that is of and about Jesus Christ. The four Gospels of the New Testament share the Good News about Jesus Christ. His life and teaching communicate to you the meaning of perseverance, sacrifice, courage, heroism, and love. When people act in Christlike ways (see image at left), others take notice.

NOTE TAKING

Describing Good News. Make a chart like the one here. As you read through this section, write down adjectives listed in this section and others that you come up with on your own that describe "good news." In the second column, write a name or event that reminds you of the good news described by the adjective. Add as many rows as needed.

Describing "Good News"	
Adjective	Example
Inspiring	Injured war veteran completes marathon

The Gospels are your primary sources of information about Jesus. Three of the four Gospels are closely related. Scholars call them the **synoptic Gospels**: Matthew, Mark, and Luke. As you have learned, when you see similar stories and teachings across the three Gospels, you should suspect that they used common sources. Scholars using source criticism show that the synoptic Gospels' authors did share sources. The Gospel of John has different sources, and while it also features the main events in Jesus' life, it does so in a different way. You will read more about John's Gospel in Chapter 9.

synoptic Gospels The synoptic Gospels are Matthew, Mark, and Luke. They can be looked at together because they shared some, but not all, of the same sources.

SECTION ASSESSMENT

NOTE TAKING

Use the chart you created to help you complete the following item.

1. Of the adjectives you listed, which best describes "good news" for you? Explain why.

VOCABULARY

2. Define *synoptic Gospels*.

REFLECTION

3. Why do you think the media believes that bad news sells?

USING YOUR GIFTS FOR OTHERS

Review the following talents. Write about an incident from your own experience in which you have witnessed or personally practiced some or all of these gifts.

- *Service*: I sense when others need help and often respond to them.

- *Teaching*: I am good at explaining things to others. I can help others learn.

- *Encouragement*: I can see the good in others and know what to say to spur them on.

- *Generosity*: I have the ability to share my time, possessions, and friendship.

- *Leadership*: I can organize people to get things done. I am also dependable when put in charge of things.

- *Compassion*: I sense when others are hurting and can respond in a loving, supportive way.

REFLECTION

- What was your initial reaction to the sportsmanship exhibited by Iván Fernández Anaya?

- How have you helped someone to reach a goal?

The Synoptic Gospels: An Overview

MAIN IDEA
The Gospels of Matthew, Mark, and Luke share a similar structure as well as some of the same sources.

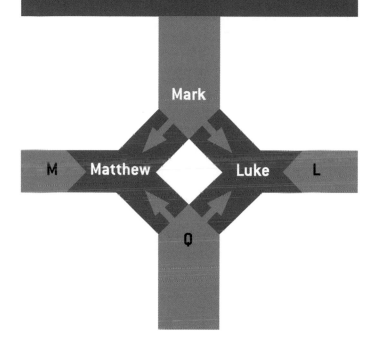

When you listen to or read the synoptic Gospels, you will notice that Matthew, Mark, and Luke share quite a bit in common. Biblical scholarship has further revealed the following facts:

- There are 661 verses in Mark's Gospel; eighty percent of these appear in Matthew's Gospel, and sixty-five percent occur in Luke's Gospel.

- Matthew's (1,068 verses) and Luke's (1,149 verses) Gospels are considerably longer than Mark's, but they follow the general outline of Mark's Gospel in reporting the events of Jesus' life.

- The three Gospels have the name *synoptic* (from the Greek *synoptikos,* meaning "see together") because they are similar enough that you can look at the three side by side and find common elements. When lined up in parallel columns, the synoptic Gospels exhibit many similarities.

Note the following similarities and subtle differences between the three Gospels' versions of Jesus' words about salt:

NOTE TAKING

Assessing Information. Use the material in this section to help you create an approximate percentage pie graph to represent the sources of the verses in Matthew's and Luke's Gospels. Include the Mark, Q, M, and L sources. Remember: the graph will be a rough estimation.

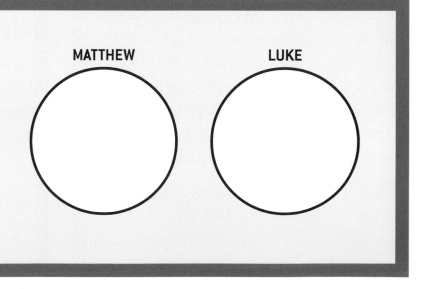

Matthew 5:13	Mark 9:50	Luke 14:34–35
You are the salt of the earth. But if salt loses its taste, with what can it be seasoned? It is no longer good for anything but to be thrown out and trampled underfoot.	Salt is good, but if salt becomes insipid, with what will you restore its flavor? Keep salt in yourselves and you will have peace with one another.	Salt is good, but if salt itself loses its taste, with what can its flavor be restored? It is fit neither for the soil nor the manure pile; it is thrown out. Whoever has ears to hear ought to hear.

The Gospel of Matthew is a well-ordered work with detailed lessons especially in the area of Christian morality. In the early Church, it became popular for liturgy and as a catechetical manual. Matthew also emphasizes the fulfillment of Old Testament prophecies, thus beautifully linking the Old and New Testaments. Early Church writers like Papias, St. Irenaeus, and Origen taught that the Apostle Matthew, writing for his fellow Jews, wrote his Gospel in the language Jesus spoke—Aramaic. Until the nineteenth century, scholars believed that Matthew's Gospel was the first Gospel written, thinking that Mark's Gospel was an abridged, later version. Later, biblical scholars found evidence that Mark's Gospel is the oldest of the four and that Matthew and Luke used Mark in composing their own Gospels.

The date of the authorship of Mark's Gospel is between AD 67 and 73, either shortly before or after the destruction of the Jewish Temple by the Romans in AD 70. Sometime in the 80s Matthew and Luke wrote their Gospels and used these three sources (note the image on page 183):

1. Mark's Gospel

2. a shared source known as *Q* (from the German *Quelle*, meaning "source") that Mark did not use

3. their own distinct sources (*M* for Matthew and *L* for Luke—easy to remember!)

The Q source contributed approximately 220 to 235 verses (in whole or part) to both Gospels. This source was probably a collection of Jesus' sayings that came down to Matthew and Luke in written or perhaps oral form.

Some examples of sources of material from Matthew's and Luke's Gospel are listed in the chart on page 185. Remember, Q is material common to Matthew and Luke, M is unique to Matthew and L is unique to Luke.

Sharing the Mysteries of Salvation

The synoptic Gospels present the mysteries of Christ's life. The term *mystery* refers to God. God is mystery because his infinite greatness, **omnipotence**, and perfect love are far beyond human understanding. In the

omnipotence An attribute of God meaning that he is all-powerful. His power is universal, loving, and mysterious.

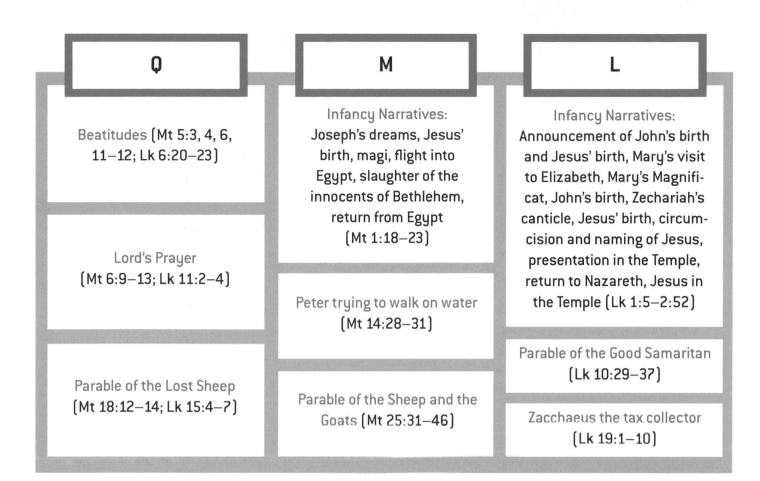

Q	M	L
Beatitudes (Mt 5:3, 4, 6, 11–12; Lk 6:20–23)	**Infancy Narratives:** Joseph's dreams, Jesus' birth, magi, flight into Egypt, slaughter of the innocents of Bethlehem, return from Egypt (Mt 1:18–23)	**Infancy Narratives:** Announcement of John's birth and Jesus' birth, Mary's visit to Elizabeth, Mary's Magnificat, John's birth, Zechariah's canticle, Jesus' birth, circumcision and naming of Jesus, presentation in the Temple, return to Nazareth, Jesus in the Temple (Lk 1:5–2:52)
Lord's Prayer (Mt 6:9–13; Lk 11:2–4)	Peter trying to walk on water (Mt 14:28–31)	Parable of the Good Samaritan (Lk 10:29–37)
Parable of the Lost Sheep (Mt 18:12–14; Lk 15:4–7)	Parable of the Sheep and the Goats (Mt 25:31–46)	Zacchaeus the tax collector (Lk 19:1–10)

At his Resurrection, Christ's body is filled with the power of the Holy Spirit. He shares in the divine life in his glorious state.

New Testament, the Greek word *mysterion* also refers to God's saving plan—"the mystery of Salvation" that gradually unfolded in human history. Both meanings of the word are intimately connected. The God who is mystery is the very same God who revealed himself in human history. God's fullest Revelation took place when he assumed human nature in order to accomplish Salvation for all people. Therefore, everything about Jesus—his words, deeds, teachings, Passion, Death, and Resurrection—reveals God as infinitely loving and merciful. The Gospels record these sacred and essential events.

SECTION ASSESSMENT

NOTE TAKING

Use the pie graph you created to help you answer the following question.
1. Why do you think it is essential to sample and read all three synoptic Gospels rather than reading only one of them?

VOCABULARY

2. The word _____ came from a Greek word meaning "see together."
3. What is the meaning of the word *omnipotence*?

COMPREHENSION

4. Provide two aspects of the mystery of God.
5. Which three sources did the Gospel of Luke's author use?

REFLECTION

6. How has your understanding of the formation of the Gospels changed after reading this section?

Jesus' Early Life

MAIN IDEA
The events of Jesus' early life reveal his identity and his love for people who were considered outsiders.

This section describes the early years of Christ's life: his birth, circumcision, presentation in the Temple, and later visit to the Temple.

Birth of Jesus

The Gospel writers carefully selected the material that they would include about Jesus' childhood. Aside from one story in Luke about Jesus at twelve years of age, Matthew (1:1–2:23) and Luke (1:1–2:52) focus only on the events surrounding Jesus' birth, called the **Nativity**. Mark's Gospel does not include any stories about Jesus' birth at all, but begins with John the Baptist announcing the advent of the Messiah.

Think for a moment about a Nativity scene. Imagine the physical environment. Who is present? What other items or creatures are there? Do the people stand in specific places or just anywhere? You will likely find that the Nativity scene of your imagination represents some aspects of the Christmas story from Matthew and some from Luke. For example, the magi are not included in Luke's Gospel, and the shepherds are not found in Matthew's Gospel.

> **Nativity** The story of the Savior's birth in Bethlehem. Two different accounts of the Nativity are given in the New Testament: one in the Gospel of Matthew, the other in the Gospel of Luke.

NOTE TAKING

Categorizing Information. Create a timeline like the one below for the events in the early life of Jesus. As you read the section, note key events below the timeline. Note connecting Scripture passages above the timeline.

- Mt 1:1–2:23
- Lk 1:1–2:52

●————————————————●————————————————————————————————●

Birth of Jesus   Presentation in the Temple   Hidden Years

There are similarities between the infancy accounts. Both Matthew and Luke highlight Jesus, Mary, and Joseph, the foster father of Jesus. You also learn the following pieces of information from the combination of both accounts:

- Mary, Jesus' Mother, was a virgin. She freely consented to God's action in her life and so became the Mother of God and the spiritual mother of everyone.

- Mary conceived Jesus by the Holy Spirit.

- Mary gave birth to Jesus during the reign of King Herod the Great in the town of Bethlehem, as the prophets had foretold.

- Jesus received his name before birth. The name **Jesus** comes from the Hebrew word *Yehoshua* (Joshua), meaning "God saves." This name points to both Jesus' identity and his mission. From all eternity, the Trinity had planned that Jesus would save the world from sin and death.

- Jesus was King David's descendant, as the prophets foretold.

- The Holy Family settled in the town of Nazareth.

The infancy narratives in Matthew and Luke foreshadow Jesus' humble ministry. Jesus was born in poverty. Luke tells you that the shepherds were the first to see him. In that day, pious Jews looked down on shepherds because their occupation did not allow them to keep the ritual precepts of the Law faithfully. From the

> **Jesus** The origins of the name are from the Hebrew word *Yehoshua* (Joshua), meaning "God saves," "God is Salvation," or simply "Savior."

beginning, you can see that Jesus came to minister to humble people. Jesus' humble infancy is also a model for human relationship with God.

Jesus' Circumcision and Presentation in the Temple

Mary and Joseph raised Jesus according to the Jewish Law. Recall that the Law, beginning with Abraham, required male infants to undergo circumcision as a sign of the covenant. Jesus' circumcision marked him as a member of the covenant of the Chosen People and a descendant of Abraham.

Mary and Joseph also followed Jewish tradition when they presented Jesus in the Temple (see Lk 2:22–38), a ritual that consecrated the firstborn son to

Mary and Joseph gave a Temple offering of "a pair of turtledoves or two young pigeons" (Lk 2:24) reflecting that they could not afford to offer the required year-old lamb.

God. At the Temple, the righteous man Simeon and the prophetess Anna recognized him as the long-awaited Messiah, a fulfillment of the Old Testament promises. They blessed and thanked God for the privilege of seeing the Messiah; Simeon predicted that Jesus would bring Salvation to both Jews and Gentiles.

The Magi, the Flight into Egypt, and Herod's Slaughter of the Innocents

Matthew's story of the journey of the **magi** (sometimes called the "three kings" or the "wise men" in Christmas stories), guided by the star to visit the Holy Family, illustrates that Christ from the very beginning came for all people, not exclusively for Jews. The Christian feast of the **Epiphany** commemorates Jesus' manifestation to the world during the visit of the magi to the Holy Family.

Matthew's Gospel also describes King Herod's treachery (Mt 2). When King Herod learned of the birth of a new king, he lied to the magi about wanting to show respect to the infant. The Lord appeared to Joseph in a dream and told him of Herod's plan to search for Jesus and kill him, urging the Holy Family to flee to Egypt (see image at right). This slaughter of the children indicates that the forces of evil were gathering against Jesus from the very beginning. Unfortunately, Herod's son was no better than his father, which meant that after Mary and Joseph returned from Egypt, they had to settle with Jesus in Galilee (Nazareth) rather than return to Judea.

> **magi** Priests of the ancient Persian religion of Zoroastrianism who paid special attention to the stars.
>
> **Epiphany** The feast that celebrates the mystery of Christ's manifestation as the Savior of the world.

Jesus' Hidden Years

The Gospels share only one story about Jesus between his return to Nazareth as a toddler and his emergence as an adult, which is why these years are called the "hidden years." The one Gospel story from Jesus' early adolescence is important, however.

Luke's Gospel reports that when Jesus was twelve, he accompanied his parents to Jerusalem for the feast of Passover. After the feast, his parents headed home, but Jesus stayed back in Jerusalem without their knowledge. He was missing for three days. You may wonder how Mary and Joseph could let a twelve-year-old get out of sight for that long. It was actually quite normal for children to mingle in the large caravan of friends and relatives from the same village as they walked along. Mary and Joseph would have assumed at first that he was well cared for. But when they could not find Jesus among their friends and family, Mary and Joseph returned to Jerusalem to find him.

Jesus had stayed in Jerusalem to talk with the Jewish teachers in the Temple, astounding them with his knowledge (see image on page 187). When Mary expressed how worried she and Joseph had been, he said to her, "Why were you looking for me? Did you not know that I must be in my Father's house?" (Lk 2:49).

Luke's Gospel tells that the boy Jesus went home with his parents and lived a life of humble obedience to them in the Galilean town of Nazareth. Notice how Jesus' submission to his mother and foster father contrasts sharply with Adam's disobedience to God in the Garden. Jesus' obedience to his parents and to his Father reminds you to be obedient: would you rather resemble Adam and Eve or Jesus? This account reveals that Jesus' attachment to his heavenly Father came before his relationship with his earthly parents.

At home in Nazareth, Jesus most likely learned the carpentry trade from Joseph. Because Mary and Joseph observed the Jewish traditions, they likely took his education in the Jewish faith seriously. Routine and work with our hands and minds are part of the human experience. Because Jesus grew up living an everyday life of hard work in his family, you can encounter him in all of your daily tasks, as well as in the ups and downs of family life.

SECTION ASSESSMENT

NOTE TAKING

Refer to the timeline you created to help you complete the following task.

1. Read the infancy narratives in Matthew 1:1–2:23 and Luke 1:1–2:52. Note three differences in the accounts.

COMPREHENSION

2. What do Mary and Joseph learn about Jesus from Simeon and Anna?

3. What does the story about Jesus as a boy in the Temple reveal about his relationships with Mary, Joseph, and God the Father?

REFLECTION

4. What does the name of Jesus have to do with his mission?

5. What do you think Mary and Joseph talked about on the way home to Nazareth *after* they found Jesus in the Temple?

SECTION 3
Jesus' Public Life

MAIN IDEA
Jesus' baptism, temptation by the devil, and call of the Apostles prepared him for the duties of his public ministry.

Every element of Jesus' life is important because he is **Emmanuel**: "God is with us." The events of Jesus' public life teach us about the Father's love for each human being through his Son. The following events are meaningful because they prepared Jesus to proclaim this love.

Baptism by John the Baptist

In all three synoptic Gospels, Jesus' public ministry began with his baptism by John the Baptist. John, the son of the priest Zechariah and his wife Elizabeth, was Jesus' cousin. Isaiah prophesied that a prophet would be sent to announce the coming of the Messiah; John called the people to baptism for the repentance of their

> **Emmanuel** A name for Jesus that means "God is with us." This is the name given to Jesus as foretold in the Old Testament (see, for example, Isaiah 7:14 and 8:8) and recounted to Joseph, the foster father of Jesus, in a dream.

NOTE TAKING

Compare and Contrast. Create a chart like the one below. Use the text section and the referenced Gospel passages to note the similarities and differences of each Gospel account of Jesus' baptism (e.g., John's Gospel never clearly mentions that it was John the Baptist who baptizes Jesus).

	Mt 3:13–17	Mk 1:9–11	Lk 3:21–22	Jn 1:29–34
Who sees the sky opened?				
Who sees the dove descending?				
Who hears the voice of the Father?				

sins and told them that someone greater would come after him. He was

> A voice of one crying out in the desert:
> "Prepare the way of the Lord,
> Make straight his paths." (Mk 1:3)

At the time of Jesus' baptism, the Gospels indicate that the Holy Spirit came down in the form of a dove and that God the Father said: "You are my beloved Son; with you I am well pleased" (Mk 1:11) (see image on page 191). The presence of all Three Persons of the Holy Trinity at Jesus' baptism emphasizes that Jesus is God. Because Jesus was sinless, he clearly did not *need* Baptism either for repentance or for the cleansing of sin. Jesus' willingness for John to baptize him emphasized Jesus' humility and his readiness to accept the Father's mission to save people from their sins.

Baptism today involves humility as well. You were immersed in water with Jesus in order to be reborn of water and the Holy Spirit with him.

Temptations in the Desert

Luke's Gospel reports that after Jesus was baptized, the Holy Spirit led him into the desert to pray, fast, and face the devil's temptation for forty days. This number recalls the forty years the Chosen People wandered in the desert after the Exodus from Egypt. Unlike the Israelites, who fell when tempted, Jesus was faithful. The Church recollects these forty days of Jesus' trial in the forty days of Lent.

A temptation is a test. The Letter to the Hebrews explains that Jesus underwent testing so that he might sympathize with human weaknesses (see Heb 4:15–16). He underwent many other tests in his life but never sinned. This is why, when you face your own temptations, you can turn to Jesus for help and strength. The devil often tempts you by telling you to take the easier option even if it is sinful or encourages you to think that Jesus will not help you. (After all, the snake waited

until God was elsewhere before tempting Adam and Eve.) Jesus has intimate knowledge of human weaknesses and wants to give you his strength. Jesus conquered Satan and temptation himself on your behalf.

Notice once again that Jesus responded to temptation in a radically different way than Adam and Eve did. When the serpent told them about a way to become like God, they disobeyed God. Instead of going his own way, Jesus remained faithful to his Father's mission for him. In Genesis, the man and woman sinned to become like God, whereas Jesus is God and accepted the human condition in order to redeem humanity.

Jesus' Followers

After his temptations in the desert, Jesus began to call and attract **disciples**, some of whom would become his Apostles. Jesus described the meaning and mission of discipleship several times in the synoptic Gospels.

> Behold, I am sending you like sheep in the midst of wolves; so be shrewd as serpents and simple as doves. (Mt 10:16)

> You are the light of the world. A city set on a mountain cannot be hidden. Nor do they light a lamp and then put it under a bushel basket; it is set on a lampstand, where it gives light to all in the house. Just so, your light must shine before others, that they may see your good deeds and glorify your heavenly Father. (Mt 5:14–16)

> If anyone wishes to come after me, he must deny himself and take up his cross daily and follow me. (Lk 9:23)

Jesus had many disciples, including a special group of seventy (see Lk 10:1–17) that included female members, whose presence would have been unusual in his

disciple A follower of Jesus. The word means "learner."

Jesus Remained Faithful in the Face of
TEMPTATION

THE FIRST TEMPTATION

Satan challenged Jesus to use his power to satisfy his own physical needs by commanding a stone to become bread. Jesus responded by quoting Deuteronomy 8:3: *"One does not live by bread alone"* (Lk 4:4).

THE SECOND TEMPTATION

Satan offered Jesus all worldly power and glory if he would worship him. (Did Satan really have the power to offer him this? Was this another lie, as in the Garden of Eden?) Jesus replied to Satan, quoting Deuteronomy 6:13:

It is written:
"You shall worship the Lord, your God,
and him alone shall you serve." (Lk 4:8)

Later on in his ministry, people who wanted to make Jesus a king also tempted him this way. Even his own Apostles thought the Messiah should be a worldly ruler, but Jesus rejected this temptation repeatedly. He came to serve, not to be served.

THE THIRD TEMPTATION

The devil suggested that Jesus test his Father by sensationally jumping off the top of the Temple. Surely the Father would send angels to rescue Jesus, and such a spectacular deed would attract people to him, prove his identity, and seemingly further the aims of his ministry. Quoting Deuteronomy 6:16, Jesus responded: *"You shall not put the Lord, your God, to the test"* (Lk 4:12).

male-dominated era. Some of these women helped him financially, traveled with him and his other followers, supplied meals and lodging, witnessed his Crucifixion, and visited his tomb on Easter Sunday.

Call of the Twelve

Jesus selected the Twelve Apostles from among his disciples to assist him in his work. Their number represents the twelve tribes of Israel and therefore symbolizes a renewed People of God. Jesus commissioned the Twelve to preach the coming of God's Kingdom to the Chosen People. Their main job was to "fish" for people (see Mk 1:17); that is, to draw people toward the Gospel.

Most of the Apostles were from humble backgrounds, though they were skilled in a craft or trade. Several were fishermen. In some ways, their relationship with Jesus resembled the bond between students of the time and their teachers or rabbis. Jesus expected the Apostles to learn carefully from his words *and* actions so that they could pass on his message to others.

Jesus' relationship to his Apostles differed, however, in two ways. First, Jesus *chose* the Apostles, whereas rabbinical students commonly selected their teachers. Second, Jesus taught on his *own authority*, directly interpreting the will of his Father. Although rabbis rigorously trained other rabbis to interpret the Law, their opinions relied on others' teachings. Jesus was different.

Jesus gave Peter a special leadership role among the Apostles, saying that the Church would be built on him. He gave Peter and his successors the authority to govern the Church with the assistance of the Apostles' successors, the bishops.

SECTION ASSESSMENT

NOTE TAKING

Use the chart you created that compares the Gospel accounts of Jesus' baptism to help you answer the following questions.

1. What are two ways that all four accounts of Jesus' baptism are similar?
2. Name three examples in which different Gospel authors offer unique pieces of information about Jesus' baptism.

COMPREHENSION

3. How did John's baptism of the Jews differ from his baptism of Jesus?
4. Explain how the Trinity was present at Jesus' baptism.

ANALYSIS

5. What is the difference between a disciple and an Apostle?

REFLECTION

6. Which of Jesus' temptations in the desert do you think was most difficult for Jesus? Why?
7. How can resisting temptation strengthen you?

SECTION 4
Jesus Proclaims the Gospel

MAIN IDEA
Jesus revealed the essential message of the Gospel by proclaiming the coming of God's Kingdom.

In the Gospel of Mark, Jesus summarizes his message this way: "This is the time of fulfillment. The kingdom of God is at hand. Repent, and believe in the gospel" (Mk 1:15).

What does this statement mean? Though it is short, it communicates quite a bit:

- *"This is the time of fulfillment."* Fulfillment here refers to the fulfillment of God's promises to the Chosen People.

- *"The **Kingdom of God** is at hand."* This means several things, including the following:

  - God's rule has come to God's People.

  - Humans will obey God's word.

  - God has triumphed over physical evils and death.

  - The Kingdom will come after a period of judgment.

- *"Repent."* To repent is to have a change of heart and to turn away from sin and toward God.

> **Kingdom (or reign) of God** The process of the Father's reconciling and renewing all things through his Son; the fact of his will being done on earth as it is in Heaven. The Kingdom of God was proclaimed by Jesus and began in his Life, Death, and Resurrection. The process will be perfectly completed at the end of time.

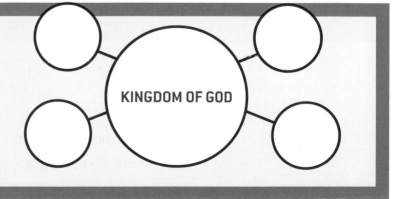

NOTE TAKING

Naming Main Ideas. Draw a concept web like the one shown below. As you read, fill in the blank circles with ways in which Jesus revealed the Kingdom of God. Add more circles as needed.

KINGDOM OF GOD

- *"Believe in the Gospel."* Jesus came to proclaim that God's Kingdom is in his very person. Jesus *is* the Good News. He *is* the Gospel. He *is* the Revelation of the Father.

This announcement in the very first chapter of the Gospel of Mark is a bold one. The final stage for the coming of God's everlasting Kingdom has begun in the person of Jesus Christ. What will this Kingdom be like? In his ministry, Jesus revealed more about the meaning of the Kingdom of God.

How Jesus Revealed the Kingdom of God

He taught about the Kingdom through stories and sermons.

(See more about Jesus as Teacher in Chapter 7.)

He worked mighty works, wonders, and signs or miracles that proved that he was the Messiah, the Son of God.

(See more about Jesus' miracles in Chapter 8.)

He revealed the Kingdom through moments of divine glory, such as the **Transfiguration**.

His Passion, Death, Resurrection, and Ascension (the **Paschal Mystery**) most clearly proclaimed the Kingdom.

(See the next page and Chapter 8 for more about the Paschal Mystery.)

Transfiguration The mystery from Christ's life in which God's glory shone through and transformed Jesus' physical appearance while he was in the company of the Old Testament prophets Moses and Elijah. Peter, James, and John witnessed this event.

Paschal Mystery Christ's work of Redemption, accomplished principally by his Passion, Death, Resurrection, and glorious Ascension. This mystery is commemorated and made present through the sacraments, especially the Eucharist.

The Transfiguration

Jesus gave his Apostles a quick vision of the Kingdom of God through his Transfiguration (see image on page 195). During this event on a high mountain, Jesus revealed his divine glory before Peter, James, and John: "His face shone like the sun and his clothes became white as light" (Mt 17:2). Through this manifestation, Jesus foreshadowed the Kingdom of God.

In *Jesus of Nazareth*, Pope Benedict XVI reflects that the Transfiguration took place while Jesus was praying.

> [I]t displays visibly what happens when Jesus talks with his Father: the profound interpenetration of his being with God, which then becomes pure light. In his oneness with the Father, Jesus is himself "light from light."[2]

During Jesus' Transfiguration, two Old Testament figures—Moses and Elijah—also appeared. Their presence recalled that the Law (given to Israel through Moses) and the Prophets (symbolized by Elijah) had announced the coming Messiah. In addition, this vision revealed all Three Persons of the Blessed Trinity: the Father (in the voice), the Son (Jesus), and the Holy Spirit (in the shining cloud).

The Transfiguration also serves as a reminder that God will transform your life in the Resurrection.

The Paschal Mystery

Jesus most clearly proclaimed the Kingdom through the Paschal Mystery. This mystery of God's infinite love revealed that Jesus Christ is the way to Salvation through all ages. Jesus' Passion, Death, Resurrection, and Ascension rescued humanity from sin and death. All four Gospels teach you this truth: Jesus, the Christ, the Son of God, has risen from the dead. Reality is different than it was before. Believe this Good News. Accept the Lord and Holy Spirit into your lives. Share the truth of faith with others. Let the Good News truly sink in.

SECTION ASSESSMENT

NOTE TAKING

Use the concept web you created to help you answer the following question.

1. If you lived in Palestine during Jesus' life, which of the four ways that Jesus proclaimed the Kingdom of God would you be most attracted to? Why?

VOCABULARY

2. What happened at the Transfiguration?

REFLECTION

3. When you hear that Jesus was in a transfigured state, what do you imagine he looked like?

4. What would it take for you to really let the Good News of Jesus' Resurrection fill and transform your life?

SECTION 5
Individual Characteristics of the Synoptic Gospels

MAIN IDEA
While they share much in common, each of the synoptic Gospels focuses on specific qualities of Jesus.

Now that you are more familiar with some important events in Jesus' life, it is possible to look more closely at each of the synoptic Gospels.

Overview of Mark's Gospel

The author of Mark's Gospel is unknown. The early Church held that the author of the Gospel of Mark was John Mark, a disciple of Peter, and that his writing included themes of Peter's preaching. The Gospel highlights Jesus' deeds more than his words and presents a vivid, human, and down-to-earth portrait of Jesus.

Remember that the real-life situations of the early Christian communities—years after Jesus' Death—influenced the focus and content of the Gospels. Mark likely wrote his Gospel for a Gentile-Christian audience that was undergoing persecution, perhaps in Rome. He chose to focus on this central theme: following Jesus often means suffering as Jesus did. Theologically, Mark emphasized Jesus Christ's role as a Suffering Messiah for Christians to imitate.

A Direct Style

In the Gospel's very first verse, Mark clearly tells readers who Jesus is: "Jesus Christ [the Son of God]" (Mk 1:1). Interestingly, the disciples portrayed in the Gospel struggle to reach the same conclusion that the readers hear in this very first verse. Mark also stressed Jesus' humanity throughout his Gospel, even if this meant presenting a more direct or blunt view of Jesus than the other Evangelists:

NOTE TAKING

Assessing Information. As you read this section, highlight or make note of a few aspects of each Gospel.

Mark	Matthew	Luke
• • •	• • •	• • •

- Mark described Jesus feeling a very human emotion: "Looking around at them *with anger* and grieved at their hardness of heart . . ." (Mk 3:5, italics added). In their versions of the story, Matthew and Luke do not mention that Jesus was angry.
- Mark minced no words when he reported that Jesus' family said "He is out of his mind" (Mk 3:21). Matthew and Luke do not include this quote in their accounts.

While it is impossible to know what was going through the minds of the Evangelists, it is appropriate to assume that Matthew and Luke nuanced their accounts from Mark to present a different if not softer view of Jesus.

Titles for Jesus in Mark

Mark used several titles for Jesus. This central passage from Mark 8:27–34 offers two titles and hints at a third Try to identify these three titles as you read.

> Now Jesus and his disciples set out for the villages of Caesarea Philippi. Along the way he asked his disciples, "Who do people say that I am?" They said in reply, "John the Baptist, others Elijah, still others one of the prophets." And he asked them, "But who do you say that I am?" Peter said to him in reply, "You are the Messiah." Then he warned them not to tell anyone about him.
>
> He began to teach them that the Son of Man must suffer greatly and be rejected by the elders, the chief priests, and the scribes, and be killed, and rise after three days. He spoke this openly. Then Peter took him aside and began to rebuke him. At this he turned around and, looking at his disciples, rebuked Peter and said, "Get behind me, Satan. You are thinking not as God does, but as human beings do."
>
> He summoned the crowd with his disciples and said to them, "Whoever wishes to come

after me must deny himself, take up his cross, and follow me."

In this passage, you find that Jesus accepted the title *Christ* that Peter gave him, but then immediately began to use the title *Son of Man* to describe himself. Though Jesus does not use the term here, he also describes himself as a *Suffering Servant* for his people. Here is more information on these three titles:

CHRIST

The title *Christ* comes from the Greek word *Christos* and is the English translation of the Hebrew word *Messiah*, meaning "anointed one." Various groups within Judaism at the time of Jesus had different ideas of who the Messiah would be: an earthly king, a religious leader, a priest, a revolutionary. After Jesus accepted Peter's proclamation about his identity as the Messiah, he warned Peter not to tell anyone; he was reluctant to let many people know his identity, perhaps because his understanding of the "anointed one" was radically differed from that of the people and of his disciples. His approach here is sometimes referred to as the *messianic secret*.

SON OF MAN

Jesus revealed to his disciples that he was the Son of Man who would suffer and die for his people. The title *Son of Man* comes from a prophecy in the Old Testament Book of Daniel where the author calls the glorious Messiah the "Son of Man" (Dn 7:14). Throughout the Gospels, Jesus referred to himself this way.

SUFFERING SERVANT

Jesus understood the titles Messiah and Son of Man in light of the prophecies in Isaiah 42–53 (see page 161) that call the Messiah a "Suffering Servant."

All three titles fit Jesus because Jesus, the Son of Man, is a Messiah who will come in glory, but only after he has suffered and sacrificed his life for his people. Peter had difficulty accepting Jesus' understanding of the Messiah as the "Suffering Servant." Peter was judging Jesus by human standards, not divine ones. Not until the Resurrection and Ascension of Jesus

Christ would the early Church begin to understand that Jesus' way was that of the Cross.

Mark's Gospel shows that to follow Jesus is to pick up your own cross daily. God does not want you to suffer unnecessarily, but offering up your suffering for and with the Lord leads to Salvation and your participation in his glorious Resurrection.

Overview of Matthew's Gospel

The author of Matthew's Gospel was probably a Jewish scribe writing sometime in the AD 80s. Matthew's Gospel emphasizes the link between Judaism and Christianity.

Matthew wrote to at least two different groups: Jews who followed Jesus and Gentiles who followed Jesus. Matthew's Gospel emphasized to Jewish-Christian readers, as well as to new Gentile converts, that Jesus Christ—*Emmanuel*—is indeed the Messiah prophesied in the Old Testament. Matthew did this in several ways, explained in the following section.

Connections between Jesus and the Old Testament

Matthew's Gospel makes several connections between Moses and Jesus, portraying Jesus as the "New Moses":

- Moses made the Sinai Covenant on behalf of the Chosen People. Jesus made a New Covenant with all people.

- Moses presented the Ten Commandments to the Israelites from a mountain. Jesus offered his primary moral teaching, the Beatitudes, in the Sermon on the Mount.

- The Gospel is divided into five sections between the infancy and the Passion narrative. This five-book arrangement, centered on five important sermons of Jesus, parallels the five books of the Pentateuch that present the Old Testament Law.

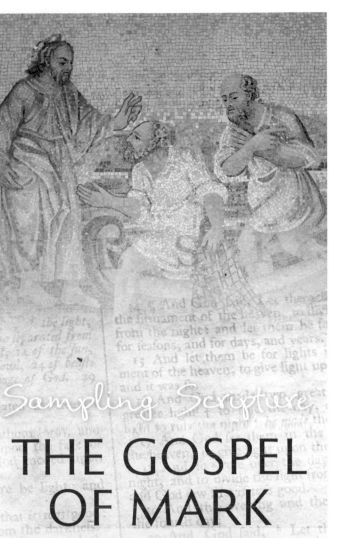

Sampling Scripture

THE GOSPEL OF MARK

Mark's is the shortest Gospel, written in a simple style. Reading it can help you understand the other synoptic Gospels. Read the entire Gospel of Mark in one sitting (this should take about an hour or so). If you want to break your reading into two segments, then first read to Mark 9:1. Read for the big picture. Record in a notebook or journal or as a separate written assignment the following:

- your ten favorite quotes or sayings of Jesus
- a list of ten key events in the Gospel
- five passages that raise questions in your mind, passages that you want to revisit for further discussion or study

COMPARING PROPHECIES

Read the following passages from Matthew's Gospel and their corresponding Old Testament prophecies. In parallel columns in your notebook, record what each passage says.

MATTHEW	EVENT	OLD TESTAMENT
1:22–23	Jesus born of a virgin	Isaiah 7:14
2:5–6	Born in Bethlehem	Micah 5:1
2:15	Flight into Egypt	Hosea 11:1
2:18	Slaughter of the Innocents	Jeremiah 31:15
4:15–16	Ministry in Galilee	Isaiah 8:23–9:1
12:18–21	Serving by leading	Isaiah 42:1–4
13:14–15	Spiritual blindness	Isaiah 6:9–10
13:35	Teaching in parables	Psalm 78:2
21:5	Entry into Jerusalem on a donkey	Isaiah 62:11; Zechariah 9:9
27:9–10	Judas betrays Jesus	Zechariah 11:12–13

The Evangelist made other connections between Judaism and Jesus. The Gospel quotes many Old Testament prophecies to proclaim Jesus' identity as the promised Messiah. See the chart, "Comparing Prophecies," above.

Matthew used the title *Son of David*, a Jewish title, more than any other Evangelist. His Gospel attempts to show that Jesus Christ fulfilled all of God's promises to the Chosen People and, through them, to all people. At the end of the Gospel, Jesus instructed his disciples to go to the ends of the earth to preach the Good News and make disciples of all the nations.

Overview of Luke's Gospel

Traditionally, the author of Luke's Gospel is identified as a Gentile Christian. The same author also wrote the

A Universal Savior:
JESUS IS FOR EVERYONE

Luke's Gospel stresses Jesus' practice of looking out for everyone: Jew and Gentile, rich and poor, women and men. He sought out those whom society considered lowly or "outcasts," including the following:

COMMON PEOPLE

Jesus appealed to the simple Jews who were open to his message of conversion, repentance, and Salvation. These were Jews who tried to follow the Law, pray, and participate in the synagogue services. Some of the Pharisees thought that the common people's ignorance kept them from holiness. Some Pharisees attributed ignorance to Jesus and his disciples because they did not strictly follow the Law in regard to fasting (see Lk 5:33) and washing (see Mt 15:2).

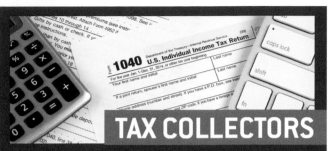

TAX COLLECTORS

Jews who collected taxes for the Romans were generally despised by their fellow Jews. Some tax collectors were further corrupt, in that they charged people more than the prescribed tax and kept the extra money. Jesus associated with tax collectors, accepted dinner invitations from them, and called one, Matthew, to be his Apostle.

THIEVES

Jesus' compassion is evident throughout the Gospel, even in his dying moments. With his last ounce of energy, he spoke to the good thief hanging in misery next to him, promising him paradise.

SAMARITANS

Jesus made a point to praise this traditional enemy by making a Samaritan the hero of a parable (see Lk 10:25-37).

PEOPLE WITH LEPROSY

Jesus embraced lepers and cured them. Leprosy was a serious and contagious skin disease, and those who suffered from it were avoided by everyone else. Jesus praised one leper, a Samaritan, for returning to thank him for his cure (see Lk 7:11–19).

WOMEN

Luke's Gospel also highlights Jesus' revolutionary approach to women in his culture. Women came to him for cures, anointed his feet, and were his constant companions. Mary and Martha were his friends. Jesus' Mother Mary is the first disciple and the model believer. (See "Women in the Gospels," page 261.)

EXECUTIONERS

While he was being crucified, taunted, and tormented by his executioners, Jesus said, "Father, forgive them, they know not what they do" (Lk 23:34).

Jesus is *everyone's* compassionate Savior. His love has no limits. The message of Luke is clear: you should allow Jesus to live in you so you can love everyone—saint and sinner—in imitation of our Lord.

Compassionate TOUCH

Jesus' healing power of touch in Luke's Gospel highlights his compassion. Read the following passages in Luke and take note of the ways that Jesus touched people literally and figuratively:

- 4:40–41
- 5:12–16
- 7:11–17
- 8:40–56
- 13:10–13
- 18:15–17

Continuing, determine a list of people who might need the healing touch of compassion. (For example, consider the elderly, who may be lonely and yearn for visitors.) Make a list of at least ten groups of people who have this need. Then decide what you can do as an individual to show God's compassion to someone who needs your loving presence. Follow through, and then report what you felt when sharing your love.

Acts of the Apostles; he thus wrote about one-fourth of the New Testament. A second-century Church Father, St. Irenaeus, also believed that Luke was a doctor and a traveling companion and friend of St. Paul.

Luke wrote to a largely Gentile-Christian audience about AD 75–90, perhaps around 85. His writing style was highly polished. He featured the city of Jerusalem as an important symbol in both of his works. His Gospel emphasizes that the Messianic age began in Jerusalem and that the second part of Jesus' ministry centers on his journey to this Holy City where the drama of Salvation unfolded. Acts of the Apostles tells of the Apostles' journeys, also beginning in Jerusalem, where they received the Holy Spirit to take the message of Jesus Christ to the end of the world. Luke highlights two major themes throughout his literary masterpiece:

1. Jesus is a universal Savior who brings Salvation to Jew and Gentile alike.

2. The Gospel of Jesus Christ is truly Good News and thus a cause of celebration.

A Message of Forgiveness and Joy

The Gospel of Luke's author also emphasized Jesus' forgiving nature. Jesus is not simply Savior for everyone, but he forgives everyone as well.

Chapter 15 is the heart of Luke's Gospel. It contains the parables of the Lost Sheep, the Lost Coin, and the Prodigal Son. These parables (covered in greater depth in Chapter 7 of this book) announced that God searches out and forgives sinners. Jesus proclaimed, "I tell you, there will be rejoicing among the angels of God over one sinner who repents" (Lk 15:10).

Through his actions and his message, Jesus reveals God to the world. Jesus' gentleness, his compassion, and his sensitivity are all divine signs of healing love. Luke writes, "The whole crowd rejoiced at all the splendid deeds done by him" (Lk 13:17).

Canticle of Joy

Read the verses of Zechariah's canticle from Luke 1:68–79. Design an artistic prayer card displaying the canticle, or choose instrumental music to accompany it. Lead a recitation with your classmates or with younger students in a parish religious education program.

SECTION ASSESSMENT

 NOTE TAKING

Use the notes you recorded on the synoptic Gospels to help you to complete the following directive.

1. Write a one-sentence summary for each of the three synoptic Gospels.

 VOCABULARY

2. _____ is a name for Jesus that means "God is with us."

 COMPREHENSION

3. Identify the primary audience for each of the synoptic Gospels.
4. What does the Gospel of Matthew mean when it refers to Jesus as the "Son of David" and suggests that he is the "New Moses"?

 REFLECTION

5. Choose one theme from each Gospel, and link the themes to your life today.
6. What does it mean to pick up your cross and follow Jesus?
7. What is your understanding of the theme that Jesus is for everyone?

Section Summaries

Focus Question

What do the synoptic Gospels reveal about Jesus?

Complete one of the following:

→ Even though each synoptic Gospel focuses on different aspects of Jesus, how do they all portray him as a man for others?

→ Create illustrated multimedia slides for each of the synoptic Gospels that summarize the stories about Jesus up until just before his Passion and Death. Work with a small group of classmates to assemble a presentation showing what the synoptic Gospels reveal about Jesus.

→ How would you summarize the Good News to these audiences: a young child, a non-Christian teen, an adult who has fallen away from the Catholic Church?

INTRODUCTION (PAGE 181–182)

Good News

Good news about human beings is inspiring, but the greatest news is the Good News of Jesus Christ revealed through the Gospels. Matthew, Mark, and Luke shared similar sources and then contributed unique material as well to their synoptic Gospels. While John's Gospel is as important as the other Gospels, his sources differ greatly.

→ What makes the Gospel message of Jesus Christ such Good News?

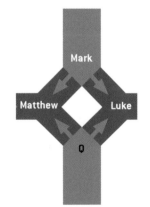

SECTION 1 (PAGES 183–186)

The Synoptic Gospels: An Overview

Matthew, Mark, and Luke share a similar structure as well as some of the same sources. Both Matthew and Luke used over half of Mark when they composed their Gospels. They also shared a source, Q, and each had his own unique source, M and L respectively. All four Gospels present the mysteries of Christ's life.

→ Why is Jesus God's fullest Revelation?

SECTION 2 (PAGES 187–190)

Jesus' Early Life

The events of Jesus' early life reveal his identity and love for people considered outsiders. Only Matthew and Luke talk about Jesus' early life; they concur regarding some essential information but differ on other details. Luke tells stories about Jesus' humble beginnings and the visit from the shepherds. Matthew emphasizes that Christ came for all people, as illustrated by the story of the magi, and tells why the Holy Family had to flee to Egypt. Luke relates the account of Mary and Joseph losing Jesus in Jerusalem and finding him in the Temple.

 How would the events Matthew and Luke included in their infancy narratives have connected with their original primary audiences?

SECTION 3 (PAGES 191–194)

Jesus' Public Life

Jesus' baptism, temptation by the devil, and call of the Apostles readied him for his public ministry. Jesus' Baptism began his mission and emphasized his faithfulness to his Father's will. The devil's efforts to tempt Jesus to sin failed as Jesus called on the Scriptures to defend himself. The temptations helped Jesus sympathize with humans who do sin. Jesus naturally attracted many disciples, but called twelve men to the special role of being Apostles.

 Look up and share a Scripture passage that helps you during a time of temptation. Explain its significance to you.

SECTION 4 (PAGES 195–197)

Jesus Proclaims the Gospel

Mark summarizes Jesus' message: "This is the time of fulfillment. The kingdom of God is at hand. Repent, and believe in the gospel" (Mk 1:15). Jesus came to preach that the Kingdom of God is present in his very person. The Transfiguration was an event in which Jesus, in divine glory, taught about the Kingdom of God to the three Apostles who came with him. Through the Paschal Mystery of his Passion, Death, Resurrection, and Ascension Jesus rescued humanity from sin and death.

 Describe what you think Jesus means by "This is the time of fulfillment."

SECTION 5 (PAGES 198–205)

Individual Characteristics of the Synoptic Gospels

The synoptic Gospels share many similarities. They also offer unique glimpses at the life and message of Jesus. Mark presents a vivid, human, and down-to-earth portrait of Jesus, focusing on Jesus' suffering as a means of encouraging suffering Christians. Matthew emphasizes the connection between Judaism and Christianity by creating a parallel between Moses and Jesus, quoting Old Testament prophecies, and calling Jesus the "Son of David." Luke's Gospel emphasizes that Jesus is a universal Savior and that the Gospel is very Good News and a cause for celebration.

→ How do you imagine the Evangelists compiling information about Jesus?

Chapter Assignments

Choose and complete at least one of these assignments to assess your understanding of the material in this chapter.

1. Represent Gospel Scenes

→ Research and write several paragraphs about the history of the Christmas crèche—a three-dimensional portrayal of Jesus' birth and related events. Choose one of the *other* events in Jesus' life (Baptism, Transfiguration, or the call of the disciples) and design a three-dimensional presentation that provides as much visual information as possible about the event. This design can be a sketch, electronic, or a combination of various objects you gather for this purpose.

2. Create a Newsletter

→ Choose either the events from Matthew's Nativity story or the events that prepared Jesus for his public ministry (Baptism, Transfiguration, and call of the Disciples). Create a newsletter (with graphics) or a comic strip to cover the events. The newsletter should be primarily serious but could have tastefully humorous features or ads. The comic strip should have at least five panes.

3. Make a Profile of Christian Leadership

→ Read one of Jesus' sermons in Matthew 10 or 18. Using the wisdom Jesus imparts in the sermon, carefully create a description of the most important qualities needed for Christian leadership. For each of these qualities, find a Christian leader who embodies that particular trait. Write a description of each quality. Include photos of Church leaders, past or present, who embody each of the qualities.

Faithful Disciple

St. Peter

St. Peter

Impetuous. Brave. Headstrong. Compassionate. Heroic. A born leader. These words all describe Simon bar Jonah, who we now refer to as St. Peter. Both he and his brother Andrew were humble fishermen working out of the village of Capernaum on the Sea of Galilee. Peter was married. (Note that Mark 1:29–30 reports that Jesus cured Peter's mother-in-law of a disease.) Jesus nicknamed Peter "Rock" to indicate that Peter would be the rock-like foundation on which he would build his Church.

Peter was unusually perceptive, yet he did not understand Jesus' mission. He recognized who Jesus was when he proclaimed him to be the Messiah, the Son of God. He argued with Jesus, however, when the Lord told him he must go to Jerusalem to die. Christ had to rebuke him, comparing Peter to the devil for trying to turn Jesus away from his mission. Peter declared his loyalty to Jesus; yet after the Lord was arrested, Peter three times denied knowing him. Peter repented for this sinful error and wept bitter tears of sorrow, and the Lord forgave him.

After his Resurrection, the Risen Lord gave Peter authority over the other Apostles and his Church. The Acts of the Apostles recounts how Peter boldly preached to the nations and describes some of his missionary activity. Tradition has it that he died a martyr in Rome in AD 64 under the Emperor Nero. He requested to be crucified upside-down, feeling that he was not worthy to die as his master did.

Jesus said to Peter: "You are Peter, and upon this rock I will build my church, and the gates of the netherworld shall not prevail against it. I will give you the keys to the kingdom of heaven. Whatever you bind on earth shall be bound in heaven; and whatever you loose on earth shall be loosed in heaven" (Mt 16:18–19). This power to forgive sins in Christ's name works through the Sacrament of

The Latin cross turned upside-down symbolizes the manner of St. Peter's execution.

Penance, in which Christ proclaims his mercy and love to sinners. Artists often depict St. Peter as having the keys to the "pearly gates" of Heaven.

Reading Comprehension

1. How do the Gospels indicate St. Peter was married?

2. Why did Jesus nickname St. Peter "Rock"?

3. Where are the accounts of St. Peter's missionary activities recorded?

4. What do the symbolic keys given to St. Peter represent?

Writing Task

- Read the following passages about St. Peter: Mt 4:18–22; Mt 8:14–15; Mt 16:15–28; Lk 9:28–36; Mk 14:27–31, 66–72; Jn 21:1–19. Write down one or two lessons from any of the passages that give you special insight into the life of St. Peter.

Explaining the Faith
Why are the Gospels the most important books of the Bible?

| Matthew | Mark | Luke | John |

The Second Vatican Council taught that "the Gospels have a special place, and rightly so, because they are our principal source for the life and teaching of the incarnate Word, our Savior" (*Dei Verbum*, 18). The four Gospels faithfully hand on what Jesus "really did and taught for their eternal Salvation" (*Dei Verbum*, 19). Their purpose is to confirm the truth about Jesus Christ. Luke, writing in the prologue of his Gospel, explains that "I too have decided, after investigating everything accurately anew, to write it down in an orderly sequence for you, most excellent Theophilus, so that you may realize the certainty of the teachings you have received" (Lk 1:3–4).

Reflection

- Summarize the message of the Gospels in one sentence.

Prayer
The Magnificat

My soul proclaims the greatness of the Lord;
>   my spirit rejoices in God my savior.

For he has looked upon his handmaid's lowliness;
>   behold, from now on will all ages call me blessed.

The Mighty One has done great things for me,
>   and holy is his name.

His mercy is from age to age
>   to those who fear him.

He has shown might with his arm,
>   dispersed the arrogant of mind and heart.

He has thrown down the rulers from their thrones
>   but lifted up the lowly.

The hungry he has filled with good things;
>   the rich he has sent away empty.

He has helped Israel his servant,
>   remembering his mercy,

according to his promise to our fathers,
>   to Abraham and to his descendants forever.

—Luke 1:46–55

JESUS' TEACHING

THE GOOD CATHOLIC HIGH SCHOOL SCIENCE TEACHER

Ms. Linda Messina teaches biology and environmental science at St. Joseph's Academy in Baton Rouge, Louisiana. Messina prefers a hands-on learning style and has empowered many of her students to win at science fairs at the state, national, and international levels. "Linda seeks opportunities to make principles of teaching come alive for students of all ages," stated one colleague.

Ms. Linda Messina

Messina began a nationally recognized "Coastal Roots Program" that enables students to explore strategies for sustaining coastal ecosystems and to practice ecological stewardship. In 2008, she won the prestigious American Stars of Teaching award from the United States Department of Education. Messina also received the 2009 Secondary Schools Department of Excellence Award from the National Catholic Education Association.[1]

"This year's award was given to teachers who collaborated with others in the educational process. Collaboration is one of the skills we practice at SJA," said St. Joseph's Academy President Sr. Adele Lambert, C.S.J.[2]

Dr. Christine Celestino is another stellar science teacher at Juan Diego Catholic High School in Draper, Utah. She teaches high school science because she did not like the way her teachers taught when she was in college. "I try to make it interesting and relatable, to keep their attention." For example, she helps the students see that, in science fiction movies such as *Star Wars*, *Star Trek*, and *Avatar*, the presence or absence of a key muscle—the sternocleidomastoid—in an alien can communicate whether the character is good or bad.

Dr. Christine Celestino

Celestino has developed a program to encourage students to pursue careers in science, technology, engineering, and math, and she has created the Summer Science Internship Program. Said senior Alex Gudac: "She's outstanding, different from a lot of other teachers. There's a lot of hands-on experience that really gets you in the mode and goes into your long-term memory." Celestino was named Utah's Biology Teacher of the Year.[3]

FOCUS QUESTION

What are the ESSENTIAL LESSONS of Jesus' teaching?

Chapter Overview

Introduction	Good Teachers
Section 1	Jesus the Teacher
Section 2	Jesus and the Kingdom of God
Section 3	Jesus' Sermon on the Mount

INTRODUCTION
Good Teachers

MAIN IDEA
Good teachers share some of the qualities of Jesus Christ, the perfect teacher.

How do the two science teachers from the opening story resemble each other? On the surface, you can

see that both are women who teach science in Catholic high schools. These teachers also share these qualities:

- a passion for their subject matter
- a love for students
- creative minds
- a "hands-on" learning approach
- the desire to make science interesting and relevant
- a mission to make the world a better place with the help of their students
- the vocation to encourage young people to go into science

In this chapter, you will be learning about Jesus the Teacher, using passages from the three synoptic Gospels. You will see that Jesus shares some common characteristics with these two Catholic school teachers. Jesus possessed the following qualities.

- a passion for his mission
- a love for those who were listening
- creative means of sharing his message
- the ability to teach in a way that made sense to his audience
- a desire to share the Good News with the help of his disciples
- a mission to encourage his disciples to go and preach the Good News themselves

Many excellent Catholic high school teachers preach the Gospel while sharing their passion for science, math, or history. All good teachers share certain qualities, including some of the qualities of Jesus as Teacher. They are like Christ's ambassadors: men and women who share his love with their students, who try to excite others about making the world a better place, and who use creative means to teach their subject matter.

Jesus, the Son of God, however, is the perfect Teacher.

NOTE TAKING

Applying Concepts. Reread the story about the two science teachers, and write down two or three characteristics you particularly value in a teacher.

I like hands-on learning activities.

FOLLOWERS OF CHRIST THE TEACHER

Students follow their master, or favorite, teachers. For Christians, Jesus is the Master Teacher. St. Jerome said of his followers, "Anyone is rich enough who is poor with Christ." Reflect on the meaning of this statement by completing the following three-step exercise.

1. List the names of people (famous or not so famous) who you believe have found a spiritually rich life by following Jesus. Do not consider only priests, religious, and lay parish helpers. Think of friends, relatives, neighbors, teachers, and acquaintances who have a relationship with Christ and who attend Mass regularly but who may not be very involved in parish life.

2. Write a wise insight about faith in Jesus or life in general that you have heard someone on your list say.

3. Write some words of your own that reflect your faith in Jesus and your willingness to follow him.

SECTION ASSESSMENT

NOTE TAKING

Review the notes you made before answering the following question.

1. What do you think is the most important characteristic a teacher should possess? Why is this characteristic so important?

COMPREHENSION

2. Identify two similarities between the qualities of Jesus and those of the high school science teachers.

REFLECTION

3. How do Catholic high school teachers who do not teach religion teach about faith?

SECTION 1
Jesus the Teacher

MAIN IDEA
Jesus possessed skills that made him a very effective teacher for the people of his time.

People reacted both positively and negatively to Jesus as he started teaching. The Gospel of Luke reports that when Jesus came out of the desert after his forty days of fasting and temptation, he returned to Galilee in the power of the Holy Spirit. He then began to teach in the synagogues throughout the whole region, and people began to praise him for his message.

One Sabbath, Jesus came to his hometown of Nazareth and went to the synagogue. On this particular day, he did the public Scripture reading (see image at left). Jesus unrolled the scroll of the prophet Isaiah until he found the following passage, which he read aloud:

> The Spirit of the Lord is upon me,
> because he has anointed me
> to bring glad tidings to the poor.
> He has sent me to proclaim liberty
> to captives
> and recovery of sight to the blind,
> to let the oppressed go free,
> and to proclaim a year acceptable
> to the Lord. (Lk 4:18–19)

After reading this prophecy describing the Messiah, he said, "Today this scripture passage is fulfilled in your hearing" (Lk 4:21). With the power of his words, Jesus amazed those gathered in the synagogue. As they began to realize the full implications of his

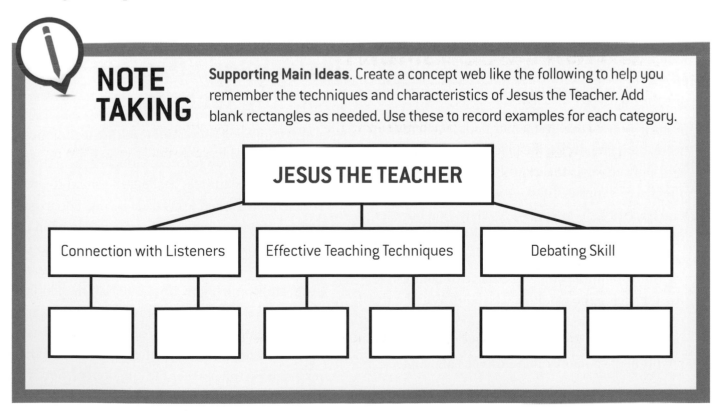

NOTE TAKING

Supporting Main Ideas. Create a concept web like the following to help you remember the techniques and characteristics of Jesus the Teacher. Add blank rectangles as needed. Use these to record examples for each category.

JESUS THE TEACHER

Connection with Listeners | Effective Teaching Techniques | Debating Skill

claim (that Jesus himself was the Messiah), however, they showed outrage, saying things like "Isn't this the son of Joseph?" (Lk 4:22). Jesus referred to the prophets Elijah and Elisha in his response: "Amen, I say to you, no prophet is accepted in his own native place" (Lk 4:24). Then the people tried to kill him.

Notice that by choosing this passage from Isaiah, Jesus gave his listeners a sense of what type of Messiah he would be. His ministry would be to the poor, captives, the blind, and the oppressed.

Jesus was an exceptional teacher, and he was effective for many reasons. Some of the major reasons are listed in the next subsections.

Jesus Connected with His Listeners

Jesus did not simply teach to an anonymous audience. Rather, he knew and cared for those who listened to him. Jesus came from a humble background and knew how to reach those whom others called outcasts in society. How did he do this?

- *Jesus was genuine.* Jesus' listeners could tell that he believed and lived what he preached. Jesus taught that the greatest love a person can have is to lay down his or her life for another (Jn 15:13); of course Jesus did this when he freely gave up his life for us all.

- *Jesus was available.* Jesus met people where they were, both literally (in the places where they lived) and figuratively (in the problems and concerns they were experiencing). A wandering preacher and teacher, Jesus taught everywhere—on hillsides, on dusty roads, and at the tables of the rich and poor, as well as in the synagogues and the Temple. He didn't require people to change or conform to his way before he would teach them. Witness the woman caught in adultery (see Jn 7:53–8:11). Jesus was interesting and engaging in order to keep the attention of so many different types of people.

"Let the one among you who is without sin be the first to throw a stone at her" (Jn 8:7).

- *Jesus used everyday language.* Jesus spoke Aramaic like his contemporaries. He also did not preach over people's heads. Instead of using big words as in "Charity should not be ostentatious," Jesus said, "When you give alms, do not let your left hand know what your right is doing" (Mt 6:3).

Jesus Used Effective Teaching Techniques

Jesus also employed successful teaching techniques:

- *Jesus challenged his listeners.* Good teachers stretch their students' minds, challenging them to grow. A rich official asked Jesus what he must do to gain eternal life, assuring Jesus that he had kept all the commandments. Jesus then invited him to sell everything he owned, distribute his money to the poor, and come follow him. The rich man looked sad. Jesus said, "How hard it is for those who have wealth to enter the kingdom of God! For it is easier for a camel to pass through the eye of a needle than for a rich person to enter the kingdom of God" (Lk 18:24–25).

What is the meaning of Jesus' saying? After all, a camel cannot pass through the eye of a needle. This saying involves *hyperbole* (exaggeration) as well as a *paradox*, an apparent contradiction or nonsense (see "Jesus and Paradox" at right). Jesus gave his own solution to the problem when some people questioned him, saying, "What is impossible for human beings is possible for God" (Lk 18:27).

- *Jesus used metaphors and similes.* He created vibrant images that made his listeners take notice. For example, Jesus explained that the Son of Man would appear very quickly and be immediately clear to all. "For just as lightning comes from the east and is seen as far as the west, so will the coming of the Son of Man be. Wherever the corpse is, there the vultures will gather" (Mt 24:27–28).

- *Jesus appealed to his listeners' senses.* He used the sense of taste to illustrate this point: "You are the salt of the earth. But if salt loses its taste, with what can it be seasoned? It is no longer good for anything but to be thrown out and trampled underfoot. You are light for the world" (Mt 5:13–14).

- *Jesus spoke in parallel statements.* Jesus often repeated thoughts a second time in a slightly different form to drive home an idea. For example, he said, "Give to the one who asks of you, and do not turn your back on one who wants to borrow" (Mt 5:42).

- *Jesus used hyperbole or exaggeration to make a point.* This speech pattern was common in Aramaic. Examples of hyperbole in English are "I have a ton of homework" and "It's raining cats and dogs." Hyperbolic language drives home a point but should not be taken literally. Jesus said,

> If your right eye causes you to sin, tear it out and throw it away. . . . And if your right hand causes you to sin, cut it off and throw it away. It is better for you to lose one of your members than to have your whole body go into Gehenna. (Mt 5:29–30)

Jesus' point is clear: avoid temptation rather than risk eternal loss. He does not want you to

Jesus and PARADOX

A paradox is "a comparison that appears to contradict" or "something that leads to a situation that defies intuition." Paradox was around in Jesus' time. Petronius, a member of the Roman court in the first century AD, is reported to have said: "Moderation in all things, including moderation."

Likewise, Jesus used thought-provoking paradoxes in his teaching—short, memorable sayings of great significance. Here are three examples:

1. For whoever wishes to save his life will lose it, but whoever loses his life for my sake will save it. What profit is there for one to gain the whole world yet lose or forfeit himself? (Lk 9:24–25)

2. For the one who is least among all of you is the one who is the greatest. (Lk 9:48)

3. For everyone who exalts himself will be humbled, but the one who humbles himself will be exalted. (Lk 14:11)

What do you think is the meaning of each of Jesus' paradoxical statements? Also, write about one or more experiences from your life when you have seen the truth of these statements by Jesus.

The Regions
WHERE JESUS TAUGHT

The Gospels report that Jesus limited his teaching ministry to Galilee, Samaria, and Judea. Gaining a perspective on the lands and populations of these three important regions can give you insight into some of Jesus' teachings.

Galilee

Jesus and most of his Apostles were natives of Galilee. Galilee was a region north of Judea and Samaria that had fertile land and rolling hills watered by the Jordan River and the **Sea of Galilee**. Jesus grew up in Nazareth, a small town of perhaps no more than five hundred people at the time. Nazareth was about an hour's walk from Galilee's largest, Roman-influenced city of Sepphoris. The people of Sepphoris might have provided work for Joseph and Jesus.

The land supported many of the region's residents. Farmers and shepherds were relatively prosperous because of the fertility of the land. The Sea of Galilee provided a living for fishermen. Most of the population was Jewish, though some Gentiles also lived in the area. Jews from Judea sometimes doubted the religiosity of Galilean Jews because of their relationships with Gentiles. Galilean Jews also spoke with a distinctive Aramaic accent. Many Galileans, however, were zealous about their religion.

Some of the colorful details of Jesus' parables came from his keen observation of Galilean life: birds, flowers, farmers at work in the fields, fishing nets straining under a heavy load. Cana (the site of Jesus' first miracle), Bethsaida (the home of Peter, Andrew, and Philip), and Capernaum were all in Galilee.

Eastern shores of Sea of Galilee

Sea of Galilee

Samaria

Samaria was the region to the south of Galilee and the north of Judea. The Samaritans were the descendants of the northern kingdom of Israel who intermarried with foreigners back at the time of Assyria's conquest. Recall that when the Jews of Jerusalem returned to Judea after the Exile, the Samaritans wanted to help rebuild the Temple. The Jews, however, found that Samaritan beliefs differed too much from Judaism: the Samaritans accepted the Mosaic Law but did not accept the Jewish prophetic or wisdom writings. They rejected the Jerusalem Temple because they believed that God chose Mount Gerizim as the proper place to worship. Because the Judeans had destroyed the Mount Gerizim Temple in 128 BC, tension between Jews and Samaritans remained in Jesus' day. On pilgrimages to Judea, Galileans would try to avoid Samaria if they could, fearing that the Samaritans would attack them.

Mount Gerizim

Though Jesus did not allow his Apostles to preach to the Samaritans (see Mt 10:5), he showed them only love. He made one Samaritan the hero of a parable (see Lk 10:30–35), was kind to a Samaritan woman (see Jn 4:1–42), and praised a leper from Samaria for being the only one to thank him for a cure (see Lk 17:16). Some of Jesus' enemies tried to insult him by calling him a Samaritan (see Jn 8:48).

Judea

Mount of Temptation, near Jericho

Bethlehem, Jesus' birthplace, was located in **Judea**, as was Bethany, the home of Jesus' friends Lazarus, Martha, and Mary. Another notable Judean town was Jericho, where Jesus healed a blind man and met a tax collector, Zacchaeus. Jerusalem was the region's principal city. Set on two hills 2,255 to 2,400 feet above sea level, Jerusalem was Judea's religious, political, and economic center. Religious life centered on the Temple.

Judea was the southernmost region was of the three. It was a dry, barren, craggy land; most of its inhabitants were descended from Jews who returned from the Babylonian Captivity. Most of the Judean population lived in or near Jerusalem. In Jesus' day, the city may have had a population of fifty-five to seventy thousand, with as many as 120,000 visitors swelling the population during the Jewish festivals.

A barren wilderness located in southernmost Judea was where the Spirit led Jesus to be tempted after his Baptism. The fifty-three-mile-long Dead Sea—at 1,300 feet below sea level, the lowest point on earth—is also in Judea.

Sea of Galilee A thirteen-mile by seven-mile body of fresh water through which the Jordan River runs.

Samaria The region to the south of Galilee, occupied by people descended from intermarriages between occupants of the old northern kingdom and foreigners.

Judea The southern region of the Holy Land, occupied by Jews who returned from the Babylonian Captivity. Its principal city was Jerusalem.

mutilate yourself! He exaggerated to drive home his message.

- *Jesus used* Amen *in unique ways.* Amen is a Hebrew word that comes from the same root as "believe." It carries the sense of "Yes, certainly, I believe." During Jesus' day, people used the word at the end of an oath, blessing, or curse. Jesus used *Amen* to introduce statements or strengthen them. The *Catechism of the Catholic Church* states, "Our Lord often used the word 'Amen,' sometimes repeated, to emphasize the trustworthiness of his teaching, his authority founded on God's truth" (*CCC*, 1063).

Locate a Biblical Site

Read the following Scripture passages from the synoptic Gospels. Locate on the map where each event took place.

- Where did Jesus cast out a demon (see Mk 1:21)?
- To which city was the traveler in the parable of the Good Samaritan going (see Lk 10:30)?
- On the road to which cities does Jesus predict his Passion and Death (see Mk 8:27–33)?
- To what does Jesus compare Chorazin and Bethsaida (see Mt 11:20–22)?
- Where did Jesus dine with Zacchaeus (see Lk 19:1–10)?
- Where did Jesus instruct two disciples to find a colt for him (see Mt 21:1)?
- Where did the resurrected Jesus eat a meal with two disciples (see Lk 24:13)?

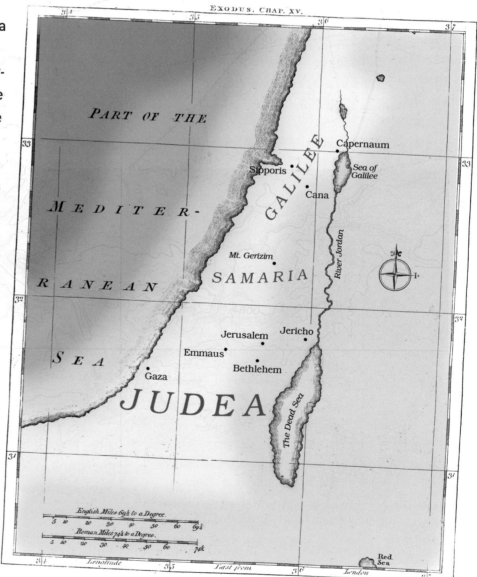

Jesus Debated Brilliantly

Jesus held his own while interacting with Jewish leaders because he was a brilliant debater. Jesus' opponents sometimes tried to find a weakness in one of his teachings, but he would have none of their tricks.

In one incident, Jesus' opponents challenged him using the coin of tribute that the Roman emperor demanded from the Jews. Pious Jews hated paying the tax. The Pharisees' disciples approached Jesus with the question "Is it lawful to pay the census tax to Caesar or not?" (Mt 22:17). If Jesus said no, his opponents could then claim that he was preaching rebellion against Rome, a crime punishable by death. If he said yes, he would lose face with zealous Jews who hated the Roman tax. Jesus clearly understood the malicious intent of the question. He asked his opponents to show him a coin. This was a clever move on his part, because his opponents produced a Roman coin, something they should not have been carrying if they hated the Romans as much as they claimed. Their hypocrisy was immediately clear to everyone. Jesus responded, "'Then repay to Caesar what belongs to Caesar and to God what belongs to God.' When they heard this they were amazed, and leaving him they went away" (Mt 22:21–22).

SECTION ASSESSMENT

NOTE TAKING

Use the concept web you created to help you to answer the following.

1. Which techniques and characteristics of Jesus as Teacher made him most successful?

COMPREHENSION

2. Give one example of Jesus' use of hyperbole.

3. What is the meaning of the word *Amen*? How and why did Jesus use it in a unique way?

4. What significant event took place when Jesus began to preach in Nazareth? How did Jesus' neighbors react? Why did they react this way?

EVALUATION

5. Tell about a favorite teacher you have had from another class who has best modeled characteristics of Jesus as Teacher.

APPLICATION

6. Rewrite one of Jesus' sayings quoted in this section to address an audience of today.

SECTION 2
Jesus and the Kingdom of God

MAIN IDEA
Jesus used parables to communicate important truths about the Kingdom of God.

From the beginning of his public ministry until his Death on the Cross, Jesus preached the coming of God's Kingdom. In doing so, Jesus accomplished the will of the Father: to share his divine life with all human beings by gathering them around his Son. The Church is, in fact, this gathering—"on earth the seed and beginning of the kingdom" (*CCC*, 541).

The *Kingdom of God* or *Kingdom of Heaven* is not really a place like an earthly kingdom. Rather, the Kingdom of God is the active presence of God's love, justice, truth, and Salvation working in the world. Jesus Christ, as God's presence in the world, is the one who brings the Kingdom. He is the one who gathers all people into the unity of the Blessed Trinity—Father, Son, and Holy Spirit—through his preaching and miracles. Ultimately, it is the Paschal Mystery—Christ's work of Redemption, accomplished principally by his Passion, Death, Resurrection, and glorious Ascension—that brings about the Kingdom. It is the Paschal Mystery that unites you to your Savior Jesus Christ and makes it possible for God to adopt you into his family.

God's Kingdom was not an easy concept for Jesus' listeners to grasp. Jesus used parables to help people understand the mystery of God's Kingdom growing in their midst. While his miracles confirmed the truth of

NOTE TAKING

Summarizing Main Ideas. As you read through this section, keep a running list of at least five phrases that describe the Kingdom of God. Put them in a chart like the following:

The Kingdom of God is . . .	like a treasure that a man sells everything to buy.

his words, his parables helped his contemporaries—and help you today—to understand the meaning of his message.

About Parables

The English word parable comes from the Greek word *parabole,* meaning "placing two things side by side in order to compare them." The parables Jesus told were simple, clear stories drawn from ordinary life that compare very familiar things—like seeds, wheat, yeast, sheep, farmers, and nets—to unfamiliar truths, usually about some aspect of God's Kingdom. Jesus told these stories to invite his listeners to use their imaginations, emotions, and minds to grapple with the truth he wanted to teach.

Parables were a brilliant way to teach about the Kingdom. Jesus' stories revealed truth in an interesting way and were so vivid that they could easily be recalled—which was important because Jesus' followers did not take notes but rather had to commit his teaching to memory.

Jesus' parables invited his listeners to look at reality from a different angle. Parables stretch the mind and engage the listener. And if people couldn't or wouldn't change their preconceptions, they would not understand the parables' point: "They look, but do not see and hear but do not listen or understand" (Mt 13:13). Jesus' parables are windows into the mystery of God's reign. Jesus' audience had to look at his stories with open eyes to discover his (often surprising) message. Despite the many years and miles separating you from first-century Palestine, you can still understand the message of his parables.

> **Hell** The eternal separation from God that occurs when a person dies after freely and deliberately acting against God's will, not repenting of a mortal sin.

Lazarus and the Rich Man

Consider the parable of Lazarus and the Rich Man (see Lk 16:19–31 and the image above). In the story, Jesus described Lazarus as poor and sick. He was so poor that he longed to eat the scraps that fell from the table of the rich man; he was so sick that sores covered his body. The rich man never even noticed Lazarus lying at his doorstep. Lazarus eventually died and went to Heaven.

Before long, the rich man also died and went to **Hell**. There he suffered every torment. He saw a vision of Lazarus, who was happy in the company of Abraham (the patriarch of the Jewish people from the Book of Genesis) in Heaven. The rich man begged Abraham to allow Lazarus to dip the tip of his finger in water to cool his tongue, for he was burning in the flames in agony. Abraham refused the rich man his request, as well as a second request to allow Lazarus to appear to his five brothers to warn them what was in store for them if they did not change their selfish ways.

PARABLES IN THE SYNOPTIC GOSPELS

Read at least five parables from the list. Be sure to select at least one from each Gospel. Find the interpretation of the parable in a biblical commentary, and summarize it. Write your own interpretation of the meaning of the parable, drawing on the information you read in the commentary.

	MATTHEW	MARK	LUKE
Lamp under a bushel	5:15–17	4:21–22	8:16–18
New cloth on old garments	9:16	2:21	5:36
New wine in old wine skins	9:17	2:22	5:37
The sower	13:3–23	4:2–20	8:4–15
Mustard seed	13:31–32	4:30–32	13:18–19
Yeast	13:33		
Wicked tenants of the vineyard	21:33–45	12:1–12	20:9–19
Budding fig tree	24:32–35	13:28–32	21:29–33
Two foundations	7:24–27		6:47–49
Wayward children	11:16–19		7:31–35
Leaven	13:33		13:20–21
Lost sheep	18:12–14		15:3–7
Weeds among the wheat	13:24–30		
Hidden treasure	13:44		
Pearl of great price	13:45–46		
Dragnet	13:47–50		
Unmerciful servant	18:23–25		
Workers in the vineyard	20:1–16		
Father and two sons	21:28–32		
Marriage feast for the king's son	22:1–14		
Wise and foolish maidens	25:1–13		
Servants and their talents	25:14–30		
Judgment of the nations	25:31–46		
Seed growing silently		4:26–29	
Doorkeeper on watch		13:34–37	
Two debtors			7:41–43
Good Samaritan			10:25–37
Friend at midnight			11:5–10
Rich fool			12:16–21
Watchful servants			12:35–38
Wise steward	24:45–51		12:42–48
Barren fig tree			13:6–9
Great feast			14:16–24
Lost coin			15:8–10
Prodigal son			15:11–32
Dishonest steward			16:1–13
Rich man and Lazarus			16:19–31
Useless servants			17:7–10
Persistent widow			18:1–8
Pharisee and tax collector			18:9–14
Ten pounds			19:11–27

Abraham replied, "If they will not listen to Moses and the prophets, neither will they be persuaded if someone should rise from the dead" (Lk 16:31).

The message of the parable is that wealthy people must share their riches with poor people. If they do not, God will punish them in eternity. How could anyone forget the story of Lazarus and the rich man or its religious message once he or she heard it?

The Pearl of Great Price

Now consider this short parable. Jesus said:

> The kingdom of heaven is like a merchant searching for fine pearls. When he finds a pearl of great price, he goes and sells all he has and buys it. (Mt 13:45–46)

The meaning of this story is clear and urgent. The perfect pearl the man discovered is so valuable that he surrenders his entire fortune to buy it. When you discover God's Kingdom, you should follow the merchant's example. God's Kingdom is so valuable that you should stake your whole life on it.

The Principal Themes of the Parables

The parables in the synoptic Gospels have several key themes. A common theme in most of these parables is the Kingdom of God—who it is for and what it is like. The parables highlighted in the following sections focus on the Kingdom of God.

God's Kingdom Is for All

The parables of the Mustard Seed and the Sower communicate that God's Kingdom is for all.

The parable of the Mustard Seed (Lk 13:18–19) teaches that though the Kingdom of God may have a small beginning like a seed, it can grow into a very large bush with room for all. The large mustard bush

includes not only Jews who follow Jesus but also Gentiles.

In the parable of the Sower (Mk 4:2–20), the seed is the Word of God. To receive the Word of God successfully, you must have "rich soil" (a receptive heart). However, there are many obstacles—symbolized by birds scavenging on the path, rocky ground, and thorns—that can prevent you from receiving and accepting the Word. In the hearts of those who are able to hear and accept God's Word and overcome the obstacles, his Word grows well and bears much fruit.

Sinners Are Welcome in the Kingdom

The parables of the Lost Sheep, the Lost Coin, and the Prodigal Son teach that God not only welcomes sinners but actively seeks them out.

Those who self-righteously believed in their own holiness severely criticized Jesus for associating with "outcasts." They believed that if a person associated with sinners, then he or she must also be evil. Jesus replied, "Those who are well do not need a physician, but the sick do. I did not come to call the righteous but sinners" (Mk 2:17). On one occasion, when certain Pharisees and scribes complained about Jesus' association with sinners, Jesus responded by telling three important parables. These are found in Luke 15, which, you remember, is the "heart" of his Gospel.

In the parable of the Lost Sheep (Lk 15:1–7), Jesus tells of a shepherd who goes out of his way to rescue one lost sheep. This would have been unusual, because shepherds at the time could not risk losing the rest of their flock to find one stray sheep. Instead, they accepted that they would lose a sheep from time to time. Jesus' story would have surprised his audience. The clear teaching is that God spares no effort to reach every person who is lost and away from him.

The parable of the Lost Coin (Lk 15:8–10) tells the story of a woman who sweeps the whole house to retrieve one lost coin and then announces to her friends and neighbors that she has found it. Notice that Jesus compares God to a woman, something no rabbi of his day would ever have done. Like the parable of the Lost Sheep, this parable shows that God persists in seeking those who have deviated from his way until they are at home again with him.

The parable of the Prodigal Son (Lk 15:11–32) is probably Jesus' most famous parable (see image on page 226). It is about a compassionate father and his two sons. The prodigal (carelessly spending) younger son foolishly wasted his inheritance, ending his spending spree by taking care of swine, the most demeaning work possible for a Jew.

When the son realized how low he had sunk, he returned to his father, hoping to become his father's servant. His father saw him coming, rushed out to meet him, embraced him, and threw a welcome-home party. It is the father's love that is prodigal—that is, generous beyond all expectations. The father was likewise generous toward the older son, who (like the Pharisees) complained about his father's generosity toward his disgraced brother. He told the older son: "You are here with me always; everything I have is yours" (Lk 15:31).

The Kingdom Is Here

Using the parables of the Workers in the Vineyard and the Great Feast, Jesus taught that the day of Salvation had arrived.

In the parable of the Workers in the Vineyard (Mt 20:1–16), a landowner hires men in the morning to work in his vineyard, promising them a certain wage. When he sees idle laborers later in the day, he hires them too for the remaining hours. At the end of the day, the landowner pays them all the same wage, which makes the ones who worked the full day upset. Jesus taught that God does not reward people the way humans do. The landowner did not cheat his earliest hires because they agreed to work for the wage offered. He could be generous with later hires if he wanted to.

In the parable of the Great Feast (Lk 14:16–24), a man prepares a dinner, but the people he has invited seemingly have better things to do. Consequently, the man asks his servants to go and find those considered outcasts (the blind and the lame) to come to his dinner. When there is still more room, the man tells the servants to "beat the bushes" to find more people to come.

These two parables show the generous way God saves. God does not reward only those who repent and listen to his word early on; he also rewards those

Christian disciples follow Jesus through all facets of their lives: learning, prayer, study, and work.

who take longer to come to him. And you should never scoff at God's offer of Salvation—whenever it comes—knowing that God invites all people in *his* time, not yours.

Repentance Is a Prerequisite for Entering the Kingdom

Two parables from the Gospel of Matthew teach about the importance of having faith in Jesus and the power of **repentance** from sin.

In the parable of the Two Foundations (Mt 7:24–27), people who listen to Jesus' words, believe them, and then act on them have built their house on a foundation of rock. When the flood comes, their house stands firm. Those who listen to the Word, but neither believe nor act, are like people whose house is built on

> **repentance** A feeling of sorrow for one's actions or "changing one's mind" (from the Greek *metanoia*); a turning away from sin and toward the amendment of one's life.

sand. When the flood comes, their house collapses and is destroyed. This parable teaches that building a life around God's Word creates a strong foundation that can help you to resist spiritual challenges.

In the parable of the Two Sons (Mt 21:28–32), the father asks his sons to go and work in the vineyard. One son at first refuses but then changes his mind and does the work. When the father makes the same request to the second son, this son tells his father that he will go, but in fact does not. Jesus asked his listeners to identify which of the two sons did his father's will, and they responded that it was the first.

The first son represents the People of Israel, who repented when John the Baptist called them—even though they were sinners. The second son represents religious leaders who did not repent when John the Baptist asked them to. Though people considered them to be holy, they did not express sorrow for their sins.

The Kingdom Belongs to the Poor and Lowly

Jesus came to preach to the poor, and he blessed them. He lived as a poor person himself, experiencing hunger, thirst, and privation. In the parable of the Last Judgment (Mt 25:31–46), Jesus spoke of the need to prepare for the coming of God's Kingdom. He requires that you love vulnerable people as a condition of entering his Kingdom, for the Kingdom belongs to the poor and lowly—to those who accept Christ in humility.

In fact, when Christ comes in judgment, he will separate the saved and the lost as sheep from the goats based on this criterion: "Whatever you did for one of these least brothers of mine, you did for me" (Mt 25:40). Jesus will ask those who ignore the needs of the least ones to depart from the Lord to the "eternal fire prepared for the devil and his angels" (Mt 25:41).

Christ's warning, echoed by the Church, is of the eternal punishment of Hell for those who die separated from God in the state of mortal sin.

There Is Rejoicing in God's Kingdom

Jesus uses the parables of the Weeds among the Wheat, the Hidden Treasure, and the Rich Fool to teach people to rejoice that the Kingdom of God will triumph in the end.

The Good News, which Jesus came to preach, met with resistance. Perhaps in some ways Jesus' words were so good they were almost impossible to accept. Jesus' enemies saw him as a threat to their power over people and worked to get rid of him. Jesus knew that some people would oppose the Kingdom, but he assured his listeners that God will triumph in the end. Apparent setbacks in working for God's Kingdom and Salvation are like the weeds among the wheat. Though you encounter many hardships along the way (the "wheat"), you can be assured of eternal happiness and

"But God said to him, 'You fool, this night your life will be demanded of you; and the things you have prepared, to whom will they belong?' Thus will it be for the one who stores up treasure for himself but is not rich in what matters to God" (Lk 12:20–21).

joy when God removes the difficulties of this life once and for all.

The parable of the Hidden Treasure (Mt 13:44) teaches that those who accept God's Kingdom (and Jesus, who proclaimed it) have found the hidden treasure. Jesus says that you should stake everything you own and your very life on Jesus. He has revealed to you his Father's goodness, his generosity, his forgiving love, and his Salvation. Therefore, you should accept this Good News with joy and deep conviction.

Finally, the parable of the Rich Fool (Lk 12:16–21) points out that tomorrow might be too late! This is the lesson that the foolish man did not understand. He tore down his old barns that were too small for his growing abundance and built new, larger ones to secure a future of leisure for himself. Unfortunately, he did not count on dying that night. The time to choose Jesus and his Father's Kingdom is *right now*.

The Lord needs your help. He wants you to believe in him and his message because he expects you to share the Good News with others. Think of people you know who emit God's joy and love through their very being.

You have the same opportunity to share the Good News of Salvation by your own life. This isn't an act of fakery or phoniness; rather, it is living the very goodness God intends for you. You are an instrument of God's love. Repent, believe the Good News, and live a life of love—this is the message of the Savior, Jesus Christ.

SECTION ASSESSMENT

NOTE TAKING

Use the phrases you jotted down while reading this section to help you complete the following task.

1. Describe the Kingdom of God.

VOCABULARY

2. Define *parable*.
3. What does it mean to repent?

COMPREHENSION

4. Why did Jesus tell parables?
5. What made parables helpful for disciples who could not write down Jesus' teaching?
6. Write a summary sentence for each of the following parables.

   - The Sower
   - The Lost Sheep
   - The Weeds among the Wheat
   - The Rich Fool

APPLICATION

7. Apply at least one of the themes of the Kingdom of God parables to life today.

REFLECTION

8. The Pharisees and scribes thought that Jesus should not associate with people whom society considered outcasts. Contrast their view with Jesus' statement: "Those who are well do not need a physician, but the sick do. I did not come to call the righteous but sinners" (Mk 2:17). What might Jesus' statement mean for the Church today?

SECTION 3
Jesus' Sermon on the Mount

MAIN IDEA
The Sermon on the Mount (especially the Beatitudes) shares the essential moral teaching of Jesus.

The Gospel of Matthew records Jesus' **Sermon on the Mount**, delivered on a mountainside to a great crowd (Mt 5–7). Recalling that Matthew wrote his Gospel primarily for a Jewish-Christian audience, compare this scene to Moses's deliverance of the Law from Mount Sinai. Recall also that Matthew's Gospel shows Jesus as the New Lawgiver, the New Moses. His instructions guide those who have accepted the Good News and wish to live as his faithful followers.

The Sermon on the Mount contains blessings (the Beatitudes), instructions about how to live, and additional reflections about what is important in life. Luke's Gospel contains a shortened version (thirty-two verses) of these teachings in the "Sermon on the Plain" (Lk 6:17–49). The following sections provide more detail on Jesus' teachings from the Sermon on the Mount.

> **Sermon on the Mount** A section from Matthew's Gospel (Mt 5:1–7:29) in which Jesus delivers the first of five discourses.
>
> **Beatitudes** A key portion of the Sermon on the Mount from Matthew 5, in which Jesus reveals to his listeners how to fulfill their desires for happiness and achieve the Kingdom of God.

NOTE TAKING

Identifying Main Ideas. Create an outline like the one below to record Jesus' main teachings from the Sermon on the Mount.

I. What Did Jesus Teach in the Sermon on the Mount?
    A. The Beatitudes
        1.
        2.
    B. Additional Instructions on How to Live

THE BEATITUDES

The moral teaching offered in the Sermon on the Mount is a roadmap to eternal happiness or *beatitude*. In Chapter 1, you read that every human being longs for happiness. In the **Beatitudes**, Jesus' blessings reveal how you can fulfill your desire for happiness and achieve your goal in life: the Kingdom of God. The life-giving words of the Beatitudes show us how to love God and others in imitation of our Lord. The Beatitudes also complete the promises that God made to Abraham. In fact, Jesus extends the promises beyond earthly gift to the eternal gift of the Kingdom of God.

Blessed are the poor in spirit, for theirs is the kingdom of heaven.

Jesus associated with poor, weak, and vulnerable people, and he expected his followers to do so also. However, this beatitude does not condone the condition of material poverty, which is an evil that humans should strive to eliminate. The "poor in spirit" are to those who put their confidence in God rather than in material possessions.

Blessed are they who mourn, for they will be comforted.

Jesus refers here to those who mourn because they suffer. He also refers to those who mourn because they see evil reign on earth. Only God can comfort people who mourn in this way.

Blessed are the meek, for they will inherit the land.

To be meek is to be humble and patient. Meekness is *not* equated with weakness. The land that the meek will inherit is the Kingdom of God.

Blessed are they who hunger and thirst for righteousness, for they will be satisfied.

Here, Jesus refers to those who submit to the saving action of God. Your restless heart cannot find true happiness until you find God.

Blessed are the merciful, for they will be shown mercy.

To be merciful means to pardon one's neighbors, to love those in need, and to love one's enemies.

Blessed are the clean of heart, for they will see God.

In Psalm 24:4, only a person "whose heart is clean" can take part in Temple worship. The promise of this beatitude is that the clean of heart will see God in his Kingdom. A person with a clean heart has a single, focused commitment to God.

Blessed are the peacemakers, for they will be called children of God.

Peace here refers to total well-being, not simply the absence of war. Peacemaking closely connects to loving one's neighbor and being merciful. It involves truly treating *all* people as brothers and sisters in Christ.

Blessed are they who are persecuted for the sake of righteousness, for theirs is the kingdom of heaven.

Those who encounter persecution do so because they are acting in conformity with God's will. They will be rewarded with eternal happiness in Heaven.

How Well Are You
LIVING THE BEATITUDES?

Examine how well you are putting the teachings of the Beatitudes into practice. Read each statement below, and rate your own behavior. First, write a short summary of how well you are doing and in what ways you need to improve. Next, answer the questions that follow.

- I work to put my confidence in God rather than in material things.

- I ask God to help me understand the evil that I see and work as I can against it.

- I am a gentle, humble person who works to build others up.

- I work to align my own will with the saving activity of God.

- I ask for God's help in forgiving others.

- I am growing in holiness—for example, I receive the Eucharist at least once a week. My priorities are as follows: God is number one, family is number two, and friends are number three.

- I am an instrument of God's peace in my family and school.

- I am willing to suffer criticism for doing the right thing. I resist peer pressure.

QUESTIONS

1. Explain which of the Beatitudes you believe the world needs most.

2. What are practical ways that you might put each of the Beatitudes into practice?

3. Read Luke's version of the Beatitudes (see Lk 6:20–23). What are some differences between Luke's and Matthew's versions?

Additional Instruction on How to Live

Many of the sayings from the next section of the Sermon on the Mount come from sources Q and M, and therefore are shared with Luke or unique to Matthew's Gospel. Begin your study of Jesus' words by first reading each referenced passage. Then use the text summary in the following sections as commentary and application for each passage from the Bible.

Be the Salt of the Earth and Light of the World (see Mt 5:13–16)

Jesus uses the metaphors of salt and light to indicate that disciples must influence the world for good. Just as salt flavors food, committed disciples "flavor" the world with Christ's love. Christians are also like light because light dispels darkness. If the disciples share Jesus' love, they will attract notice like a city set on a mountain. If they do not, they are as useless as flavorless salt or a covered lamp.

External Observance of the Law Is Not Enough (see Mt 5:17–48)

The Old Law that God gave Moses on Mount Sinai prepared people for the Gospel. Jesus said that he did not come to abolish the Law and the prophets of the Old Testament but to fulfill them. Jesus stressed that external observance of the Law alone is not enough. (Does this remind you of the prophets' message? Clearly, their warnings were not heeded.) Jesus explained several ways to internalize God's Law:

- Jesus extended the Fifth Commandment prohibition against killing to include anger: "But I say to you, whoever is angry with his brother will be liable to judgment."

- Jesus said that if you have an enemy, you must reconcile with this person before approaching God in worship. This teaching makes sense in light of Jesus' connection between love of God and love of neighbor.

- Jesus affirmed the Sixth Commandment against adultery, but he went further and taught his disciples to avoid lust (defined in the *Catechism* as "a disordered desire or inordinate enjoyment of sexual pleasure" [*CCC*, 2351]). He also taught people to be faithful to each other in marriage and forbade lawfully married couples to divorce.

- Jesus said that true disciples of the Lord do not need to take oaths or swear. They should be truthful in all things, responding with a yes or a no.

- Jesus delivered two of the most difficult teachings of all. They are related: (1) refuse to retaliate against someone who is evil, and (2) love your enemies. The "eye for an eye" command existed in the ancient world to prevent a person from punishing an opponent too severely. Jesus called on his disciples not to retaliate at all. He also expected them to love their enemies.

Jesus set high standards for his followers, calling them to "be perfect, just as your heavenly Father is perfect" (Mt 5:48). From a human point of view, Jesus

seemed to be demanding the impossible. In reality, what he is calling you to do is to reach for perfection by being more loving and responsive to others. What is impossible for you to achieve by your own efforts is possible when you surrender to God's love and allow his Kingdom to be the center of your life.

Do Not Be a Hypocrite (see Mt 6:1–24)

Jesus warned against doing good deeds in order that others might see those deeds and admire you. Having good intentions is essential for moral living. Jesus instructed his followers to examine their motives when they performed virtuous works. Jesus tells you that his way to holiness is the path of humble love.

To emphasize this teaching, Jesus contrasted the way that hypocrites perform good works with the way that his disciples should perform them. While the hypocrites seek praise and attention ("blow trumpets") when giving alms, his followers should prevent one hand from knowing what the other one is doing. While the hypocrites pray in public, Jesus' followers should pray secretly in their rooms. Instead of looking gloomy like the hypocrites when fasting (that is, limiting food intake or other types of consumption for a religious cause), disciples should make a special effort to hide any outward signs of their fast.

Trust God (see Mt 6:25–34)

Jesus said that you should trust God because he will watch out for you. If the Father takes care of the birds in the sky and the flowers of the field by providing them with food, water, and nourishment, how much more will he watch over you, his children? Worrying about things you cannot control is empty and leads nowhere. If you make doing God's will your priority, then he will lead you and provide you with everything you truly need.

The Our Father

As with the Beatitudes, the Our Father or Lord's Prayer appears in both Matthew and Luke. In the Gospel of Matthew (6:9–13), Jesus gave the Lord's Prayer as an example while instructing his disciples to be authentic (not hypocritical) when they prayed, to speak to God without using a lot of empty words, and to pray with forgiveness in their hearts. Some have described the Lord's Prayer in Matthew's Gospel, directed to a Jewish-Christian audience, as "the Gospel in miniature."

In Luke's Gospel, the Lord's Prayer (11:2–4) appears right after Jesus prayed alone. His disciples then asked him how they should pray. Luke's Gentile-Christian audience did not have much experience with prayer. Luke presents the Lord's Prayer as a formula, the model prayer for followers of Jesus. Luke then relates two of Jesus' parables that emphasize the need to be persistent when you pray because God will surely answer your prayers. This may have been a new message for Gentile Christians, since they did not grow up with the Jewish experience of YHWH, who answered the prayers of his Chosen People.

Follow the Golden Rule (see Mt 7:1–29)

The last chapter of the Sermon on the Mount describes several requirements for Christian living, beginning with Jesus' admonition not to judge others. Jesus did not approve of those who thought they were morally superior to others. Just as God will forgive you as you forgive others, so he will judge you as you judge others.

Jesus instructed his disciples to trust God always, especially when they pray. God the Father knows what is good for you, and if you ask for it, he will grant it.

Jesus taught the **Golden Rule**, the summary of his Law of Love: "Do to others whatever you would have them do to you" (Mt 7:12). He warned about false prophets, perhaps a problem in the community for which Matthew wrote.

The Sermon on the Mount concludes with Jesus encouraging his listeners to take his words to heart and build their lives on them. These teachings are a solid foundation for a Christian life, a foundation that nothing can shake.

> **Golden Rule** Described by Jesus and recorded in Matthew 7:12: "Do unto others whatever you would have them do to you."

SECTION ASSESSMENT

NOTE TAKING

Use your outline of this section to help you answer the following questions.

1. What are the Beatitudes?
2. How are practicing Christians like salt and light?
3. In the Sermon on the Mount, what does Jesus have to say about giving alms, praying, and fasting?

APPLICATION

4. Give an example from your experience of a person who lives (or lived) by the Golden Rule.
5. If you and your classmates really put into practice Jesus' teaching about judging others, how might your high school change?

REFLECTION

6. Write a practical and contemporary definition of what it means to be "poor in spirit."

Section Summaries

Focus Question

What are the essential lessons of Jesus' teaching?

Complete one of the following:

Identify a profession or vocation in which you could shine, seek perfection, follow the Golden Rule, and "bear good fruit." (A *vocation* in this sense is a state of life, either married or consecrated to the service of God.) Explain.

Research the mission of Catholic school teachers. The National Catholic Educational Association is a good resource.

Explain why the Our Father can be understood as "the gospel in miniature."

INTRODUCTION (PAGES 217–218)

Good Teachers

Good teachers share common qualities, like passion for their subject matter, love for their students, desire to make their subject interesting, and the wherewithal to encourage and excite their students for learning. Jesus himself is the perfect teacher, who exhibits these same characteristics while leading all people to share and take part in his Good News.

Reflecting on your own skills, interests, and talents, how might Christ call you to be his ambassador?

SECTION 1 (PAGES 219–225)

Jesus the Teacher

Jesus possessed skills that made him a very effective teacher for the people of his time. He understood his listeners. He used a variety of effective teaching techniques and appealed to his listeners' senses. Jesus taught on his own authority, recognized when his opponents were trying to trap him, and used strong debating skills to respond.

Describe the differences between a teacher or speaker who does understand and connect with his or her audience and one who doesn't.

SECTION 2 (PAGES 226–233)

Jesus and the Kingdom of God

Jesus' brilliant use of parables helped him communicate important truths about the Kingdom of God. Because parables are stories, they were easy for listeners to remember, yet they challenged people by inviting them to look at reality in a new way. The parables had several recurring themes. The primary message of the parables is that the Kingdom of God is for all—sinners, the poor, and the lowly; that Jesus himself is Salvation; and that repentance is a prerequisite for entering the Kingdom.

 How many stories can you remember that you learned from your teachers?

SECTION 3 (PAGE 234–239)

Jesus' Sermon on the Mount

Jesus' Sermon on the Mount taught his disciples more about how to gain the Kingdom of God, stretched their understanding of the Law, explained how to worship with the proper motive, and taught them how to pray. The Beatitudes provided characteristics of people who would gain entrance to the Kingdom of God. Other teachings in the Sermon on the Mount encouraged Jesus' followers to continue to strive and search for perfection.

How do you define perfection for your own life? What excites you about the possibilities of being perfect?

Chapter Assignments

Choose and complete at least one of these assignments to assess your understanding of the material in this chapter.

1. Create a Guide for Living

Using ten of Jesus' teachings, create a resource to guide a person through middle school. For each teaching, write a paragraph applying the teaching to a facet of middle-school life, and add a one-to-two-sentence prayer. Format this resource in a way that would appeal to someone a few years younger than you. Arrange for a group to share your project with a religious education or Catholic grade school class.

2. Explore the Parables

Do one of the following activities on the parables:

- Write an original parable to exemplify one theme in the teaching of Jesus. Create your own artwork to illustrate your story.

- Rewrite the parable of the Good Samaritan in a modern urban setting.

- After choosing one of the parables from the synoptic Gospels, research at least two biblical commentaries to discover more about its meaning. Write a two-page report using appropriate footnotes. Conclude the paper with your own interpretation of the parable.

- With several other students, enact a skit of the parable of the Prodigal Son or the Good Samaritan. Set the skit in a contemporary setting.

3. Discover the *Anawim*

Read the following quotation:

Jesus Is the Parable

The real novelty of the New Testament lies not so much in new ideas as in the figure of Christ himself, who gives flesh and blood to those concepts—an unprecedented realism. In the Old Testament, the novelty of the Bible did not consist merely in abstract notions but in God's unpredictable and in some sense unprecedented activity.

This divine activity now takes on dramatic form when, in Jesus Christ, it is God himself who goes in search of the "stray sheep," a suffering and lost humanity. When Jesus speaks in his parables of the shepherd who goes after the lost sheep, of the woman who looks for the lost coin, of the father who goes to meet and embrace his prodigal son, these are no mere words: They constitute an explanation of his very being and activity.

—Pope Benedict XVI (*Deus Caritas Est*, 12)

Do the following:

Research the meaning of the term *anawim*. How are the *anawim* another way to describe the poor in spirit? Who are *anawim* in your community? How can you serve them? Write a one-page essay that describes them.

Faithful Disciple

St. Scholastica

St. Scholastica with her brother, St. Benedict

St. Scholastica was born in 480 into a wealthy Italian family. Her twin brother was St. Benedict of Nursia, the founder of the Benedictine order. Our information about Scholastica comes from another saint, the famous reformer St. Gregory the Great, who wrote about her in his *Dialogues*.

Gregory tells that Scholastica was dedicated to God from a young age. She was a nun who founded and led a community of women a few miles away from her brother's abbey at Monte Cassino.

Scholastica visited her brother near his abbey once every year; during the visit, they would spend time praying together and discussing sacred writings and topics. One year, sensing that her death was near, Scholastica asked Benedict to stay the night so that they might continue their conversations, but Benedict resisted because his own Rule said that he must stay in his room (known as a "cell") each night. So Scholastica bowed her head in prayer, and immediately a tremendous storm began outside of the place where they were, preventing Benedict from returning to the abbey. When Benedict asked Scholastica what she had done, she replied, "I asked a favor of you and you refused. I asked it of God and he granted it."

Scholastica died several days later. According to Gregory, Benedict saw her soul in the form of a dove leaving earth and ascending to Heaven. Benedict passed away shortly afterwards.

St. Scholastica is the patron saint of nuns and convulsive children, and people ask her intercession against storms and rain.[4]

Reading Comprehension

1. Where did St. Scholastica live?

2. How was St. Scholastica able to change her brother's mind about staying longer to speak with her?

244

ⓘ Writing Task

- Why might siblings from the same family each choose the religious life? Why might they choose different vocations from each other?

Explaining the Faith

Is God male? If not, then why do we address God as "Father"?

God is a pure Spirit beyond gender distinctions. God has both feminine and masculine characteristics, as evidenced by the fact that both men and women are created "in the image and likeness of God." (God is not in humanity's image.) When he taught the Lord's Prayer, Jesus called God his Father and invited everyone to do the same. That he would refer to God as Father when he could have used a number of other words and titles from Hebrew Scriptures is significant. It showed clearly that Jesus had come to earth to tell us about God, his Father and our Father.

❝❞ Reflection

- What are some human characteristics people attribute to God when they call him "Father"?

Prayer
The Lord's Prayer

The Lord's Prayer as it appears in the Gospel of Luke is slightly different from the version you are used to praying. Read and pray these words several times, meditating on each phrase:

> Father, hallowed be your name,
> your kingdom come.
> Give us each day our daily bread
> and forgive us our sins
> for we ourselves forgive everyone in
> debt to us,
> and do not subject us to the final test.
> —Luke 11:2–4

JESUS' MIRACLES
AND THE PASCHAL MYSTERY

Gloria's Miracle

Even after receiving the grim diagnosis of stage IV cancer, Gloria Strauss hoped to make it on *American Idol* some day and dreamed of being an actress after college. With her natural talent, gift for humor, and love for dancing, her nickname "Glow" seemed natural.

In 2007, by age eleven, she had already fought a virulent form of cancer called neuroblastoma for four years. She prayed for a miracle—God's healing—as did her parents, their parish community, and their friends and family. Gloria's mom, Kristen, said that God told her that he would heal Gloria and that she would change the lives of many people. Gloria said,

> I hope people get that it's going to be a miracle, and I'm going to make it. A lot of people will cry and go, "I really hope." I know for a fact that I'm going to make it. I'm really sure about that.

Many people talked about Gloria's generous heart. From her first chemotherapy treatments, she asked her family to give some of the toys and gifts she received to other children in the hospital. Gloria offered her suffering to God for the other children in the hospital. She prayed, "So I really just ask right now, dear Jesus, that you hold each and every one of us in your arms. Our bodies, hold them tight and squeeze them hard. Put us on your shoulders, so that we can feel it. Amen."[1]

A series of articles in *The Seattle Times* told Gloria's story and related her family's experience of the illness. These articles inspired people around the country to pray for her and to gain their own strength from Gloria's faith and courage. Gloria touched many people in big and small ways. Gloria inspired her cousin Michael to run a marathon, another cousin to quit smoking, a stranger across the country to stop drinking, another to return to church, and so on.

Gloria did pass away in September 2007. Soon after, Gloria's parents founded a nonprofit agency called Gloria's Angels, the mission of which is "to lift burdens with loving care." Support for a family with a sick member is most often patchy and disorganized. Gloria's Angels attempts to inform well-meaning people about how they can help. Gloria's Angels' staff assembles a group of people who are connected to the sick person and family and help them develop teams that will sustain the family's quality of life over the long haul by fundraising and scheduling meals, prayer, house repairs, and so on. While many were hoping for a miracle of healing for Gloria, Gloria and her family have inspired real miracles of a different kind.

Kristen Strauss, Gloria Strauss's mother

FOCUS QUESTION

How do MIRACLES AFFECT YOUR LIFE?

Chapter Overview

Introduction	**Miracles**
Section 1	**Jesus, the Miracle Worker**
Section 2	**Gospel Accounts of Jesus' Passion, Death, Resurrection, and Ascension**
Section 3	**Church Teaching on the Paschal Mystery**
Section 4	**The Paschal Mystery and Your Life**

Miracles

God continues to author miracles for the benefit of humankind.

God granted Gloria Strauss the grace to love life in the midst of a battle with cancer. She embodied faith and hope. She was ready for God to work a miracle through her on earth, but instead, in her own suffering and death, Gloria experienced a deep connection with the Paschal Mystery of Christ. This sharing of Christ's Passion and Death resulted in the miracle of Gloria sharing in his Resurrection as well. The miracle is also witnessed in the way her life impacted others.

God worked through Gloria to change the hearts of people she left behind. The way she handled her illness created miracles in the Strauss family's faith community: many people, both friends and strangers, came together to support the eight people who loved Gloria most: her parents and siblings. They not only came together to work, but they gathered to pray with hope that God could and would heal this little girl. Their spiritual lives grew.

Miracles for the World Today

Miracles are defined simply as signs or wonders that can be attributed to God. A true miracle has its source in God, whether the miracle suspends the laws of nature or whether ordinary events lead to extraordinary outcomes. An inexplicable healing has its origin in Christ the Healer. The greatest miracle is that God became a human being in Jesus and redeemed the world from the everlasting consequences of sin. The sacraments miraculously draw from the amazing miracle of the Paschal Mystery, taking away sin and putting you in communion with God. Each of these types of miracles can change your life. Gloria Strauss's

> **miracle** A powerful sign of God's Kingdom worked by Jesus.

NOTE TAKING

Applying Concepts. Use the basic definition of *miracle* from this section and the story of Gloria Strauss and Gloria's Angels to help you recall signs and wonders associated with God's action in your life. In words and images, name those times.

Dad's **NEW** Job      *YOSEMITE SUNSET*

life is evidence that miracles can and do occur today. (The image on page 251 is of the Grotto at Lourdes, France, where the Blessed Mother appeared to St. Bernadette Soubirous in 1858 and where many miraculous healings have resulted in the years since.) As you read more about miracles in this chapter, look for amazing ways that God is changing your own life.

In the example written about here, Gloria's Angels continues to facilitate God's miraculous way of bringing people together in his name. The organization is a blessing for families with sick loved ones as well as for the community, supporting them in physical and spiritual ways.

This chapter defines miracles and their place in the world today. All miracles lead to the Paschal Mystery, the ultimate miracle that has won forgiveness of sin and eternal life for you, as it did for Gloria. This chapter explains how you are called to live the pattern of the Paschal Mystery—life, suffering, death, and resurrection.

SECTION ASSESSMENT

NOTE TAKING

Use your notes to help you answer the following questions.

1. How do the experiences you named fit the definition of *miracle*?
2. Which experience most helps you to recognize God's presence in your life?

SECTION 1
Jesus, the Miracle Worker

MAIN IDEA
Each of the several types of miracles Jesus worked enabled people to understand who he was and to get a glimpse of the Kingdom of God.

Jesus' miracles healed people, showed them that the Kingdom of God was present in him, and proved that he was the Messiah.

Types of Miracles

Jesus performed several different types of miracles: physical healings, nature miracles, exorcisms, and raisings from the dead. He addressed particular problems and provided solutions for each type of problem.

Physical Healings

Jesus caused blind people to see, deaf people to hear, and lame people to walk. He cured dreaded skin diseases, healed a woman who bled for twelve years, and relieved others' suffering.

> When it was evening, after sunset, they brought to him all who were ill or possessed by demons. The whole town was gathered at the door. He cured many who were sick with various diseases, and he drove out many demons. (Mk 1:32–34)

Jesus performed miracles to confirm that God the Father sent him; he did not perform miracles on demand to satisfy people's curiosity or desire to see something magical. He wanted to strengthen people's faith in God and ease their pain and difficulties. Jesus had great sympathy for those who suffered.

NOTE TAKING

Refining a Definition. Create a flowchart like the one here. Before beginning your reading, write your own definition of a miracle in the first circle. As you read through this section, revise your definition as needed. Your last circle should reflect your most up-to-date definition.

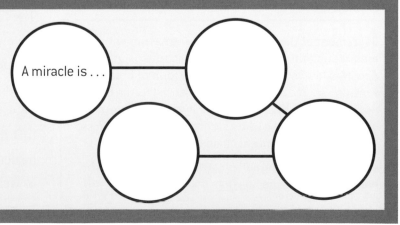

A miracle is . . .

Nature Miracles

Jesus demonstrated a miraculous mastery over the elements. He calmed a storm and walked on water. He cursed a fig tree that then withered. He changed water into wine. In another example, Jesus fed five thousand people on the shores of Lake Galilee with five loaves of bread and two fish. (Matthew and Luke record a second such miracle as well: the feeding of four thousand people.)

Jesus' feeding of the five thousand appears in all four Gospels and is probably very familiar to you (see image on page 253). According to the accounts in Matthew 14:15–21 and Luke 9:12–17, Jesus had gone to the Sea of Galilee to be by himself, but the people followed him there. Their faith moved Jesus, so he healed the sick among them. He also taught them about the Kingdom of God. When evening came, the disciples approached Jesus with a suggestion: "This is a deserted place and it is already late; dismiss the crowds so that they can go to the villages and buy food for themselves" (Mt 14:15).

Jesus wanted the people to stay, however, so he told his disciples to feed the crowd. This request confused the disciples; the available food for the whole crowd consisted only of five loaves of bread and two fish. Jesus instructed the disciples to bring him the food they had. He took it, looked up to Heaven, blessed and broke the loaves, and gave them to the disciples, who in turn distributed them to the crowds. "They all ate and were satisfied, and they picked up the fragments left over—twelve wicker baskets full" (Mt 14:20).

This miracle is meaningful in more than one way. First, notice the use of the number twelve, and think of some other times this number has featured prominently in the Old Testament and New Testament. The twelve baskets bring to mind the twelve tribes of Israel. As with Jesus' choice of Twelve Apostles, the use of twelve in relation to the baskets of leftovers connects Jesus' miracle to the Old Testament.

Also, Jesus' actions—blessing, breaking, and giving—point to the Last Supper and Jesus' institution of the Eucharist. This miracle foreshadows the **Sacrament of the Holy Eucharist**, a powerful sign of Christ's love for you on your earthly journey. The Holy Eucharist is the food that will sustain you until you reach the messianic banquet in God's Kingdom at the end of time.

Exorcisms

The Gospels describe evil spirits that tormented people and sometimes drove them to insanity. In Mark's Gospel, among Jesus' **exorcisms** was his expulsion of a legion (or multitude) of spirits from a suffering man. These spirits were transferred into a herd of swine that then ran off a cliff (see Mk 5:1–20). The Lord also healed a possessed man who was both blind and mute, as well as other people who may have had epilepsy.

> **Sacrament of the Holy Eucharist** The sacrament commemorating the Last Supper, at which Jesus gave his Apostles his Body and Blood in the form of bread and wine. The source and summit of Christian life, the Eucharist is one of the Sacraments of Initiation. It re-presents, or makes present, the Lord's sacrificial Death on the Cross. The word *eucharist* means "thanksgiving."
>
> **exorcism** A public and authoritative act, by Christ or in his name, to liberate a person from the devil.

"He took the child by the hand and said to her, 'Talitha koum,' which means, 'Little girl, I say to you, arise!'" (Mk 5:41).

The evil spirits or demons driven out in several of these miracles seemed to recognize Jesus. In Luke 4:31–37, Jesus cured a man possessed by an "unclean spirit" while he was teaching on the Sabbath in a synagogue in Capernaum. Those assembled were astonished at his teaching because he spoke with authority. The possessed man cried out, "Ha! What have you to do with us, Jesus of Nazareth? Have you come to destroy us? I know who you are—the Holy One of God!" (Lk 4:34). Jesus rebuked—that is, spoke sharply to—the demon and ordered him to be quiet and come out of the man. "Then the demon threw the man down in front of them and came out of him without doing him any harm" (Lk 4:35). The people who observed this powerful deed were amazed, saying, "What is there about his word? For with authority and power he commands the unclean spirits, and they come out" (Lk 4:36).

Jesus had and still has the power to make broken people whole. Significantly, Jesus had power over evil. Miracles of this kind made people ask themselves just who this man was.

Raisings from the Dead

Jesus brought several dead people back to life in the Gospels. According to all three synoptic Gospels, Jesus raised Jairus's daughter from the dead. Jairus, the head of a local synagogue in Galilee, sought Jesus out, fell at his feet, and begged him to come to his house and cure his dying daughter. Before Jesus reached the house, word came that the daughter had died. Jesus told Jairus, "Do not be afraid; just have faith" (Mk 5:36).

Reading and Interpreting Jesus' Miracles

On the following pages are a complete list of Jesus' miracles in the Bible. Work through the following steps to learn more about the miracles of Jesus:

1. Read all versions of each miracle listed in **boldface type** (e.g., "**Stilling of the Storm**").

2. Briefly summarize what took place and why the event is miraculous.

3. Assign each miracle to one of the four categories of miracle discussed in this section: physical healing, nature, exorcism, or raisings from the dead.

4. Interpret the deeper meaning of the miracle. How does it show God's *power*? What *significance* does it have; that is, what is it a sign of?

FEEDING OF THE FOUR THOUSAND
MT 15:32–39
MK 8:1–9

CHANGING WATER INTO WINE	HEALING OF THE NOBLEMAN'S SON	DISCIPLES' CATCH OF FISH	DEMONIACS OF GERASENE	HEALING OF THE BLEEDING WOMAN
			MT 8:28–34	MT 9:20–22
			MK 5:1–20	MK 5:24–34
JN 2:1–11	JN 4:46–54	LK 5:1–11	LK 8:26–39	LK 8:43–48

STILLING OF THE STORM	RAISING OF JAIRUS'S DAUGHTER	CURING THE BARREN FIG TREE	HEALING OF THE TWO BLIND MEN	HEALING OF THE POSSESSED MUTE
MT 8:23–27	MT 9:18–26			
MK 4:35–41	MK 5:21–43	MT 21:18–22		
LK 8:22–25	LK 8:40–46	MK 11:12–24	MT 9:27–31	MT 9:32–34

SECOND MIRACULOUS CATCH OF FISH	CLEANSING OF THE LEPER	HEALING OF THE PARALYTIC	HEALING OF MALCHUS'S EAR	HEALING OF THE CENTURION'S SERVANT
	MT 8:1–4	MT 9:1–8		
	MK 1:40–45	MK 2:1–12		MT 8:5–13
JN 21:1–14	LK 5:12–16	LK 5:17–26	LK 22:49–51	LK 7:1–10

RAISING OF THE WIDOW'S SON	WALKING ON WATER	DEMONIAC AT CAPERNAUM	HEALING OF THE BLIND AND MUTE MAN	HEALING AT THE POOL OF BETHESDA
	MT 14:22–23			
	MK 6:45–52	MK 1:23–27		
LK 7:11–17	JN 6:14–21	LK 4:33–36	MT 12:22	JN 5:1–15

FEEDING OF THE FIVE THOUSAND	HEALING OF THE TWO BLIND MEN AT JERICHO	HEALING OF SIMON'S MOTHER-IN-LAW	HEALING OF THE DEAF MAN WITH A SPEECH IMPEDIMENT	HEALING OF THE MAN'S WITHERED HAND
MT 14:15–21				
MK 6:34–44	MT 20:29–34	MT 8:14–15		MT 12:9–13
LK 9:12–17	MK 10:46–52	MK 1:29–31		MK 3:1–5
JN 6:5–14	LK 18:35–43	LK 4:38–39	MK 7:31–33	LK 6:6–11

HEALING OF THE SYROPHOE-NICIAN WOMAN'S DAUGHTER	HEALING OF THE MAN WITH DROPSY	FINDING THE COIN IN THE FISH'S MOUTH	OPENING THE EYES OF THE MAN BORN BLIND	HEALING OF THE WOMAN ON THE SABBATH
MT 15:21–28				
MK 7:24–30	LK 14:1–6	MT 17:24–27	JN 9:1–41	LK 13:10–17

HEALING OF THE BLIND MAN AT BETHSAIDA	CLEANSING OF THE TEN LEPERS	HEALING OF THE SUFFERING	RAISING OF LAZARUS	HEALING OF THE LUNATIC CHILD
				MT 17:14–21
				MK 9:14–29
MK 8:22–26	LK 17:11–19	MT 15:29–31	JN 11:1–54	LK 9:37–42

When Jesus reached the official's house, he found people weeping and wailing over the child's death. Jesus said to them, "Why this commotion and weeping? The child is not dead but asleep" (Mk 5:39).

People ridiculed his words, but this reaction did not deter Jesus. He took the child's father and mother with him as well as Peter, James, and John, and entered the child's room. Taking her by the hand, he commanded her to get up (see Mk 5:41). Immediately, the girl got up and started to walk around. This incredible deed of power over death utterly astounded those who witnessed it. As was typical of him, Jesus also ordered the witnesses to the miracle not to spread word about it. He did not want people to misunderstand his identity and his mission. He was the Messiah, but not a king intent on earthly power. He was the Suffering Servant who would die to save the people.

This miracle of raising the child from the dead, like all Jesus' miracles that brought people back to life, clearly foreshadowed the resurrected life of Jesus.

Miracle Skeptics

Some people who encountered Jesus felt offended because he would not work miracles on demand to satisfy their curiosity or to prove that he possessed the powers of a magician. Others refused to believe in him in spite of his great deeds. The Gospels indicate that Jesus differed from other people of his time who claimed to do miraculous things.

The Skeptics' Arguments

Jesus' adversaries had many "logical" explanations for his miracles. John's Gospel reports the story of a man Jesus cured of his blindness (see Jn 9:1–34). Jesus' opponents first claimed that the man was never blind to begin with. Then they took that claim back and acknowledged that Jesus could heal but gave the credit to Satan because, in their eyes, Jesus was a sinner. Yet this accusation made no sense. Why would someone doing miraculous *good* deeds actually be *evil*? Elsewhere, Jesus said, "Every kingdom divided against itself will be laid waste and house will fall against house" (Lk 11:17).

In today's secular society, skeptics deny the reality of supernatural events. They claim to debunk miracles with statements like these:

- It is impossible that God would suspend the laws of nature to get directly involved in the natural universe.

- Science can explain away apparent miracles, both those that Jesus performed and ones today.

- Jesus was nothing more than a clever healer who could diagnose people's mental disorders and say the right words to make them heal themselves.

- In the miracle of the loaves and fishes, Jesus did not multiply the loaves and fishes; he merely inspired the people to share their food.

- Jesus did not really raise anybody from the dead, but simply used a form of artificial respiration that revived an apparently dead person.

Notice how each of these explanations limits God's power. Jesus is the Second Person of the Blessed Trinity, truly God and truly man. God's power is unlimited. He is able to do *anything*. The real basis for some of this disbelief is denial of the divinity of Jesus or misunderstanding of Jesus' miracles in the context of the New Testament.

Historical Criticism's Response to Skepticism

There were other healers in Jesus' time in both the Jewish and Roman world, but Jesus was unique among them. The New Testament itself mentions other people who had the power to heal. Even so, historical criticism suggests that Jesus' miracles were distinctive in several ways:

- There is no record that anyone else cured such a variety of problems—blindness, paralysis, a severed ear, leprosy, and death.

- Jesus did not engage in any bizarre rituals to bring about the cures, as did so many of his contemporaries. He healed on his own authority, using his own power, and often stressing the need for the afflicted to have faith.

- Jesus did not perform miracles for pay.

Jesus' miracles were absolutely unequaled. He did his works out of the goodness of his heart and to further God's will.

Miracles in the New Testament Worldview

The premise of the New Testament is that God continues to work in human history. God cares for you and demonstrated this by sending his Son to live on earth. This is the real miracle of God's love—that God became human in Jesus Christ. The miracles that Jesus performed are powerful signs of God's compassionate love for you. Through these miracles, Jesus freed people from conditions resulting from Original Sin, such as disease, disability, or emotional distress. The greatest freedom that Jesus gives you, however, is freedom from the eternal effects of sin.

The New Testament uses three different but related words to describe miracles. The synoptic Gospels use the Greek word *dynamis*, which means "act of power." (Note how the English words *dynamic* and *dynamite* are derived from this word.)

On the other hand, John's Gospel uses the Greek words *ergon* ("work") and *semeion* ("sign") when referring to miracles. In John's Gospel, Jesus' "works and signs" reveal his glory, purpose, identity, and relationship to his Father. For John, Jesus' mighty works were both *power*ful and *sign*ificant. These three nouns tell you two important things about Jesus' miracles:

- Jesus' miracles revealed God's power.

- Jesus' works were signs of God's Kingdom.

The miracles also demonstrate these truths:

JESUS IS GOD.

Anyone who has God's power—over nature, over sickness and death, over Satan and the forces of evil, over sin itself—must be God himself. The miracles help show that Jesus is God's Son.

God's power has broken into human history.

God rules the natural world he created. When Jesus calmed the storm, for example, he demonstrated his connection to YHWH, the Master of the universe. The miracles help reveal who Jesus is and where he came from.

JESUS MASTERED SATAN AND THE FORCES OF DARKNESS.

When Jesus drove out demons, he revealed that God has power over sickness and the evil it brings upon people. When he raised someone from the dead, Jesus showed that God has power over the worst evil of all—eternal death. Jesus' miracles crushed Satan's power.

God's Kingdom is here, and Satan's kingdom is ending.

Sin, sickness, and death entered the world when Adam sinned. Jesus, the New Adam, has inaugurated God's Kingdom, where there will be no sickness and death.

JESUS HAD AND HAS POWER TO FORGIVE SINS.

Sin alienates you from God, other people, and yourself. When Jesus forgave sin, he was speaking for God.

PEOPLE WHO ENCOUNTERED JESUS

You should know something about how Jesus interacted with powerful people in his own time—the religious leaders—as well as some of the most oppressed people in his time—women. Jesus' approach to religious leaders and women differed significantly from that of others in his culture.

RELIGIOUS LEADERS IN THE GOSPELS

The Gospels mention two religious parties frequently: the Sadducees and the Pharisees. These were Jewish religious sects that were influential among the common people. Some of their members did not approve of Jesus and his message. It is helpful to know more about these sects and what they believed. Also be aware that other groups of Jewish leaders—such as elders, chief priests, and scribes—are mentioned in the Gospels. These people too had various roles to fulfill with the Jewish community. *Scribes*, for example, interpreted Jewish Law and transcribed the Torah (the Pentateuch). See below for more information about the Sadducees and Pharisees.

SADDUCEES	PHARISEES
OCCUPATION	
Sadducees were priests and aristocrats who cared for Temple practices and worship in Jerusalem. There were many Sadducees in the Sanhedrin.	Pharisees were experts in Jewish Law. The Pharisees preserved Judaism after the Romans destroyed the Temple in AD 70. They separated themselves from people who did not follow the Law closely.
BELIEFS	
The Sadducees believed that only the Torah was inspired. They did not believe in the resurrection of the dead, immortality, or angels. They interpreted the Law literally.	The Pharisees believed in resurrection, divine judgment, and the value of spiritual practices like prayer, fasting, and almsgiving. They developed an elaborate system of oral interpretation of the Law perceived to be almost as sacred as the Law itself. They believed that keeping the Law could earn them eternal life, and they claimed Mosaic authority over the Law.
NAME ORIGIN	
The word *Sadducee* comes from Zadok, the priest King Solomon appointed to care for the Ark of the Covenant.	The word *pharisee* means "separated ones"—those who distinguish themselves from lukewarm believers.
FOCUS	
The Temple	The Synagogue and the Torah
RELATIONSHIP TO ROMANS	
Sadducees collaborated with the Romans	Pharisees separated themselves from Gentile influence
OTHER	
Sadducees disappeared from Jewish life after the destruction of the Temple	Pharisees were in every neighborhood. They studied the Law, and their pious attempts to live it gave them influence over the common people. Although the Pharisees have a relatively poor reputation in the New Testament, many of them were very good and pious Jews. Some Pharisees, like St. Paul, later became staunch followers of Jesus.

WOMEN IN THE GOSPELS

Of course, half the people in Jewish society were female. By his own respectful actions, Jesus challenged the ways that his society treated them. Note the way women were commonly treated in first-century Jewish society in comparison to the revolutionary way Jesus interacted with and spoke of women during the same time.

HOW FIRST-CENTURY JEWISH SOCIETY VIEWED WOMEN	HOW JESUS VIEWED WOMEN
Men considered women to be property.	Jesus elevated the position of women, treating them in a revolutionary way.
A general male attitude toward women in Jesus' time was represented in a daily prayer recited by men: "Praised be God that he has not created me a Gentile; praised be God that he has not created me a woman; praised be God that he has not created me an ignorant man."	Women played an important role in Jesus' ministry.
In public, men were not supposed to speak with women who were not their wives, daughters, or sisters.	Jesus spoke in public with women who were not his relatives. • Jesus had friends who were women, such as Mary and Martha. He spoke to them in public. • Jesus' interaction with the Samaritan woman at the well surprised his Apostles.
A Jewish man could divorce his wife for any reason as long as he gave her a legal document saying she was free to remarry. It was much more difficult for a woman to divorce her husband.	When his enemies wanted him to take sides about divorce, Jesus simply forbade divorce altogether. He also told men to treat women with respect: "Everyone who looks at a woman with lust has already committed adultery with her in his heart" (Mt 5:28).
Women could not participate fully in religious devotions.	Jesus taught women and allowed them to follow him as disciples.
Women could not study the Torah (Law), and they only rarely learned to read or write. Women were not required to recite morning prayers, prayers at meals, and other Jewish prayers.	Jesus used positive female characters to illustrate his stories and sayings, something the rabbis of his day rarely did. Recall the woman in Luke's parable of the Lost Coin as an image of God. After his Resurrection, Jesus appeared first to Mary Magdalene.

Jesus responded to women's needs in several ways:

- He raised Jairus's daughter and the son of the widow of Nain.
- He responded compassionately to the heartfelt emotion of Mary and Martha when their brother Lazarus died.
- When his enemies wanted to trap Jesus into condemning a woman caught in adultery, Jesus forgave her instead and told her to sin no more.

- When his enemies criticized him for allowing a sinful woman to anoint his feet, Jesus refused to judge her negatively; rather, he told her to go in peace.

The way Jesus treated everyone with dignity reminds you that, in God's Kingdom, there are no second-class citizens. The way he treated others—with love, gentleness, strength, sensitivity, honesty, and humility—shows you how best to live as his brothers and sisters.

What does this mean for you? It means that you should put your faith in Jesus. Faith played a role in Jesus' miracles. On two occasions in Mark (5:34 and 10:52) and one in Luke (17:19), Jesus said, "Your faith has saved you." In some cases, miracles increased faith.

You should continue to work toward believing that your own resurrection will occur through Jesus. Jesus' Resurrection was a powerful sign that Jesus has power to conquer death for you.

SECTION ASSESSMENT

NOTE TAKING

Use the flowchart you made to help you answer the following questions.

1. How did reading this section lead you to refine your definition of a miracle? Explain.
2. Write your own definition of *miracle*.

COMPREHENSION

3. What were the four kinds of miracles Jesus performed?
4. Why would Jesus refuse to perform miracles on demand to satisfy people's curiosity?
5. What is the meaning of the miracle of the multiplication of the loaves and fishes?
6. What is the significance of the exorcisms performed by Jesus?
7. What did Jesus' healing of the synagogue official's daughter foreshadow?
8. Why was it ridiculous for Jesus' opponents to claim that Jesus' power to heal came from Satan?
9. How did Jesus differ from other wonder-workers of his time?

ANALYSIS

10. Which of the skeptics' arguments about miracles is the strongest, and which is the weakest? How would you refute each one?

REFLECTION

11. How does God work miracles today?
12. Give an example of a modern-day miracle.
13. Of the Sadducees and Pharisees, which sect do you think you would have identified with most if you lived in Jesus' time? Explain.
14. How does Jesus' treatment of women contain an important message for Christians today?

Gospel Accounts of Jesus' Passion, Death, Resurrection, and Ascension

MAIN IDEA

Several significant events recounted in the Gospels form the basis for belief in the Paschal Mystery.

Up to this point in the book, you have learned or reviewed important events in Jesus' life such as his birth, Baptism, temptation in the desert, and selection of his Apostles. You have learned that Jesus spent his time walking with his disciples in Galilee, teaching in various ways, and performing miracles to help people.

How did such a loving man end up dying on a cross? You can answer this question by reading the *Passion narratives*—the story, found in all four Gospels, of the events leading up to Jesus' Death.

The Passion or suffering of Jesus is a response to God's plan foretold in the Old Testament: "Christ died for our sins in accordance with the Scriptures" (1 Cor 15:3). Recall the *Protoevangelium*: God will defeat evil. The Passion narratives explain how God did defeat evil. The narratives begin when Jesus arrived triumphantly in Jerusalem and celebrated the Passover with his Apostles.

The Passion Narratives

Why call these events the "Passion narratives"? You are familiar with several meanings for the word *passion*. Passion can describe a person's intense devotion to a cause or describe the intensity of love. As used in the Passion narratives, however, the word *passion* has the

---

NOTE TAKING

Understanding Concepts. As you read through this section, keep a list of questions that you would like to ask an Evangelist about one of the important events from the Passion, Death, Resurrection, and Ascension of Jesus. Also think and write about how the Evangelists might really answer your questions.

Q&A for Evangelists
Example:
Q: Where did the Apostles (aside from Peter) go when Jesus was arrested, tried, condemned, and executed?
A: Most of them went back to their homes; some of them stood farther on the outskirts of the crowd than Peter.

---

meaning "to suffer," from the Greek *paschō*. Jesus did indeed suffer greatly during these historical events.

Jesus Enters Jerusalem

The palm branches you receive on Palm (or Passion) Sunday, the Sunday that opens Holy Week, commemorate Jesus' triumphant entry into Jerusalem in a manner befitting the type of Messiah many Jews had been expecting: a King of Glory. The people placed their capes and palm branches on the ground before him (Mt 21:8), a sign of honor somewhat like a red carpet, and asked Jesus to save them. This dramatic entry showed that the pivotal events of Jesus' Death and Resurrection and his coming Kingdom were nearing.

The Last Supper

The Passover meal that Jesus ate with his Apostles was his Last Supper. Remember that the annual Jewish Passover meal celebrated God's action to free the Israelites from slavery. Just as Exodus tells you that the Israelites celebrated the Passover meal prior to their liberation, Jesus celebrated the memorial of this Exodus event before he liberated humanity from sin and death. The central part of the Last Supper was the institution of the Sacrament of the Holy Eucharist. The Eucharist would be the memorial of Jesus' sacrifice.

> While they were eating, Jesus took bread, said the blessing, broke it, and giving it to his disciples said, "Take and eat; this is my body." Then he took a cup, gave thanks, and gave it to them, saying, "Drink from it, all of you, for this is my blood of the covenant, which will be shed on behalf of many for the forgiveness of sins." (Mt 26:26–28)

The Agony in the Garden

After the Passover meal, Jesus went to a garden called Gethsemane with several Apostles to spend time in prayer before his arrest, torture, and Death. As Jesus contemplated the horror of Death, he recoiled. Unfortunately, his Apostle companions could not stay awake to comfort him through this desperate time.

The Apostle Judas identified and thus betrayed Jesus to the authorities with a kiss, usually a sign of friendship. Jesus did not use violence to resist his arrest, though the Apostle Peter cut off the ear of the high priest's servant (Jn 18:10). In Matthew's Gospel, Jesus says, "Put your sword back into its sheath, for all who take the sword will perish by the sword" (Mt 26:52). The Prince of Peace refused to be a political or military Messiah.

Before the Sanhedrin

The Gospel accounts all relate that after his arrest, Jesus had a hearing before the **Sanhedrin**, where the high priest, Joseph Caiaphas, and other priests interrogated him. False witnesses testified against him. In Mark's Gospel, Jesus acknowledged that he was the Christ, the Son of the Living God, predicting that the Son of Man would come in glory. This acknowledgment led the Jewish authorities to accuse Jesus of **blasphemy**, a sin but also a crime punishable by death under Jewish Law. They believed him to be a **false prophet**. They then spat on, struck, and ridiculed him.

Meanwhile, out in the courtyard, Peter three times denied knowing Jesus, as Jesus had predicted he would. When the rooster crowed the third time, Peter realized what he had done, broke down, and wept (see Lk 22:54–62). Peter, the one who had acknowledged Jesus

---

Sanhedrin The seventy-one-member supreme legislative and judicial body of the Jewish people during Jesus' life on earth. Many of its members were Sadducees.

blasphemy Any thought, word, or act that expresses hatred or contempt for God, Christ, the Church, saints, or holy things.

false prophet A person who claims to speak in the name of God without being inspired by him.

Pilate questioned Jesus: "Are you the King of the Jews?" (see Jn 18:33).

to be the Messiah and Son of God, had turned his back on his Lord out of fear.

Pilate Condemns Jesus to Death

In lands under Roman occupation, only the Romans had the authority to approve the death penalty. According to Roman law, blasphemy was not a capital crime (that is, punishable by death). *Sedition* (creating a revolt against civil leaders), however, was a capital offense. Even though the Jewish authorities condemned Jesus for blasphemy, they redefined the charges against him as sedition when they went to the Roman prefect, Pontius Pilate. They told Pilate that Jesus was claiming to be a king in competition with Caesar.

Pilate had been appointed by the governor to rule over part of the Roman Empire, in this case Judea. Secular history recognizes Pilate as a competent leader, but one also capable of harshness and arrogance. The Gospels indicate that Pilate recognized Jesus' innocence but tried to escape personal responsibility for his Death by invoking a Passover custom of freeing one

prisoner of the citizens' choosing, no doubt thinking that they would choose Jesus. But Pilate had miscalculated, because the Jewish people, inflamed by their leaders, asked for freedom for Barabbas, a convicted murderer. Pilate caved in to crowd pressure, pronounced Jesus guilty, sentenced him to crucifixion, and told his men to scourge him—that is, to whip him severely. He then turned Jesus over to the soldiers, who mocked him by calling him the "King of the Jews." (Unknowingly, the soldiers spoke the truth, because Jesus is king not only of the Jews but of the entire universe.)

The Way of the Cross

You are likely familiar with the Stations of the Cross, a devotion of contemplating fourteen different stages of Jesus' suffering. People who received the sentence of *crucifixion* often carried the horizontal beam of their cross to the place of execution. The vertical beam was already in the ground at Golgotha or Calvary, the hill outside Jerusalem where these executions took place. Crucifixion not only prolonged the sentenced person's agony, but it also allowed other citizens to watch and learn what would happen if they broke Roman law. Historical criticism indicates that the Gospel description of Jesus' crucifixion was typical of Roman executions of the time. In Jesus' day, crucifixion consisted of stretching a person's arms on the crossbeam and nailing or tying the person's extremities to the wood. The Romans would also crucify people upside-down.

The traditional image of Jesus' wrists and feet nailed to a cross in an elongated plus sign is historically plausible. Whether Jesus' Cross had a support for his feet or a seat for his buttocks is hard to determine. The purpose of the support on the vertical beam was to keep the victim breathing and thus prolong the agony. Ultimately, crucifixion resulted in a horrible death, usually by dehydration, loss of blood, shock, or respiratory arrest due to suffocation.

The Church of the Holy Sepulcher in Jerusalem is believed to house Jesus' tomb as well as Golgotha, the place where he was crucified. Roman emperor Constantine had the church built after his mother, Helena, discovered what she believed to be the true cross and tomb on the site.

As stated above, the condemned usually carried their own horizontal crossbeams. The scourging had so severely weakened Jesus, however, that at some point he was no longer able to carry his Cross. The soldiers enlisted a bystander, Simon of Cyrene, to help carry it.

Jesus' time on the Cross was painful and humiliating. He refused to take the wine mixed with myrrh offered for pain relief, so he experienced the full pain of the crucifixion. An inscription written in Hebrew, Greek, and Latin ironically advertised Jesus' crime as having claimed to be the "King of the Jews." Bystanders mocked and taunted Jesus. Among the last words he spoke came from Psalm 22:1, "My God, my God, why have you forsaken me?" (Mt 27:46). Observers thought he was calling on Elijah for help, showing that people continued to misunderstand who Jesus was.

Jesus' Death and Burial

Not everyone abandoned Jesus at the end. Matthew's Gospel reports that there were many women looking on from a distance, including Mary Magdalene, Mary the mother of James and Joseph, and the mother of the sons of Zebedee (see Mt 27:55–56). Mark reports that the women looking on from a distance included Mary Magdalene, Mary the mother of the younger James and of Joses, and Salome (see Mk 15:40–41), while Luke refers to them collectively as "his acquaintances . . . including the women who had followed him from Galilee and saw these events" (Lk 23:49).

After Jesus cried out, he breathed his last. The veil in the Temple sanctuary was torn into two pieces, top to bottom. Amazed by the earthquakes and tombs opening after Jesus' Death, a Roman centurion and his men professed, "Truly this man was the Son of God!" (Mt 27:54). Is it not ironic and interesting that a Gentile understood and recognized Jesus, while many of his fellow Jews and closest followers did not?

Joseph of Arimathea, a member of the Sanhedrin and secret follower of Jesus, asked Pilate for permission to bury Jesus. The women who had witnessed Jesus' crucifixion also participated by preparing spices and oils to anoint him (see Lk 23:55–56). According to the Gospel of Matthew, Pilate stationed a guard at the tomb to prevent the disciples from stealing Jesus' body (see Mt 27:65).

Jesus' Resurrection

The Resurrection was a mysterious, real event that surprised Jesus' disciples. The Gospels of Matthew and Mark relate that Mary Magdalene, another Mary, and Salome (in Mark) went to the tomb on Sunday morning to anoint Jesus' body. They had not carried out this Jewish burial custom on the night of Jesus' Death because their first opportunity to do so had come after sunset on Friday, when the Jewish Sabbath had begun and no work was to be done. Matthew reports that after the women arrived at the tomb, an angel told the women that "Jesus is risen," instructing them to go to Galilee to meet the other Apostles.

In Luke's Gospel, after the women told the Apostles the news, the Apostles did not believe them. Peter, however, ran to the tomb to see for himself and was amazed when he found the tomb open and only the burial cloths inside. The first step toward belief in the Resurrection occurred when the disciples discovered that Jesus' tomb was empty. But the Apostles and other disciples came to believe in the Resurrection when they actually *saw* Jesus.

The reality is that the Apostles had doubts about the Risen Jesus, thinking he was a ghost or being stubborn in their disbelief like the Apostle Thomas. By allowing Thomas to touch his wounds and by eating with the Apostles, Jesus helped them see that he was the same man who had been crucified. Face-to-face meetings with the Risen Lord transformed the frightened and disillusioned disciples into bold eyewitnesses who spread the Good News of Jesus Christ far and wide. Their testimony, aided by the Holy Spirit's gifts of faith and fortitude, led many of them to suffer martyrdom for their firm conviction and belief that Jesus Christ rose from the dead.

More details of the Resurrection are included in all four Gospels and in other places in the New Testament. Jesus appeared to his disciples several times after the Resurrection prior to his Ascension to Heaven. These visits are known as "post-Resurrection appearances" and are summarized here:

- Jesus appeared to two followers on the road to Emmaus, although they did not recognize him until they shared a meal together.

- Jesus appeared to Mary Magdalene.

- Jesus appeared to the Apostles in the upper room twice.

- In the First Letter to the Corinthians, St. Paul lists various people to whom Jesus appeared. These people include Peter, the Twelve Apostles, five hundred other disciples (some of whom were still living when Paul wrote his letter), James, and all the Apostles yet again.

- Jesus appeared to Saul, a Pharisee known for persecuting Christians. After this experience, Saul became St. Paul (see 1 Cor 15:1–11).

The Ascension of Jesus

Forty days after Jesus rose from the dead, he ascended or "was taken up" into Heaven to sit at the right hand of God the Father and to be glorified. The Gospel of Luke provides the fullest account of the Ascension (see Lk 24:50–52). In the Acts of the Apostles, Luke reports that Jesus appeared to the disciples over a period of forty days after his Resurrection. Right before he was lifted up and taken from their sight, Jesus promised to send them the Holy Spirit. Two messengers in white garments were standing there with the Apostles and told them that Jesus would return one day the same way he went into Heaven (see Acts 1:6–12).

SECTION ASSESSMENT

NOTE TAKING

Use your notes to help you answer the following questions.

1. What is the question you would you most like to ask an Evangelist? What do you think he would say in reply?

VOCABULARY

2. What does the word *passion* in the phrase "Passion narratives" mean?
3. Define *blasphemy*.
4. Why did the Jewish priests accuse Jesus of blasphemy?
5. Define *Eucharist*.

COMPREHENSION

6. Why was the Jewish feast of Passover an appropriate occasion for the Last Supper?
7. To whom did Jesus appear first after his Resurrection?

REFLECTION

8. How was Judas's kiss of Jesus symbolic of his betrayal?
9. What evidence have you seen to support Jesus' statement that "all who take the sword will perish by the sword"?
10. What do you think were some of the thoughts that went through the Apostles' minds after Jesus' crucifixion?

SECTION 3
Church Teaching on the Paschal Mystery

MAIN IDEA
The Paschal Mystery of Jesus Christ is central to the Christian faith and to your Redemption.

You have read about the events of Salvation History beginning with the covenants in the Book of Genesis. All of Salvation History led up to the coming of Jesus Christ, whose mission is completed in the Resurrection. By conquering death, Christ restored humanity's relationship with God that was destroyed by Original Sin; after physical death, human beings can once again be in an intimate relationship with God. This new relationship will no longer exist in a garden paradise, but in Heaven.

The Apostles did not know what to expect after Jesus' Death. Fear of arrest and persecution overwhelmed them, so they hid in Jerusalem. When some women they knew reported they had seen the tomb empty, at first the Apostles did not believe them. As time passed, they realized that the events of their last days with Jesus had even more meaning than the other years they had spent together. These last events of the Paschal Mystery are so rich in meaning that it is important to treat them separately so you can better understand their significance. The Paschal Mystery has two aspects. First, by his Death, Jesus liberated you from sin. Second, through his Resurrection, Jesus opened the way for a new way to live.

NOTE TAKING

Summarizing Material. As you read through this section, keep notes by writing two theological truths connected to each event:

Jesus' Death	1. Jesus died because all humans sinned. 2.
Descent into Hell	1. 2.
Resurrection	1. 2.
Ascension	1. 2.
Second Coming of Christ	1. 2.

{defining the}
Paschal Mystery

Understanding the meaning of the Paschal Mystery is essential to being a Christian. Breaking down the meaning of both words can help you to better comprehend why the Paschal Mystery is so significant.

The first word, *Paschal*, comes from the Jewish word for Passover, *pasch*, which points to a journey from slavery to freedom like the Israelites had in the Book of Exodus. When Christians use the word *Paschal*, however, they are usually referring to the Easter celebration of the Resurrection of Christ—though without losing the meaning of a passage from slavery to freedom and new life.

Recall that one meaning of *mystery* is "God's saving plan." The events leading up to Easter were clearly part of God's plan to save his people. Even though Jesus had mentioned to his friends that he would suffer and die, even his closest disciples, the Apostles, did not understand what was going on. They did not understand God's plan until after the Resurrection. In the time between the crucifixion and the Resurrection, Jesus' Death just seemed to be a plan gone very wrong.

A second meaning of *mystery* is "something that is hidden." Even when the Apostles had a greater sense of God's plan after the Resurrection, they could never *fully* understand its meaning. Although the Father did send the Son to earth to walk and talk like you, God's ways are always far above human ways, and aspects of the truth will remain hidden.

The divine plan, the Paschal Mystery, was accomplished for all time by the redemptive Passion, Death, Resurrection, and Ascension of Jesus Christ. The Paschal Mystery is at the center of the Good News that the Apostles, and the Church after them, needed to proclaim to the world. The Paschal Mystery of Christ's sacrifice repaired the broken relationship between God and humans in the New Covenant.

The Meaning of Jesus' Death

Jesus died to liberate you from sin.

It has probably never occurred to you to blame Jews today for what the Jewish leaders did to Jesus two thousand years ago. Unfortunately, many Christians in history have wrongly blamed Jesus' Death on the Jewish people as a whole. The Passion narratives reveal that Jesus' trial was complex. Even then, only a few Jewish leaders opposed Jesus and collaborated with Pontius Pilate to crucify Jesus. In fact, some Pharisees (like the leading figure of Nicodemus) and a prominent ally in the Sanhedrin (Joseph of Arimathea) were Jesus' strong supporters.

Sin is responsible for Jesus' crucifixion. The real authors and instruments of Jesus' crucifixion are sinners—that is, every human being.

You may wonder why Jesus had to die in order to save you. The Passion of Jesus is a response to God's plan foretold in the Old Testament. Remember what God said to the snake (Satan) as he expelled Adam and Eve from the Garden (the *Protoevangelium*):

I will put enmity between you and the woman,
and between your offspring and hers;
They will strike at your head,
while you strike at their heel. (Gn 3:15)

God said that a human would defeat the power of evil. The Passion narratives explain how God did defeat evil through his Son, Jesus Christ.

It is important to understand some key theological truths about Jesus' Death.

- Jesus' Death was part of God's plan. It was not a random act. God does not experience time and space as you do. He knew ahead of time that some Jewish leaders would collaborate with Pontius Pilate to kill Jesus. God allowed this to happen to fulfill his plan of Salvation.

- Jesus' Death was consistent with Jewish belief, even though not all Jews accepted Jesus as the Messiah and the Son of God. Referring to the Old Testament, St. Paul said, "Christ died for our sins in accordance with the scriptures" (1 Cor 15:3). Recall the prophet Isaiah's verses about the Suffering Servant and what he would endure (see page 161). As you have seen, God the Father, especially through his prophets, reassured the Chosen People that they would experience Salvation.

- The Father did not force his son to die; rather, Jesus died freely out of love for you. How can you be assured of this? Here are four ways:

  1. Out of an immense love for you, Jesus, like many prophets before him, headed to Jerusalem knowing he would die.

  2. Throughout his entire life, Jesus obediently embraced his Father's will, courageously accepting his mission and the plan of redeeming love.

  3. John the Baptist pointed out that Jesus was the Lamb of God (Jn 1:29), thus showing not only that Jesus was the Suffering Servant, but also that he willingly took on the role of the Paschal Lamb, the symbol of Israel's redemption at the first Passover.

  4. Jesus loves sinful humans as much as his Father and wanted to save you from the consequences of sin and provide you with the opportunity to live in communion with the Holy Trinity now and forever.

- Jesus did not have any illusions about human holiness, for "while we were still sinners, Christ died for us" (Rom 5:8). Jesus loves you. Love is what makes Jesus' act of **reparation** so powerful. Jesus' unique sacrifice is the source of eternal Salvation

> **reparation** Repairing a relationship by making amends for a personal wrong or injury. A secular meaning of reparation is to take financial responsibility for damaging someone's property.

for all. "For just as through the disobedience of one the many were made sinners, so through the obedience of one the many will be made righteous" (Rom 5:19). Jesus is the Suffering Servant from Isaiah who makes himself an offering for sin, substituting for you.

- Jesus asked his Apostles to memorialize his voluntary offering of himself to the Father for your Salvation in the Sacrament of the Eucharist. Jesus' offer of his Body and Blood as he instituted the Eucharist at the Last Supper prefigured the death he would freely undertake out of love for humanity. By celebrating this memorial with his Apostles, he made the Apostles priests of the New Covenant.

- Jesus Christ died for all human beings. Throughout the Old Testament, the Jewish people were prophesied to be the means through which *all* people came to God:

  > I, the LORD, have called you for justice,
  >
  > I have grasped you by the hand;
  >
  > I formed you, and set you
  >
  > as a covenant for the people,
  >
  > a light for the nations. (Is 42:6)

- The Father did not condemn Jesus as if Jesus, himself, had sinned. Rather, Jesus lived in solidarity with sinners. He experienced much human suffering and even Death on the Cross in solidarity with humanity's sufferings. Jesus' lack of sin made it possible for him to ransom humanity from death, the punishment for sin. Jesus' sacrifice was not only a gift from God the Father to sinful humanity, but also a gift of the Son to his Father who offered himself out of love.

- Humans could not have saved themselves from death. Jesus is the only being who could offer himself up to save you from sin. Not even the holiest of humans could take upon himself or herself the sins of the world.

- Jesus died like a human being, yet his Death also differed in a mysterious way. In God's plan of Salvation, Jesus was to taste death, the separation of his soul from his body, just as all humans do. This does not mean, however, that Jesus somehow lost his human body or became two persons. Jesus' stay in the tomb linked his prior human body to his glorious and risen body after the Resurrection. Given these similarities to human death, it is important to realize that death could not hold Jesus and that his body did not begin to decay.

Why Jesus Descended into Hell

Jesus' descent into Hell was part of his conquest of death. Since the expulsion of Adam and Eve from the Garden, the souls of everyone who died—"good" and "bad"—were in a place that was not necessarily subject to time and space as humans know it. These souls were neither connected to God, nor were they punished. They just remained dead after their physical death on earth.

Jesus changed this reality. Jesus made life come from the depths of death. Jesus' soul joined the other dead souls after his Death. He went to share the Good News with those who were in the realm of the dead,

JESUS' *Last Words*

The Gospels report several of Jesus' last words. Each saying in some way typifies the way he lived. Each example helps you form a deeper connection with the mystery of Christ's saving Death.

"Father, forgive them, they know not what they do." (Lk 23:34)

In his dying moments, Jesus showed the loving forgiveness that characterized his entire ministry. He died as he lived. His forgiveness extends not only to those who crucified him, but to everyone. All human beings are sinners, implicated in the Death of Christ.

"Amen, I say to you, today you will be with me in Paradise." (Lk 23:43)

Jesus assures the good thief hanging on the cross next to him of Salvation on the very day it is accomplished for everyone. In his own moment of suffering, Jesus' thoughts were on others.

"Woman, behold, your son. . . . Behold, your mother." (Jn 19:26, 27)

Jesus showed concern for his Mother in his dying moments. He also entrusted his Mother to the Church, represented by the beloved disciple, believed to be John. Thus, by Jesus' desire, Mary is Mother of the Church.

"Eli, Eli, lema sabachthani?" . . . "My God, my God, why have you forsaken me?" (Mt 27:46)

Here Jesus prayed Psalm 22, but he did not despair as some of the bystanders thought. These lines suggest that he prayed the entire Psalm, which ultimately proclaims God's mercy to his Suffering Servant.

"I thirst." (Jn 19:28)

John includes these words to show that Jesus fulfilled a prophecy about the Messiah: "For my thirst, they gave me vinegar" (Ps 69:22). Jesus accepted the agony of Death until the divine plan was fulfilled.

"It is finished." (Jn 19:30)

The plan of Salvation had been accomplished: Jesus' work of preaching the Good News, working miracles, and bringing Salvation to all was now complete. Jesus allowed sin and death to overcome him, but by his Resurrection, he overcame both. God's will for Jesus included his Death on the Cross, but it also included the magnificent Resurrection to superabundant life and the remission of sin through his Son.

"Father, into your hands I commend my spirit." (Lk 23:46)

Jesus quoted Psalm 31 here. He entrusted his life to his Father in an act of supreme faith and love. With these words, Jesus Christ stood for all people; he feared death, but trusted his Father to rescue him out of the depths. He gave to his Father his very life on behalf of all. Thus, his Death became the perfect proof of God's love.

which meant that he preached the Good News to people of all time. He offered them eternal life.

Though the Apostles' Creed says that Jesus descended into Hell (see page 360), he did so not to save those who had freely chosen on their own to be eternally separated from God, but rather to save the just and righteous people who had been waiting for a Savior. By going into the depths of death, Jesus was able to give eternal life to the just among the dead, thus defeating Satan, the Lord of death.

The Meaning of the Resurrection

The Resurrection was at the same time a historic event and a mysteriously transcendent breakthrough of Christ's humanity into the glory of God. In addition, the Resurrection opened the way to new life for you. Without the Resurrection, there would be no New Testament and no Catholic Church. You wouldn't be reading this book. St. Paul put it this way: "If Christ has not been raised, then empty [too] is our preaching; empty, too, your faith" (1 Cor 15:14). As the *Catechism of the Catholic Church* teaches,

> The Resurrection of Jesus is the crowning truth of our faith in Christ, a faith believed and lived as the central truth by the Christian community; handed on as fundamental by Tradition; established by the documents of the New Testament; and preached as an essential part of the Paschal mystery along with the cross. (*CCC*, 638)

THE RESURRECTION IS IMPORTANT FOR YOU FOR SEVERAL REASONS:

1. The Resurrection gives you confidence in all of Christ's works and teaching, because it proves that he is divine.

2. The Resurrection tells you that promises from the Old Testament and Jesus' own words are authentic.

3. Jesus' Resurrection makes possible and gives you hope for your own future resurrection.

4. The Resurrection further reveals the unending loving communion of God as Trinity: the Father glorifies the Son, the Son makes a sacrifice that merits this glory, and the Holy Spirit contributes life and resurrection.

Jesus' glorified body did not have the same restrictions of time and space as his body before death. The *Catechism* puts it this way: "In his risen body he passes from the state of death to another life beyond time and space" (*CCC*, 646). It is important to realize that Jesus did not return to ordinary life like Lazarus did after Jesus raised him. The Resurrection was a historical event; at the same time, it transcends human experience and remains present to you today.

Theological Truths of the Ascension

The Ascension of Jesus refers to the time when Jesus stopped appearing to his disciples in visible, human form. Jesus in his glorified resurrected body went up to Heaven to sit at the Father's right hand in even greater glory. The Ascension marks the end of Jesus' time on earth. Yet Jesus also promises to come again (see Jn 16:22).

Jesus is present and active today in the Church and in the sacraments, especially the Eucharist. From Heaven, Jesus advocates for you to the Father. Jesus' return to his Father's heavenly Kingdom gives you and other members of the body of Christ the hope of one day joining him there for eternity.

Jesus' presence in Heaven inaugurated the transition from Christ's risen presence on earth to his presence at his Father's right hand.

The Second Coming of Christ

At Jesus' Ascension, the angels told the Apostles that the Lord would come again. They were referring to a future event called the **Parousia**, when Jesus will arrive on earth in all his glory. In a Memorial Acclamation at Mass, the Church prays: "We proclaim your Death, O Lord, and profess your Resurrection until you come again."

Christians look forward to the Parousia and proclaim belief in it in her creeds. On that day, the world you know will end. All of God's creatures everywhere will acknowledge that Jesus is Lord. The glorious Lord Jesus will then fully bring about the Father's Kingdom of justice, love, and peace. Jesus said that the time and date when this will take place is already hidden in God's almighty plan. However, you should be ready at all times. "Be watchful! Be alert! You do not know when the time will come" (Mk 13:33).

All of the events surrounding the Paschal Mystery marked a transition for the Apostles from being Jesus' followers to being his witnesses in the new era of the Church. The early Church grew in great part because there were eyewitnesses to these events—especially the Resurrection—who in turn told new believers about Jesus. St. Paul mentions that Jesus also appeared to others in addition to the women and the Apostles.

Annually, the Church remembers these events during Holy Week. You know that Palm Sunday begins Holy Week and that you celebrate Jesus' Last Supper on Holy Thursday and his Death on Good Friday. Easter, the most important feast on the Church calendar, celebrates the Resurrection of Christ.

> **Parousia** A Greek term for the Second Coming of Christ, when the Lord will judge the living and the dead.

SECTION ASSESSMENT

NOTE TAKING

Review the notes you made on the theological truths connected to the Paschal Mystery. Then answer these questions.

1. Why did Jesus have to die in order for you to be saved?
2. Name another key theological truth about Jesus' Death.
3. Why did Jesus descend to Hell?
4. Why is it accurate to say that without the Resurrection there would be no New Testament or Christianity?
5. What transition did Jesus go through during the Ascension?

VOCABULARY

6. Describe the Parousia.

COMPREHENSION

7. What are two aspects of the Paschal Mystery?
8. How do you know that Jesus died freely?
9. How does the Church annually celebrate the events of the Paschal Mystery?

ANALYSIS

10. How is the Paschal Mystery related to the events of Genesis?

REFLECTION

11. Has your understanding of the Paschal Mystery changed after reading this section? If so, how?

SECTION 4
The Paschal Mystery and Your Life

The graces of the Paschal Mystery are not limited to eternal life, but rather offer you many blessings now, especially in the sacraments.

Through the Paschal Mystery, God has saved you from sin and has given you the opportunity for eternal life with him. Although you may understand the consequences of the Paschal Mystery for you *after* your physical death, you may not be as familiar with the impact of the Paschal Mystery on your everyday life right now.

Salvation from Sin

You still commit sins even though Christ died to save the world from sin. Everyone does. Jesus has made it possible to be saved from the everlasting consequences of Original Sin, including a weakened human nature that is subject to ignorance, suffering, and death, and an inclination to sin known as *concupiscence*. To avoid concupiscence, Jesus has given you **graces** through the Holy Spirit to help fend off sin and Satan. However, because of human freedom, it is still possible to make sinful choices and suffer those consequences. Christ's grace in the Paschal Mystery has **justified** you and has given you the freedom to avoid sin and the strength to grow in holiness. Christ's grace can restore the damage that sin has done to you.

concupiscence An inclination to commit sin that arises from a disordered human desire or appetite. It is one of the temporal consequences of Original Sin that remains even after the Sacrament of Baptism.

graces Free and undeserved gifts that God gives people to respond to their vocation to become his adopted children.

justified To be justified is to receive remission for sins, sanctification, and inner renewal through the gracious action of God.

NOTE TAKING

Understanding Main Ideas. As you read this section, keep notes in a diagram like the one here on how the rites and graces of the sacraments help you to connect with the Paschal Mystery.

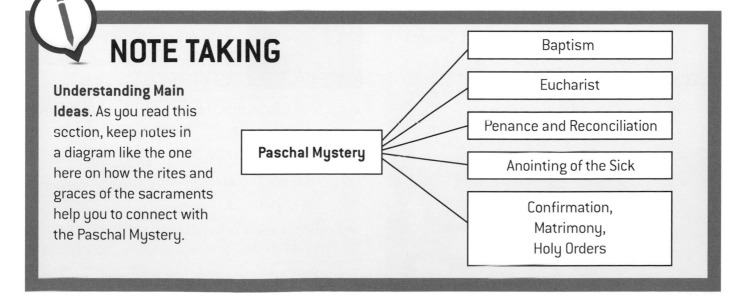

Paschal Mystery
- Baptism
- Eucharist
- Penance and Reconciliation
- Anointing of the Sick
- Confirmation, Matrimony, Holy Orders

BEING HOSPITABLE

Jesus welcomed everyone and challenges you to do the same. This is done by practicing the virtue of hospitality, a virtue that extends a friendly and generous welcome to strangers and guests.

Today, there are both *shut-ins* and *shut-outs*. Shut-ins are housebound because of age, sickness, or some other inability to get around. Shut-outs are people who are ignored and not included in certain groups simply because of who they are.

"I was . . . a stranger and you welcomed me" (Mt 25:35). When you are welcoming to others, Jesus promises you the gift of eternal life.

- With a partner, devise some practical strategies to show hospitality to shut-ins and shut-outs. Create a list of ten concrete things you can do. (For example, you can befriend a classmate who is lonely, invite a lonely classmate to join your extracurricular activity, engage in a conversation with a neighbor with whom you have never spoken, or visit a person who is bedridden.) Put at least one of your strategies into effect during the coming week. Report on what happened.

The Sacraments and the Paschal Mystery

Jesus can heal you from the effects of your own sins and the sins of others. You and your classmates did not grow up in perfect families. You may have experienced painful loss through divorce or death. In an imperfect world, you encounter lies, violence, discrimination, poverty, and disappointments of all kinds. Bring these wounds to Jesus in the sacraments for healing and transformation, an important blessing of the Paschal Mystery.

Your life is bound up in the ongoing pattern of the Paschal Mystery, including "little deaths"—experiences like pain and suffering—as well as "little resurrections" of joy and happiness that offer glimpses of God's eternal Kingdom. The Seven Sacraments of the Catholic Church—Baptism, Confirmation, Holy Eucharist, Penance and Reconciliation, Anointing of the Sick, Holy Orders, and Holy Matrimony—are means by which the Holy Trinity strengthens you in this pattern of the Paschal Mystery. Each of the sacraments reveals the saving power of the Paschal Mystery.

Baptism

The Sacrament of Baptism conferred justification upon you. This means that you "descended into the tomb" (represented by the triple immersion or blessing with holy water) with Jesus, died to sin with Christ, and rose to new life. Your Baptism confers several graces:

- Baptism conforms you to the righteousness of God. The sacrament cleanses you of all sin—including Original Sin.

- Baptism also strengthens you to resist sin. God continually gives you graces throughout your life because of your Baptism.

- Baptism brings glory to God and Christ and enables you to achieve eternal Salvation.

Holy Eucharist

The Sacrament of the Holy Eucharist brings you into communion with Jesus and commemorates the Paschal Mystery directly. Here are several truths about this sacrament:

- The Eucharist is a sacrificial meal.
- The sacrifice of the Eucharist and the sacrifice of Christ on the Cross are one single sacrifice.
- The Eucharist re-presents, or makes present, the sacrifice of the Cross.
- In the Mass, the priest offers the sacrifice, but the victim, Jesus, is the same.
- The manner of the sacrifice also differs because during Mass, the priest offers Christ in an unbloody manner.
- The Eucharist confers the graces that Christ won on the Cross. The Eucharist will commemorate Jesus' sacrifice until the end of time.

At Mass, during the Eucharistic Prayer, the priest takes wheat bread and grape wine, asks for the blessing of the Holy Spirit, and says the words of consecration. These are the essential signs of the Eucharist. At the consecration, the bread becomes the Body of Christ, and the wine becomes the Blood of Christ (though still under the form of bread and wine).

The Eucharist is the sacrament that brings you, as a baptized Catholic, into communion with Jesus. People sometimes refer to the sacrament as "The Lord's Supper" and the "Breaking of Bread," both of which are appropriate because they refer to what Jesus did at the Last Supper. Receiving the Sacrament of the Eucharist not only brings you into communion with Christ and other members of the Body of Christ, but also builds up the Church. The Sacrament of the Holy Eucharist offers you the daily strength to offer up the difficulties that come your way while also living and anticipating your future glory. These are some effects of the Eucharist:

- The Eucharist reminds you that Christ has pledged his love to you and promised you future glory in Heaven.
- The Eucharist enables Christ to connect with you. When you consume his Body and Blood, Christ fills your mind with grace, giving you a taste of what eternal life will be like. Jesus wants to be in communion with you.
- Jesus knew that the Eucharist would be a sign and a bond of love. Christ left all of humanity a sacrament that brings love, unity with others, communion with him, and grace.
- Christ instituted the Eucharist so that you could remember his Death and Resurrection. By commanding his Apostles to celebrate the Eucharist until his return, he called them to be priests of the New Covenant.
- Jesus instituted the Eucharist so that his followers could receive the grace connected with the sacrament to apply to the forgiveness of daily sins.
- Through the Eucharist, the People of God become one body in Jesus Christ.

Penance and Reconciliation

Like Baptism and Holy Eucharist, the Sacrament of Penance and Reconciliation (Confession) visibly re-creates the Paschal Mystery for your own life. In this sacrament, you are able to confess your personal sins, both mortal and venial, to the priest and receive God's **absolution** through him. God can forgive a mortal sin that jeopardized your eternal life with him; this brings you back into relationship with him and restores the possibility of eternal life in Heaven.

Not only does Confession cleanse you from sin, but it also strengthens you to resist sin in the future. It is always necessary to confess any mortal sin, but it is also wise to frequently confess your venial sins—perhaps at least once per month—in order to receive the graces of this sacrament.

Anointing of the Sick

In the Garden of Eden, Adam and Eve had everything they could ever want. God did not intend for them to suffer. Suffering was a consequence of their Original Sin rather than an experience that God wanted for them. Likewise, sickness, pain, and suffering are not God's intention for you. They, too, all result from Original Sin.

Modern society communicates the message that you should avoid suffering at all costs, that suffering has no value. This is not accurate. When you unite your own suffering with the Paschal Mystery of Christ, you also unite yourself with the entire People of God and contribute to their good.

By becoming human, Jesus united himself to all humans, inviting you to personally participate in his redemptive suffering. Uniting your suffering with Christ's Passion gives new meaning to suffering.

Painful physical suffering as well as emotional suffering due to trauma, depression, and loss can seem unbearable. Uniting your suffering with Christ enables you to gain grace and strength for yourself and for others.

The grace that comes with uniting your suffering with Christ's Paschal Mystery occurs very visibly in the **Sacrament of the Anointing of the Sick**. When a person who is terminally or chronically sick receives this sacrament, he or she receives strength in being united deeply to the Passion and Death of Christ. His or her suffering then also contributes to the holiness of the Church and the good of all people.

Special graces from the Sacrament of the Anointing of the Sick include

- unity with Christ for your own good and the good of the Church
- strength, peace, and courage to endure suffering
- forgiveness of sins when a person cannot receive the Sacrament of Penance
- restoration of health according to God's will
- preparation for death and eternal life according to God's will

Confirmation, Holy Matrimony, and Holy Orders

The other three sacraments also deeply connect those who receive them with Christ's Paschal Mystery.

---

absolution Forgiveness of sins; remission of guilt; also the statement by which a priest, speaking as the official minister of Christ's Church, declares forgiveness of sins to a repentant sinner in the Sacrament of Penance and Reconciliation. The formula of absolution reads: "I absolve you from your sins in the name of the Father, and of the Son, and of the Holy Spirit. Amen."

Sacrament of the Anointing of the Sick The sacrament administered by a priest through prayer and the anointing of the body with the oil of the sick to a baptized person who is ill or in danger of dying. The sacrament's effects are a special grace of healing and comfort to the person suffering.

In Confirmation, you receive the **gifts of the Holy Spirit** and the grace to handle the different spiritual challenges that you encounter as you grow older. God knows that you will make mistakes but also that, with his help, you will be courageous, cultivate virtue, and discern what is of God and what is not.

The graces of Confirmation help you to choose a state in life, whether marriage or religious life. Both marriage (Matrimony) and priesthood (Holy Orders) begin with sacraments. In a marriage, couples who maintain their relationship with God and receive the sacraments regularly can find new closeness, depth, and commitment in the "little deaths" or sufferings of their lives: illness, disability, loss of a job, loss of a loved one, a forced move, and so on. Though a couple experiences any of these "little deaths," they can rise again to new life because of their participation in the Paschal Mystery.

Priests also experience various little deaths that they can unite to the Paschal Mystery with prayer and participation in the sacraments. Priests may experience periods of self-doubt, have family losses, encounter conflict in their parishes, and otherwise struggle with daily challenges like every other adult. When priests connect with the Paschal Mystery, they emerge stronger and wiser.

Though their state of life is not conferred by a sacrament, women and men in consecrated religious life face some of the same ups and downs as married people and priests. They too draw strength from uniting their challenges to the Paschal Mystery of Christ.

Rewards of the Paschal Mystery

By conquering Satan and death, Jesus not only gave meaning to unavoidable suffering, but also ensured that suffering does not have the last word in your life.

You will pass through the "phases" of the Paschal Mystery, from little death to little resurrection, many times over in your life. During some periods, you may

St. Pius X decreed in 1910 that all children who reached the age of reason should receive First Communion. He also encouraged all Catholics to frequently partake in the "Bread of Life."

identify closely with the Jesus of Good Friday, experiencing physical or emotional suffering. In other times, you may feel more like the shocked Apostles of Holy Saturday who experienced emptiness while wondering how anything good could come from their suffering. Yet at other times, as on the first Easter, you will experience a little resurrection or rebirth: a sense that you have found new life out of suffering through hope, faith, love, or forgiveness.

> **gifts of the Holy Spirit** An outpouring of God's gifts at Confirmation to help a person lead a Christian life. The traditional seven gifts of the Holy Spirit are wisdom, understanding, counsel, fortitude, knowledge, piety, and fear of the Lord.

Never forget that you have indeed experienced a miracle in your life. The miracle of God's Son coming to earth, saving humanity from the consequences of sin, and offering people the opportunity for eternal life is truly miraculous. You experience this every time you receive the Eucharist. In addition, God works miracles in the most difficult life situations. No situation is too dark for God.

SECTION ASSESSMENT

NOTE TAKING

Use the notes you kept to help you answer the following questions.

1. Name at least two ways that the sacraments re-present the pattern of Christ's Passion, Death, and Resurrection.

2. How do the graces of the sacraments help you to connect with the Paschal Mystery?

VOCABULARY

3. What does it mean to be justified?

4. Fill in the blanks. A sacrament is a _____ and _____ of _____ instituted by _____ _____ and entrusted to the _____ by which _____ _____ is bestowed on us through the _____ _____.

COMPREHENSION

5. What are two graces that the Sacrament of Baptism confers?

6. How does the Eucharist re-present the sacrifice of the Cross yet do so in an unbloody manner?

7. What are the essential signs of the Eucharist?

8. How does the Sacrament of Penance and Reconciliation parallel the Paschal Mystery?

9. Identify two ways that the Anointing of the Sick blesses you.

ANALYSIS

10. How does Christ save you from Satan in your life here on earth?

REFLECTION

11. What does it mean for you to pick up your cross daily?

12. What types of "little deaths" and "little resurrections" do people your own age encounter?

Section Summaries

Focus Question

How do miracles affect your life?

Complete one of the following:

 Research the origins of the crucifix and its popularity in people's private devotions, especially as displayed in homes or worn as jewelry. Why do you think that many people wear crosses rather than images of the empty tomb?

→ How does one's view of God affect one's understanding of miracles?

→ Do you think that a miracle has to defy science? For example, could you consider the separation of conjoined twins miraculous, even if God works through surgeons to achieve such a result? Share your opinion.

INTRODUCTION (PAGES 251–252)

Miracles

Though God is the author of miracles, human beings can participate in miraculous events. Sometimes people come to know God better when they see him work in the lives of real people.

 Do an Internet search for "Gloria's Angels." Write two facts about the mission of the organization that are not found in this chapter.

SECTION 1 (PAGES 253–262)

Jesus, the Miracle Worker

Jesus performed physical healings, nature miracles, exorcisms, and raisings from the dead to help people to know and understand him and to give them a glimpse of the Kingdom of God. Just as many people today do not believe in miracles, some in Jesus' time came up with many reasons why Jesus' actions did not reveal that he is God. Jesus' miracles were unmatched and unique.

 Read paragraph 548 in the *Catechism of the Catholic Church*. What is the connection between faith and miracles?

Gospel Accounts of Jesus' Passion, Death, Resurrection, and Ascension

Several significant events occurred prior to Jesus' Resurrection that are important for your Salvation. Jesus freely went to Jerusalem, knowing what was coming. He celebrated the Passover with his Apostles, instituting the Eucharist to commemorate his loving sacrifice. After his arrest, the Jewish authorities accused Jesus of blasphemy and handed him over to the Romans on the charge of sedition. The Romans scourged and crucified Jesus, and his friends buried him. He descended into Hell and rose from the dead. Jesus then ascended to Heaven and joined his Father in glory.

> Put the following events that Jesus experienced in the order in which they occurred: Death, Last Supper, Entry into Jerusalem, Resurrection, Agony in the Garden, going before the Sanhedrin, Ascension, Pilate's condemnation, carrying the cross, burial.

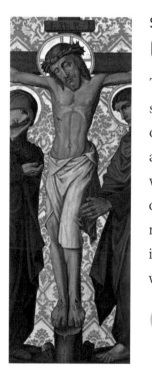

Church Teaching on the Paschal Mystery

The Paschal Mystery describes Jesus' Passion, Death, Resurrection, and Ascension. By his Death, Jesus liberated the world from sin. By his Resurrection, Jesus opened the way to new life. Jesus freely gave up his life for you, taking on your sin and the sin of all human beings. The Resurrection confirmed Jesus' teaching and works, as well as the promises from the Old Testament, and is the source for your own resurrection. Although the Resurrection was a historical event, seeing the resurrected Christ and later receiving the Holy Spirit transformed fearful Apostles into bold Evangelists. At his Ascension, the angels told the Apostles that the Lord would come again in all his glory at the Parousia.

> Imagine that Christ is going to return tomorrow. What would you do differently today? Which people would you absolutely want to see? What would you tell them?

SECTION 4 (PAGES 277–282)

The Paschal Mystery and Your Life

While the most important outcome for you from the Paschal Mystery is Salvation from the eternal consequences of sin and the possibility of life everlasting, the Paschal Mystery can affect your life now, primarily through the sacraments. Your life follows a pattern of "little deaths" and "little resurrections." Baptism erases Original Sin. The Eucharist brings you into communion with Jesus. The Sacrament of Penance and Reconciliation brings you absolution from your sins. The Anointing of the Sick brings goodness and Redemption out of suffering.

 How can you understand and compare the truths that God does not intend humans to suffer with the redemptive nature of suffering?

Chapter Assignments

Choose and complete at least one of these assignments to assess your understanding of the material in this chapter.

1. Imagine What It Was Like

 Learn the Stations of the Cross and use creative media to share your deeper reflection on the Stations. For example, you could do one of the following:

- Retell the Passion story from the point of view of one of the Apostles.

- Write your own short reflections and prayers for each station.

- Create a multimedia or other visual presentation of the Stations.

- Make a detailed sketch of a station that particularly strikes you.

- Compose a song or create a playlist that connects to the Stations.

2. Explore the Resurrection Appearances

Listed below are the Resurrection appearances of Jesus recorded in the New Testament. Read and summarize at least six of these references. Then imagine yourself to be one of the persons to whom Jesus appeared. Write three to five paragraphs describing the following: what you feel about Jesus being alive; what he looks like; what he says to you.

- Disciples on the road to Emmaus (Lk 24:13–35)

- Women (Mt 28:9–10)

- Mary Magdalene (Jn 20:11–18)

- Peter (Lk 24:34; 1 Cor 15:5)

- Four separate appearances to the Eleven and some other disciples (Jn 20:19–23; Jn 20:24–29; Mt 28:16–20; Acts 1:6–9)

- Seven disciples (Jn 21:1–14)

- More than five hundred brethren (1 Cor 15:6)

- James (1 Cor 15:7)

- Paul (Acts 9:3–8)

3. Research Miracles

When the Vatican beatifies people or canonizes them, the committee needs to associate one miracle with the person for each step toward becoming a saint. Following are a few people whose healings have been considered miraculous and have been used in recent canonization processes. Research and report on two of the three people below. Find another example of a person whose miraculous healing has contributed to a beatification or canonization.

- Jake Finkbonner (St. Kateri Tekakwitha)

- Maria Isabel Gomes de Melo (St. Carmen Salles y Barangueras)

- Floribeth Mora (St. John Paul II)

Faithful Disciple

St. Martin de Porres

St. Martin de Porres

St. Martin de Porres was a Dominican brother of African and Spanish descent living in sixteenth-century Peru who was widely known for his miraculous healings.

Juan Martin de Porres was born December 9, 1579, in Lima, Peru. He was the illegitimate son of a Spanish nobleman and a former slave from Panama of Native American or African descent. Martin's family was poor, and early on he became an apprentice of a surgeon and barber. From an early age, he prayed for hours at night.

Martin asked to enter a Dominican convent as a lay helper because his race prevented him from any other role. First he was a servant boy and then an *almoner* (a person who distributed alms to the poor). He soon became associated with some miraculous healings of the poor he served. Because of these healings and Martin's piety, the Dominican friars decided to ignore the prejudicial racial limits on admission to the order, and Martin became a full Dominican brother.

As a brother, Martin did not eat meat, fasted often, and collected alms to give to the poor and hungry. He founded a residence for orphans and abandoned children. He loved animals and worked to heal them, too. Though he had always wanted to be a missionary and travel to different parts of the world, he stayed in Lima for his entire life. Amazingly, people attested to seeing him in other regions of the world, such as China, Africa, and Japan. A merchant from Lima was ill in Mexico and prayed for Brother Martin to be with him. Immediately, Martin entered the man's room.

After his death, miracles and graces increased when people asked for his intercession. After twenty-five years, his body was found intact. Pope Gregory XVI beatified Martin de Porres in 1837, and St. John XXIII canonized him in 1962. He is the patron saint of people of mixed race, public health workers, and barbers.

Reading Comprehension

1. Where did St. Martin de Porres grow up?

2. Why did the Dominicans first reject and then later accept St. Martin de Porres as a brother?

3. Name a miracle associated with St. Martin de Porres.

Writing Task

- Write a short prayer to St. Martin de Porres calling on his intercession for a sick loved one.

Explaining the Faith

Why do some crucifixes have the letters INRI at the top of the cross?

The letters *INRI* are related to the Roman custom of posting the crime of condemned criminals on their crosses. The idea was to advertise the crime to deter others from doing something similar. In the Holy Land, Romans would have affixed a sign in three languages: Greek, Hebrew, and Latin. Visitors to Jerusalem during the religious festivals could understand at least one of these languages. INRI abbreviates the Latin words that would have been posted: *Iesus Nazarenus Rex Iudaeorum*, which translates to "Jesus the Nazorean, King of the Jews"—which Jesus in fact was.

Reflection

- Read John 19:19–20. Why do you think Pilate included this inscription on the Cross of Christ?

Prayer
Scripture Meditation

Then the king will say to those on his right, "Come, you who are blessed by my Father. Inherit the kingdom prepared for you from the foundation of the world. For I was hungry and you gave me food, I was thirsty and you gave me drink, a stranger and you welcomed me, naked and you clothed me, ill and you cared for me, in prison and you visited me."

—Matthew 25:34–36

Meditate on Jesus' words in Matthew's Gospel concerning the Last Judgment. Follow these steps:

1. Assume a comfortable position. Relax, and get ready for your time with Jesus.

2. Become aware of the Lord's presence. Feel his love surround you.

3. Slowly, meditatively, read Matthew 25:31–46. Put yourself into the scene. Engage all your senses: What do you see? Hear? Taste? Smell? Feel? The Lord is separating the sheep from the goats. Listen carefully once again to his words.

4. Reflect by reviewing your life right now. What if you were to meet our Lord tonight at midnight? What could you say to him?

5. Thank the Lord for his time with you.

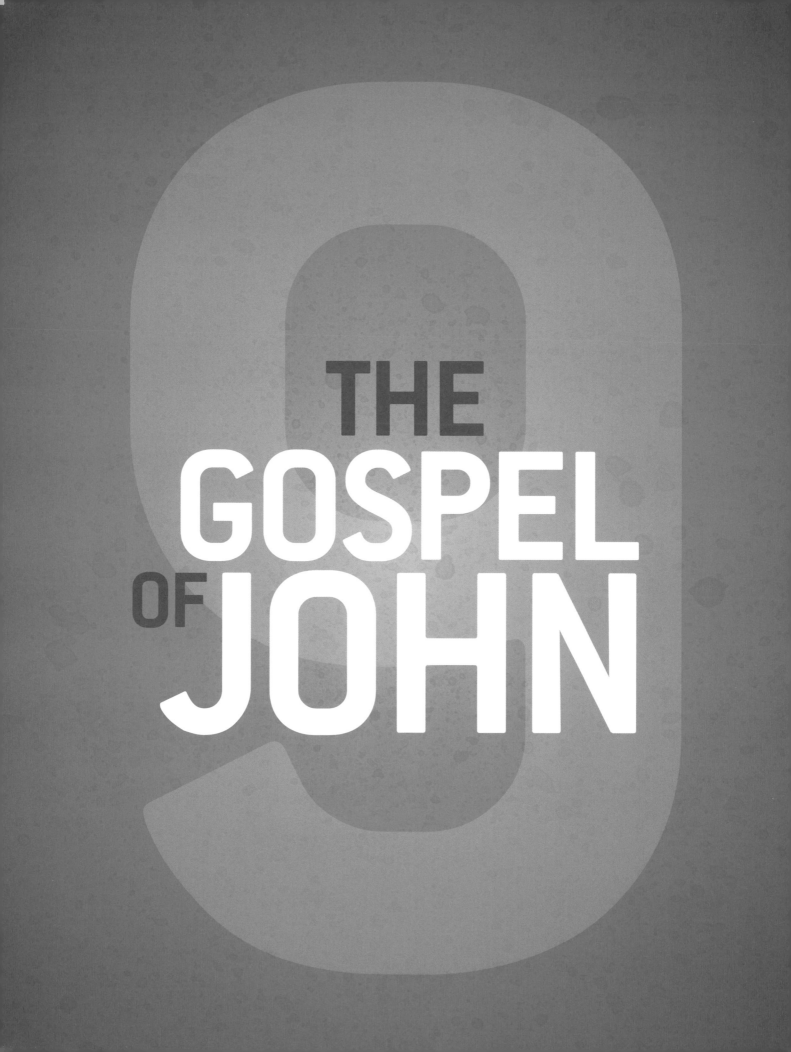

THE GOSPEL OF JOHN

LATE NIGHT
WITH GOD

For years at Georgetown University, the first Catholic college in the United States, the last weekday Mass was at 11:15 at night. As students filed in, the chapel was in darkness with candles on the altar. There was an impressive silence, a feeling of holiness permeating the sacred space.

Everything remained simple when the Mass began. The lights stayed dim. If there was music, it was reflective and still. The different priests who celebrated the 11:15 Mass all seemed to deliver their homilies in an almost hushed voice, to keep in touch with the reflective ambiance. When it was time to exchange the Sign of Peace, college students—usually known for their boisterousness—calmly and quietly greeted only their immediate neighbors.

Something memorable took place after the reception of Holy Communion. No one was in a hurry for Mass to end. Minutes passed, with priest and students sitting still in silent reflection. The old saying "the silence was deafening" applied during these moments. Finally, the priest would rise and move to the lectern. Nightly, no matter which priest, his words would be the same. He would read the entire prologue from John's gospel (1:1–18):

> In the beginning was the Word,
> and the Word was with God,
> and the Word was God. . . .
> "No one has ever seen God. The only Son, God, who is at the Father's side, has revealed him."

After reading the final blessing, the priest dismissed the congregation, and the students walked out in the night to return to their dorms for sleep, study, or socializing.

FOCUS QUESTION

How does John's Gospel reveal SOMETHING UNIQUE ABOUT JESUS?

INTRODUCTION
Contemplating Jesus

MAIN IDEA
The Gospel of John focuses on Jesus' divinity without diminishing his humanity.

The late-night Mass at Georgetown seemed to exist apart from regular time on the university campus. While others were fretting over study for exams, frolicking in neighborhood pubs, or competing loudly in intramural sports, those in attendance at Mass

contemplated the "otherness" or holiness of God, the divine nature of Jesus who is the light in the darkness. Darkness, candles, silence, the late hour, and the celebrant himself invited them to contemplation. Reflecting on the Gospel of John after Holy Communion was appropriate in this context.

During the other daily Masses at Georgetown, the chapel was well lit. Students greeted one another as they came in and engaged in conversation before and after Mass. The celebrants did not read John's Prologue at the end of these Masses. Jesus was present in each Mass: in the sacred readings from Scripture, in the priest himself, and especially in the consecrated bread and wine which became Christ's Body and Blood. But you might say that the nighttime Mass had a stronger emphasis on the divinity of Jesus, the daytime Masses on his humanity.

Likewise, the Gospel of John is known for its focus on Jesus' divinity. The synoptic Gospels had a stronger focus on Jesus' humanity. The term **Christology** captures these two approaches using a simple visual comparison. "Below" refers to the earth and thus to Jesus' human nature. "Above" refers to heaven, God, and Jesus' divine nature.

You know that in Matthew, Mark, and Luke, the Gospel authors initially teach about Jesus' human nature through his birth, baptism, temptation, and calling of his disciples. Later on, the reader encounters his miracles, teachings, and discussion of the Kingdom of God, all of which indicate that Jesus is no ordinary human being. Ultimately, the reader can see that Jesus is both God and human through Jesus' Death, Resurrection, and Ascension. The synoptic Gospels emphasize a Christology *from below*.

NOTE TAKING

Understanding Main Ideas. Draw a sketch to help remind you that John's Gospel focuses first on Jesus' divinity, whereas the synoptic Gospels emphasize his humanity.

Divinity   The Gospel of John
                       ↑ ↓
Humanity   The synoptic Gospels

> **Christology** The study of Jesus Christ; the academic effort to understand who he is.

In contrast, John tells his readers of Jesus' divinity in his first verses and later introduces his humanity. John's Gospel reflects a Christology *from above*. Though the Gospels have different starting points and emphases, both approaches articulate the truth of the Incarnation: Jesus is fully human and fully divine.

John's Gospel is organized in four sections, all of which highlight Jesus' divinity:

> I. *Prologue (Jn 1:1–18).* The Prologue highlights Jesus' divinity and states the preexistence of Jesus as the incarnate *Logos* or Word.

> II. *The Book of Signs (Jn 1:19–12:50).* This section of the Gospel contains seven signs (miracles) of Jesus (including the Wedding at Cana, pictured on page 295).

> III. *The Book of Glory (Jn 13:1–20:31).* The entire Gospel reveals Jesus' glory, but in this section, John explains the meaning of Jesus' Passion, Death, and Resurrection.

> IV. *Epilogue: Resurrection Appearance in Galilee (Jn 21:1–25).* The Epilogue describes the resurrected Jesus' encounter with his Apostles.

SECTION ASSESSMENT

NOTE TAKING

Use your sketch to help you answer the following questions.

1. What does it mean to say John's Gospel reflects a Christology "from above"?

2. How do the synoptic Gospels emphasize a Christology "from below"?

REFLECTION

3. Imagine yourself a student at Georgetown University. Which daily Mass would you prefer—one during the day or late at night? Give more than one reason for your response.

MAIN IDEA

The many differences between John's Gospel and the synoptic Gospels include audience, characters, emphasis on Jewish feast days, the centrality of Jerusalem, and literary styles.

Why did God choose to become human? The famous passage from John 3:16 provides an answer: "For God so loved the world that he gave his only Son, so that everyone who believes in him might not perish but might have eternal life." St. Irenaeus, the second-century Church Father, stated it this way:

> For this is why the Word became man, and the Son of God became the Son of Man: so that man, by entering into communion with the Word and thus receiving divine sonship, might become a son of God. (quoted in *CCC*, 460)

The Gospel of John helps you to know the incredible love God showed you through his Son, Jesus Christ. The next sections provide background and context for the creation and purpose of this Gospel.

Authorship

St. Irenaeus was also the first to attribute the fourth Gospel to the Apostle John, the "beloved disciple" of the Lord and the son of Zebedee. Further study of the Gospel reveals that several writers and editors may have contributed to its formation. For example, some material appears twice with only slight changes in the wording (see Jn 6:35–50 and 6:51–58). In addition,

NOTE TAKING

Compare and Contrast. Create a Venn diagram with one circle labeled "synoptics" and one circle labeled "John." They should share some space. As you read about the formation and uniqueness of John's Gospel, write in the circles several ways that the Gospels resemble one another and ways that they differ.

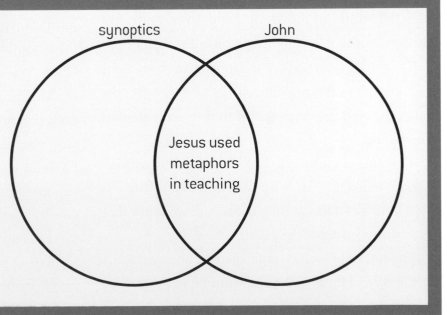

synoptics | John

Jesus used metaphors in teaching

St. John the Evangelist's tomb lies within the ruins of the Basilica of St. John in Ephesus. The basilica was the third structure to have been built on the site dedicated to St. John.

John 21 reads like an appendix that someone other than the original author added to the end of the Gospel.

A solid tradition places John, the son of Zebedee, in Ephesus (in present-day Turkey) where he likely gathered around him a community of believers. Papias, a Church bishop, described meeting one of these followers, a certain priest called Presbyter John. This John was a close associate of John, son of Zebedee (and was likely the author of the Second and Third Letters of John). It is probable that disciples like Presbyter John took the beloved disciple's testimony, prayed about his words, and later produced, in stages, a Gospel that addressed the concerns of their own Christian community.

The author of John's Gospel was an eyewitness to Jesus' public life: "It is this disciple who testifies to these things and has written them, and we know that his testimony is true" (Jn 21:24).

The author of John's Gospel focused on strengthening the faith of the believer and winning new converts.

Now Jesus did many other signs in the presence of [his] disciples that are not written in this book. But these are written that you may [come to] believe that Jesus is the Messiah, the Son of God, and that through this belief you may have life in his name. (Jn 20:30–31)

Sources

John's Gospel describes many of the same events as the synoptic Gospels, but in a different way, suggesting that he possessed a unique source or sources.

The Evangelist drew from written and oral traditions that he shared in common with Mark and Luke's Gospels and possibly also with Matthew's Gospel. The final editor of John's Gospel used the synoptic Gospels as sources, though he did not greatly rely on them. One of John's major sources included seven miracles, three of which appear only in his Gospel: Jesus' transformation of water into wine in Cana, his cure of a man born blind, and his raising Lazarus from the dead. Another major source was a version of the Passion and Resurrection narratives that would have been in circulation for many years before the composition of all of the Gospels.

Date of Composition

The Gospel of John was likely composed between AD 90 and 100. The earliest fragment of any New Testament writing found to date is a short piece of papyrus discovered in Egypt with a verse from John's Gospel. Known as the John Rylands Greek papyrus, it dates to around AD 130. This finding indicates that Christians circulated John's Gospel widely throughout the Mediterranean world only a few decades after its composition.

Audience

John wrote for Christians who may have needed to differentiate themselves from other groups—such as the followers of John the Baptist, the Jews who had expelled Jewish Christians from the synagogues, Samaritan converts, Gentile Christians, and other Christians who may have separated themselves from the Church over the topic of Jesus' divinity.

The Gospel also challenged certain followers of John the Baptist who, even as late as the last decade of the first century, wrongly believed that John the Baptist was the Messiah. In contrast, the Gospel of John insists that Jesus is superior to John the Baptist, who proclaimed that there was one coming "whose sandal strap I am not worthy to untie" (Jn 1:27).

The Uniqueness of John's Gospel

The Gospel of John differs from the synoptic Gospels in several ways:

John has characters not found in any synoptic Gospel, including Nicodemus, Lazarus, a man born blind, and a Samaritan woman.

John's Gospel mentions Jewish feasts as part of Jesus' ministry. For example:

- In John 5, Jesus cured a crippled man on the Sabbath during "a feast of the Jews."
- Jesus attended three Passover festivals, not just one as in the other three books.
- John 7–9 reports that Jesus goes to Jerusalem for the Feast of Tabernacles, a multi-day autumn festival recalling the tents the Israelites camped in during the Exodus.
- Jesus also attended the Feast of Dedication—that is, the Festival of Lights, or Hanukkah—in John 10.

John characterizes Jesus' ministry as divided between Galilee and Jerusalem, while the synoptic Gospels describe his ministry as almost exclusively in Galilee.

This Gospel contains no stories of Jesus curing people with demonic possessions.

The focus of God's Revelation is Jesus and his relationship to his Father. Jesus shows the way to the Father. John's Gospel offers Jesus' great "I AM" statements that reveal who he is in relationship to God and you, while the synoptic Gospels put greater emphasis on the Kingdom of God.

Jesus speaks in long, extended discourses or speeches, rather than in the short sayings and parables of the synoptic Gospels.

The Gospel of John is very poetic. The authors used literary techniques like irony, wordplay, metaphors, and figurative language.

The Gospel of John is more *mystical* than any of the synoptic Gospels. Recall that *mystery* is a word that points to something hidden as well as to the plan of God's saving action in human history—that is, "the mystery of Salvation." To describe John's Gospel as mystical highlights both aspects of this definition: the God who is mystery and his plan of Salvation come together in Jesus Christ.

The Gospel of John emphasizes that Jesus Christ is the One who mediates between God and humanity, because he is true God and true man, in the unity of the Divine Person.

SECTION ASSESSMENT

NOTE TAKING

Use the Venn diagram you drew to help you complete this task.

1. Defend or oppose this statement: "The Gospel of John shares more similarities than differences with the synoptic Gospels." Explain.

COMPREHENSION

2. Where did John the Apostle most likely live?

3. When was the Gospel of John written?

4. What does the discovery of the John Rylands Greek papyrus tell scholars about John's Gospel?

ANALYSIS

5. Why do you think that some people thought for many decades that John the Baptist was the Messiah?

The Prologue: And the Word Became Flesh

MAIN IDEA
The Prologue of the Gospel of John highlights the Incarnation, an essential dogma of the Faith.

The first eighteen verses of John's Gospel celebrate Jesus Christ, the preexistent Word; his participation in Creation; and his role in guiding humans, who often reject divine wisdom. All of these beautiful teachings culminate in the dogma of the Incarnation, God's becoming a human being. The Prologue contains different language (*Logos* or Word) from the later chapters and features parallel sentence structure.

The Incarnation

Recall that the Incarnation of Jesus Christ is an essential dogma of the Faith. Because the Word of God took on human flesh from his Mother Mary by the power of the Holy Spirit, Jesus is fully God and fully human. The Prologue to the Gospel of John (see Jn 1:1–18) provides scriptural evidence for the Church's belief in the Incarnation.

The Evangelist used a word that you could use to describe yourself—flesh—in order to make it clear that the *Logos* or Word of God became a *real* human being. Incarnation means "enfleshment." John likely chose the word *flesh* to counteract a first-century heresy

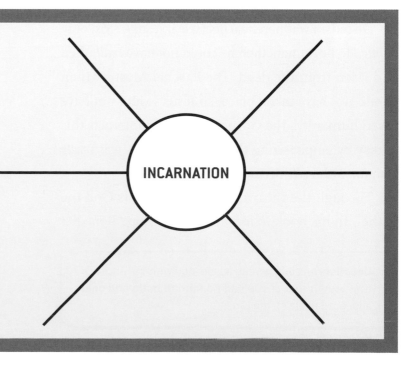

NOTE TAKING

Summarizing Content. Create a spoked wheel like the one here to help you track some of the main descriptions of the Incarnation. Write one description on each spoke. Use both the information in this section and the Prologue of the Gospel of John (1:1–18) for naming the descriptions.

INCARNATION

This image of Jesus by Louis Glanzman captures the humanity of the Son of Man. In describing his painting, Glanzman quoted John 14:6–7a, "I am the way, and the truth, and the life. No one comes to the Father except through me. If you know me, you will also know my Father."

known as **Docetism**. Docetists did not believe that the almighty God became human, so they taught that Jesus only *seemed* to be a man.

Docetism was heretical because if Jesus Christ only *seemed* to be human, then he could not have *really* died and risen from the dead. The Paschal Mystery then would not have taken place, so Jesus would not have saved humanity. The Gospel of John counteracts this heresy by emphasizing the truth that Jesus was *really* human and *really* divine.

Through the Incarnation, Jesus reveals God the Father. In his book *Jesus of Nazareth*, Pope Benedict

> **Docetism** An early heresy associated with the Gnostics that taught that Jesus had no human body and only appeared to die on the Cross.

XVI stressed that only the Son of God can reveal God perfectly. The prophet Moses spoke to God as a friend but was never able to see God's face. John's Prologue speaks to this truth: "No one has ever seen God. The only Son, God, who is at the Father's side, has revealed him" (Jn 1:18). Pope Benedict XVI wrote:

> Jesus' teaching is not the product of human learning, of whatever kind. It originates from immediate contact with the Father, from "face-to-face" dialogue—from the vision of one who rests close to the Father's heart. It is the Son's word. . . . Jesus is only able to speak about the Father in the way he does because he is the Son.[1]

The Incarnation has several implications for your life today. Because Jesus Christ is God and human, he can be your perfect model of holiness. Later in John's Gospel, you see that Jesus is "the way and the truth and the life" (Jn 14:6), who teaches that the path to holiness is to imitate him by giving yourself to others: "Love one another as I love you" (Jn 15:12). Significantly, by becoming human, the Word of God made it possible for you to share in God's nature. As John's Prologue states, "But to those who did accept him he gave power to become children of God" (Jn 1:12).

♥ THE "I AM" STATEMENTS
FROM JOHN'S GOSPEL

These are some of the titles that the author of John's Gospel gives to Jesus in the Prologue: the Word of God, the Son of God, the Christ, the greatest Prophet, the Lamb of God, Teacher, King of Israel, and the Son of Man.

Later in the Gospel, other designations for Jesus are recorded. In the titles listed below, Jesus reveals himself by first proclaiming "I AM," a reference to the name YHWH (I AM) revealed to Moses (see Ex 3:14). Jesus' divine nature shines through these self-designations. In John 8:58, Jesus clearly stated his true identity: "Amen, amen, I say to you, before Abraham came to be, I AM." His opponents knew exactly what he was claiming. They picked up stones to throw at him because they thought he had blasphemed, "but Jesus hid and went out of the temple area" (Jn 8:59).

Read the references below. Note which title means the most to you and why. Write a prayer to Jesus using your favorite title. Design the prayer using a form of creative media (e.g., electronic formatting, collage, prayer card). Share and pray your prayer with others.

VERSE	TITLE	MEANING
6:35f	**BREAD OF LIFE** Sign: Jesus feeds five thousand (Jn 6:5–14)	Jesus gives true life— eternal life. When you receive him in the Eucharist, he lives in you.
8:12	**LIGHT OF THE WORLD** Sign: Jesus cures the man born blind (Jn 9:1–41)	Jesus is the beacon of truth who points you to his Father. Living in the light brings true life.
10:7	**SHEEP GATE** Words: "I am the gate."	Jesus is the way into God's Kingdom, Heaven.
10:11	**GOOD SHEPHERD** Words: "I am the good shepherd. A good shepherd lays down his life for his sheep."	Jesus tenderly loves each person and has surrendered his life for humanity. He is the Messiah who watches out for his flock.
11:25	**RESURRECTION AND LIFE** Sign: Jesus raises Lazarus from the dead (Jn 11:1–44)	Jesus has power over death. Believe in him, live in his light, and you will have eternal life.
14:6	**WAY, TRUTH, LIFE** Words: "I am the way and the truth and the life. No one comes to the Father except through me."	This summarizes the Word's purpose for joining humanity: He is the Way to God; he proclaims the true message of Salvation; and he bestows eternal life on humankind.
15:5	**TRUE VINE** Words: "I am the vine, you are the branches. Whoever remains in me and I in him will bear much fruit, because without me you can do nothing."	Jesus is the source of life; you must remain attached to him.

SECTION ASSESSMENT

NOTE TAKING

Use the notes you kept on the Incarnation to help you complete the following item.

1. Name and describe two ways of thinking about the Incarnation.

COMPREHENSION

2. Define *Incarnation* in your own words.

3. What is *Docetism*?

4. What does the heresy of Docetism teach about Jesus? What does this imply for the Resurrection?

5. How is Jesus the Word of God?

ANALYSIS

6. How do you think that John's use of the word *flesh* would have made it clear to the early Church that Docetism was heretical?

7. Why was Docetism such a challenge to core Christian beliefs?

SECTION 3
The Book of Signs

MAIN IDEA
Seven signs (or miracles) are included in John's Gospel that reveal Jesus' identity, his mission, and his glory.

Although the Book of Signs covers other material, its main focus is on Jesus' miracles and their implications. In John's Gospel, Jesus' miracles (called works or signs) reveal his identity, explain his reason for coming to earth, display his heavenly glory, and illuminate his relation to his heavenly Father. You too need the faith of Jesus' first witnesses to grasp the deeper meaning of his signs.

This section highlights the material in John 1:19–12:50—the seven signs and the transitional words and actions between them.

First Sign: The Wedding at Cana (Jn 2:1–12)

The miracle Jesus performed at a wedding feast in Cana marked the first time Jesus publicly revealed his glory. When Mary heard that the host was running low on wine, she told Jesus about the problem. Although he resisted helping at first, Jesus changed

NOTE TAKING

Analyzing Information. As you read through this section, note down some basic information about each sign in your own version of this chart:

Sign Name	Miracle	Who Else Involved?	What Else Involved?	Outcome	Reaction
1. Wedding at Cana	Water into wine	Mary/people at wedding	Jars of water	Water became wine	This is better wine
2.					
3.					
4.					
5.					
6.					
7.					

This Franciscan church in the modern city of Kafr Kanna, Israel, marks the place where the wedding at Cana took place and Jesus turned water into wine.

Death, Resurrection, and Ascension, the full manifestation of his glory.

Jesus' first sign helped the disciples to believe, revealed his power over nature, and foreshadowed his ministry of helping others by acting with authority. Jesus' attendance at a wedding feast showed that he enjoyed and celebrated ordinary life and blessed marriage as a sacrament.

The Woman at the Well (Jn 4:4–42)

Before performing his next sign, Jesus headed back to Galilee by way of Jerusalem and then Samaria. Recall that there was a historical basis for the bad feeling between the Samaritans and the Jews. In Samaria, thirsty and tired, Jesus met a woman at a well in the town of Sychar. What Jesus did was unheard of for a self-respecting, first-century Jewish man: he spoke in public to a woman and, even more scandalously, to a hated Samaritan who was also a notorious sinner. This behavior would have offended his contemporaries. John likely wanted to emphasize that Jesus is the Savior of the world rather than only the Savior of the Jews.

The conversation revealed that the woman longed for the "living water" of which Jesus spoke. The woman thought literally and wondered aloud how Jesus could provide this special water from an underground river when the old well collected only ground runoff. Jesus patiently explained. When he knew that she had five husbands, she proclaimed, "You are a prophet" (Jn 4:19). Jesus satisfied the woman's thirst for true knowledge: He is the Messiah, the source of eternal life, the one who refreshes and renews and brings life. He also told her that his life enabled a person to worship God in Spirit and truth. It is possible to meet God everywhere, not just on Mount Gerizim, as the Samaritans believed, or in the Jerusalem Temple, as the Jews believed. "God is Spirit, and those who worship him must worship in Spirit and truth" (Jn 4:24).

some of the water stored for ceremonial washings into wine that was superior to the wine that had originally been served. (John may have shown Jesus' reluctance because some of the heretical gospels in circulation at that time told of Jesus performing special miracles for family and friends.)

Mary, the perfect model of faith, played an important role in the story. Hospitality was important in Jesus' society, so running out of wine would have shamed the wedding hosts. Mary's concern for others moved her to intercede. She had faith in her Son's compassion, even though his time to reveal himself openly had not yet come. When he mentioned, "My hour has not come" (Jn 2:4), Jesus was referring to his Passion,

The ruins of the pool of Bethesda, where Jesus healed the lame man, were discovered in the nineteenth century near the Church of Saint Anne in Jerusalem.

The woman told the people in her town of her meeting with Jesus. Many came, listened to him, and believed for themselves that he "is truly the savior of the world" (Jn 4:42). Interestingly, this Samaritan woman was really the first missionary to spread the word about Jesus.

Second Sign: Cure of the Official's Son (Jn 4:46–54)

Jesus' second sign also occurred in Cana. The power of Jesus' word was enough to heal the son of a court official, who was likely a Gentile. This royal official heard that Jesus had returned to Galilee and sought him out, seeking healing for his son. At first Jesus suggested that people would not believe unless they witnessed signs and wonders. When the father repeated his request, Jesus recognized that the father already had faith. The father's faith moved Jesus to act. Jesus assured the official that his son would live. At that very moment, miles away, the boy's condition began to improve. The boy's recovery led the father and his entire household to believe in Jesus.

Prayer for others—**intercessory prayer**, or prayer of intercession—has power. Jesus responds to your concern for others as he did for the father who wanted health restored to his boy.

Third Sign: Cure on a Sabbath (Jn 5:1–47)

Jesus encountered a man who had been lame for thirty-eight years and who waited to immerse himself in a pool that was thought to bring healing. Although the injured man only asked for help getting to the pool, Jesus ordered him to rise, take his mat, and walk.

> **intercessory prayer** Prayer in which you ask for something on behalf of another person or group of people.

JESUS *and* Judaism

What was Jesus' relationship with Judaism? Jesus was a faithful Jew and saw his ministry in the context of the Old Testament. Many ordinary Jews liked what he had to say and appreciated his miracles. Others did not. Those who opposed him tended to be powerful men who carefully followed the Law and did not appreciate what Jesus said, those with whom he associated, and how he interpreted the Law.

Jesus actually agreed with many of the truths that these religious leaders taught. Within this educated group who studied and followed the Law, there were also men who followed Jesus. Those who disliked Jesus thought that he was disregarding some of the main tenets of Judaism, including the following:

- Complete submission to the Law, both written and oral traditions (the latter were important, especially to the Pharisees)

- The centrality of the Temple in Jerusalem as a holy place where God dwelt in a special way

- Faith in one God

You can understand why Jesus upset these religious leaders charged with worship and stewardship of the Law. Jesus had a new understanding of each of these aspects of Judaism.

Jesus and the Law

Near the beginning of the Sermon on the Mount, Jesus said, "Do not think that I have come to abolish the law or the prophets. I have come not to abolish but fulfill" (Mt 5:17). Why did some Jewish leaders disagree?

The Pharisees advocated perfect obedience to the Law. Of course, this was not humanly possible. This is why every year, on the **Day of Atonement**, Jews asked God's forgiveness for violating the Law. The Pharisees' focus on perfect adherence to the Law had prompted many Jews at the time to extreme religious zeal, leading them to judge others. Jesus fulfilled the Law to the point of taking upon himself the sins against it and redeeming those who could not follow it well.

God had given the Law to Moses. The Jewish people and their leaders thought of Jesus as a rabbi, but Jesus interpreted the Law in a divine way. His tendency to "upgrade" his listeners' understanding of the Law ("you have heard that it was said to your ancestors . . . but I say to you . . .") under his own authority made religious leaders uncomfortable. Jesus' interpretation of dietary and Sabbath laws especially offended the religious leaders.

Jesus and the Temple

Jesus went to the Temple for religious celebrations with his family. Recall that Mary and Joseph presented Jesus at the Temple after his birth and that Jesus risked scaring his earthly parents to spend time in his Father's house.

Jesus understood the Temple to be a place where he could encounter his Father and pray. This helps explain his rage at seeing the merchants turning the Temple into a business district (Jn 2:13–16). Jesus taught in the Temple, paid taxes to the Temple, and identified himself with the Temple as a dwelling place for God. Unfortunately, near the end of his life, when Jesus predicted the fall of the Temple, his words were distorted and used against him by false witnesses at the high priest's house (see Mt 26:57–68).

Jesus and One God

Of all of the issues that disturbed Jewish religious leaders, Jesus' professed role in the forgiveness of sins was the greatest stumbling block. The Pharisees did not like that Jesus ate with sinners, nor his saying that the Pharisees were blind because they did not feel the need for Salvation. Jesus' merciful relationship with sinners and his forgiveness of sins led the leaders to see Jesus as a man who was trying to make himself equal with God or claim to be God, since only God could forgive sins.

Jesus' claims to be divine further frustrated them. They believed that Jesus was guilty of blasphemy, a serious crime in their community, and took action according to the Law (see Lk 18:28–40). When you read the Bible, you read it through the lens of your belief in Jesus, your knowledge of him, and your experiences of Christianity. The Jewish leaders during his lifetime were following a tradition that was over one thousand years old when they encountered Jesus. It would have been difficult (but not impossible) for them to immediately believe in him.

Some Jews told the man that he should not be carrying his mat because it was the Sabbath. The Jews asked who told him he should walk with his mat, and they began to persecute Jesus because he had done this cure on the Sabbath. Jesus sided with some rabbis who believed that God does not rest from all things on the Sabbath, using the logic that, after all, people die and are born on the Sabbath: "My Father is at work until now, so I am at work" (Jn 5:17). Jesus' claim to be equal with God irritated his adversaries even more than did his work on the Sabbath.

Note that Jesus boldly claimed equality with God in several ways:

- First, Jesus indicated that the unique Son, like the Father, actively works on the Sabbath.

- Second, he said that like his Father, the Son also gives life to whomever he wants.

- Finally, he asserted that the Father gave his Son the right to judge.

Jesus' clear claim of divine authority enraged his opponents: "For this reason the Jews tried all the more to kill him, because he not only broke the Sabbath but he also called God his own father, making himself equal to God" (Jn 5:18).

In describing this sign, the Evangelist uses the expression "the Jews" in a negative way. Several times throughout John's Gospel the antagonism between Jesus and "the Jews" is so intense that it appears that Jesus is *anti-Semitic*—that is, prejudiced against Jewish people. Remember, though, that Jesus and all his early disciples were Jews also. John wrote for a largely Jewish-Christian community.

In John's Gospel, a mention of "the Jews" does not refer to all those who practice Judaism. Instead, it

> **Day of Atonement** The Day of Atonement, also called Yom Kippur, is the holiest day of the year for the Jewish people, its central themes being atonement and repentance.

The Sea of Galilee where Jesus walked on water and calmed the storm. Jesus said to the disciples, "It is I. Do not be afraid" (Jn 6:20).

represents those who persisted in not accepting Jesus while at the same time persecuting Jewish Christians. The term also describes anyone who stubbornly refused to accept Jesus or who engaged in lifeless religious practices and missed out on a vital relationship with Jesus.

Recall from Chapter 5 the story of the friendship St. John Paul II had with his Jewish friend Jerzy Kluger. Remember that the Church condemns prejudice against Jews—against all people. It is wrong to assign responsibility for the Death of Jesus to the Jews of Jesus' time or to Jews today (see pages 271–272 and *CCC*, 597).

Fourth and Fifth Signs: Multiplication of the Loaves and Walking on the Water (Jn 6:1–14, 16–24)

These two signs go together because they bring to mind God's miracles in the desert from the Book of

Exodus: manna in the desert and the walk through the Red Sea. In the first, Jesus fed the hungry crowd that followed him because of the signs he performed for the sick. After the miracle, the people wanted to make him king, so he withdrew from them to the mountain. In John's account of the multiplication of the loaves, Jesus asked Philip how they could provide food for the crowds as a test rather than a request, because "he himself knew what he was going to do" (Jn 5:6).

Jesus' walk on the water also appears in the synoptic Gospels (see image on page 305). Jesus revealed his true identity to his disciples when he said, "It is I. Do not be afraid" (Jn 6:20). "It is I" refers to the name God revealed to Moses: YHWH, or "I AM." Jesus pointed to his divine identity by using that term.

The Bread of Life Discourse (Jn 6:25–70)

In conjunction with Jesus' sign of the multiplication of loaves, John presents Jesus' teaching about his identity as the "bread of life." Speaking in a Capernaum synagogue, Jesus says *he* replaces the manna of the Exodus. He is the new bread God has given to his disciples, their source of eternal life. Through Jesus, all of his followers will pass over from death to new life.

> I am the bread of life; whoever comes to me will never hunger, and whoever believes in me will never thirst. . . . Amen, amen, I say to you, unless you eat the flesh of the Son of Man and drink his blood, you do not have life within you. Whoever eats my flesh and drinks my blood has eternal life, and I will raise him on the last day. (Jn 6:35, 53–54)

You have the advantage of reading these words in light of the Eucharist, knowing that no one would actually consume Christ in the form of human flesh or blood, but instead under the forms of bread and wine. You know that the Eucharist brings about an intimate relationship between Jesus and his Church, those who believe in him. He lives in you and you in him. As the Father is the source of Jesus' life, so Jesus is the source of your life.

Consider what Jesus' words might have sounded like to his listeners hearing them for the first time. Jesus' shocking teaching about his Body and Blood caused many to abandon him. But Peter and the Apostles put their trust in him: "Master, to whom shall we go? You have the words of eternal life. We have come to believe and are convinced that you are the Holy One of God" (Jn 6:68–69).

Sixth Sign: The Cure of the Man Born Blind (Jn 9:1–41)

In this sign, a man born blind received sight after Jesus smeared clay on his eyes and he obeyed the Lord's instructions to wash in the Pool of Siloam. The story has a comical side, as the Pharisees repeatedly interrogate the man with restored sight about what happened to him, while he challenges their irrational thinking. Even the formerly blind man's parents want nothing to do with the Pharisees' concerns and remind them that their son is of age himself to answer any questions.

The man's physical cure brought growth in his faith. Responding to the Pharisees' questions, he at first referred to Jesus as "the man called Jesus" (Jn 9:11); then he called him a prophet (Jn 9:17); next he testified that Jesus is a man from God (Jn 9:33). Finally, the healed man confessed belief that Jesus is the Son of Man and worshipped him (Jn 9:38). Even though the authorities severely challenged him, and he risked being thrown out of the synagogue, he refused to criticize Jesus. (This risk was quite real. Later, the Apostle John's own community would be thrown out of the synagogue for preaching the Gospel of Jesus.)

Some of the Pharisees, in contrast to the blind man, were people with physical sight but spiritual blindness. In this story, they called Jesus "a sinner" (Jn 9:24). As the light who had come into the world (Jn 1:4–5), however, Jesus dispelled the darkness of ignorance and sin with his truth and light. He asked people to have faith in him so as to overcome their spiritual blindness. Their narrow interpretations of the Law blinded some Pharisees to God's presence in their midst. Jesus taught that spiritual blindness is worse than physical blindness (Jn 9:41).

The Good Shepherd (Jn 10:1–21)

Jesus' discourse about the Good Shepherd continues some of the themes found in John 9 about the man born blind. This appears to be the parallel he is drawing:

- Jesus = the Good Shepherd
- Sheep = Jewish people who hear Jesus' voice (like the blind man)
- Stranger/Hired Hand = Pharisees (as in the story of the blind man)

- Other sheep that do not belong to this fold = possibly the Gentiles

Jesus suggested that the Jewish people who, like the blind man, recognize him by his voice and follow him are like sheep following their shepherd. He then identified himself as the gate for the sheep. In some societies, a sheepfold would not have a gate, because the shepherd would sleep across the fence opening at night to defend the sheep against enemies with his body. In this role, a shepherd might easily have to sacrifice his life trying to protect his herd. Jesus contrasted the role of the Good Shepherd with someone who is simply hired to guard the sheep, a person who will not risk his life for them.

The "other sheep" (Jn 10:16) may refer to Gentiles, followers in the future, or possibly other groups of Christians. Notice that Jesus emphasized that he gives up his life freely, an important truth in the synoptic Gospels as well. The crowd had a mixed response to Jesus, though most of it was negative. Some thought that Jesus was possessed. Others thought that he had committed blasphemy. Some tried to stone him and arrest him.

The tomb of Lazarus, where Jesus took pity on Martha and Mary's grief and raised their brother from the dead, is located at modern al-Eizariya in the West Bank.

Seventh Sign: The Raising of Lazarus (Jn 11:1–44)

Jesus' raising of Lazarus from the dead prefigured Jesus' own Death and Resurrection, not only because Lazarus "rose" from the dead, but also because performing the miracle brought attention to Jesus that hastened Jesus' own death.

On his way to Jerusalem, Jesus learned that his friend Lazarus was ill and near death, but he waited two days before going to see Lazarus. This delay allowed God the Father to glorify Jesus through this marvelous sign. Once Jesus arrived, Lazarus's grieving sister Martha and Jesus had this exchange: "I am the resurrection and the life; whoever believes in me, even if he dies, will live, and everyone who lives and believes in me will never die. Do you believe this?" (Jn 11:25–26). Martha replied, "Yes, Lord. I have come to believe that you are the Messiah, the Son of God, the one who is coming into the world" (Jn 11:27).

Though Lazarus's sisters believed that their brother would rise on the last day, their sorrow at losing their brother moved Jesus to tears. John 11:35 is the shortest verse in the Bible: "And Jesus wept." Jesus also prayed to his Father. Then he called Lazarus out of the grave, and the dead man came out.

Jesus' miracle led many to believe but caused others, such as the members of the Sanhedrin, to feel threatened by Jesus. They feared that if people began to follow Jesus, the Romans would come and take away the land and nation of the Jewish people (Jn 11:48). Joseph Caiaphas, the high priest, said that "it is better for you that one man should die instead of the people, so that the whole nation may not perish" (Jn 11:50).

Ironically, Caiaphas did not realize the prophecy he spoke: that Jesus' Death would save the Jewish people, as well as all people—not just from the Romans, but from death.

SECTION ASSESSMENT

NOTE TAKING

Using the chart you created as a guide, answer these questions.

1. Why might Jesus have wanted these signs to be public?

2. Which miracle involved the Apostles only?

3. What might you name as a common theme for all seven signs?

COMPREHENSION

4. Choose one of Jesus' seven signs, and explain its meaning.

5. Why did so many of Jesus' followers leave him after the Bread of Life discourse?

6. How is Jesus the Good Shepherd?

REFLECTION

7. After Jesus spoke to the Samaritan woman, other Samaritans came to listen to Jesus for themselves. This highlights another theme in John's Gospel: *Each person must come into personal contact with Jesus.* Write about how you can personally come into contact with Jesus.

The Book of Glory and Epilogue

MAIN IDEA
The messages in the third part of John's Gospel are about service, love, and the promise of the Holy Spirit.

The third major part of John's Gospel is the Book of Glory. The first half of the Book of Glory, John 13–17, concerns the Last Supper. John 18–21 narrates Jesus' Passion, Death, and Resurrection, in which Christ reveals his glory, marking the victory of Salvation he won for you.

The Last Supper (Jn 13:1–17:26)

John's account of the Last Supper differs in several ways from the story in the synoptic narratives. For example, John's Gospel places the Last Supper on the day before Passover; that is, the day on which Jews killed the lambs for the Passover meal.

In John's account of the Last Supper, Jesus humbly washed his disciples' feet. Jesus explained, "If I, therefore, the master and teacher, have washed your feet, you ought to wash one another's feet. I have given you a model to follow, so that as I have done for you, you should also do" (Jn 13:14–15). If any of the Apostles still believed that Jesus would be a conquering Messiah, his words here clarify the type of Messiah he was. Their discipleship will reflect the servant mission of the Messiah.

As Jesus spoke about his imminent departure, he offered a new commandment:

NOTE TAKING

Compare and Contrast. Recall the material on the Paschal Mystery from the synoptic Gospels (see Chapter 8). Find at least four examples of differences between the synoptic Gospels' account of Jesus' Passion, Death, Resurrection, and Ascension and the account in John's Gospel.

The Gospel of John	Synoptic Gospels
The Last Supper is the day before Passover.	The Last Supper is on Passover.

Love one another. As I have loved you, so you also should love one another. This is how all will know that you are my disciples, if you have love for one another.

(Jn 13:34–35)

Interestingly, although John's Gospel shares some elements of the synoptic Gospels' narrations of the Last Supper (such as the prediction that Peter would deny Jesus), it does not include the institution of the Eucharist.

The Last Supper Discourses

John 14–17 contains Jesus' Last Supper discourses. These are important statements of faith spoken by Jesus at the Last Supper. In these statements, Jesus encouraged his followers to stay close to him. He offered the following:

- "I am the way and the truth and the life. No one comes to the Father except through me. . . . Whoever has seen me has seen the Father" (Jn 14:6, 9). In John's Gospel, truth is equated with the Father's presence in the life and works of Jesus.

- "Peace I leave with you; my peace I give to you. Not as the world gives do I give it to you. Do not let your hearts be troubled or afraid" (Jn 14:27). Peace ("Shalom") is a traditional Jewish salutation. Jesus' gift of peace is the gift of Salvation.

- "I am the vine, you are the branches. Whoever remains in me and I in him will bear much fruit, because without me you can do nothing" (Jn 15:5). Jesus used a vine and its branches to illustrate how necessary it is for his followers to remain attached to him.

SERVING as Jesus Served

In John 13:1–20, Jesus teaches the disciples of the importance of serving others. He washes the feet of his disciples—a task that even slaves were not required to do—to teach them that leaders must serve and that love requires humility.

In your journal, write a short reflection about your current commitment to service. How helpful are you at home, at school, with your friends? Do you participate in a parish or school service program? Do you share some of your "time, talent, and treasure" with people in need? In the past couple of months, have you helped someone without expecting to be repaid financially or otherwise? Take stock of how well you are doing. Then, write up three practical ways that you might be of service to others in the coming month. Set up a timetable for them, and follow through.

- "This is my commandment: love one another as I love you. No one has greater love than this, to lay down one's life for one's friends" (Jn 15:12–13). Jesus called you his friend, teaching you to keep his commandments and to love one another. This is the heart of the Good News. Jesus has chosen you, his friend, to continue his work of love.

Jesus also promised to send "another Advocate": the Holy Spirit, also called the **Paraclete** (a Helper or Counselor). The Spirit will open your mind and heart, helping you understand and live Jesus' teaching.

> **Paraclete** A name for the Holy Spirit that means "Advocate." In John 14:26, Jesus promised to send an Advocate, a Helper, who would continue to guide, lead, and strengthen the disciples.

The High Priestly Prayer of Jesus (Jn 17)

The Last Supper ended with a prayer that Jesus prayed directly to his Father. This is called Jesus' *High Priestly Prayer*, likely because Jesus prayed directly to his Father on behalf of his people, just as the Jewish high priest prayed in the Temple on behalf of the Jewish people. Jesus prayed on behalf of his disciples, asking his Father to protect them and then bring them to be with him. Jesus extended his prayer to people in the future who would believe in him.

> Holy Father, keep them in your name that you have given me, so that they may be one just as we are. . . . Consecrate them in the truth. Your word is truth. As you sent me into the world, so I sent them into the world. . . . I pray not only for them, but also for those who will believe in me through their word, so that they may all be one, as you, Father, are in me and I in you, that they also may be in us, that the world may believe that you sent me. (Jn 17:11, 17–18, 20–21)

This prayer marked a transition in the way that the disciples would relate to Jesus. Up to this point, they had followed him in the physical world, but in this prayer, Jesus spoke about connecting with him and the Father in a spiritual way.

Passion, Death, and Resurrection of Jesus (Jn 18–20)

The discourses in John 13–17 serve as a prologue to the traditional narratives of the Passion, Death, and Resurrection in John 18–20. In the Resurrection account, Jesus reveals his glory and confesses the need for testimony to the Resurrection.

Jesus' Passion and Death (Jn 18–19)

John portrays Jesus as in control of the events of his Passion. Jesus revealed God's glory every step of the way, willingly accepting his Death as an atoning sacrifice for all humanity. Unlike the synoptic authors, John does not include Jesus' anguished prayer in the garden. When the soldiers arrested Jesus, they fell to the ground in fear of the divine majesty when he identified himself as "I AM" (Jn 18:6). You can sense in this scene Jesus' readiness to accept his Death. When Peter came to his defense by attacking one of the servants of the high priest, Jesus admonished Peter: "Put your sword into its scabbard. Shall I not drink the cup that the Father gave me?" (Jn 18:11).

Only in John's Gospel does Jesus go before Annas prior to his encounter with Caiaphas, the high priest. The meeting with Caiaphas is not described; you, the reader, are left to infer that the meeting with Caiaphas went poorly because Jesus is bound and brought before Pilate.

During his meeting with Pilate, Jesus remained in control. Jesus and Pilate conversed about his royal identity, the meaning of truth, and the source of Pilate's power. Pilate said that he could not find Jesus guilty and gave responsibility for his Death to the Jewish crowd, appealing to the custom of releasing one prisoner to the people. The people chose Barabbas, a revolutionary. The crowd cried that they opposed any king but Caesar and that they wanted Jesus crucified. Ironically, the Jewish crowd acclaimed, "We have no king but Caesar" (Jn 19:15).

Jesus carried the Cross to Golgotha, where the Romans crucified him between two men. The inscription read "Jesus the Nazorean, the King of the Jews" (Jn 19:19), a title that bothered many of his opponents. The "disciple there whom he loved" (Jn 19:26) and several women stood close to the Cross. In an event found

The ornate Crucifixion Altar within the Church of the Holy Sepulcher in Jerusalem marks the spot called Golgotha where Jesus was crucified, and a view of the exterior of the church (foreground) set in the hilly terrain of Jerusalem.

only in John's Gospel, Jesus asked his Mother Mary to be the beloved disciple's Mother and the disciple to be Mary's son.

John's Gospel also highlights the Old Testament prophecies concerning the crucifixion. Jesus is the persecuted just man of Psalms 22 and 69: the soldiers gambled for his seamless tunic (see Ps 22:18) and someone offered him sour wine (see Ps 69:21). Treating Jesus like the Paschal lamb of Exodus 12:46, the soldiers did not break his legs.

These prophecies remind you that Jesus was lifted up on the Cross for your Salvation. God is in charge. Jesus freely obeyed his Father's will. Finally, Jesus freely gave up his spirit only when he decided to do so (see Jn 19:30).

Jesus' Resurrection (Jn 20–21)

The Resurrection is the central event of human Salvation and an indication of the glory of the Father and the Son. The four Gospels together provide fourteen stories about the Resurrection. Mark emphasizes the empty tomb. Matthew stresses God's power and majesty. Luke highlights the Risen Jesus alive in the Word of God and the breaking of the bread.

In John's Gospel, Jesus appeared first to a woman, Mary Magdalene, who stayed at the tomb, weeping. At first, she did not recognize the transformed, glorified Lord (she thought he was a gardener), but when he called her by name, Mary knew it was the Lord. Mary Magdalene exhibited a great abundance of faith and love. Perhaps this is why she was the first to see and believe in the Risen Lord. Mary told the Apostles about

Comparing the
RESURRECTION NARRATIVES

READ MARK 16:1-8, 9-20; MATTHEW 28:1-20; LUKE 24; AND JOHN 20-21.

All four Gospels proclaim the Resurrection as a real event with historically verifiable elements. As mentioned, some details differ. However, all four Gospels agree on the following essentials:

1 The Resurrection took place early in the morning on the first day of the week.

2 Women were present at the tomb, definitely including Mary Magdalene.

3 The stone had been rolled away, and the tomb was empty. An empty tomb is important to the Resurrection stories. It is an essential sign of Jesus' Resurrection, a first step in acknowledging God's work in bringing the Son back to life. It corroborates that something happened. The early Christians' enemies were never able to produce Jesus' corpse, though they probably tried to do so.

4 A messenger or messengers spoke to the women at the tomb, providing them with a message for the disciples.

5 Most importantly, Jesus appeared to his disciples on several occasions. These appearances convinced the frightened disciples that the crucified Jesus was alive, that he was Lord, and that he was God's Son. Strengthened with the Holy Spirit's gifts of faith and fortitude, Jesus' frightened, confused, and disappointed followers became bold, courageous witnesses.

6 Jesus' disciples were slow to recognize him. Jesus' resurrected body shone with the glory of God's life. They needed the Lord's own words of peace and reassurance to help them come to Resurrection faith. The resurrected Jesus is not a ghost, but neither is he a corpse that breathes. He is alive in a transformed, glorified body.

One of the most significant testimonies about the Resurrection is St. Paul's account in 1 Corinthians 15:1–19. In addition to testifying that the Lord appeared to him, St. Paul mentions several other post-Resurrection appearances, including a most significant one to more than five hundred people. At the time of his writing in the early 50s, St. Paul assured his readers that many of these eyewitnesses were still alive and could easily be called on to verify that the Lord rose from the dead.

Jesus prepared the disciples for his Ascension and the Descent of the Holy Spirit. In Mark, Jesus instructed the Apostles to wait for him (see Mk 16:7). In Luke, Jesus helped them reflect on scriptural prophecies concerning him (see Lk 24:25–27). He commissioned them to preach (see Mt 28:18–20) and forgive sin (see Jn 20:21–23). Jesus told them to wait for the Spirit, who would empower them to accomplish marvels in his name (Lk 24:49).

The Resurrection of Jesus is the heart of the Gospel, giving new meaning to our lives. Death does not have the last word! Jesus gives every person the opportunity for superabundant, eternal life with him in community with the Father and the Holy Spirit and all others who love the Lord.

what she saw. They came and verified that Jesus was no longer in the tomb.

Jesus also appeared to the Apostles in a locked room. The Risen Jesus, not bound by the laws of ordinary physics, suddenly appeared in their midst. The Apostles "rejoiced when they saw the Lord" (Jn 20:20). The Lord wished them peace and commissioned them to continue his work. He breathed on them, signifying the descent of the Holy Spirit, and he instructed them to forgive sins in his name.

The Risen Jesus' next appearance came eight days later, to St. Thomas the Apostle, who was absent when Jesus first appeared to the others. By showing him his hands and side, Jesus taught "doubting Thomas" that he was the same Jesus who lived and died. Thomas acknowledged Jesus' divinity, saying "My Lord and my God!" (Jn 20:28). In answer to Thomas, Jesus blessed all people who believe without seeing him.

Resurrection Appearance in the Epilogue

Scholars believe that John's Gospel originally ended with chapter 20. However, its final edition includes chapter 21, Jesus' appearance to the Apostles in Galilee. There Jesus helped the disciples catch fish, symbolic of their future role as "fishers" of people. He also prepared a breakfast for them. Jesus recommissioned Peter, who earlier had denied him three times. This time the Lord elicited from Peter a threefold promise of his love (see Jn 21:15–19).

SECTION ASSESSMENT

NOTE TAKING

Refer to your comparison between John's Gospel and the synoptic accounts of the Paschal Mystery to answer the following questions.

1. How can the total years of Jesus' ministry be dated by the number of Passovers recorded in John's Gospel?
2. Which story of service was unique to the Last Supper account in John's Gospel?
3. Finish this sentence: Only in John's Gospel does Jesus go before _____ prior to his encounter with _____, the high priest.
4. Who was the first person to look into the empty tomb in John's Gospel?

ANALYSIS

5. Explain the reason for the different stories about the Resurrection in the four Gospels.
6. What is the meaning of Jesus' Resurrection for Christians?

REFLECTION

7. In what ways do you personally find the Lord today?

Section Summaries

Focus Question

How does John's Gospel reveal something unique about Jesus?

Complete one of the following:

→ Research and report on the difference between "high Mass" and "low Mass."

→ St. John the Divine is a name given to the Apostle John. Why is this an appropriate name?

→ Which of Jesus' signs recorded in John's Gospel helps you most to connect with him? Explain.

INTRODUCTION (PAGES 295–296)

Contemplating Jesus

While all four Gospels focus on both Jesus' humanity and his divinity, the synoptic Gospels reflect a Christology that emphasizes Jesus' humanity ("from below") whereas John's Gospel emphasizes Jesus' divinity ("from above").

→ Transcribe John 3:16 from memory. Explain its meaning.

SECTION 1 (PAGES 297–300)

Formation of John's Gospel

Some differences between John's Gospel and the synoptic Gospels include audience, characters, emphasis on Jewish feast days, the centrality of Jerusalem, and literary styles. The principal author, John the beloved disciple, settled in Ephesus and likely composed the Gospel between AD 90 and 100. John wrote for a diverse audience. While he shared some material with Mark and Luke, his unique sources featured miracles and another version of the Passion and Resurrection narratives.

Ephesus, in modern-day Turkey, includes tours of sites connected with St. John the Apostle. Look up tours in Ephesus to find out what you could learn about St. John if you went there.

SECTION 2 (PAGES 301–304)

The Prologue: And the Word Became Flesh

The first eighteen verses of John serve as a prologue or introduction to some of the Gospel's major themes. They tell you who Jesus is and help you understand the meaning of his life and ministry. The Prologue provides scriptural evidence for the Church's belief in the Incarnation, a key doctrine of faith. Because he is fully human and fully divine, Jesus can be your model of holiness.

 If you could take on one of Jesus' human characteristics, which would it be and why?

SECTION 3 (PAGES 305–313)

The Book of Signs

The Book of Signs tells you about miracles that Jesus performed. John used these miracles to share Jesus' teachings. Jesus' first sign during the wedding in Cana helped the disciples to believe, revealed his power over nature, and foreshadowed his ministry of helping others. The power of Jesus' word was enough to heal the son of a Gentile court official. When Jesus healed a lame man on the Sabbath, his clear claim of divine authority enraged his opponents. The multiplication of the loaves and the walking on water go together because they bring to mind God's miracles in the desert from the Book of Exodus. The blind man's physical cure brought growth in the man's faith as well. Jesus taught that the Pharisees' spiritual blindness was worse than physical blindness. Jesus' raising of Lazarus from the dead prefigured Jesus' own Death and Resurrection.

 How do the seven signs reveal Jesus' presence and mission for you?

SECTION 4 (PAGES 314–319)

The Book of Glory and Epilogue

Jesus' Last Supper discourses (Jn 14–17) are a prologue to his Passion, Death, and Resurrection (Jn 18–20), where Christ revealed his glory while ensuring the victory of Salvation. The Book of Glory appears to end with chapter 20. Chapter 21 relates a post-Resurrection meeting between Jesus and the Apostles over breakfast in Galilee.

 "Blessed are those who have not seen and have believed" (Jn 20:29). What does Jesus' Resurrection mean to you?

Chapter Assignments

Choose and complete at least one of these assignments to assess your understanding of the material in this chapter.

1. Create a Stained-Glass Image

Choose a story from John's Gospel, short or long, and create a stained-glass window of the scene. Stained glass is basically pieces of colored glass, traditionally held together by lead, arranged to create a window. Via computer or using black construction paper and colored tissue paper, create a simple image that depicts the scene or symbolizes the meaning of the scene. You can find many examples of stained glass on the Internet. Write a short reflection about your process of familiarizing yourself with the story or event.

2. Explore the Theme of Light

Locate different passages on the theme of light in John's Gospel. Examples include John 3:19–21; 8:12; 11:9–10; 12:35–36, 46. Do both of the following:

- Write a short report on how the image of light is used in the Gospel.

- Report on the customs of lighting candles that Catholics use to show their faith. Examples include votive lights, the Paschal candle, baptismal candle, Christmas candles, and luminaria.

3. Research Devotions to Mary

Jesus entrusted Mary, his Mother, to the beloved disciple (see Jn 19:25–27). She is your Mother and the Mother of the Church. Catholics in many countries have a strong devotion to Mary under various titles. For example, in the United States, Mary is honored as Our Lady of the Immaculate Conception. In Mexico, she is honored as Our Lady of Guadalupe. Research and list at least five other titles for Mary from other nations. Write one paragraph of explanation for each title.

Faithful Disciple

St. Margaret Mary Alacoque

St. Margaret Mary Alacoque

St. Margaret Mary Alacoque was a seventeenth-century nun of the Visitation order who received visions from Jesus asking her to encourage devotion to his Sacred Heart.

Margaret Mary was born in Burgundy, France, the fifth of seven children of a prosperous public servant and his wife. She developed a case of rheumatic fever at age ten that kept her confined to bed for about four years, during which she developed a devotion to the Blessed Sacrament—that is, to Jesus in the Eucharist, reserved in the tabernacle after Mass. When she vowed that she would enter a convent, she immediately returned to health. Margaret Mary entered the Visitation convent at Paray-le-Monial. She experienced visions of Christ from the age of twenty. On December 27, 1673, she began to receive a series of visions that lasted over a year.

In the visions, Christ told her that she was his chosen instrument to spread devotion to his Sacred Heart, but not everyone believed she was telling the truth. Her confessor, St. Claude de la Colombière, did believe that her visions were authentic. Margaret Mary finally won her superior over, but she could not convince theologians that the visions were true. When Margaret Mary became the assistant superior of her community, the convent finally began to observe the feast of the Sacred Heart, a devotion that spread to other Visitation convents.

After Margaret Mary's death in 1690, the Jesuits helped preserve the devotion to the Sacred Heart of Jesus, but it was not officially recognized by the Church until seventy-five years after Margaret Mary's death. Pope Pius IX declared Margaret Mary Blessed in 1864. When they opened her tomb, her body had not been corrupted (had not decayed); it now lies in a chapel that attracts many pilgrims from around the world. Pope Benedict XV canonized St. Margaret Mary Alacoque in 1920.

Reading Comprehension

1. What led to St. Margaret Mary Alacoque's devotion to the Blessed Sacrament?

2. What was the relationship between St. Margaret Mary Alacoque's illness and her decision to enter the convent?

3. What devotion did Christ want St. Margaret Mary Alacoque to promote?

Writing Task

• Why do you think it was significant that St. Margaret Mary Alacoque's body had not been corrupted? Why might God offer this sign?

Explaining the Faith

Was Jesus really human in the same way you are human?

"Jesus became truly man while remaining truly God" (*CCC*, 464). Jesus Christ is true God and true man. Jesus was a real man who was born of a woman and who lived and walked on the same earth that you live on now. He lived in a town in Israel nearly two thousand years ago, in a place you can still visit today—Nazareth. Christ was like you in all things except sin. In his human nature, Christ also had the immediate knowledge of the Father and of the secret thoughts of people he encountered. Jesus Christ had two wills, divine and human. His human will was always conformed to his divine will.

 Reflection

- The Second Vatican Council taught that "by His incarnation the Son of God has united himself in some fashion with every human being" (*Gaudium et Spes*, 22). How is Jesus united with you?

Prayer
Prayer to Become More Like Jesus

God, our Father, you redeemed us and made us your children in Christ. Through him you have saved us from death and given us your Divine life of grace. By becoming more like Jesus on earth, may I come to share his glory in Heaven. Give me the peace of your Kingdom, which this world does not give. By your loving care protect the good you have given me. Open my eyes to the wonders of your love that I may serve you with a willing heart.

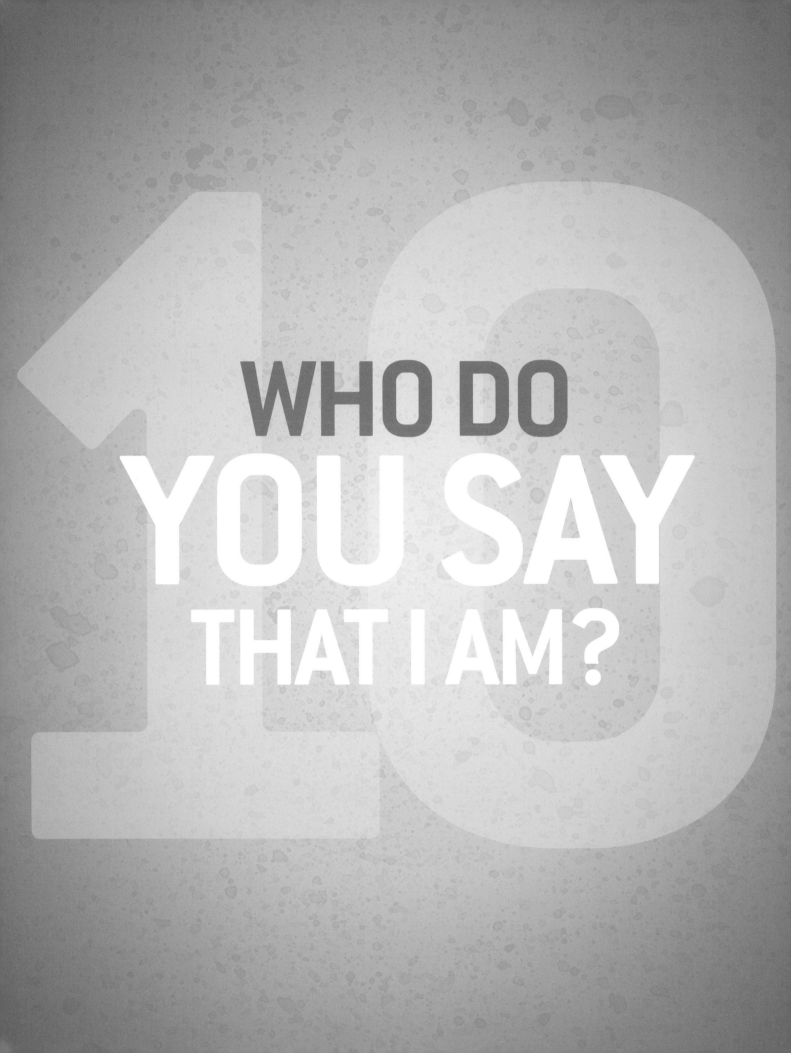

10

WHO DO YOU SAY THAT I AM?

A SERVANT SOLDIER

With bullets and explosions around him, United States Army military chaplain Fr. Emil Kapaun walked peacefully among the wounded and dying, giving the Anointing of the Sick to some men, while dragging others to safety. The US troops had entered North Korea during the Korean War of the 1950s.

Though he had had the opportunity to retreat with some other able-bodied soldiers, he chose to stay among the wounded even though he knew that the Chinese would capture him along with his men. After the Chinese came into their area, a Chinese officer stood over one wounded American soldier, aiming a rifle at him. Fr. Kapaun bravely prevented the American's death by simply moving the officer's gun aside.

Survivors at Fr. Kapaun's ceremony in Washington, DC.

After capturing the unit, the Chinese forced the men to march eighty-seven miles to prisoner-of-war (POW) camps. For much of the distance, Fr. Kapaun carried the wounded man he had saved, at times helping the man hop along to give his back a break.

At the camp, Fr. Kapaun and the other soldiers faced incessant lice, freezing cold temperatures, daily hunger, dysentery, and untreated wounds. Fr. Kapaun removed the soldiers' lice, gave them his own food, risked his life to forage for more food, boiled fresh water, made socks out of clothing scraps, prayed with the soldiers, and offered encouragement.

The prisoners in Fr. Kapaun's camp had the highest survival rate of all the American POW camps in Korea, due in great part to Fr. Kapaun's work. Fr. Kapaun, however, died in the camp at the age of thirty-five. Afterward, his fellow prisoners recalled his spirit and secretly made a crucifix in his honor. His body has never been recovered.

On April 11, 2013, Fr. Kapaun was posthumously awarded the Medal of Honor, the nation's highest military award. Several of the survivors from his camp were present at the ceremony in Washington, DC, including the soldier Fr. Kapaun had saved from the Chinese officer and carried on the march. These survivors have been part of a movement not only to award Fr. Kapaun the Medal of Honor but also to declare Fr. Kapaun a saint. The Vatican has begun the process. A convincing miracle has occurred, and people believe it is due to Fr. Kapaun's intercession. He is officially a "Servant of God," the first of four steps in the canonization process.

FOCUS QUESTION

Who do YOU say that JESUS IS?

INTRODUCTION
Who Is Jesus to You?

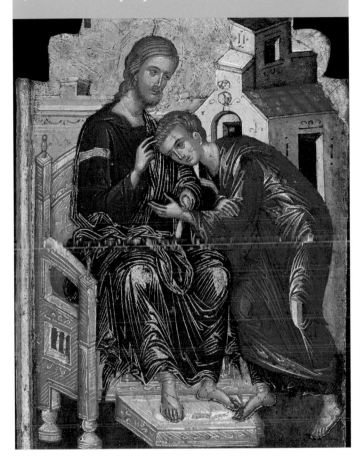

MAIN IDEA
Jesus attracted people for varied reasons.

By examining Fr. Kapaun's life and choices, you can make an informed guess about how he understood Jesus. He likely saw Jesus as faith-filled and fearless, someone who followed his Father's mission despite criticism from Jewish leaders and even in the face of death. He probably admired Jesus' tireless dedication to other people as he spent his time teaching, healing, and empowering his disciples. He undoubtedly understood Jesus' great desire to heal the human body and spirit.

The American prisoners viewed Fr. Kapaun as a person who lived like Jesus, though in very different circumstances. Fr. Kapaun touched the soldiers in so many ways. Some found strength in his prayers. Others appreciated his simple acts of kindness in such a difficult situation. Still others admired his bravery and generosity.

Similarly, the people of Jesus' day found Jesus attractive for different reasons. You too probably understand Jesus differently than the other students in your class based on your own life story and experiences.

Jesus asked one of his most important questions of his followers on the road to Philippi: "But who do you say that I am?" (Mt 16:15). Peter had a ready answer.

NOTE TAKING

Understanding Main Ideas. As you begin to answer the question "Who is Jesus to you?" keep notes on who Jesus is for others. Add more panels for each person or group who answers this question.

Who is Jesus for . . .

| His Followers | Fr. Kapaun | Society Today | |

| Your Peers | | Your Family |

He knew Jesus as the Messiah. Further, Peter called Jesus "the Son of the living God" (Mt 16:16).

Unfortunately, some people write Jesus off when they do not really know him. If Jesus does not immediately fix everything for them, they try something else—or worse, they attempt to convince others not to believe in him. Think how dangerous it is to make snap judgments about people before really getting to know them.

Some people today believe that Jesus was a great teacher but nothing more. Others say that he was a holy man and prophet like Moses or Elijah of the Old Testament. Still others admit only that he was a historical figure: a good-hearted yet misguided philosopher, whose teachings led to his tragic death.

"But who do you say that I am?"

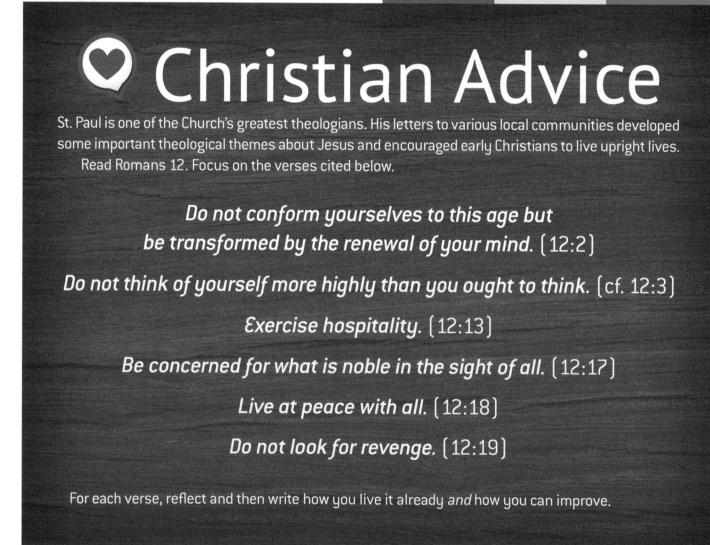

♥ Christian Advice

St. Paul is one of the Church's greatest theologians. His letters to various local communities developed some important theological themes about Jesus and encouraged early Christians to live upright lives. Read Romans 12. Focus on the verses cited below.

Do not conform yourselves to this age but be transformed by the renewal of your mind. (12:2)

Do not think of yourself more highly than you ought to think. (cf. 12:3)

Exercise hospitality. (12:13)

Be concerned for what is noble in the sight of all. (12:17)

Live at peace with all. (12:18)

Do not look for revenge. (12:19)

For each verse, reflect and then write how you live it already *and* how you can improve.

In his book *Crossing the Threshold of Hope*, St. John Paul II talks about St. Paul's understanding of Jesus:

St. Paul is profoundly aware that Christ is absolutely original and absolutely unique. If he were only a wise man like Socrates, if he were a "prophet" like Muhammad, if he were "enlightened" like Buddha, without any doubt he would not be what he is. He is the one mediator between God and humanity.

Ultimately, you must make your own decision about Jesus Christ, answering his question, "Who do you say that I am?" This is an important question, and it deserves your time, prayer, and attention. Your study of Salvation History and the important figures in the Bible can help you answer this for yourself. This chapter presents some of the ways that Jesus' earliest followers understood him. Notice which of Jesus' qualities resonate with your own understanding of him.

SECTION ASSESSMENT

NOTE TAKING

Use your notes on what various people and groups think of Jesus to help you answer the following questions.

1. What are three adjectives to describe Jesus?
2. What insight does the example of Fr. Kapaun give you about who Jesus is?

COMPREHENSION

3. How old was Fr. Kapaun when he died?
4. How did the other soldiers honor Fr. Kapaun after he died?
5. Who did St. Peter say that Jesus is?

REFLECTION

6. Explain why it is dangerous to make judgments about other people before getting to know them.
7. Why is it important for you to come up with a personal response to Jesus' question, "But who do you say that I am?"

SECTION 1
The Gospel Portrait of Jesus

MAIN IDEA
The Gospel accounts of Jesus' life help you understand why Jesus attracted so many people to follow him.

Everyone who reads the Gospels comes away with a distinct impression of Jesus, so much so that Jesus has been the subject of more books, articles, and films than anyone else in human history.

You have gained knowledge *about* Jesus during this course, but do you *know* him personally? What is so special about this man? What do *you* find attractive about Jesus? How do you answer these questions? In this section, you will review some of Jesus' personal qualities.

Jesus Was a Friend

In the Gospels, Jesus had many different kinds of friends. Consider, for example, what an interesting and varied group of Apostles he chose. Peter was headstrong and impetuous. The brothers James and John—Zebedee's sons—had such hot tempers that

Jesus nicknamed them "sons of thunder." Matthew was a tax collector. Ordinary fishermen were part of Jesus' inner circle.

As he walked the roads of Palestine, sick, maimed, undesirable, and sinful people flocked to Jesus. Recall that some Jewish leaders criticized Jesus about the outcasts with whom he associated, yet Jesus also numbered among his friends leading members of the Sanhedrin such as Joseph of Arimathea and Nicodemus.

Jesus interacted with people in unique ways:

- He ate with tax collectors.

- He forgave Peter, who sinned by denying Jesus' love prior to his crucifixion.

- He spoke to the Samaritan woman at the well even though she was a Samaritan, a woman, and someone who "lived in sin."

- He forgave the people who put him to death.

Jesus was a "friend for everyone." Anyone in the Gospels who was not a friend of Jesus seemed to have

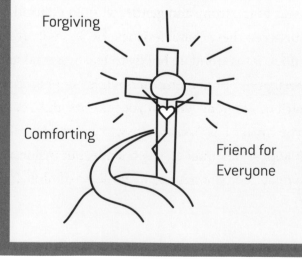

NOTE TAKING

Understanding Main Ideas. Sketch a simple portrait of Jesus in your notes. As you read the text section, jot down around the sketch personal qualities that describe the Lord.

Forgiving

Comforting

Friend for Everyone

only themselves to blame. This did not mean that Jesus did not make demands of people whom he considered friends. Remember, for example, that Jesus said to Peter: "Get behind me, Satan! You are an obstacle to me. You are thinking not as God does, but as human beings do" (Mt 16:23). Yet some people did not want a friendship with Jesus badly enough to change their ways of life or views. Recall the rich official who would not part with his possessions, or the many Jewish leaders who could not or would not believe in him.

Jesus shared true human emotions with his friends. For example, he wept when he saw how much Lazarus's family was suffering from Lazarus's death (see Jn 11:33–35). He had an especially close relationship with John, the beloved disciple. He was disappointed by his Apostles' lack of support during his agony in the garden.

Jesus likewise calls you to accept his offer of friendship. He sees in each person something so worthwhile that he chooses you to continue his work: "I . . . chose you and appointed you to go and bear fruit" (Jn 15:16). His call and direction to you is clear: "I have called you friends. . . . It was not you who chose me, but I who chose you. . . . This I command you: love one another" (Jn 15:15–17).

Jesus Had a Gentle Strength

Jesus was both strong and gentle, with no contradictions between these characteristics. He was not afraid of conflict. Jesus stood up boldly to teachers who laid heavy religious burdens on others while not practicing the spirit of religion: "Woe to you, scribes and Pharisees, you hypocrites. You are like whitewashed tombs, which appear beautiful on the outside, but inside are full of dead men's bones and every kind of filth" (Mt 23:27).

The sheep and oxen in the Temple area were intended for sacrifice. Doves were the offering of the poor.

Jesus exhibited a dramatic show of physical strength when he cleared the Temple precinct of money-changers because they were misusing the sacred place: "He made a whip out of cords and drove them all out of the temple area, with the sheep and oxen, and spilled the coins of the money-changers and overturned their tables, and to those who sold doves he said, 'Take these out of here, and stop making my Father's house a marketplace'" (Jn 2:15–16).

Jesus had passionate convictions that he would not compromise. But that did not translate into his forcing people to abide by his convictions. He was not loud or arrogant, qualities often associated with people who attempt to give off an air of strength. Rather, he was tender, loving, and sensitive to others. Picture the little children coming to Jesus. He warmly accepted them

THE FACE OF JESUS

Have you ever read a book and then later watched its movie version? As you read the book, you likely developed mental images of the characters and scenery based on the author's descriptions. Then, when you saw the movie, the characters and environment might or might not have matched your own images. Have you found that it is difficult not to see those movie images when you reread the book or its sequel? Images are very powerful. Consider this power as you encounter images of Jesus.

Jesus Christ is the most famous person who ever lived, yet there are no accurate pictures of him. To prevent idolatry, the Jews of Jesus' day forbade personal portraits. The Gospels do not even give you a physical description of Jesus. You simply do not know if he was short or tall, for example.

In the early centuries, Christians began to create images of Jesus. The catacombs of Rome contain the earliest images. There he sometimes appeared as a curly-haired young man who resembled young King David. At other times, he was a bearded man with long hair, the style worn by pious Jewish men of Jesus' own day.

St. Jerome concluded that some of God's majesty must have shone through Jesus' human body. He wrote, "Had he not had something heavenly in his face and his eyes, the Apostles never would have followed him at once, nor would those who came to arrest him have fallen to the ground."

In later centuries, Christian artists largely shared St. Jerome's view. Although a true representation of Jesus would be impossible to capture, artists decided that paintings and statues of Jesus should be compatible with the beauty of the mystery of God becoming flesh.

Interestingly, it was not until after the first millennium that artists widely portrayed Jesus as a suffering, crucified Savior. Depictions of the crucified Jesus appeared first in the art of Byzantine Christians and then spread to the Western, Latin-speaking Church. By the Renaissance, artists increasingly portrayed Jesus' humanity. Rembrandt, for example, chose Jewish men from his city of Amsterdam as his models for Jesus. His paintings are excellent classic representations of a truly human Jesus.

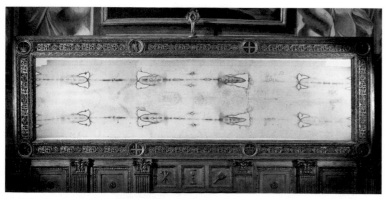

This is the Shroud of Turin, an image of Jesus that many Christians believe is the cloth he was wrapped in when buried.

In the nineteenth century, some artists began to paint Jesus with delicate, soft features. Certainly, Jesus could not have been such an unassertive, waxen, or plastic man. He was a strong carpenter, suntanned from walking throughout Palestine. It is hard to imagine the waxen Jesus attracting as many people as he did.

It is important to think critically about images of Jesus, because the images are so powerful. Your reaction to movie portrayals, statues, and paintings of Jesus can give you insight into your own understanding of Jesus. In addition, you need to be careful not to rely too much on the visuals you have seen. In some biblical films, Jesus does not smile very much, for example. He is very solemn, so much so that without other input, a viewer might think, "I don't know if I want to get to know this Jesus." Make sure you find images that fit with the Jesus you have come to know in the Gospels.

over the objections of his disciples (see Mk 10:13–16). He embraced them and made them feel welcomed and loved.

The Gospels contain other examples of Jesus' strength of personality and character.

- Jesus comforted Peter, James, and John when they become frightened at the time of his Transfiguration (see Mt 17:7).

- His loving touch reached out to heal unwanted lepers as well as countless other sick people. For example, he extended sympathy to the woman with an incurable blood flow who merely touched the tassel of his cloak. In the midst of the many who were reaching out to him, he sensed her need and cured her (see Lk 8:47–48).

Jesus Lived What He Taught

Jesus taught his followers to be humble, forgiving, and loving—and he lived these virtues himself.

Jesus modeled humility when he washed the feet of his disciples at the Last Supper. He said, "I have given you a model to follow, so that as I have done for you, you should also do" (Jn 13:15). He had previously taught his followers to be humble by instructing them not to parade good deeds in public to attract

Volunteers build new houses at a Habitat for a Humanity project.

attention. His followers were to give alms discreetly without drawing attention to their individual acts of charity.

Jesus taught his followers that they should forgive others, even enemies. He then forgave those who crucified him.

Jesus' primary lesson and example was to love others. He taught about love, saying "No one has greater love than this, to lay down one's life for one's friends" (Jn 15:13). Clearly, Jesus' own Passion and Death testify to his heartfelt love for each human being. He practiced what he preached.

SECTION ASSESSMENT

NOTE TAKING

Use the sketch and personal qualities you wrote down for Jesus to help you complete the following item.

1. List and discuss three character traits of Jesus revealed in the Gospels. Give scriptural evidence to illustrate your choices.

COMPREHENSION

2. What is an example of Jesus' humility?

3. When did Jesus share his emotions with his Apostles?

4. How was Jesus both strong and compassionate?

REFLECTION

5. What do you find most special about Jesus?

6. Discuss what it might mean for someone to have Jesus call that person his friend.

7. Select three passages from the Gospels that you believe capture the essential character of Jesus. Explain what they reveal about him.

SECTION 2
The Early Church Preaches about Jesus

MAIN IDEA
It is important to "listen" to how the Apostles describe Jesus because they knew him personally.

The Acts of the Apostles and the New Testament Letters narrate stories about the early days of the Church and the spread of the Gospel around the Roman Empire. The ways that St. Peter, St. Paul, and the other Apostles described Jesus can help you to know Jesus more deeply. The Apostles knew Jesus personally and were the most reliable witnesses to Jesus' identity.

Description of Jesus in the Kerygma

Although God had the Church in mind for all eternity, the history of the Church is known to have begun at Pentecost (see Acts 2). On that day, the Holy Spirit showered spiritual gifts on the Apostles, including the courage to proclaim the Gospel with faith and conviction as well as the ability to speak in various languages. A new human community known as the Church was created under the power of the Holy Spirit.

Remember that the Apostles preached the *kerygma*—the essential message or proclamation about Jesus Christ—in the years after Jesus' Death. A typical example of a sermon using the kerygma is the one preached by Peter on Pentecost (see Acts 2:14–40; 3:11–26). Acts records eighteen different sermons that capture what the early Church preached about Jesus. The great saints Peter, Paul, and Stephen delivered these sermons. St. Peter's famous sermon delivered from the window of the Upper Room on Pentecost contains these truths about Jesus:

NOTE TAKING

Summarizing Content. As you read the section, list descriptions of Jesus found in the following sources in a chart similar to the one below.

Descriptions of Jesus				
Acts of the Apostles	Letters of St. Paul	Letter to the Hebrews	Catholic Letters	Book of Revelation

IN THE KERYGMA

- Jesus of Nazareth **FULFILLS** the Old Testament **PROPHECIES**.
- Jesus was **BORN** of David's family.
- God worked **MIGHTY DEEDS** through Jesus.

- The Jewish leaders put Jesus to Death on a Cross, but as was prophesied, God **RAISED** him **FROM THE DEAD**. His disciples witnessed his appearances after the Resurrection.
- Jesus **ASCENDED TO HEAVEN**, is exalted at the right hand of the Father, and reigns as the Lord of the living and the dead.
- The crucified Jesus is **BOTH LORD AND MESSIAH**.

- As he promised, **CHRIST SENT THE HOLY SPIRIT**, whom he received from the Father. The Spirit is the sign and assurance of the Lord's presence in the Church until the Lord comes again at the end of time as **JUDGE AND SAVIOR** of the world.
- Because all of the above is true, people must respond to **THE GOOD NEWS**. "Repent and be baptized, every one of you, in the name of Jesus Christ for the forgiveness of your sins; and you will receive the gift of the Holy Spirit" (Acts 2:38).

Peter's Pentecost sermon had an electrifying effect on his hearers. Three thousand people accepted his message and were baptized on that day alone. The Church was well underway.

St. Paul's Portrait of Jesus

A good portion of the Acts of the Apostles tells the story of the great missionary and theologian St. Paul. Initially called Saul, Paul was born around AD 10 in Tarsus (modern-day Turkey).

Paul had a varied background. He was both a Jew and a Roman citizen. He received a classical Greek education and also studied to be a Jewish rabbi under the famous rabbi Gamaliel. As a young man, Paul chose to be a strict Pharisee, but his upbringing in Tarsus exposed him to Gentile religions, philosophies, and customs. All of these experiences were valuable after Paul converted to Christianity.

Prior to his conversion, Paul was hostile to Jews who believed in Jesus and violently opposed people preaching that the condemned criminal Jesus was the Messiah. In his mind, this claim was blasphemy, a charge that demanded the proclaimer's death. Paul was present at the execution of St. Stephen (Acts 7:54–8:1), the first Christian martyr.

Paul's conversion to Christ was a great turning point in history.

FAMOUS SERMONS
IN ACTS

Read the following sermons from Acts. Indentify the various kerygmatic elements contained in each.

- Peter and Cornelius: Acts 10:34–48.
- Paul at the Synagogue in Perga: Acts 13:16–41

St. Paul was beheaded in Rome in AD 67. His martyrdom was the eventual result of his conversion.

On his journey, as he was nearing Damascus, a light from the sky suddenly flashed around him. He fell to the ground and heard a voice saying to him, "Saul, Saul, why are you persecuting me?" He said, "Who are you, sir?" The reply came, "I am Jesus, whom you are persecuting. Now get up and go into the city and you will be told what you must do." The men who were traveling with him stood speechless, for they heard the voice but could see no one. Saul got up from the ground, but when he opened his eyes he could see nothing; so they led him by the hand and brought him to Damascus. (Acts 9:3–8)

Paul's conversion initiated his work as a Christian evangelist. After God called Ananias to restore Paul's sight, Paul was baptized in Damascus. Paul preached for a time in that city and then made his way to Jerusalem, where Barnabas had to assure the disciples that Paul had truly turned away from persecuting Christians and was instead proclaiming the Good News.

Paul wrote letters to the communities he founded around the Mediterranean Sea. Theologians believe that Paul wrote at least seven of the letters preserved in the New Testament himself: Romans, 1 and 2 Corinthians, Galatians, Philippians, 1 Thessalonians, and Philemon. The Church has not determined definitively that Paul alone wrote Ephesians, Colossians, 2 Thessalonians, 1 and 2 Timothy, and Titus. One or more of Paul's closest disciples may have written the other six letters, though all are attributed to Paul.

In his letters, Paul explains Jesus' identity and mission. The letters are rich in theology. St. Paul's inspired insights help Christians from every era to a deeper understanding of Jesus. Some of St. Paul's most prominent teachings about Jesus are summarized in the feature on page 342.

ST. PAUL'S Teachings on Jesus

Jesus is the Son of God.

In the Letter to the Galatians, Paul wrote, "I live by faith in the Son of God who has loved me and given himself up for me" (Gal 2:20).

Jesus is the Christ.

The title Christ (Messiah) appears 379 times in the Pauline Letters. After his conversion, it was very clear to St. Paul that Jesus was the Messiah promised to the Chosen People. He understood the need to preach the Good News of Jesus Christ to Jew and Gentile alike.

Jesus is the New Adam.

The first Adam disobeyed and brought sin and death to the world, but "through the obedience of one [Jesus Christ] the many will be made righteous" (Rm 5:19).

The crucified Jesus truly rose from the dead.

The Paschal Mystery is unequaled in Salvation History. Christ's Resurrection is essential to the Salvation of the world. St. Paul writes, "If Christ has not been raised, then empty [too] is our preaching; empty, too, your faith. Then we are also false witnesses to God. . . . If Christ has not been raised, your faith is vain; you are still in your sins" (1 Cor 15:14–15; 17). Your faith is intimately tied to your belief in the Resurrection of Jesus Christ.

Jesus sent the Holy Spirit to give spiritual life to his followers.

Jesus works through the power of the Holy Spirit. The Spirit's life unites followers to the Risen Christ and enables them to proclaim, "Jesus is Lord." The Holy Spirit showers spiritual gifts on the members of Christ's Body, the Church, for the benefit of all: to build up the Church and to attract nonbelievers to worship Jesus Christ.

Jesus is the Savior and Redeemer of the World.

The Son of God became man and died to atone for the sins of humanity: "the Lord Jesus Christ . . . gave himself for our sins that he might rescue us from the present evil age" (Gal 1:3–4). Jesus took on the sins of all to make you righteous before the Father. He is your Redeemer.

The Father exalted the Risen Christ.

Although Christ sits in glory at the right hand of the Father in Heaven, he is the perfect example of humility.

The Letter to the Philippians teaches that Jesus,

. . . though he was in the form of God,
did not regard equality with God something
to be grasped.
Rather, he emptied himself,
taking the form of a slave,
coming in human likeness;
and found human in appearance,
he humbled himself,
becoming obedient to death,
even death on a cross.
Because of this, God greatly exalted him
and bestowed on him the name
that is above every name,
that at the name of Jesus
every knee should bend,
of those in Heaven and on
earth and under the earth,
and every tongue confess
that Jesus Christ is Lord,
to the glory of God
the Father. (Phil 2:6–11)

These theological teachings of St. Paul merely scratch the surface of the mystery of Jesus Christ, but they offer an idea of the exciting truths this great Apostle preached to people in the early decades of the Church.

Lessons about Jesus in Other New Testament Epistles

The Bible contains nine non-Pauline Epistles that reveal key truths about Jesus and offer guidance for Christian living, as well as the Book of Revelation.

Jesus in the Letter to the Hebrews

The Letter to the Hebrews (composed in the AD 60s or 80s) is a written homily that develops the theme that Jesus Christ is supreme High Priest, the model of faith.

Nineteenth-century fresco of Jesus Christ as Priest

In Judaism, priests offered sacrifices. Jesus willingly offered his life as a sacrifice for the sins of all. He is not only the Priest who offered the sacrifice on behalf of all, but he himself is the sacrifice offered. Christ's sacrifice instituted the New Covenant foretold by Jeremiah.

The Letter to the Hebrews often refers to Jesus as "the Son" and compares him to other biblical figures. It is also the only New Testament writing that calls Jesus an Apostle—that is, a messenger or representative of

> **Redeemer** Redemption is the process that frees you from the slavery of sin. Jesus Christ is your Redeemer because he paid the price of his own sacrificial Death on the Cross to save you from sin.

God (see Heb 3:1). Hebrews stresses that Jesus is far superior to angels and greater than any Old Testament prophet. Jesus "is worthy of more 'glory' than Moses, as the founder of a house has more 'honor' than the house itself" (Heb 3:3).

The Letter to the Hebrews encourages a community of dispirited Christians to persevere in their faith. The author offers the example of Jesus Christ, who himself was tempted and suffered, yet remained faithful.

The advice given in Hebrews holds true for you today. If you feel distracted by a world that often ignores Christ and his message, you should take to heart the words of Hebrews: "Let us rid ourselves of every burden and sin that clings to us and persevere in running the race that lies before us while keeping our eyes fixed on Jesus, the leader and perfecter of faith" (Heb 12:1–2).

Jesus in the Catholic Epistles

The seven Catholic Epistles contain general advice that was helpful to all the churches—hence the name catholic, which means "universal." Both the Western and Eastern churches universally accepted these letters, all of which offer unique insights to help you better know Jesus.

The *Letter of James* contains practical advice about how to live a Christian life: how to handle temptation, control your tongue, love your neighbor, and more. The letter stresses that Jesus' followers must put their faith into action. Good works go hand-in-hand with faith in Jesus.

Recall that the prophet Isaiah and the Gospel of Mark emphasized the suffering the Messiah would have to endure. The *First Letter of Peter* also presents Jesus as the Suffering Servant. Christ's followers should imitate Jesus' patient suffering. When Christians endure trials for Christ, they enter into his suffering and attract others to him. Jesus is the model for this way of living.

The *Letter of Jude* and the *Second Letter of Peter* are both addressed to converts to Christianity who entered the Church only to engage in immoral behavior or teach heretical beliefs. The letters condemn both the immoral practices and the false teachings, especially the teachings that deny that Christ will come again. The Second Letter of Peter emphatically states that there will be a Parousia because the Lord said he would return and the Lord keeps his word. The Second Letter of Peter concedes that people do not know the time when this will occur, but they should always be ready.

All three letters of John, written around AD 100, deal with false teachings that had crept into the Church. The *First Letter of John* counters people who said that Jesus came to give only *some* people special knowledge and eternal life. This is not true: Christ came for everyone. The First Letter of John also attacks the heretical views of Docetism (see 1 Jn 9) by teaching that Christians must have true belief in Jesus Christ as Son of God and the Messiah. The central teaching of the letter is "God is love." If this is true, Jesus is love. The letter contains this famous and beautiful passage:

> Beloved, let us love one another, because love is of God; everyone who loves is begotten by God and knows God. Whoever is without love does not know God, for God is love. In this way the love of God was revealed to us: God sent his only Son into the world so that we might have life through him. In this is love: not that we have loved God, but that he loved us and sent his Son as expiation for our sins. Beloved, if God so loved us, we also must love one another. No one has ever seen God. Yet, if we love one another, God remains in us, and his love is brought to perfection in us.
> (1 Jn 4:7–12)

This truth is profound for your understanding of Christ. Any time you experience love, you also experience Jesus.

Jesus in the Book of Revelation

The Book of Revelation, also known as the *Revelation of John* or the *Apocalypse*, is the last book in the Bible, and it is one of the most difficult to understand. Filled with elaborate symbolism, it is written in the apocalyptic style.

The Book of Revelation is clear in communicating that Jesus has brought victory over death and will triumph in other situations of sin and suffering. Final Salvation will take place at the end of the present age, when Jesus Christ will return in glory at his Second Coming. Therefore, although there is suffering and hardship in the present world, a Christian should endure these in order to achieve God's reward.

These titles of Jesus from the Book of Revelation reveal the deep faith of a persecuted Christian community that Lord will triumph at the end of time:

LAMB. The author of Revelation calls Jesus the Lamb twenty-eight times. The title refers to Jesus' great sacrifice that won you Salvation. He is the perfect Passover Lamb who liberates you from sin.

ALPHA AND OMEGA. These are the first and last letters of the Greek alphabet. They reveal the eternal nature of Jesus Christ, who is Lord God. He is the beginning and the end. "'I am the Alpha and the Omega,' says the Lord God, 'the one who is and who was and who is to come, the almighty'" (Rv 1:8).

THE AMEN. Jesus is the Amen or Yes to God the Father. He is the God of Truth.

LION OF THE TRIBE OF JUDAH. Just as the lion is the king of the animals, this title emphasizes Jesus as the Messiah, the promised King in the royal line of David. "The lion of the tribe of Judah, the root of David, has triumphed" (Rv 5:5).

KING OF KINGS AND LORD OF LORDS. Perhaps you are familiar with Handel's *Messiah*. These words are in the famous "Hallelujah Chorus." They affirm that Jesus is supreme and will conquer the evil one and his servants.

MORNING STAR. Near the end of Revelation, Jesus says, "I, Jesus, sent my angel to give you this testimony for the churches. I am the root and offspring of David, the bright morning star" (Rv 22:16).

Revelation also uses many of the familiar titles of other New Testament writings such as Son of God, Lord, Word of God, and Christ. The Book of Revelation ends the Bible with these words: "Amen! Come, Lord Jesus! The grace of the Lord Jesus be with all" (Rv 22:20–21).

LETTER OF Encouragement

Imagine you are an early Christian missionary. Write a short letter to your converts to encourage them to remain strong in their faith in Jesus Christ. Include at least three practices of faith applicable to all generations.

SECTION ASSESSMENT

NOTE TAKING

Use the chart you made to help you match the following teachings with the book of the Bible where it was most prominently taught.

1. Jesus is the Supreme High Priest.

2. Jesus is the Alpha and the Omega.

3. Jesus fulfilled the Old Testament prophecies.

4. Jesus is the New Adam.

5. Jesus is love.

A. The Letters of St. Paul

B. The Letter to the Hebrews

C. The Catholic Letters

D. The Acts of the Apostles

E. The Book of Revelation

VOCABULARY

6. Define *Redeemer*.

COMPREHENSION

7. What is Pentecost, and why is it so important?

8. What is the main kerygma of the Church?

9. How was St. Paul's background unique?

10. Discuss three titles for Jesus that appear in the Book of Revelation.

REFLECTION

11. List three ways the Lord has shown his love for you. Reflect on your life. Write a short paragraph telling Jesus how you show your love for him by sharing it with others.

12. When was a time you had to defend your faith in Jesus Christ? What was the result?

SECTION 3
Make a Commitment to Really Know Jesus

MAIN IDEA
It is not enough to know about Jesus Christ; rather, it is important to develop a personal relationship with him.

The grace you have received at Baptism; the gifts of faith, hope, and love; and the virtues necessary for discipleship offer you a firm and lasting foundation for knowing and following Jesus. The conclusion of this course and text—*Jesus Christ: God's Revelation to the World*—is a good time for you to reflect even more deeply on your own understanding and beliefs about Jesus Christ. You might ask yourself questions like these:

- How has God revealed Jesus to you in your life?
- How has the Holy Spirit led you to love and serve Jesus?

It is important to *know about* the Savior of the world, but it is more important to *know him personally*. Do you know Jesus? Is he your friend? Do you want to grow closer to him? Will you say yes to these questions as you imagine him asking you?

- Do you accept me as God's only Son, your Savior, a friend who loves you beyond what you can imagine?
- Will you spend time talking to me in prayer, listening to my word in Scripture, enjoying the love I have for you?
- Will you receive me in the Eucharist every week?
- Are you willing to express your sorrow to me in the Sacrament of Penance and Reconciliation, where you can ask for my forgiveness and be assured of my love and the strength of the Holy Spirit?

NOTE TAKING

Making a Timeline. Create a timeline like the one below. Along with ideas you glean from this section, write a strategy for deepening your friendship with Jesus at various stages of your life.

Go on a retreat   Adopt a foster child

/_____/_____/_____/_____/_____/_____
Today   Next Year   In 5 Years   In 10 Years   In 25 Years   In My Last Year

- Will you make an effort to recognize me in other people?

- Will you form your conscience in light of my teachings and example in the Gospels and the teachings of the Magisterium, my representatives on earth?

- Will you try to imitate me, especially by serving others? Will you reach out in a special way to help those who are especially close to me—like the poor, the handicapped, the sick, victims of injustice?

Becoming Jesus' Friend

Jesus personally invites you to accept his friendship. In John 15:15–17, he says:

- I have called you friends.

- It was not you who chose me, but I who chose you.

- This I command you: love one another.

Jesus sees in you something so worthwhile that he chooses you to continue his work of love. With his Father and the Holy Spirit, he has given you everything you need to do his work.

It may sound like a good idea to become Jesus' friend, but how does a person actually do that? Some of the saints, people who were definitely friends with Jesus, have insight into this process. Read and reflect on what they had to say in the feature that follows.

4 STEPS TO BECOMING JESUS' FRIEND

1 FOCUS ON CHRIST

According to St. John Baptist de La Salle, you should remember that you are always in the presence of God. This awareness leads you to Jesus. St. John Baptist de La Salle wrote, "One consequence of living in the presence of God is that all our actions will be referred to Jesus Christ and will tend towards him as towards their center."[1] Calling to mind that you are in the presence of Christ enables you to see events and people more like God does. According to St. Benedict, a focus on Christ changes your behavior:

> Your way of acting should be different from the world's way; the love of Christ must come before all else. You are not to act in anger or nurse a grudge. Rid your heart of all deceit. Never give a hollow greeting of peace or turn away when someone needs your love. Bind yourself to no oath lest it prove false, but speak the truth with heart and tongue.[2]

St. John Baptist de La Salle

2 LEARN ABOUT AND LIVE MORE LIKE JESUS

Reading the Gospels for homework and reading them prayerfully are quite different experiences. St. Ignatius of Loyola in his *Spiritual Exercises* asks participants to meditate on various events in Jesus' life in order to get to know him better. St. John of the Cross advises you to study Jesus' life and then try to imitate him. If you make an effort to live in a Christlike way, the stories about Jesus from the Scriptures will make more sense to you.

St. Ignatius of Loyola

3 SERVE OTHERS

Serving others is vital to following Jesus. St. Francis de Sales says that you should seek opportunities for serving Jesus and practice virtue as much as you can. St. John of the Cross writes, "You should strive in your prayer for a pure conscience, a will that is wholly with God and a mind truly set upon him."[3] God revealed to St. Catherine of Siena this thought: "So they offend me more by abandoning charity for their neighbor. For in charity for their neighbors they find me, but in their own pleasure, where they are seeking me, they will be deprived of me."[4]

St. John of the Cross

4 TALK WITH JESUS

You may have heard that prayer is simply "talking with God." This is true. What does God want you talk with him about? St. Teresa of Avila describes prayer this way:

> The soul can also picture itself as in the presence of Christ, and accustom itself to feel deep love for His blessed humanity. It can have Him always with it, and talk to Him, and ask Him for what it needs and complain to Him of its troubles and rejoice with Him in its pleasures, and yet never allow them to make it forgetful of Him.[5]

St. Teresa described the advantages of such a friendship.

> With the Lord by our side, there is nothing we cannot do. Separated from Him, we will collapse almost immediately. With so good a friend and Captain ever present, Himself the first to suffer, everything can be borne. He helps. He strengthens. He never fails. He is the true friend.

St. Teresa of Avila

SECTION ASSESSMENT

NOTE TAKING

Use some of the ideas from your timeline to help you to answer the following questions.

1. What are three ideas for deepening your relationship with Jesus?
2. How will other people help you be a better friend of Jesus?

CRITICAL THINKING

3. Take a side in one of the following debates and write a response.
   - Is it possible to be Jesus' friend without believing that he is the Savior?
   - Is it possible to be Jesus' friend without being part of the Church?

COMPREHENSION

4. What is one consequence of living in the presence of God?
5. What does St. Teresa of Avila say you can do if you are friends with Jesus?

REFLECTION

6. How has God revealed Jesus to you in your life?

Section Summaries

Focus Question

Who do you say that Jesus is?

Complete one of the following:

→ Select two saints not mentioned in this chapter, and research some advice they gave for getting to know Jesus better.

→ Research the miracle that is unofficially attributed to Fr. Kapaun. Does this miracle seem authentic to you?

→ Pick two stories from the Gospels to pray with in order to know Jesus better.

INTRODUCTION (PAGES 331–333)

Who Is Jesus to You?

Jesus attracts people to him for varied reasons. Jesus appeals to different people in different ways. It is important to determine who Jesus is to you in order to cultivate a deeper friendship with him.

 If someone were to say that Jesus was only a prophet or wise man, what would you say in response?

SECTION 1 (PAGES 334–338)

The Gospel Portrait of Jesus

The Gospel accounts of Jesus' life help you understand why Jesus attracted so many people to be near to him. Jesus was strong but gentle. He showed his strength when interacting with people who were oppressive or hypocritical and his gentleness with oppressed people. Jesus walked his talk. He did not ask anyone to do something that he would not do himself.

 Following Jesus' example is a characteristic of discipleship; how might you imitate Jesus by expanding your group of friends to include a greater variety of different people?

SECTION 2 (PAGES 339–346)

The Early Church Preaches about Jesus

The Apostles preached the kerygma, a set of statements of faith that were essential to include in introducing Jesus. Their main message was that Jesus Christ, the Son of God, is risen from the dead. St. Paul also emphasized certain points as he traveled around the Mediterranean world and founded Christian communities in several places. The other New Testament Letters emphasized different elements of Christology. The Book of Revelation includes many symbols along with some unique titles for Jesus to help you to better understand him.

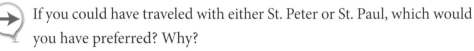 If you could have traveled with either St. Peter or St. Paul, which would you have preferred? Why?

SECTION 3 (PAGES 347–350)

Make a Commitment to Really Know Jesus

To become Jesus' friend is to pray and participate in the life of the Church, keep your focus on him, learn more about him, follow his way of life, serve others, and talk with him. Getting to know Jesus and becoming his friend involves specific choices. Great friends of Jesus, the saints, offer some guidance about how to come to know Jesus as a friend.

From your own experience, how would you coach someone else who wanted to grow in friendship with Jesus?

Chapter Assignments

Choose and complete at least one of these assignments to assess your understanding of the material in this chapter.

1. Forge a Deeper Relationship with Jesus

Write an essay focusing on these two points:

- How you are most like Jesus

- Why Jesus would want to be your friend

In your essay, describe how you imagine the face of Jesus. If you like, you may sketch the face of Christ as you imagine him.

2. Analyze a Christian Hymn

Philippians 2:5–11 is recognized as an early Christian hymn. Research several traditional and contemporary Catholic musicians. After listening to their works, pick out two favorite songs from two different eras. Copy down their lyrics, and write a two-page reflection on the Christian themes or virtues each song highlights. If you like, play or sing one or both songs for your classmates.

3. Share the Faith

Construct a set of twenty-five questions and answers on beliefs about Jesus that can be used as a quiz with grade school students. Present it as a booklet or an online quiz. Work with a religious education or Catholic school teacher to administer the test. Score the questions. Arrange to visit with the students after they have taken the test. Share with them about your faith and friendship with the Lord.

Faithful Disciple

St. Robert Bellarmine

St. Robert Bellarmine

St. Robert Bellarmine was born in 1542, the third of ten children to Italian nobles who had fallen on hard times. Robert received a Jesuit education as a boy, joined the order in September 1560, and was ordained a priest in 1570. The sixteenth century, remember, was the century of the Protestant Reformation when there was a need for the Catholic Church to defend her teachings and practices against Protestant challenges. The Council of Trent, the Catholic response to the Reformation, ended during Robert's first years as a Jesuit.

After completing his own education, Robert was a professor of Theology at the University of Louvain for six years before Pope Gregory XIII asked him to teach at the Roman College. While he was in Rome, Robert wrote the most complete work of his day, *Disputations on the Controversies of the Christian Faith*, defending Catholicism against Protestant critique. He also wrote catechisms for students and for teachers and served on a commission to revise the Latin Bible, the Vulgate. He wrote additional works defending the Church from heresies. Later, he became an archbishop and implemented the teachings of the Council of Trent in his archdiocese.

While he was not immersed in scholarship, Robert was embroiled in other tumultuous affairs. He was theologian to Pope Clement XIII for several years and served as a bishops' examiner. This same pope raised Robert to the level of cardinal. Robert defended the pope against anti-clerics in Venice and against the political ideas of King James I of England. At home, he lived a simple life. He was a great preacher, and gave his money to the poor. At one point, he gave some wall hangings from his home so that they could become clothes for the less fortunate. As he noted, "the walls won't catch cold." Robert died at age seventy-eight.

Robert Bellarmine was canonized by Pope Pius XI in 1930 and declared a Doctor of the Church in 1931. His feast day is September 17 and he is the patron saint of canon lawyers, catechists, and catechumens.

Reading Comprehension

1. How many years as a Jesuit did it take before St. Robert Bellarmine became a priest?

2. What was the subject of St. Robert Bellarmine's most famous writing?

3. Who did St. Robert Bellarmine defend Pope Clement XIII from?

Writing Task

- St. Robert Bellarmine is the patron saint of catechists. Look up and define the meaning of the word. How do you think St. Robert himself was a model catechist?

Explaining the Faith
Why do some people try to change what the Church teaches about Jesus Christ?

False teaching has been a problem in the Church from the earliest years. For example, *Gnosticism* tried to restrict Jesus' message to a very few. The heresy claimed that Jesus taught secret knowledge that only select people could understand. The Church condemned this approach, as you can imagine, because it excluded most people from the Good News. Jesus came for all people, and his message is open to all people. The Church invites all people to approach Christ. The Gospel must be preached to everyone, and it can be understood by less educated people as well as learned scholars.

Some distortions of Jesus and the Good News appeared because people did not like what Jesus taught or found his teachings hard to follow. Others resulted from downplaying Jesus' suffering and Death. That is precisely what the Docetists did, because they had a hard time seeing how God would lower himself to become a man who could suffer like other humans. Again, the Church condemned false teachings like these because they simply did not correspond with apostolic teaching. The author of the First Letter of John made it very clear that "what we have heard, what we have seen with our eyes, what we looked upon and touched with our hands concerns the Word of life" (1 Jn 1:1).

Between the second and fourth centuries, some authors, curious about the life of Jesus, made up their own Gospels to fill in details that did not appear in the canonical Gospels or to present a different angle. One example is the *Gospel of Judas*, a relatively recent discovery. It is a Gnostic text that made

Judas Iscariot, the Apostle who betrayed Jesus, a hero. It obviously clashes with the true portrait of Judas given in the four Gospels, and it was excluded from the canon and condemned by Church authorities.

In those early centuries, heresies also sometimes arose as errors about who Jesus was. A classic example was **Arianism**, started by the priest Arius in the fourth century. Arius accepted that Jesus was the Son of God, but he claimed that the Son was *created* by God and thus was not equal to God. In short, he denied the divinity of Jesus. This teaching clearly contradicted what the Apostles and St. Paul taught. The first ecumenical Church council, the Council of Nicaea (325), condemned Arianism.

Today, people are still trying to figure out who Jesus is. Most theologians and biblical scholars are responsible scholars. They respect Sacred Tradition and look to the Magisterium to guide them in their studies. Others, though, deny that God can intervene in the natural world. For example, one group of mostly Protestant scholars—the "Jesus Seminar"—denies God's unique intervention and Revelation in human history in the Incarnation and calls into question the true divinity of Jesus Christ.

For each generation, the Church must call all followers of Christ to true belief, belief that rests ultimately on Sacred Scripture and Sacred Tradition. Simply put, the Incarnation itself is the great miracle. If God could become man in Jesus of Nazareth, then Jesus could certainly perform miracles. The Church reminds us of this simple truth.

> **Arianism** A fourth-century movement named for an Alexandrian priest, Arius, who denied the true divinity of Christ.

Reflection

- Look up the term *relativism*. How is this term connected with the heresies described above? How is this issue present in the Church today?

Prayer
The Prayer of St. Patrick

Christ with me, Christ before me,
Christ behind me,
Christ in me, Christ beneath me,
Christ above me,
Christ on my right, Christ on my left,
Christ where I lie, Christ where I sit,
Christ where I arise,
Christ in the heart of every man who
thinks of me,
Christ in the mouth of every man who
speaks to me,
Christ in every eye that sees me,
Christ in every ear that hears me.

APPENDIX
CATHOLIC HANDBOOK for FAITH

Beliefs

From the beginning, the Church expressed and handed on its faith in brief formulas accessible to all. These professions of faith are called creeds *because their first word in Latin,* credo, *means "I believe." The following creeds have special importance in the Church. The Apostles' Creed is a summary of the Apostles' faith. The Nicene Creed developed from the Councils of Nicaea and Constantinople and remains in common between the Churches of the East and West.*

Apostles' Creed

I believe in God,
the Father almighty,
Creator of heaven and earth,
and in Jesus Christ, his only Son, our Lord,
who was conceived by the Holy Spirit,
born of the Virgin Mary,
suffered under Pontius Pilate,
was crucified, died, and was buried;
he descended into hell;
on the third day he rose again from the dead;
he ascended into heaven,
and is seated at the right hand of God the
   Father Almighty;
from there he will come to judge the living and
   the dead.

I believe in the Holy Spirit,
the holy catholic Church,
the communion of saints,
the forgiveness of sins,
the resurrection of the body,
and life everlasting. Amen.

Nicene Creed

I believe in one God,
the Father almighty,
maker of heaven and earth,
of all things visible and invisible.

I believe in one Lord Jesus Christ
the Only Begotten Son of God,
born of the Father before all ages.
God from God, Light from Light,
true God from true God,
begotten, not made, consubstantial with the
Father;
through him all things were made.
For us men and for our salvation
he came down from heaven,
and by the Holy Spirit was incarnate of the
   Virgin Mary,
and became man.

For our sake he was crucified under Pontius
Pilate,
he suffered death and was buried,
and rose again on the third day
in accordance with the Scriptures.
He ascended into heaven
and is seated at the right hand of the Father.
He will come again in glory
to judge the living and the dead
and his kingdom will have no end.

I believe in the Holy Spirit, the Lord, the giver
of life,
who proceeds from the Father and the Son,

who with the Father and the Son is adored and
  glorified,
who has spoken through the prophets.

I believe in one, holy, catholic and apostolic
Church.
I confess one Baptism for the forgiveness of
sins
and I look forward to the resurrection of the
dead
and the life of the world to come. Amen.

Faith in God: Father, Son, and Holy Spirit

The Church's profession of faith begins with God, for God is the First and the Last, the beginning and end of everything.

Attributes of God

St. Thomas Aquinas named nine attributes of God (characteristics that tell us some things about God's nature):

1. *God is eternal.*
   He has no beginning and no end. Or, to put it another way, God always was, always is, and always will be.

2. *God is unique.*
   There is no other God like YHWH (see Is 45:18). God is the designer of a one-and-only world. Even the people he creates are one of a kind.

3. *God is omnipotent.*
   God is Almighty. This is the only attribute of God mentioned in the Creed. God's power is over all the universe, which remains totally at his disposal. God rules everything and can do everything. His power is both loving and mysterious.

4. *God is omnipresent.*
   God is not limited to space. He is everywhere. You can never be away from God.

5. *God contains all things.*
   All of creation is under God's care and jurisdiction.

6. *God is immutable.*
   God does not evolve. God does not change. God is the same God now as he always was and always will be.

7. *God is pure spirit.*
   Though God has been described with human attributes, God is not a material creation. God's image cannot be made. God is pure spirit and cannot be divided into parts. God is simple, but complex.

8. *God is alive.*
   We believe in a living God, a God who acts in the lives of people. Most concretely, he came to this world in the incarnate form of Jesus Christ.

9. *God is holy.*
   God is pure goodness. God is pure love.

The Holy Trinity

The Trinity is the mystery of one God in three Persons—Father, Son, and Holy Spirit. Viewed in the light of faith, some of the Church *dogmas*, or beliefs, can help our understanding of this mystery:

• *The Trinity is One.* There are not three Gods, but one God in Three Persons. Each one of them—Father, Son, and Holy Spirit —is God whole and entire.

• *The Three Persons are distinct from one another.* The Three Persons of the Trinity are distinct in how they relate to one another. "It is the Father who generates, the Son who is begotten, and the Holy Spirit who proceeds" (Lateran Council IV, quoted in *CCC*, 254). The Father is not the Son, nor is the Son the Holy Spirit.

- *The Three Persons of the Blessed Trinity are related to one another.* While the Three Persons are truly distinct in light of their relations, we believe in one God. The Three Persons do not divide the divine unity. The Council of Florence taught: "Because of that unity the Father is wholly in the Son and wholly in the Holy Spirit; the Son is wholly in the Father and wholly in the Holy Spirit; the Holy Spirit is wholly in the Father and wholly in the Son" (quoted in *CCC*, 255).

St. John of Damascus used two analogies to describe the doctrine of the Blessed Trinity.

Think of the Father as a root,
of the Son as a branch,
and of the Spirit as a fruit,
for the substance of these is one.

The Father is a sun
with the Son as rays
and the Holy Spirit as heat.

Read more about the Holy Trinity in paragraphs 232–260 of the *Catechism of the Catholic Church.*

Deposit of Faith

Deposit of Faith *refers to both Sacred Scripture and Sacred Tradition handed on from the time of the Apostles, from which the Church draws all that she proposes is revealed by God.*

Canon of the Bible

There are seventy-three books in the canon of the Bible (that is, the official list of books the Church accepts as divinely inspired writings): forty-six Old Testament books and twenty-seven New Testament books. Listed on the following page are the categories and books of the Old Testament and New Testament.

The Old Testament				The New Testament			
The Pentateuch		**The Prophetic Books**		**The Gospels**		**The Catholic Letters**	
Genesis	Gn	Isaiah	Is	Matthew	Mt	James	Jas
Exodus	Ex	Jeremiah	Jer	Mark	Mk	1 Peter	1 Pt
Leviticus	Lv	Lamentations	Lam	Luke	Lk	2 Peter	2 Pt
Numbers	Nm	Baruch	Bar	John	Jn	1 John	1 Jn
Deuteronomy	Dt	Ezekiel	Ez			2 John	2 Jn
The Historical Books		Daniel	Dn	Acts of the Apostles	Acts	3 John	3 Jn
Joshua	Jos	Hosea	Hos	**The New Testament Letters**		Jude	Jude
Judges	Jgs	Joel	Jl	Romans	Rom		
Ruth	Ru	Amos	Am	1 Corinthians	1 Cor	Revelation	Rv
1 Samuel	1 Sm	Obadiah	Ob	2 Corinthians	2 Cor		
2 Samuel	2 Sm	Jonah	Jon	Galatians	Gal		
1 Kings	1 Kgs	Micah	Mi	Ephesians	Eph		
2 Kings	2 Kgs	Nahum	Na	Philippians	Phil		
1 Chronicles	1 Chr	Habakkuk	Hb	Colossians	Col		
2 Chronicles	2 Chr	Zephaniah	Zep	1 Thessalonians	1 Thes		
Ezra	Ezr	Haggai	Hg	2 Thessalonians	2 Thes		
Nehemiah	Neh	Zechariah	Zec	1 Timothy	1 Tm		
Tobit	Tb	Malachi	Mal	2 Timothy	2 Tm		
Judith	Jdt			Titus	Ti		
Esther	Est			Philemon	Phlm		
1 Maccabees	1 Mc			Hebrews	Heb		
2 Maccabees	2 Mc						
The Wisdom Books							
Job	Jb						
Psalms	Ps(s)						
Proverbs	Prv						
Ecclesiastes	Eccl						
Song of Songs	Sg						
Wisdom	Ws						
Sirach	Sir						

The Relationship between Sacred Scripture and Sacred Tradition

The Church does not derive the revealed truths of God from the Sacred Scriptures alone. Sacred Tradition hands on God's word, first given to the Apostles by the Lord and the Holy Spirit, to the successors of the Apostles (the bishops and the pope). Enlightened by the Holy Spirit, these successors faithfully preserve, explain, and spread God's Word to the ends of the earth. The Second Vatican Council fathers explained the relationship between Sacred Scripture and Sacred Tradition:

> It is clear therefore that, in the supremely wise arrangement of God, Sacred Tradition, Sacred Scripture, and the Magisterium of the Church are so connected and associated that one of them cannot stand without the others. Working together, each in its own way, under the action of the one Holy Spirit, they all contribute effectively to the salvation of souls. (*Dei Verbum*, 10)

Church Teaching on Reading and Studying Scripture

If one carefully reads the Scriptures, he will find there the word on the subject of Christ and the prefiguration of the new calling. He is indeed the hidden treasure in the field—the field in fact is the world—but in truth, the hidden treasure in the Scriptures is Christ. Because he is designed by types and words that humanly are not possible to understand before the accomplishment of all things, that is, Christ's second coming.

—St. Irenaeus (second century)

[Christ's words] are not only those which he spoke when he became a man and tabernacled in the flesh; for before that time, Christ, the Word of God, was in Moses and the prophets. . . . [Their words] were filled with the Spirit of Christ.

—Origen (third century)

You recall that one and the same Word of God extends throughout Scripture, that it is one and the same Utterance that resounds in the mouths of all the sacred writers, since he who was in the beginning God with God has no need of separate syllables; for he is not subject to time.

The Scriptures are in fact, in any passage you care to choose, singing of Christ, provided we have ears that are capable of picking out the tune. The Lord opened the minds of the Apostles so that they understood the Scriptures. That he will open our minds too is our prayer.

—St. Augustine of Hippo (fifth century)

My dear young friends, I urge you to become familiar with the Bible, and to have it at hand so that it can be your compass pointing out the road to follow. By reading it, you will learn to know Christ. Note what St. Jerome said in this regard: "Ignorance of the Scriptures is ignorance of Christ" (PL 24,17; cf. *Dei Verbum*, 25). A time-honoured way to study and savor the Word of God is *lectio divina* which constitutes a real and veritable spiritual journey marked out in stages. After the *lectio*, which consists of reading and rereading a passage from Sacred Scripture and taking in the main elements, we proceed to *meditatio*. This is a moment of interior reflection in which the soul turns to God and tries to understand what his Word is saying to us today. Then comes *oratio* in which we linger to talk with God directly. Finally we come to *contemplatio*. This helps us to keep our hearts attentive to the presence of Christ whose Word is "a lamp shining in a dark place, until the day dawns and the morning star rises in your hearts" (2 Pet 1:19). Reading, study and meditation of the Word should then flow into a life of consistent fidelity to Christ and his teachings.

St. James tells us: "Be doers of the word, and not merely hearers who deceive themselves. For if any are hearers of the word and not doers, they are like those who look at themselves in a mirror; for they look at themselves and, on going away, immediately forget what they were like. But those who look into the perfect law, the law of liberty, and persevere, being not hearers who forget but doers who act—they will be blessed in their doing" (Jas 1:22–25). Those who listen to the Word of God and refer to it always, are constructing their existence on solid foundations. "Everyone then who hears these words of mine and acts on them," Jesus said, "will be like a wise man who built his house on rock" (Mt 7:24). It will not collapse when bad weather comes.

To build your life on Christ, to accept the Word with joy and put its teachings into practice: this, young people of the third millennium, should be your programme! There is an urgent need for the emergence of a new generation of Apostles anchored firmly in the Word of Christ, capable of responding to the challenges of our times and prepared to spread the Gospel far and wide. It is this that the Lord asks of you, it is to this that the Church invites you, and it is this that the world—even though it may not be aware of it—expects of you! If Jesus calls you, do not be afraid to respond to him with generosity, especially when he asks you to follow him in the consecrated life or in the priesthood. Do not be afraid; trust in him and you will not be disappointed.

—Pope Benedict XVI (twenty-first century)

Church

The Church is the Body of Christ; that is, the community of God's People who profess faith in the risen Lord Jesus and love and serve others under the guidance of the Holy Spirit. The Roman Catholic Church is guided by the pope and his bishops on the foundation of the Apostles.

Marks of the Church

1. *The Church is one.*

   The Church remains one because of its source: the unity, in the Trinity of Persons, of one God, the Father and the Son in the Holy Spirit. The Church's unity can never be broken and lost because this foundation is itself unbreakable.

2. *The Church is holy.*

   The Church is holy because Jesus, the founder of the Church, is holy, and he joined the Church to himself as his Body and gave the Church the gift of the Holy Spirit. Together, Christ and the Church make up the "whole Christ" (*Christus totus* in Latin).

3. *The Church is catholic.*

   The Church is catholic ("universal" or "for everyone") in two ways. First, she is catholic because Christ is present in the Church in the fullness of his Body, with the fullness of the means of Salvation, the fullness of faith, the sacraments, and the ordained ministry that comes from the Apostles. The Church is also catholic because she takes its message of Salvation to all people.

4. *The Church is apostolic.*

   The Church's apostolic mission comes from Jesus: "Go, therefore, and make disciples of all nations" (Mt 28:19). The Church remains apostolic because she still teaches the same things the Apostles taught. Also, the Church is led by leaders who are successors to the Apostles and who help guide us until Jesus returns.

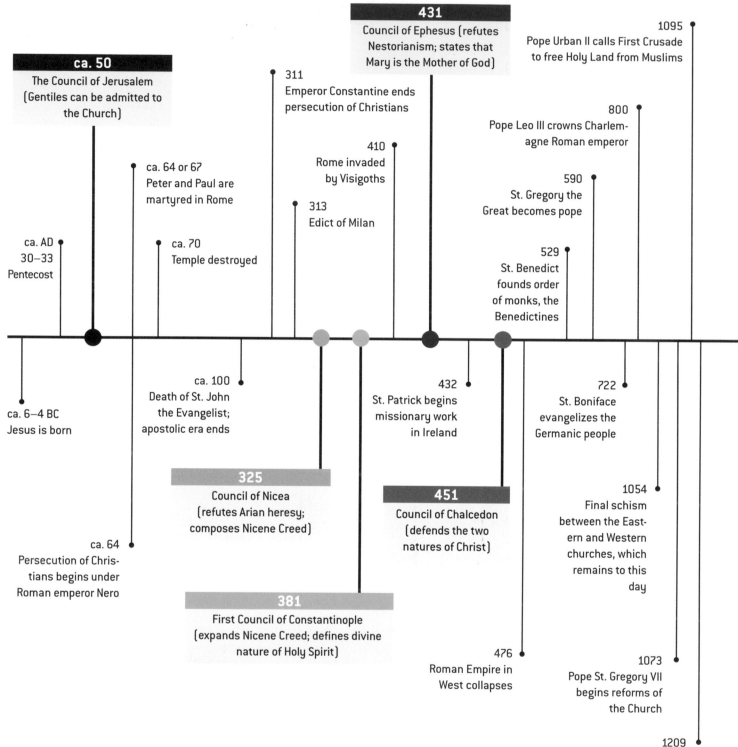

431
Council of Ephesus (refutes Nestorianism; states that Mary is the Mother of God)

1095
Pope Urban II calls First Crusade to free Holy Land from Muslims

311
Emperor Constantine ends persecution of Christians

ca. 50
The Council of Jerusalem (Gentiles can be admitted to the Church)

800
Pope Leo III crowns Charlemagne Roman emperor

410
Rome invaded by Visigoths

590
St. Gregory the Great becomes pope

ca. 64 or 67
Peter and Paul are martyred in Rome

313
Edict of Milan

529
St. Benedict founds order of monks, the Benedictines

ca. AD 30–33
Pentecost

ca. 70
Temple destroyed

ca. 100
Death of St. John the Evangelist; apostolic era ends

432
St. Patrick begins missionary work in Ireland

722
St. Boniface evangelizes the Germanic people

ca. 6–4 BC
Jesus is born

325
Council of Nicea (refutes Arian heresy; composes Nicene Creed)

451
Council of Chalcedon (defends the two natures of Christ)

1054
Final schism between the Eastern and Western churches, which remains to this day

ca. 64
Persecution of Christians begins under Roman emperor Nero

381
First Council of Constantinople (expands Nicene Creed; defines divine nature of Holy Spirit)

476
Roman Empire in West collapses

1073
Pope St. Gregory VII begins reforms of the Church

1209
St. Francis of Assisi founds Franciscan order

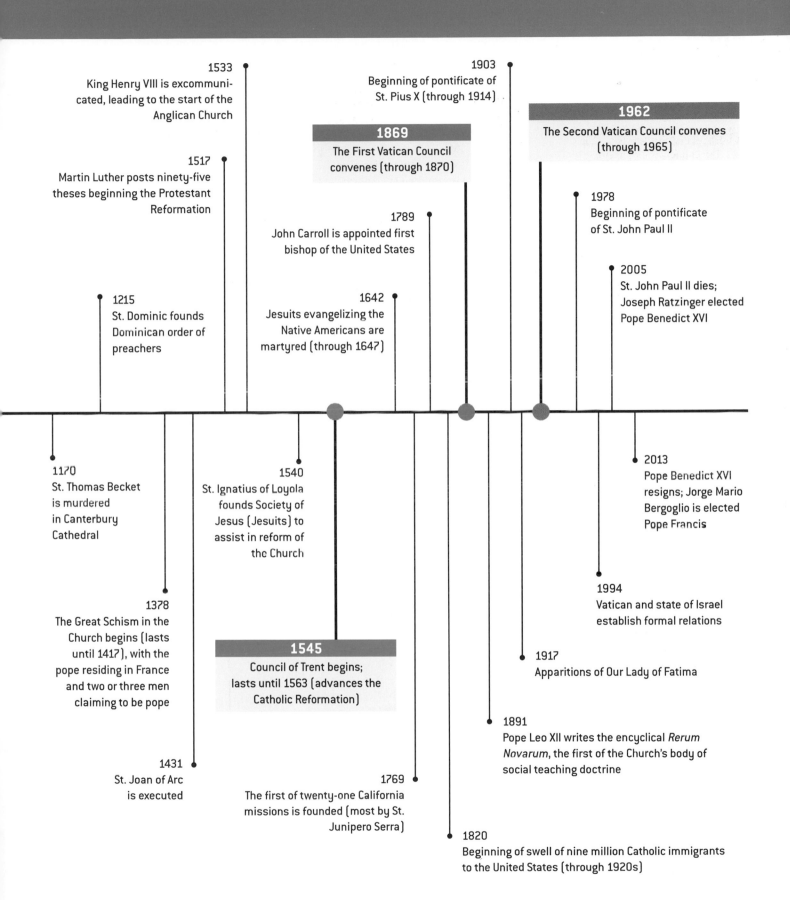

1533
King Henry VIII is excommunicated, leading to the start of the Anglican Church

1517
Martin Luther posts ninety-five theses beginning the Protestant Reformation

1215
St. Dominic founds Dominican order of preachers

1170
St. Thomas Becket is murdered in Canterbury Cathedral

1378
The Great Schism in the Church begins (lasts until 1417), with the pope residing in France and two or three men claiming to be pope

1431
St. Joan of Arc is executed

1540
St. Ignatius of Loyola founds Society of Jesus (Jesuits) to assist in reform of the Church

1545
Council of Trent begins; lasts until 1563 (advances the Catholic Reformation)

1769
The first of twenty-one California missions is founded (most by St. Junipero Serra)

1869
The First Vatican Council convenes (through 1870)

1789
John Carroll is appointed first bishop of the United States

1642
Jesuits evangelizing the Native Americans are martyred (through 1647)

1903
Beginning of pontificate of St. Pius X (through 1914)

1820
Beginning of swell of nine million Catholic immigrants to the United States (through 1920s)

1891
Pope Leo XII writes the encyclical *Rerum Novarum*, the first of the Church's body of social teaching doctrine

1917
Apparitions of Our Lady of Fatima

1962
The Second Vatican Council convenes (through 1965)

1978
Beginning of pontificate of St. John Paul II

2005
St. John Paul II dies; Joseph Ratzinger elected Pope Benedict XVI

2013
Pope Benedict XVI resigns; Jorge Mario Bergoglio is elected Pope Francis

1994
Vatican and state of Israel establish formal relations

The Apostles and Their Emblems

St. Andrew

Tradition holds that Andrew was crucified on an X-shaped cross, called a *saltire*.

St. Bartholomew

Bartholomew was flayed alive before being crucified. He was then beheaded.

St. James the Greater

James the Greater, the brother of John, was beheaded by Herod Agrippa. It is the only death of an Apostle mentioned in Scripture (Acts 12:2). The shell indicates James's missionary work by the sea in Spain. The sword is of martyrdom.

St. James the Less

James the Less is traditionally known as the first bishop of Jerusalem. The saw for his emblem is connected with the tradition of his body having been sawed into pieces after he was pushed from the pinnacle of the Temple.

St. John the Evangelist

John was the first bishop of Ephesus. He is the only Apostle believed to have died a natural death, in spite of many attempts by his enemies to murder him. One attempt included his miraculous survival after drinking a poisoned drink.

St. Jude

Some traditions have Sts. Jude and Peter martyred together. It is thought that Jude traveled throughout the Roman Empire with Peter.

St. Matthew

Matthew's shield depicts three purses, reflecting his original occupation as tax collector.

St. Matthias

Matthias was the Apostle chosen by lot to replace Judas. Tradition holds that Matthias was stoned to death and then beheaded with an ax.

St. Peter

Simon Peter was the brother of Andrew. The first bishop of Rome, Peter was crucified under Nero, asking to be hung upside-down because he felt unworthy to die as Jesus did. The keys represent Jesus' giving Peter the keys to the Kingdom of Heaven.

St. Philip

Philip may have been bound to a cross and stoned to death. The two loaves of bread at the side of the cross refer to Philip's comment to Jesus about the possibility of feeding the multitudes of people (Jn 6:7).

St. Simon

The book with fish depicts Simon as a "fisher of men" who preached the Gospel. He was also known as Simon the Zealot.

St. Thomas

Thomas is thought to have been a missionary in India, where he is thought to have built a church—hence the carpenter's square. He may have died by arrows and stones. It is thought that he then had a lance run through his body.

The Pope

The bishop of Rome has carried the title *pope* since the ninth century. *Pope* means "papa" or "father." St. Peter was the first bishop of Rome and thus the first pope. He was commissioned directly by Jesus:

> And so I say to you, you are Peter, and upon this rock I will build my church, and the gates of the netherworld shall not prevail against it. I will give you the keys to the kingdom of heaven. Whatever you bind on earth shall be bound in heaven; and whatever you loose on earth shall be loosed in heaven. (Mt 16:18–19)

Because Peter was the first bishop of Rome, the succeeding bishops of Rome have had primacy in the Church. The entire succession of popes since St. Peter can be traced directly to the Apostle.

The pope is in communion with the bishops of the world as part of the Magisterium, which is the Church's teaching authority. The pope can also define doctrine in faith or morals for the Church. When he does so, he is *infallible* and cannot be in error.

The pope is elected by the College of Cardinals by a two-thirds plus one majority vote in secret balloting. Cardinals under the age of eighty are eligible to vote. If the necessary majority is not achieved, the ballots are burned in a small stove inside the council chambers along with straw that makes dark smoke. The sign of dark smoke announces to the crowds waiting outside St. Peter's Basilica that a new pope has not been chosen. When a new pope has been voted in with the necessary majority, the ballots are burned without the straw, producing white smoke and signifying the election of a pope.

Church Fathers

Church Father, or *Father of the Church*, is a traditional title that was given to theologians of the first eight centuries whose teachings made a lasting mark on the Church. The Church Fathers developed a significant amount of doctrine that has great authority in the Church. The Church Fathers are designated either Latin Fathers (West) or Greek Fathers (East). Among the greatest Fathers of the Church are:

Latin Fathers

St. Ambrose

St. Augustine

St. Jerome

St. Gregory the Great

Greek Fathers

St. John Chrysostom

St. Basil the Great

St. Gregory of Nazianzus

St. Athanasius

Doctors of the Church

The *Doctors of the Church* are men and women honored by the Church for their writings, preaching, and holiness. Originally the Doctors of the Church were considered to be Church Fathers Augustine, Ambrose, Jerome, and Gregory the Great, but others have been added over the centuries. St. Teresa of Avila was the first woman named a Doctor of the Church (in 1970); St. Catherine of Siena was designated a Doctor of the Church the same year. This is the list of Doctors of the Church:

Name	Life Span	Designation
St. Athanasius	296–373	1568 by Pius V
St. Ephraem the Syrian	306–373	1920 by Benedict XV
St. Hilary of Poitiers	315–367	1851 by Pius IX
St. Cyril of Jerusalem	315–386	1882 by Leo XIII
St. Gregory of Nazianzus	325–389	1568 by Pius V
St. Basil the Great	329–379	1568 by Pius V
St. Ambrose	339–397	1295 by Boniface VIII
St. John Chrysostom	347–407	1568 by Pius V
St. Jerome	347–419	1295 by Boniface XIII
St. Augustine	354–430	1295 by Boniface XIII
St. Cyril of Alexandria	376–444	1882 by Leo XIII
St. Peter Chrysologous	400–450	1729 by Benedict XIII
St. Leo the Great	400–461	1754 by Benedict XIV
St. Gregory the Great	540–604	1295 by Boniface XIII
St. Isidore of Seville	560–636	1722 by Innocent XIII
St. John of Damascus	645–749	1890 by Leo XIII
St. Bede the Venerable	672–735	1899 by Leo XIII
St. Peter Damian	1007–1072	1828 by Leo XII
St. Anselm	1033–1109	1720 by Clement XI
St. Bernard of Clairvaux	1090–1153	1830 by Pius VIII
St. Hildegard of Bingen	1098–1179	2012 by Benedict XVI
St. Anthony of Padua	1195–1231	1946 by Pius XII
St. Albert the Great	1206–1280	1931 by Pius XI
St. Bonaventure	1221–1274	1588 by Sixtus V
St. Thomas Aquinas	1226–1274	1567 by Pius V
St. Catherine of Siena	1347–1380	1970 by Paul VI
St. John of Avila	1499–1569	2012 by Benedict XVI
St. Teresa of Avila	1515–1582	1970 by Paul VI
St. Peter Canisius	1521–1597	1925 by Pius XI
St. John of the Cross	1542–1591	1926 by Pius XI
St. Robert Bellarmine	1542–1621	1931 by Pius XI
St. Lawrence of Brindisi	1559–1619	1959 by John XXIII
St. Francis de Sales	1567–1622	1871 by Pius IX
St. Alphonsus Liguori	1696–1787	1871 by Pius IX
St. Thérèse of Lisieux	1873–1897	1997 by John Paul II

Ecumenical Councils

An *ecumenical council* is a worldwide assembly of bishops under direction of the pope. There have been twenty-one ecumenical councils, the most recent being the Second Vatican Council (1962–1965). Here is a complete list of the Church's ecumenical councils with the years each met:

Nicaea I	325
Constantinople I	381
Ephesus	431
Chalcedon	451
Constantinople II	553
Constantinople III	680
Nicaea II	787
Constantinople IV	869–870
Lateran I	1123
Lateran II	1139
Lateran III	1179
Lateran IV	1215
Lyons I	1245
Lyons II	1274
Vienne	1311–1312
Constance	1414–1418
Florence	1431–1445
Lateran V	1512–1517
Trent	1545–1563
Vatican I	1869–1870
Vatican II	1962–1965

Moral Teaching

Morality refers to the goodness or evil of human actions. Listed below are several helps the Church offers for making good and moral decisions.

The Ten Commandments

The Ten Commandments are a main source for Christian morality. The Ten Commandments were revealed by God to Moses. Jesus himself acknowledged them. He told the rich young man, "If you wish to enter into life, keep the commandments" (Mt 19:17). Since the time of St. Augustine (fourth century), the Ten Commandments have been used as a source for teaching baptismal candidates.

I. I am Lord, your God: you shall not have strange gods before me.

II. You shall not take the name of the Lord your God in vain.

III. Remember to keep holy the Lord's day.

IV. Honor your father and your mother.

V. You shall not kill.

VI. You shall not commit adultery.

VII. You shall not steal.

VIII. You shall not bear false witness against your neighbor.

IX. You shall not covet your neighbor's wife.

X. You shall not covet your neighbor's goods.

The Beatitudes

The word *beatitude* means "happiness." Jesus preached the Beatitudes in his Sermon on the Mount. They are as follows:

Blessed are the poor in spirit, for theirs is the kingdom of heaven.

Blessed are they who mourn, for they will be comforted.

Blessed are the meek, for they will inherit the land.

Blessed are they who hunger and thirst for righteousness, for they will be satisfied.

Blessed are the merciful, for they will be shown mercy.

Blessed are the clean of heart, for they will see God.

Blessed are the peacemakers, for they will be called children of God.

Blessed are they who are persecuted for the sake of righteousness, for theirs is the kingdom of heaven.

Cardinal Virtues

Virtues—habits that help in leading a moral life—that are acquired by human effort are called moral or human virtues. Four of these are known as the cardinal virtues, *as they form the hinge that connects all the others. These are the cardinal virtues:*

- Prudence
- Justice
- Fortitude
- Temperance

Theological Virtues

The theological virtues are the foundation for moral life. They are gifts infused into our souls by God:

- Faith
- Hope
- Love

Works of Mercy

The works of mercy are charitable actions that remind you how to come to the aid of a neighbor and fulfill his or her bodily and spiritual needs.

Corporal Works of Mercy

1. Feed the hungry.
2. Give drink to the thirsty.
3. Clothe the naked.
4. Visit the imprisoned.
5. Shelter the homeless.
6. Visit the sick.
7. Bury the dead.

Spiritual Works of Mercy

1. Counsel the doubtful.
2. Instruct the ignorant.
3. Admonish sinners.
4. Comfort the afflicted.
5. Forgive offenses.
6. Bear wrongs patiently.
7. Pray for the living and the dead.

Precepts of the Church

The precepts of the Church are positive laws made by Church authorities to guarantee for Catholics the minimum in prayer and moral effort to facilitate their love for God and neighbor.

1. You shall attend Mass on Sundays and on Holy Days of Obligation and rest from servile labor.
2. You shall confess your sins at least once a year.
3. You shall receive the Sacrament of the Eucharist at least during the Easter season.
4. You shall observe the days of fasting and abstinence established by the Church.
5. You shall help to provide for the needs of the Church.

Catholic Social Teaching: Major Themes

The 1998 document Sharing Catholic Social Teaching: Challenges and Directions—Reflections of the US Catholic Bishops—*highlighted seven principles of the Church's social teaching:*

1. Life and dignity of the human person
2. Call to family, community, and participation
3. Rights and responsibilities
4. Preferential option for the poor and vulnerable

5. The dignity of work and the rights of workers

6. Solidarity

7. God's care for creation

Teaching on Sin

Being a moral person entails avoiding sin. Sin is an offense against God.

Mortal sin is the most serious kind of sin. Mortal sin destroys or kills a person's relationship with God. For a sin to be mortal, three conditions must exist:

1. The moral object must be of grave or serious matter. Grave matter is specified in the Ten Commandments (e.g., do not kill, do not commit adultery, do not steal, etc.).

2. The person must have full knowledge of the gravity of the sinful action.

3. The person must completely consent to the action. It must be a personal choice.

Venial sin is less serious sin. Examples of venial sins are petty jealousy, disobedience, "borrowing" a small amount of money from a parent without the intention of repaying it. Venial sins, when not repented, can lead a person to commit mortal sins.

Vices are bad habits linked to sins. Vices come from particular sins, especially the seven *capital sins*: pride, avarice, envy, wrath, lust, gluttony, and sloth.

The Theology of the Body

In 129 talks at his weekly Wednesday audiences from 1979 to 1984, St. John Paul II spoke of the appropriate ways that all people are to live out the gift of chastity in preparing themselves for Heaven. St. John Paul II's *Theology of the Body* talks highlight the basic principle governing sexual morality: that God intended sexual intercourse, and all actions leading directly to intercourse, to be shared exclusively by a man and woman in the union of marriage.

The 129 audiences of St. John Paul II that make up the Theology of the Body can be referenced at the Vatican website (www.vatican.va) under "Audiences." The various talks will introduce you to several new terms. Make a chart like the one below. In the second column, write what you think each term means. Then search the Theology of the Body talks to find out what St. John Paul II meant by these terms.

Term	Your Definition	Meaning in TOB
Nuptial meaning of the body		
Reverence		
Manichaeism		
Celibacy for the Kingdom		
Primordial Sacrament		
One-flesh union		
Personalism		
The Way of Beauty		
Communion of persons		
Responsible parenthood		
Utilitarianism		
Humanae Vitae		
Natural Family Planning		
Freedom of the gift		

Prayers

Some common Catholic prayers are listed below. The Latin translation for four of the prayers is included. Latin is the official language of the Church. There are occasions when you may pray in Latin (for example, at a World Youth Day when you are with young people who speak many different languages).

Sign of the Cross

In the name of the Father,
and of the Son,
and of the Holy Spirit. Amen.

In nómine Patris,
et Filii,
et Spíritus Sancti.
Amen.

Our Father

Our Father
who art in heaven,
hallowed be thy name.
Thy kingdom come;
thy will be done on earth as it is in Heaven.
Give us this day our daily bread
and forgive us our trespasses
as we forgive those who trespass against us.
And lead us not into temptation,
but deliver us from evil.
Amen.

Pater Noster qui es in caelis:
sanctificétur Nomen Tuum;
advéniat Regnum Tuum;
fiat volúntas Tua,
sicut in caelo, et in terra.
Panem nostrum
quotidiánum da nobis hódie;
et dimítte nobis débita nostra,
sicut et nos

dimíttimus debitóribus nostris;
Et ne nos inducas in tentatiónem,
sed libera nos a malo.
Amen.

Glory Be

Glory be to the Father
and to the Son
and to the Holy Spirit,
as it was in the beginning,
is now,
and ever shall be,
world without end. Amen.

Glória Patri
et Filio
et Spiritui Sancto.
Sicut erat in princípio,
et nunc et semper,
et in saécula saeculórum.
Amen.

Hail Mary

Hail Mary, full of grace,
the Lord is with thee.
Blessed art thou among women
and blessed is the fruit of thy womb, Jesus.
Holy Mary, Mother of God,
pray for us sinners now
and at the hour of our death. Amen.

Ave, María, grátia plena,
Dóminus tecum.
Benedícta tu in muliéribus,
et benedíctus fructus ventris
tui, Iesus.
Sancta María, Mater Dei,
ora pro nobis peccatóribus
nunc et in hora mortis nostrae.
Amen.

Memorare

Remember, O most gracious Virgin Mary,
that never was it known
that anyone who fled to thy protection,
implored thy help,
or sought thy intercession was left unaided.
Inspired by this confidence I fly unto thee,
O virgin of virgins, my Mother,
To thee I come, before thee I stand,
sinful and sorrowful.
O Mother of the word Incarnate,
despise not my petitions,
but in thy mercy hear and answer me. Amen.

Hail, Holy Queen

Hail, holy Queen, Mother of Mercy,
our life, our sweetness, and our hope.
To thee do we cry,
poor banished children of Eve.
To thee do we send up our sighs,
mourning and weeping in the valley of tears.
Turn then, most gracious advocate,
thine eyes of mercy toward us,
and after this our exile,
show unto us the blessed fruit of thy womb,
    Jesus.
O clement, O loving, O sweet Virgin Mary.

V. Pray for us, O holy Mother of God,
R. That we may be made worthy of the prom-
    ises of Christ.

The Angelus

V. The angel of the Lord declared unto Mary.
R. And she conceived of the Holy Spirit.
Hail Mary . . .
V. Behold the handmaid of the Lord.
R. Be it done unto me according to thy word.
Hail Mary . . .

V. And the Word was made flesh.
R. And dwelt among us.
Hail Mary . . .
V. Pray for us, O holy Mother of God.
R. That we may be made worthy of the prom-
    ises of Christ.
Let us pray: We beseech you, O Lord, to pour
out your grace into our hearts. By the message
of an angel we have learned of the Incarna-
tion of Christ, your son; lead us by his Passion
and Cross, to the glory of the Resurrection.
Through the same Christ our Lord. Amen.

Regina Caeli

Queen of heaven, rejoice, alleluia.
The Son whom you merited to bear, alleluia,
has risen as he said, alleluia.
Pray to God for us, alleluia.
Rejoice and be glad, O Virgin Mary, alleluia!
For the Lord has truly risen, alleluia.
Let us pray.
O God, who through the resurrection of your
Son, our Lord Jesus Christ, did vouchsafe to
give joy to the world; grant, we beseech you,
that through his Mother, the Virgin Mary, we
may obtain the joys of everlasting life. Through
the same Christ our Lord. Amen.

Grace at Meals

Before Meals
Bless us, O Lord,
and these your gifts,
which we are about to receive from your
bounty,
through Christ our Lord. Amen.

After Meals
We give you thanks, almighty God,
for these and all the gifts

which we have received
from your goodness
through Christ our Lord. Amen.

Guardian Angel Prayer

Angel of God, my guardian dear,
to whom God's love commits me here,
ever this day be at my side,
to light and guard, to rule and guide. Amen.

Prayer for the Faithful Departed

V. Eternal rest grant unto them, O Lord.
R. And let perpetual light shine upon them.
V. May they rest in peace.
R. Amen.

Morning Offering

O Jesus, through the Immaculate Heart of Mary, I offer you my prayers, works, joys, and sufferings of this day in union with the holy sacrifice of the Mass throughout the world. I offer them for all the intentions of your Sacred Heart: the Salvation of souls, reparation for sin, and the reunion of all Christians. I offer them for the intentions of our bishops and all Apostles of Prayer and in particular for those recommended by our Holy Father this month. Amen.

Act of Faith

O my God, I firmly believe that you are one God in three divine Persons, Father, Son, and Holy Spirit. I believe that your divine Son became man and died for our sins and that he will come to judge the living and the dead. I believe these and all the truths which the Holy Catholic Church teaches because you have

revealed them who are eternal truth and wisdom, who can neither deceive nor be deceived. In this faith I intend to live and die. Amen.

Act of Hope

O Lord God, I hope by your grace for the pardon of all my sins and after life here to gain eternal happiness because you have promised it who are infinitely powerful, faithful, kind, and merciful. In this hope I intend to live and die. Amen.

Act of Love

O Lord God, I love you above all things and I love my neighbor for your sake because you are the highest, infinite and perfect good, worthy of all my love. In this love I intend to live and die. Amen.

Act of Contrition

O my God, I am heartily sorry for having offended Thee, and I detest all my sins because of thy just punishment, but most of all because they offend Thee, my God, who art all good and deserving of all my love. I firmly resolve with the help of Thy grace to sin no more and to avoid the near occasion of sin. Amen.

Prayer for Peace (St. Francis of Assisi)

Lord, make me an instrument of your peace.
Where there is hatred, let me sow love;
where there is injury, pardon;
where there is doubt, faith;
where there is despair, hope;
where there is darkness, light;
where there is sadness, joy.

O Divine Master,
grant that I may not seek so much to be consoled as to console;
to be understood, as to understand,
to be loved, as to love.
For it is in giving that we receive,
it is in pardoning that we are pardoned,
and it is in dying that we are born to eternal
life.

NOTES

1. Searching for God

1. Frank Newport, Dan Witters, and Sangeeta Agrawal, "Religious Americans Enjoy Higher Well-being," Gallup.com, February 16, 2012, http://www.gallup.com/poll/152723/Religious-Americans-Enjoy-Higher-Wellbeing.aspx

2. Ibid.

3. "Aluminum Recycling Facts," A Recycling Revolution website, accessed February 14, 2013, http://www.recycling-revolution.com/recycling-facts.html.

4. "Everything You Need to Know About Paper Recycling," Earth911.com, accessed January 23, 2015, http://www.earth911.com/business-policy/business/paper-recycling-details-basics/. Average is as of 2011.

2. Introduction to Sacred Scripture

1. Austin, "The Bible, Pornography, and Evil," *No Question Left Behind: Teens Helping Teens* (blog), October 13, 2008, accessed May 2013, http://noquestionleftbehind.blogspot.com/search/label/Pornography.

3. Surveying the Books of the Bible

1. Philipp Harper, "In the Book World, the Rarest of the Rare: Would You Pay $25 Million for a Bible?" *Today: Books*, accessed February 26, 2015, http://www.today.com/id/6124643/ns/today-today_entertainment/t/book-world-rarest-rare.

2. "Edith Stein, Teresa Benedicta of the Cross Bibliography," ETWN.COM," ewtn.com, accessed March 8, 2013, http://www.ewtn.com/faith/edith_stein.htm.

4. The Pentateuch: Creation, Covenant, and the Exodus

1. "Army Community Covenant Comes to Idaho Falls Today," *Idaho State Journal*, October 10, 2012, *eLibrary*, accessed Nov. 27, 2012.

2. Brian Higginbotham, "Utah State University First University in Nation to Sign Community Covenant," *Utah State Today Online News*, October 31, 2012, www.usu.edu/ust/print.cfm?article=51784.

3. J. Vincent Crowne, "St. Caedmon," *The Catholic Encyclopedia*, vol. 3 (New York: Robert Appleton, 1908), accessed December 5, 2012, http://www.newadvent.org/cathen/03131c.htm.

4. "St. Caedmon," Catholic Exchange website, accessed February 9, 2012, http://catholicexchange.com/st-caedmon/.

5. Kings and Prophets Await the Messiah

1. Douglas Martin, "Jerzy Kluger, John Paul's Jewish Confidant, Dies at 90," *The New York Times*, January 7, 2012, http://www.nytimes.com/2012/01/08/world/europe/jerzy-kluger-pope-john-paul-iis-jewish-confidant-dies-at-90.html.

2. US Department of State, Office to Monitor and Combat Trafficking in Persons, "International Best Practices," § II, *Trafficking in Persons Report,* June 3, 2005, http://www.state.gov/j/tip/rls/tiprpt/2005/46608.htm.

6. The Synoptic Gospels

1. Carlos Arribas, "Honesty of the Long-Distance Runner," *El País in English* (Madrid) December 19, 2012, http://elpais.com/elpais/2012/12/19/inenglish/1355928581_856388.html.

2. Benedict XVI, *Jesus of Nazareth: From the Baptism in the Jordan to the Transfiguration*, trans. Adrian J. Walker (New York: Doubleday, 2007).

7. Jesus' Teaching

1. National Catholic Education Association, "Secondary Department Recognizes 2009 Leaders at NCEA 106th Convention," *NCEA Notes* 42, no. 5 (May 2009): 10, http://www.ncea.org/sites/default/files/documents/09_NCEA_Notes_May.pdf.

2. Mindy Brodhead Averitt, "Science Teacher Wins National Award," St. Joseph's Academy website, September 30, 2008, http://archive.sjabr.org/news/news-detail.cfm?id=1862.

3. Jon Clifford, "Juan Diego Named Best Biology Teacher of the Year," *Salt Lake Tribune*, October 12, 2012, http://www.sltrib.com/sltrib/neighborhood-southvalley/55039221-132/celestino-really-biology-diego.html.csp.

4. Saints.SQPN.com, "Saint Scholastica," Saints.SQPN.com, accessed April 2, 2013, http://saints.sqpn.com/saint-scholastica.

8. Jesus' Miracles and the Paschal Mystery

1. Jerry Brewer, "A Prayer for Gloria: 'She Teaches Us All So Much Each Day about Life,'" *Seattle Times*, September 16, 2007, http://seattletimes.com/html/localnews/2003886843_gloria16.html.

9. The Gospel of John

1. Benedict XVI, *Jesus of Nazareth: From the Baptism in the Jordan to the Transfiguration*, trans. Adrian J. Walker (New York: Doubleday, 2007).

10. Who Do You Say That I Am?

1. John Baptist de La Salle, *Explanation of the Method of Mental Prayer*, 8.

2. Benedict, *RB 1980: The Rule of Saint Benedict in Latin and English with Notes,* ed. Timothy Fry (Collegeville, MN: Liturgical Press, 1981), 4.20–28 quoted in Katherine Howard, *Praying with Benedict* (Winona, MN: Saint Mary's Press, 1996).

3. John of the Cross, *Ascent of Mt. Carmel*, bk. 3, chap. 40, no. 2, quoted in "Selected Quotes from St. John of the Cross on the Journey of the Soul to God by Contemplation," http://www.innerexplorations.com/chmystext/stquotes.htm.

4. Catherine of Siena, *The Dialogue*, trans. and intro. Susan Noffke, preface by Giuliana Cavallini (New York: Paulist Press, 1983) quoted in Patricia Mary Vinje, *Praying with Catherine of Siena* (Winona, MN: Saint Mary's Press, 1990), 66.

5. Teresa of Avila, *The Life of Saint Teresa of Avila by Herself,* trans. and intro. J. M. Cohen (New York, Penguin Books, 1957), 84.

GLOSSARY

absolution Forgiveness of sins; remission of guilt; also the statement by which a priest, speaking as the official minister of Christ's Church, declares forgiveness of sins to a repentant sinner in the Sacrament of Penance and Reconciliation. The formula of absolution reads: "I absolve you from your sins in the name of the Father, and of the Son, and of the Holy Spirit. Amen."

Adonai A name for God meaning "Lord" or "master," which the Israelites used out of respect for the sacredness of the name YHWH.

agnostic A person who practices a form of atheism that often expresses an indifference to the search for God. In some cases, an agnostic may make no judgment of God's existence while declaring it impossible to prove, affirm, or deny. When it rejects God and the religious and moral truths attainable through human reason, agnosticism, like atheism, is a serious sin.

apocalyptic *Apocalypse* is a Greek word for "revelation." It also refers to a type of highly symbolic literature that contains apparitions about the future and the Final Judgment. This form of literature was used to give hope to a persecuted people that God's goodness will triumph over evil.

apocrypha A word that means "hidden." The term describes the extra section of Protestant Bibles where the additional Old Testament books of the Greek Septuagint from Catholic Bibles are placed.

apostasy The denial of God and the repudiation of faith.

Apostle A term meaning "one who is sent." Jesus called twelve of his disciples to become his Apostles, chosen witnesses of his Resurrection, and the foundation on which he built the Church. As Jesus was sent by the Father, so he sent his chosen disciples to preach the Gospel to the whole world.

Arianism A fourth-century movement named for an Alexandrian priest, Arius, who denied the true divinity of Christ.

Ark of the Covenant The most important symbol of the Jewish faith. It served as the only physical manifestation of God on earth. The Ark was built while the Israelites wandered in the desert and was used until the building of the First Temple.

atheist A person who denies in theory and/or practice that God exists. Atheism is a sin against the virtue of religion, a requirement of the First Commandment.

Beatitudes A key portion of the Sermon on the Mount from Matthew 5, in which Jesus reveals to his listeners how to fulfill their desires for happiness and achieve the Kingdom of God.

Bible Sacred Scripture; the books that contain the truth of God's Revelation and were composed by human writers inspired by the Holy Spirit.

bishop One who has received the fullness of the Sacrament of Holy Orders, which makes him a member of the episcopal college and a successor of the Apostles. He is a shepherd of a particular church entrusted to him.

blasphemy Any thought, word, or act that expresses hatred or contempt for God, Christ, the Church, saints, or holy things.

canon The official list of inspired books of the Bible. Catholics list forty-six Old Testament books and twenty-seven New Testament books in their canon.

catholic With a lowercase *c*, *catholic* means universal.

Christ A Greek translation of the Hebrew *Messiah*, which means "anointed one." It became the name proper to Jesus because he accomplished perfectly the divine mission of the priest, prophet, and king, signified by his anointing as Messiah, "Christ."

Christology The study of Jesus Christ; the academic effort to understand who he is.

Church Father A theologian of the first eight centuries of Christianity whose teachings made a lasting mark on the Church.

circumcision The surgical removal of the male foreskin; it was the physical sign of the covenant between God and Abraham.

concupiscence An inclination to commit sin that arises from a disordered human desire or appetite. It is one of the temporal consequences of Original Sin that remains even after the Sacrament of Baptism.

covenant A binding and solemn agreement between human beings or between God and people, holding each other to a particular course of action.

Day of Atonement The Day of Atonement, also called Yom Kippur, is the holiest day of the year for the Jewish people, its central themes being atonement and repentance.

Dead Sea Scrolls Old Testament manuscripts discovered in 1947 in a cave near the Dead Sea along with other writings. The manuscripts have proved very valuable to scholars studying the Old Testament and have revealed some Jewish practices in Jesus' day.

Deposit of Faith "The heritage of faith contained in Sacred Scripture and Sacred Tradition, handed down in the Church from the time of the Apostles, from which the Magisterium draws all that it proposes for belief as being divinely revealed" (*Catechism of the Catholic Church*, Glossary).

devil The name for the fallen angel who refused to accept God or his Kingdom. Another word for the devil is Satan, or the "Evil One."

didache A Greek word that means "teaching." In a Christian context this term refers to the earliest known writing in Christianity aside from the New Testament.

disciple A follower of Jesus. The word means "learner."

divine Relating to or proceeding directly from God.

Divine Revelation The way God communicates knowledge of himself to humankind, a self-communication realized by his actions and words over time, most fully by his sending us his divine Son, Jesus Christ.

Docetism An early heresy associated with the Gnostics that taught that Jesus had no human body and only appeared to die on the Cross.

Doctor of the Church A title officially conferred on a saint by the pope or by a general council declaring that person to be holy, wise, learned, and therefore a source of sound theological teaching for the Church. See page 370 for a complete list of the Doctors of the Church.

Elohim A common Semitic word for God used in the Bible. Elohim appears in Hebrew names like Mich-a-el, Dan-i-el, and Ari-el.

Emmanuel A name for Jesus that means "God is with us." This is the name given to Jesus as foretold in the Old Testament (see, for example, Isaiah 7:14 and 8:8) and recounted to Joseph, the foster father of Jesus, in a dream.

Epiphany The feast that celebrates the mystery of Christ's manifestation as the Savior

epistle A letter. In the New Testament, epistles are letters intended for public reading.

Evangelist One who proclaims in word and deed the Good News of Jesus Christ. "The Four Evangelists" refers to the authors of the four Gospels: Matthew, Mark, Luke, and John.

exegesis The process used by scholars to discover the literal meaning of the biblical text.

Exodus A foundational event in the history of the Chosen People that occurred when Moses led the Hebrews out of Egypt and slavery.

exorcism A public and authoritative act, by Christ or in his name, to liberate a person from the devil.

faith One of the theological virtues. Faith is an acknowledgement of an allegiance to God.

Fall A short form of "the Fall of Adam and Eve" which describes their expulsion from paradise in the Garden of Eden into exile as a consequence of their disobedience. They symbolically "fell" from the state of Original Holiness and Original Justice into the state of Original Sin.

false prophet A person who claims to speak in the name of God without being inspired by him.

free will The capacity to choose among alternatives. Free will is "the power, rooted in reason and will . . . to perform deliberate actions on one's own responsibility" (*CCC*, 1731). True freedom is at the service of what is good and true.

Galilee A large region in the north of the modern nation of Israel, north of Samaria at the time of Jesus.

Gentile A term for non-Jews.

gifts of the Holy Spirit An outpouring of God's gifts at Confirmation to help a person lead a Christian life. The traditional seven gifts of the Holy Spirit are wisdom, understanding, counsel, fortitude, knowledge, piety, and fear of the Lord.

Golden Rule Described by Jesus and recorded in Matthew 7:12: "Do unto others whatever you would have them do to you."

Gospel A word meaning "Good News." *Gospel* refers to three distinct but interrelated concepts: Jesus Christ himself is the Gospel; his message is the Gospel; and the four written accounts of his Life, Death, Resurrection, and Ascension in the New Testament are Gospels.

graces Free and undeserved gifts that God gives people to respond to their vocation to become his adopted children.

Hanukkah The Jewish Feast of Dedication, which celebrates the recovery and purification of the Temple from the Syrians in 164 BC. It is an eight-day feast that takes place during December. Jews usually give gifts at this time. Hanukkah is also called the Festival of Lights.

Hasmonean Dynasty Descendants of the Maccabees who ruled in Judea after the ousting of the last of the Syrians in 141 BC until the establishment of Roman authority in 63 BC.

Hebrews The first name given by biblical authors to the Chosen People, most likely after Eber, the ancestor of several Semitic peoples who lived in Canaan.

Hell The eternal separation from God that occurs when a person dies after freely and deliberately acting against God's will, not repenting of a mortal sin.

Hellenism The diffusion of Greek culture throughout the Mediterranean world after the conquest of Alexander the Great.

Holy Trinity The central mystery of the Christian faith; there are Three Divine Persons in one God: Father, Son, and Holy Spirit.

idolatry Worshiping something or someone other than the true God.

Incarnation The assumption of a human nature by Jesus Christ, God's eternal Son, who became man in order to save humankind from sin. The term literally means "being made flesh."

intercessory prayer Prayer in which you ask for something on behalf of another person or group of people.

Jesus The origins of the name are from the Hebrew word *Yehoshua* (Joshua), meaning "God saves," "God is Salvation," or simply "Savior."

Jews The term for people who lived or were born in ancient Judea.

Judea The southern region of the Holy Land, occupied by Jews who returned from the Babylonian Captivity. Its principal city was Jerusalem.

judges Military leaders who led Old Testament Israelite tribes in battles against their oppressors.

justified To be justified is to receive remission for sins, sanctification, and inner renewal through the gracious action of God.

kerygma The core or essential message of the Gospel that Jesus Christ is Lord. One example is Acts 2:14–36.

Kingdom (or reign) of God The process of the Father's reconciling and renewing all things through his Son; the fact of his will being done on earth as it is in Heaven. The Kingdom of God was proclaimed by Jesus and began in his Life, Death, and Resurrection. The process will be perfectly completed at the end of time.

kingdom of Israel The name of the northern kingdom that split with Judah after the death of Solomon.

kingdom of Judah The name of the southern kingdom after the splitting of the monarchy. It included the territory originally belonging to just two of the twelve tribes, Judah and Benjamin.

Law The Law helped the Israelites live in conformity to God's will. There are 613 laws listed in the last four books of the Pentateuch.

lectio divina A Benedictine prayer tradition of "sacred reading"; its intent is for the person praying to meet God through the Scriptures.

literal sense (of the biblical text) "The meaning conveyed by the words of Scripture and discovered by exegesis, following the rules of sound interpretation" (*CCC*, 116).

literary genre A type of writing that has a particular form, style, or content.

Liturgy of the Hours The prayer of the Church at specific times of the day; also known as the Divine Office. The Liturgy of the Hours uses readings from Scripture, particularly the psalms, and hymns.

liturgy The official public worship of the Church. The liturgy is first Christ's work of Redemption, and of his continuing work of Redemption as he pours out his blessings through the sacraments. The Holy Spirit enlightens our faith and encourages us to respond. In this way, the liturgy is the participation of the People of God in the work of the Trinity. The sacraments and the Divine Office constitute the Church's liturgy. Mass is the most important liturgical celebration.

Lost Tribes of Israel The ten tribes of the northern kingdom who disappeared from history after being enslaved and exiled by the Assyrians.

magi Priests of the ancient Persian religion of Zoroastrianism who paid special attention to the stars.

Magisterium The official teaching authority of the Church. Christ bestowed the right and power to teach in his name on Peter and the Apostles and their successors. The Magisterium is the bishops in communion with the successor of Peter, the bishop of Rome (the pope).

Messiah The "anointed one" promised by the Old Testament prophets. He would be a descendant of David who would set up an ideal kingdom ruled by an adopted son. He would preach the Law in truth and would sacrifice his life for the people. Jesus Christ fulfills the prophecies about the Messiah.

miracle A powerful sign of God's Kingdom worked by Jesus.

monotheism From the Greek words *monos* (one) and *theos* (God); the belief in one all-powerful God. Christianity, Judaism, and Islam are the three great monotheistic religions.

Nativity The story of the Savior's birth in Bethlehem. Two different accounts of the Nativity are given in the New Testament: one in the Gospel of Matthew, the other in the Gospel of Luke.

Natural Revelation The knowledge of the existence of God and his basic attributes that can be derived by human reason while reflecting on the created order.

New Testament The twenty-seven books of the Bible written by the sacred authors in apostolic times, which have Jesus Christ, the incarnate Son of God—his life, his teachings, his Passion and glorification, and the beginnings of his Church—as their central theme.

Old Testament The forty-six books of the Bible that record the history of Salvation from Creation through the old alliance or covenant with Israel, in preparation for the appearance of Christ as Savior of the world.

omnipotence An attribute of God meaning that he is all-powerful. His power is universal, loving, and mysterious.

oral tradition The process of sharing stories and other important pieces of information by word of mouth.

Original Holiness and Original Justice The state of Adam and Eve before sin. The grace of Original Holiness was for people to share in God's life. The main gifts of Original Justice were that people would not have to suffer or die. Original Justice also guaranteed an inner harmony of the human person, the harmony between man and woman, and the harmony between Adam and Eve and all of creation.

Original Sin The sin of disobedience committed by Adam and Eve that resulted in their loss of Original Holiness and Original Justice and their becoming subject to sin and death. Original Sin also describes the fallen state of human nature into which all generations of people are born. Christ Jesus saved humanity from Original Sin. The Sacrament of Baptism restores Original Holiness, but not Original Justice (see *CCC*, 400).

parable From the Greek *parabole*, meaning "placing two things side by side in order to compare them"; a short story that illustrates a moral or spiritual lesson.

Paraclete A name for the Holy Spirit that means "Advocate." In John 14:26, Jesus promised to send an Advocate, a Helper, who would continue to guide, lead, and strengthen the disciples.

Parousia A Greek term for the Second Coming of Christ, when the Lord will judge the living and the dead.

Paschal Mystery Christ's work of Redemption, accomplished principally by his Passion, Death, Resurrection, and glorious Ascension. This mystery is commemorated and made present through the sacraments, especially the Eucharist.

Passover A sacred feast that first occurred prior to God's saving the Israelites from the Egyptians. The angel of death "passed over" the houses with lambs' blood smeared on their doorposts and lintels. The Passover then became a religious celebration reminding the Chosen People of God's deliverance, Salvation, fidelity, and love.

patriarchs A name to describe "fathers of the faith," male rulers, elders, or leaders. The patriarchs of the faith are Abraham, Isaac, and Jacob.

Pentateuch A Greek term for the first five books of the Bible.

Pentecost A Greek word that means "fiftieth day." On this day, the Church celebrates the descent of the Holy Spirit upon Mary and the Apostles. It is often called the "birthday of the Church."

polytheism The belief, in opposition to Christian doctrine, that there are many gods.

Protoevangelium A Latin term meaning "first gospel" and is the initial sign of the very good news that God did not abandon humanity's first parents or their descendants after they committed sin. Eve's offspring (Jesus) would someday destroy the snake (sin and death).

rabbi A Hebrew word for a Jewish master or teacher of the Torah.

Redeemer Redemption is the process that frees you from the slavery of sin. Jesus Christ is your Redeemer because he paid the price of his own sacrificial Death on the Cross to save you from sin.

religion The relationship between God and humans that results in a body of beliefs and a set of practices: creed, cult, and code. Religion expresses itself in worship and service to God and by extension to all people and all creation.

remnant A name for the exiles and former exiles who remained faithful to God during the time of the Babylonian Captivity and who were expected to restore Jerusalem.

reparation Repairing a relationship by making amends for a personal wrong or injury. A secular meaning of reparation is to take financial responsibility for damaging someone's property.

repentance A feeling of sorrow for one's actions or "changing one's mind" (from the Greek *metanoia*); a turning away from sin and toward the amendment of one's life.

Resurrection The rising of Jesus from the dead on the third day after his Death on the Cross. Jesus was able to conquer death because he is God.

Sabbath A day of rest and prayer for the Jewish people on the seventh day of the week.

sacrament A sign and source of grace instituted by Jesus Christ and entrusted to the Church by which divine life is bestowed on us through the Holy Spirit.

Sacrament of the Anointing of the Sick The sacrament administered by a priest through prayer and the anointing of the body with the oil of the sick to a baptized person who is ill or in danger of dying. The sacrament's effects are a special grace of healing and comfort to the person suffering.

Sacrament of the Holy Eucharist The sacrament commemorating the Last Supper, at which Jesus gave his Apostles his Body and Blood in the form of bread and wine. The source and summit of Christian life, the Eucharist is one of the Sacraments of Initiation. It re-presents, or makes present, the Lord's sacrificial Death on the Cross. The word *eucharist* means "thanksgiving."

Sacred Scripture The *written* transmission of the Church's Gospel message found in the Church's teaching, life, and worship. It is faithfully preserved, handed down, and interpreted by the Church's Magisterium.

Sacred Tradition The *living* transmission of the Church's Gospel message found in the Church's teaching, life, and worship. It is faithfully preserved, handed down, and interpreted by the Church's Magisterium.

Salvation History The story of God's saving action in human history.

Samaria The region to the south of Galilee, occupied by people descended from intermarriages between occupants of the old northern kingdom and foreigners.

Samaritans Descendants of a mixed population of Israelites who survived the Assyrian deportations and various pagan settlers imported after the northern kingdom fell. They worshipped YHWH on Mount Gerizim but considered only the Pentateuch to be divinely inspired.

Sanhedrin The seventy-one-member supreme legislative and judicial body of the Jewish people during Jesus' life on earth. Many of its members were Sadducees.

scribes People trained to write using the earliest forms of writing before literacy was widespread.

Sea of Galilee A thirteen-mile by seven-mile body of fresh water through which the Jordan River runs.

Second Vatican Council A conference of bishops from around the world called by St. John XXIII to consider the Church in the modern world. It took place from 1962 to 1965.

secularism An indifference to religion and a belief that religion should be excluded from civil affairs and public education.

Septuagint A second-century BC Greek translation of the Hebrew Bible made at Alexandria, Egypt. The term is from a Latin word meaning "seventy" for the legendary seventy scholars who worked on the translation.

Sermon on the Mount A section from Matthew's Gospel (Mt 5:1–7:29) in which Jesus delivers the first of five discourses.

Sinai Covenant The covenant God made with his Chosen People through Moses on Mount Sinai; it bound God and his Chosen People in a loving union and gave the Israelites the Law so they would know how they were to stay faithful to the covenant.

synagogue A meeting place for Jews for study and prayer to foster study of the Law and adherence to the covenant code.

synoptic Gospels The synoptic Gospels are Matthew, Mark, and Luke. They can be looked at together because they shared some, but not all, of the same sources.

tabernacle The portable sanctuary in which the Jews carried the Ark of the Covenant throughout their travels in the desert.

Ten Commandments The Ten Commandments summarize the Law, serving as its basic guide.

theist A person who believes in a personal and provident God. However, a theist may believe in one god or many gods.

theology The study of the nature of God and religious truth. Theologians are people who conduct this study.

Transfiguration The mystery from Christ's life in which God's glory shone through and transformed Jesus' physical appearance while he was in the company of the Old Testament prophets Moses and Elijah. Peter, James, and John witnessed this event.

Twelve Tribes of Israel The descendants of the twelve sons of Jacob (Israel). See Exodus 1:2–5, Numbers 1:20–43, or 1 Chronicles 1:1–2.

Vulgate St. Jerome's fourth-century translation of the Bible from Greek into the common language of the people of his day, Latin.

YHWH God's sacred name, revealed to Moses; it means "I am who I am" or "I AM" and is never pronounced by Jews.

SUBJECT INDEX

E

Ecclesiastes, Book of (Eccl), 79

Egypt, slavery in, 119–20

Elijah

    denouncing Ahab, 151

    as important prophet, 150, 151

    Jezebel's threat to kill him, 151

    as precursor to Messiah, 151

    taken to heaven in whirlwind, 151

    at Transfiguration, 197

Elisha, miracles performed by, 151

Elohim, 108, 120

Elohist (E)

    defined, 108

    name for God, 120

    style of, 108

Emmanuel, 155, 191, 201

Enemies, love your, 237

Ephesians, Letter to the (Eph), 91

Epilogue, John's Gospel, 296, 319

Epiphany, 189

Epistle, 88

Esau, 116

Esther, Book of (Est), 78

Etiology, 49

Eucharist. *See* Holy Eucharist

Evangelist, 51

Eve. *See* Adam and Eve

Exaggeration, as teaching technique, 221, 224

Exegesis, 48–49

Exodus, 55, 57, 121–22

Exodus, Book of (Ex), 119–22

    Moses, 119–20

    overview of, 75

    Passover, 121

    plagues, 120

    Sinai Covenant, 122

    Ten Commandments, 122, 123

    wandering in wilderness, 122

Exorcisms, 254–55

Eye for and eye command, 237

Ezekiel

    life of, 159–60

    visions of, 159–60

Ezekiel, Book of (Ez), 81, 159–60

Ezra, 165

Ezra, Book of (Ezr), 78

F

Fable, 49

Faith

    of the Church, 26

    defined, 25

    gifts of, 26

    Holy Spirit's help, 26

    personal faith, 25–26

Faithful disciples

    Caedmon, St., 130–31

    Jerome, St., 62

    Margaret Mary Alacoque, St., 323–24

    María Micaela, St., 173–74

    Martin de Porres, St., 288

    Newman, John Henry, 32–33

    Peter, St., 210–11

    Robert Bellarmine, St., 354–55

    Scholastica, St., 244

    Stein, Edith, St., 98

Fall, of Adam and Eve, 112

False prophet, 264

False teaching, 344, 356–57

Family Bible, 47

Father
    as Creator, 18
    God the Father, 15–16, 246
    at Transfiguration, 197

First cause, God as, 11

First Council of Constantinople, 18

First Vatican Council, 10

Flood, Noah and, 113

Forgiveness
    Jesus' power to forgive sins, 259
    message of, in Luke's Gospel, 204

Form criticism, 49–50

Form criticism, of biblical text, 49–50

Francis, Pope, 21

Francis de Sales, St., 349

Freedom, leading to God, 12

Free will, 111

Friendship
    Bible on, 138
    between God and Israelites, 137–38
    Jesus as friend, 334–35, 348–49
    qualities of, 137–38

Fundamentalism, Bible and, 50

G

Galatians, Letter to the (Gal), 91

Galilee, 85
    geography and population of, 222
    as place where Jesus taught, 222

Genealogy, as literary genre in Bible, 50

Genesis, Book of (Gn), 110–18
    Cain and Abel, 113
    covenant with Abraham, 114–16
    creation stories, 110–11
    Fall of Adam and Eve, 112
    Joseph, the favored son, 117–18
    Noah and Flood, 113
    Original Sin, 111–12
    overview of, 75
    patriarch Israel, 116–17
    promise of redemption, 112–13
    protoevangelium, 112–13

Gentile, 51

Georgetown, daily Mass at, 293, 295

Gerizim, Mount, 223

Gershom, 119

Gethsemane, 264

Gideon, 142

Gifts of the Holy Spirit, 281

Glanzman, Louis, 302

Gloria's Angels, 249, 252

Gnosticism, 356

Gnostics, 44

God
    in creation story, 110–11
    as creator, 10, 18
    desire for, 6–8
    the Father, 15–16, 246
    as first cause, 11
    friendship between God and Israelites, 137–38
    as grand designer, 11
    happiness in, 6–7
    the Holy Spirit, 18
    Holy Trinity, 15–18
    Kingdom (or reign) of, 195–97

knowing through Divine Revelation, 14–19

knowing through natural revelation, 10–12

as male, 246

Old Testament names for, 120

omnipotence of, 184

proofs of existence, 10–11

Salvation History, 15

shares his name with Moses, 119–20

the Son, 16–17

as supreme model, 11

in suzerainty covenant, 114

Transfiguration, 196, 197

as unmoved mover, 11

YHWII, 120

Golden Rule, 239

Golgotha, 265, 316, 317

Good News, Gospel as, 84, 181–82

Good Samaritan parable, 185

Good Shepherd, 303, 311–12

Gospel of Judas, 356–57

Gospels, 181–205. *See also* John, Gospel of (Jn); Luke, Gospel of (Lk); Mark, Gospel of (Mk); Matthew, Gospel of (Mt); Synoptic Gospels

    Ascension of Jesus, 268

    date of authorship, 184

    date of composition, 90

    as Good News, 84, 181–82

    importance of, 212

    Jesus' Death and burial, 266–67

    Jesus' early life, 187–90

    Jesus' last words, 273

    Jesus proclaims Gospel, 195–97

    Jesus' public life, 191–94

    kerygma, 85

    L (Luke source), 184, 185

    M (Matthew source), 184, 185

    Mark's Gospel as source, 184

    meaning of word, 84, 181

    mystery of Salvation, 184, 186

    overview of, 84, 90

    passion narratives, 263–66

    Pharisees in, 260

    portrait of Jesus, 334–37

    Q (Quelle source), 184, 185

    reasons for waiting to write, 87–88

    religious leaders in, 260

    Resurrection, 267

    Sadducees in, 260

    synoptic Gospels, 182–84, 198–205

    women in, 261

    writing of, 86–88

Graces, 277

Grand designer, God as, 11

Great Feast parable, 230

Great Flood, 113

Greek language, 43

Gregory the Great, St., 244

Grotto at Lourdes, France, 251, 252

Gutenberg, Johannes, 70

Gutenberg Bibles, 70

H

Habakkuk, Book of (Hb), 82

Haggai, 165

Haggai, Book of (Hg), 82

Hanukkah, 167, 168

Happiness

    in God, 6–7

    material world and, 6

    pursuit of, 3–5

Hospitality, virtue of, 278

Humanity of Jesus, 295–96

Human person

    beauty and truth, 12

    contemplation on, to find God, 12

    love and intelligence, 12

    moral goodness, voice of conscience and freedom, 12

Husserl, Edmund, 98

Hyperbole, as teaching technique, 221

Hypocrites, 238

I

I AM statements, 303, 316

Idolatry, 16, 147, 150

Ignatius of Loyola, St., 348

Incarnation

    defined, 16

    in Gospel of John, 301–2

Infancy narratives, 185, 188

Inspiration, of writers of Bible, 41

Intelligence, leading to God, 12

Intercessory prayer, 307

Interpretation of the Bible in the Church, The, 45

Irenaeus, St., 184, 204, 297

Isaac, 16, 76

    as father of Chosen People, 114, 116

    as patriarch, 114, 116

    prefigures Jesus, 116

    sacrifice of, 116

Isaiah, 154–55

Isaiah, Book of (Is)

    asking people to repent, 154

    authors and sections of, 154

    during exile, 160–62

    overview of, 81

    prophecy of Jesus, 155

    Servant Songs, 161

Israel, 16

    David as greatest king of, 144, 146

    Jacob as, 117

    Lost Tribes of Israel, 152

    monarchy in, 143–47

    Saul as first king of, 144

    Twelve Tribes of, 117, 121–22

    as vassal in suzerainty covenant, 114

Israel, kingdom of (northern kingdom). *See* Kingdom of Israel (northern kingdom)

Israelites, 16

    belonging to Twelve Tribes of Israel, 117, 121–22

    as Chosen People, 117

    cycle of apostasy, 140

    desire for human king, 143–44

    exile of, 152

    friendship between God and Israelites, 137–38

    Joshua leading, into Promised Land, 139–40

    leaving Egypt, 121–22

    murmurings of, 124

    wandering in wilderness, 122, 124

J

Jacob (Old Testament), 16

    deceiving Esau, 116

    encounters with God, 117

    as father of Chosen People, 114, 116

    name change, 117

    as patriarch, 114, 116

Jairus's daughter, 255, 258

James, Letter of (Jas), 92, 344

K

Kapaun, Emil, Fr., 329, 331

Kepler, Johannes, 9–10

Kerygma, 85, 339–40

Kingdom (or reign) of God

    defined, 195, 226

    God's Kingdom is for all parable theme, 229

    Jesus reveals, 195

    Jesus tells parables about, 226–27

    Kingdom belongs to the poor/lowly parable theme, 232

    Kingdom is here parable theme, 230–31

    Paschal Mystery, 196, 197, 226

    rejoicing in Kingdom parable theme, 232–33

    repentance prerequisite for entering parable theme, 231

    sinners are welcome in Kingdom parable theme, 230

    Transfiguration, 196, 197

Kingdom of Israel (northern kingdom)

    fall of, 152

    formation of, 147

    Lost Tribes of Israel, 152

    prophets of, 149–53

Kingdom of Judah (southern kingdom)

    after Babylonian exile, 164–68

    formation of, 147

    prophets of, 149–50, 154–55

King James Version of Bible, 42, 45

King of kings, 345

Kings, First Book of (1 Kgs)

    Elijah, 150–51

    Elisha, 151

    idolatry, 147

    King Jeroboam, 150

    King Solomon and divided kingdom, 146–47

    overview of, 77

Kings, Second Book of (2 Kgs), 77

Kluger, Jerzy, 135

Koine language, 43, 89, 166

L

L (Luke source), 184, 185

Lamb of God, Jesus as, 345

Lamentations, Book of (Lam), 81

La Sainte Bible, 45

Last Judgment parable, 232

Last Supper

    High Priestly Prayer, 316

    Jesus' discourses, 315

    John's Gospel, 314–16

    Passion narratives, 264

Latin language, 43

Law(s)

    in Book of Leviticus, 124

    Code of Hammurabi, 122

    external observance of law not enough, 237–38

    Jesus and, 308

    as literary genre in Bible, 49

    Mosaic Law, 124

    natural law, 132

    in Old Testament, 74, 75

Lazarus

    Lazarus and the rich man parable, 227, 229, 312–13

    raising Lazarus from dead, 312–13

Leah, 116

Lectio divina, 57, 64–65

Leo XIII, Pope, 21

Leprosy, 203

M

passion narratives, 264

pearl of great price parable, 229

portrayal of Jesus as teacher, 87

Resurrection, 317, 318

salt of the earth and light of world, 236

Sermon on the Mount, 234–39

as synoptic Gospel, 182, 183–84

Transfiguration, 197

trust God, 238

Two Foundations parable, 231

Two Sons parable, 231

Workers in the Vineyard parable, 230

written from Mark's Gospel, 184

Matthew, St., 40

Messiah

Elijah as precursor to, 151

Micah's foretelling of, 155

Peter calling Jesus, 199, 200

prophecy of, 146, 219–20

Messianic secret, 200

Messina, Linda, 215

Metaphor, as teaching technique, 221

Micah, Book of (Mi), 82, 155

Minor prophets, 82, 166

Miracles, 249–282

complete list of Jesus' miracles, 256–57

cure of man born blind, 311

cure of official's son, 307

cure on Sabbath, 307, 309–10

defined, 251

exorcism, 254–55

faith's role in, 262

loaves and fishes miracle, 254

multiplication of loaves, 310

nature miracles, 254

in New Testament, 259

physical healing, 253

raising from the dead, 255, 258

raising Lazarus, 312–13

skepticism of, 258–59

types of, 253–58

walking on water, 310

wedding at Cana, 305–6

woman at the well, 306–7

in world today, 251–52

Moderation, 221

Monotheistic, 15

Moral goodness, leading to God, 12

Moral sense, of biblical text, 57–58

Morning star, 345

Mosaic Law, 124

Moses

burning bush, 119

Death of, 139

God's call to, 119

God shares his name with, 119–20

Jesus compared to, in Matthew's Gospel, 201

leaving Egypt, 121–22

Sinai Covenant, 122

at Transfiguration, 197

wandering in wilderness, 122

Murmurings, 124

Muslims, Abraham as father of faith, 76

Mustard Seed parable, 229

Mutai, Abel, 179, 181

Mystery of Salvation, 184, 186

N

Naaman, 151

Nahum, Book of (Na), 82

Naomi, 77, 78

Nathan, 144, 146

Nativity, 187–88

Natural law, 132

Natural revelation

contemplation on human person, 12

contemplation on universe, 10–11

defined, 10

Nature, finding God in, 10, 13

Nature miracles, 254

Nazareth, 188, 189, 190, 222

Nebuchadnezzar, King, 157

Nehemiah, Book of (Neh), 78, 165

Nehemiah, governor of Judah, 165

New American Bible, Revised Edition, 42, 45

New Covenant, 343

compared to Sinai Covenant, 201

New Jerusalem Bible, 45

Newman, John Henry, 32–33

New Moses, 201

New Testament. *See also specific books of*

Acts of the Apostles (Acts), 90

Catholic Epistles, 92

defined, 21

didache, 86

formation of, 84–88

as Good News of Jesus Christ, 84

Gospels, 84, 90

Hebrews (Heb), 92

kerygma, 85

miracles in, 259

overview of, 84

Pauline Letters, 90–91

reason for name, 84

reasons for waiting to write, 87–88

in relation to Old Testament, 54–55

stage 1: historical Jesus, 85

stage 2: oral tradition, 85–86

stage 3: writing of, 86–88

survey of books of, 89–92

Nicodemus, 275, 334

Noah, 16, 113

Nonwriting prophets, 151

No Question Left Behind website, 37

Northern kingdom (Kingdom of Israel)

fall of, 152

formation of, 147

Lost Tribes of Israel, 152

prophets of, 149–53

Numbers, Book of (Nm)

murmurings, 124

overview of, 75, 124

O

Obadiah, 165

Obadiah, Book of (Ob), 82

Obed, 78

Old Testament. *See also specific books of*

Dead Sea Scrolls, 43

defined, 5

editing of, 73

formation of, 71–72

Gospel of Matthew's connection of Jesus and, 201–2

Historical Books, 77–78, 139–51

names for God, 120

oral tradition of, 72

overview of, 71

Pentateuch, 71, 75, 107–24

Prophetic Books, 81–82, 152–66

Sermon on the Mount, 234–39

Temple. *See* Jerusalem Temple

Temptation, Mount of, 223

Temptations, of Jesus, 192, 193

Ten Commandments, 122–23, 201

Sermon on the Mount and, 237

as way to apply natural law, 132

Teresa Benedicta of the Cross, 98

Teresa of Avila, St., 7, 349

Theist, 7

Theology, 17

Thessalonians, First Letter to the (1 Thes), 91

Thessalonians, Second Letter to the (2 Thes), 91

Thomas, Apostle, 267, 319

Timothy, First Letter to (1 Tm), 91

Timothy, Second Letter to (2 Tm), 91

Titus, Letter to (Ti), 91

Tobit, Book of (Tb), 78

Torah, 165

Transfiguration, 196, 197

Translations, of Bible, 42–44

True vine, 303

Truth

leading to God, 12

religious truth in Bible, 53–54

Twelve Minor Prophets, 82

Twelve Tribes of Israel, 121–22

land distributed to, by Joshua, 140

Two Foundations parable, 231

Two Sons parable, 231

U

Universe, contemplation on creation of, 10–11

Unmoved mover, God as, 11

Uriah, 146

V

Vassal, 114

Vulgate, 43, 45, 62

W

Walking on water, 310

Way, truth and life, 303

Wealthy (rich) people

Lazarus and the rich man parable, 227, 229

Rich Fool parable, 232–33

Wedding at Cana, 305–6

Weeds among the wheat parable, 232

Wisdom, Book of (Ws), 79

Wisdom Books

Ecclesiastes, Book of, 79

Job, Book of 79

Proverbs, Book of, 79

Psalms, Book of, 79, 145

Sirach, Book of, 79

Song of Songs, 79

survey of books, 79

Wisdom, Book of, 79

Wojtyla, Karol, 98, 135

Woman at the well parable, 306–7

Women

as disciples, 192, 194

in Gospels, 261

at Jesus' Death and burial, 266–67

Jewish society vs. Jesus' view of, 261

in Luke's Gospel, 203

Word, Jesus is the Word, 17

Word of God, Bible as, 34, 39–40

SCRIPTURE INDEX

OLD TESTAMENT

Mt 1:1–17, 50

Mt 1:18–23, 185

Mt 1:22–23, 202

Mt 2, 189

Mt 2:5–6, 202

Mt 2:15, 202

Mt 2:18, 202

Mt 4:4, 69

Mt 4:15–16, 202

Mt 4:18–22, 211

Mt 5–7, 234

Mt 5:3, 4, 6, 11–12, 185

Mt 5:13, 184

Mt 5:13–14, 221

Mt 5:13–16, 236

Mt 5:14–16, 192

Mt 5:15–17, 228

Mt 5:17, 308

Mt 5:17–48, 237

Mt 5:27–29, 37

Mt 5:29–30, 221

Mt 5:42, 221

Mt 5:48, 237

Mt 6:1–24, 238

Mt 6:3, 220

Mt 6:9–13, 185, 238

Mt 6:25–34, 238

Mt 7:1–29, 239

Mt 7:6, 69

Mt 7:12, 239

Mt 7:24–27, 228, 231

Mt 8:1–4, 256

Mt 8:5–13, 256

Mt 8:14–15, 211, 257

Mt 8:23–27, 256

Mt 8:28–34, 256

Mt 9:1–8, 256

Mt 9:16, 228

Mt 9:17, 228

Mt 9:18–26, 256

Mt 9:20–22, 256

Mt 9:27–31, 256

Mt 9:32–34, 256

Mt 10:5, 223

Mt 10:16, 192

Mt 11:11, 50

Mt 11:16–19, 228

Mt 11:20–22, 224

Mt 12:9–13, 257

Mt 12:18–21, 202

Mt 12:22, 257

Mt 13:3–23, 228

Mt 13:13, 227

Mt 13:14–15, 202

Mt 13:24–30, 228

Mt 13:31–32, 228

Mt 13:33, 50, 228

Mt 13:35, 202

Mt 13:44, 58

Mt 13:44, 228, 232

Mt 13:45–46, 228, 229

Mt 13:47–50, 228

Mt 14:15–21, 254, 257

Mt 14:20, 254

Mt 14:22–23, 257

Mt 14:28–31, 185

Mt 15:2, 203

Mt 15:21–28, 257

Mt 15:29–31, 257

Mt 15:32–39, 256

Mt 16:15, 331

Mt 16:15–28, 211

Mt 16:16, 332

Mt 16:18–19, 210

Mt 16:23, 335

Mt 17:2, 197

Mt 17:7, 337

Mt 17:14–21, 257

Mt 17:24–27, 257

Mt 18:12–14, 185, 228

Mt 18:23–25, 228

Mt 20:1–16, 228, 230

Mt 20:29–34, 257

Mt 21:1, 224

Mt 21:5, 202

Mt 21:8, 264

Mt 21:18–22, 256

Mt 21:28–32, 228, 231

Mt 21:33–45, 228

Mt 22:1–14, 228

Mt 22:14, 69

Mt 22:17, 225

Mt 22:21–22, 225

Mt 23:27, 335

Mt 24:27–28, 221

Mt 24:32–35, 228

Mt 24:45–51, 228

Mt 25:1–13, 228

Mt 25:14–30, 228

Mt 25:31–46, 185, 228, 232, 291

Mt 25:34–36, 291

Mt 25:35, 278

Mt 25:40, 232

Mt 25:41, 232

Mt 26:26–28, 264

Mt 26:52, 264

Mt 26:57–68, 309

Mt 27:9–10, 202

Mt 27:46, 266, 273

Mt 27:54, 266

1 Cor 15:14, 274

1 Cor 15:14–15; 17, 342

2 Corinthians

2 Cor 11:3, 88

Galatians

Gal 1:3–4, 342

Gal 2:20, 342

Philippians

Phil 2:3–4, 138

Phil 2:6–11, 343

1 Thessalonians

1 Thes 1:3, 69

1 Timothy

1 Tm 6:10, 69

Hebrews

Heb 1:1–3, 17

Heb 3:1, 344

Heb 3:3, 344

Heb 4:15–16, 192

Heb 11:1, 25, 27, 116

Heb 12:1–2, 344

Catholic Letters

James

Jas 2:24–25, 172

1 John

1 Jn 1:1, 348

1 Jn 4:7–12, 344

1 Jn 9, 344

Revelation

Rv 1:8, 345

Rv 5:5, 345

Rv 22:16, 345

Rv 22:20–21, 345

CATECHISM OF THE CATHOLIC CHURCH INDEX

CHURCH DOCUMENTS INDEX

PHOTO CREDITS

Agnus Images
p. 277, 278, 279

Army Community Covenant
p. 103 (Adam Skoczylas; Larry Sommers; Parker Rome, Fort Riley Public Affairs; Fort Drum Public Affairs)

Art Resource
p. 39, 40, 52, 70, 77, 79, 87, 110, 144, 164, 165, 188, 195, 212, 226, 341, 354

Associated Press
p. 105, 135, 160, 329

Bridgeman Images
p. 348

Corbis
p. 1, 20, 21, 22, 25, 26, 32, 67, 138, 235, 298, 306, 307, 312

www.diariodenavarra.es
p. 179

Etsy
p. 98, 323

Getty
p. 203, 329

Gloria's Angels Foundation
p. 249

Good Salt
p. 72, 73

Shutterstock
p. 185

Superstock
p. 9, 14, 18, 21, 42 , 47, 53, 55, 62, 63, 64, 72, 74, 75, 76, 77, 78, 79, 80, 81, 82, 84, 89, 100, 101, 107, 116, 117, 124, 130, 132, 137, 139, 141, 143, 145, 146, 152, 153, 155, 157, 159, 160, 161, 162, 168, 173, 175, 187, 189, 193, 196, 198, 199, 200, 218, 219, 220, 221, 222, 223, 227, 232, 234, 237, 244, 251, 253, 255, 256, 257, 263, 265, 266, 267, 272, 273, 275, 279, 280, 281, 297, 305, 314, 317, 331, 335, 336, 337, 339, 348, 349, 356, 358

Thinkstock
p. 2, 3, 6, 7, 12, 13, 34, 35, 46, 55, 67, 69, 71, 75, 77, 80, 85, 121, 133, 149, 151, 154, 166, 167, 176, 182, 201, 203, 204, 210, 212, 213, 215, 231, 235, 238, 247, 254, 259, 269, 270, 278, 290, 291, 301, 310, 325, 326, 332, 334, 343, 347

Trinity
p. 205, 246, 288, 302, 323

https://sjabr.org/parents/contacts/269-linda-messina.html
p. 215

www.nabt.org/websites/institution/index.php?p=716
p. 215

www.icatholic.org/article/juan-diego-chs-teacher-wins-national-award-7244671
p. 217